THE FATE OF THE CORPS

The Fate of the Corps

WHAT BECAME OF THE
LEWIS AND CLARK EXPLORERS
AFTER THE EXPEDITION

LARRY E. MORRIS

YALE UNIVERSITY PRESS   NEW HAVEN & LONDON

Parts of this book were adapted from the author's article "Dependable John Ordway," *We Proceeded On* 27, May 2001; used by permission. Parts of this book were adapted for the article "After the Expedition," *American History,* April 2003.

Designed by James J. Johnson and set in Bulmer & Baskerville types
by Integrated Publishing Solutions.
Printed in the United States of America

Library of Congress Cataloging-in-Publication Data

Morris, Larry E., 1951–
The fate of the corps : what became of the Lewis and Clark explorers after the
expedition / Larry E. Morris.
p.   cm.
Includes bibliographical references and index.
ISBN 0-300-10265-8 (alk. paper)

1. Lewis and Clark Expedition (1804–1806)   2. Explorers—West (U.S.)—Biography.
3. Lewis, Meriwether, 1774–1809.   4. Lewis, Meriwether, 1774–1809—Friends
and associates.   5. Clark, William, 1770–1838.   6. Clark, William,
1770–1838—Friends and associates.   I. Title
F592.7.M685   2004
917.804′2—dc22
2004000196

A catalogue record for this book is available from the British Library.

The paper in this book meets the guidelines for permanence and durability
of the Committee on Production Guidelines for Book Longevity
of the Council on Library Resources.

10 9 8 7 6 5 4 3 2 1

To Richard Lloyd Anderson

"I tried to tell her how if you could not accept the past and its burden there was no future, for without one there cannot be the other, and how if you could accept the past you might hope for the future, for only out of the past can you make the future."

—ROBERT PENN WARREN, *All the King's Men*

Contents

———

Illustrations appear following p. 88

Chronology

31 August 1803	In a keelboat loaded with supplies, Meriwether Lewis and a crew of eleven depart Pittsburgh via the Ohio River.
14 October 1803	Lewis reaches Louisville and joins William Clark and his recruits.
26 October 1803	The expedition begins as Lewis and Clark and the Corps of Discovery set out from the Falls of the Ohio, traveling together as a group for the first time.
14 May 1804	The expedition leaves Camp Dubois and heads up the Missouri River.
20 August 1804	Charles Floyd's death at age twenty-two, probably of a ruptured appendix. He is the only member of the corps to die during the expedition.
27 October 1804	The expedition reaches the Mandan villages in what is now North Dakota.
11 February 1805	Birth of Jean-Baptiste Charbonneau.
7 April 1805	The corps departs Fort Mandan with a total of thirty-three people in the group. A group of men carrying specimens and reports returns to St. Louis in the keelboat.
13 June 1805	The expedition reaches the Great Falls of the Missouri River.

12 August 1805	Meriwether Lewis leads a group of men over the Continental Divide.
7 November 1805	The Pacific Ocean comes into view.
23 March 1806	The group departs Fort Clatsop for the return journey.
3 July 1806	The corps splits into groups to explore present-day Montana. There are eventually five different groups, headed by Lewis and Clark and Sergeants Ordway, Pryor, and Gass.
27 July 1806	In the expedition's sole violent encounter with Indians, Lewis, Drouillard, and Joseph and Reubin Field kill two Blackfoot Indians.
11 August 1806	Pierre Cruzatte accidentally shoots Lewis as the two are hunting elk.
12 August 1806	The entire group is reunited.
14 August 1806	The corps reaches the Hidatsa and Mandan villages, where Charbonneau, Sacagawea, and Jean-Baptiste remain. John Colter receives permission to join two trappers heading west.
23 September 1806	The Corps of Discovery arrives back in St. Louis.
5 November 1806	Lewis and Clark arrive in Louisville, having left there a little more than three years earlier.
March 1807	Meriwether Lewis appointed governor of Louisiana Territory; William Clark appointed chief Indian agent and brigadier general of the militia for the Louisiana Territory.
April 1807	Manuel Lisa's trapping party, which includes expedition veterans George Drouillard, Peter Weiser, John Potts, Richard Windsor, and Jean-Baptiste Lepage, heads up the Missouri River. Near present-day Omaha, Nebraska, they meet John Colter, who joins them.
18 May 1807	Nathaniel Pryor's party, which includes George Shannon and George Gibson, and possibly the Field brothers, departs St. Louis in an attempt to return Mandan chief Sheheke and his family to the Mandan villages in what is now North Dakota.
September 1807	Aaron Burr acquitted of treason.

October 1807	Pryor's party returns with Sheheke after having been attacked by Arikara Indians. Joseph Field, about age twenty-seven and possibly with Pryor, is killed sometime between 27 June and 20 October. He is the first veteran to die after the expedition.
Autumn 1808	John Potts killed by Blackfeet at age thirty-two; John Colter escapes and makes his famous run back to Fort Raymond.
September 1808	George Drouillard acquitted of the murder of Antoine Bissonnet.
1809	Death of George Gibson, probably in his late twenties, in St. Louis; death of John Shields, age forty, in the Indiana Territory; death of Jean-Baptiste Lepage, age forty-eight.
March 1809	James Madison inaugurated as fourth president of United States.
September 1809	Lewis and Clark depart on separate trips east.
24 September 1809	Sheheke and his family are safely returned to the Mandan villages.
11 October 1809	Death of Meriwether Lewis, age thirty-five, by suicide at Grinder's Stand, Tennessee.
December 1809	William Clark visits Thomas Jefferson at Monticello.
April 1810	George Drouillard killed by Blackfeet near Three Forks at age thirty-six.
1811–15	Several members of the corps participate in the War of 1812.
Spring 1811	Toussaint Charbonneau and Sacagawea travel up the Missouri River with Manuel Lisa's party.
16 December 1811	At New Madrid, in what is now Missouri, William Bratton and John Ordway witness one of the most powerful earthquakes to ever strike North America.
1 January 1812	Nathaniel Pryor survives an attack by Winnebago Indians near present-day Galena, Illinois (south of Dubuque, Iowa).
7 May 1812	Death of John Colter in present-day Missouri at about age thirty-seven.

19 June 1812	President Madison officially proclaims a state of war between the United States and Britain.
Autumn 1812	Sheheke killed by Gros Ventre warriors.
20 December 1812	Death of Sacagawea at Fort Manuel at about age twenty-four.
22 January 1813	William Bratton taken prisoner at Frenchtown.
June 1813	William Clark appointed governor of Missouri Territory.
1814	Death of Thomas P. Howard in Missouri Territory at about age thirty-five.
1814	*The History of the Expedition Under the Commands of Captains Lewis and Clark* published. Nicholas Biddle receives no credit although he is the chief compiler and editor.
24 December 1814	The Peace of Ghent signed, but the War of 1812 does not actually end until the next summer.
1815	Death of John B. Thompson in the Missouri Territory at about age forty.
1817	Death of John Ordway in Missouri Territory at about age forty-two.
March 1817	James Monroe inaugurated as fifth U.S. president.
1820–24	George Shannon serves in the Kentucky House of Representatives.
1820	William Clark loses bid to become first governor of the state of Missouri.
12 August 1820	Death of Manuel Lisa in St. Louis at about age forty-eight.
August 1821	At Bexar, in what is now Texas, Stephen F. Austin takes possession of land granted to his father, Moses Austin.
1822	Nicholas Biddle becomes president of the United States Bank.
1822–38	William Clark serves as superintendent of Indian affairs for native nations along the Mississippi and Missouri Rivers.
1823	Death of Reubin Field in Kentucky at about age forty-two.
2 June 1823	John Collins killed by Arikara Indians in present-day South Dakota at about age forty-two.

June 1824	William Bratton elected first justice of the peace in Waynetown, Indiana.
1825	Henry Clay named secretary of state under John Quincy Adams.
1826–27	Jedediah Smith explores the Great Basin and California.
4 July 1826	Death of Thomas Jefferson, age eighty-three, and John Adams, age ninety.
1829	George Shannon appointed U.S. district attorney for Missouri.
March 1829	Andrew Jackson inaugurated as seventh U.S. president.
May 1831	Jedediah Smith killed by Comanche Indians in what is now Kansas at age thirty-two.
June 1831	Death of Nathaniel Pryor in the Arkansas Territory at age fifty-nine.
1832	Alexander Willard serves in the Black Hawk War.
February– March 1836	Siege of the Alamo.
30 August 1836	Death of George Shannon in Palmyra, Missouri, at age fifty-one.
September 1836	Sam Houston defeats Stephen Austin to become president of the Republic of Texas; Austin dies three months later at age forty-three.
1837	Death of Robert Frazer in Franklin County, Missouri, at about age sixty-two.
1 September 1838	Death of William Clark in St. Louis at age sixty-eight.
ca. 1840	Death of Toussaint Charbonneau at about age seventy-three.
11 November 1841	Death of William Bratton in Waynetown, Indiana, at age sixty-three.
1842	John C. Frémont begins his first exploration of the West.
1844	Death of Nicholas Biddle at age fifty-eight.
1844	James K. Polk narrowly defeats Henry Clay in the presidential election.
1846–48	Mexican War.

1846–47	Jean-Baptiste Charbonneau serves as a guide for the Mormon Battalion.
July 1847	Mormon pioneers arrive in present-day Utah.
1851	Patrick Gass petitions Congress for a pension. (In 1854 he is granted 320 acres of land by a special act of Congress.)
1852	Alexander Willard and his wife travel by wagon train from Wisconsin to California.
29 June 1852	Death of Henry Clay in Washington at age seventy-five.
1859	Sam Houston elected governor of Texas; he is deposed in 1861 when Texas secedes from the Union and Houston refuses to swear allegiance to the Confederacy.
November 1860	Abraham Lincoln elected president of the United States.
12 April 1861	Civil War begins at Fort Sumter, South Carolina.
1863	Death of Sam Houston in Huntsville, Texas, at age seventy.
6 March 1865	Death of Alexander Willard in Franklin, California, at age eighty-six.
9 April 1865	Robert E. Lee surrenders to Ulysses S. Grant at Appomattox Court House, Virginia.
15 April 1865	Abraham Lincoln dies after being shot the previous evening.
16 May 1866	Death of Jean-Baptiste Charbonneau at Inskip Station, Oregon, at age sixty-one.
20 July 1868	Fourteenth Amendment grants citizenship to all persons born or naturalized in the United States.
27 November 1868	Colonel George Custer and his troops massacre 103 Cheyenne Indians, mostly women and children, on the upper Washita River.
10 May 1869	Transcontinental railroad completed at Promontory Point, Utah Territory.
2 April 1870	Death of Patrick Gass in Wellsburg, West Virginia, at age ninety-eight.

Prologue

A steady drizzle was falling on the final day of the Lewis and Clark Expedition, Tuesday, 23 September 1806, which was perfectly fitting because the men had hit rain their first day out. They paddled through the downpour into the current of the river they loved and hated. They had drunk from a trickling stream at the edge of the Continental Divide that was a source of the Missouri River, and now, reaching the end of that waterway, they must have experienced a unique blending of joy and sorrow, excitement and nostalgia, as the muddy Missouri merged with the mighty Mississippi. The greatest adventure of their lives had ended, and with it a sense of unity and purpose that they could never duplicate.

In the 864 days since they had left St. Louis, the Corps of Discovery had traveled more than eight thousand miles. Only one man, Sergeant Charles Floyd, had died, probably from appendicitis, meaning that even the best medical treatment of the day could not have saved him. These explorers were the first Americans to cross the continent, discovering and describing 178 plant and 122 animal species previously unknown to science, compiling one of the best records on natural history ever produced.[1] They made significant contact with at least fifteen different Indian tribes, including some who had never seen white men before, treating the Indians with respect and keeping detailed records of American Indian culture and language. (Through all this they refrained from violence except for one brief, unavoidable skirmish with hostile Blackfeet.) They kept meticulous records of their position and the surrounding geography, constructing a map of the region between St. Louis and the Pacific that was surprisingly accurate. For the next half century, explorations led by everyone from William Ashley to John C. Frémont, from Wilson Price Hunt to Kit Carson, from Etienne Provost to Jim Bridger, were unmistakably influenced by the Lewis and Clark Expedition.

Thirty-three people had made the momentous trek to the Pacific and back to the Mandan villages. The first death among those who completed the journey occurred a year later when Private Joseph Field, one of the best hunters in the party, died violently at about age twenty-seven. Over the next six decades, expedition veterans saw the opening of the West they had explored, from Andrew Henry's trapping venture in present-day Idaho to the discovery of gold at Sutter's Fort. They saw conflicts from the War of 1812 to the War Between the States. They defended Crow and Osage Indians and fought Blackfeet and Arikara. They befriended both mountain men and statesmen, from Joe Meek and Jedediah Smith to Henry Clay and Stephen F. Austin. They reminisced with Thomas Jefferson and Daniel Boone. They witnessed the rough-and-tumble world of Missouri politics and the march of the Mormon Battalion. Some settled down, married, and had children. Others turned back west, continually seeking adventure, only to be slain and scalped by Blackfoot warriors. Several held public office; two were charged with murder. Some faded into obscurity and were lost to history.

At age thirty-five, Meriwether Lewis died a premature death in the Tennessee wilderness, with the key witness contradicting herself in various accounts. To this day, historians debate whether he died by suicide or murder.

Sacagawea, the young Shoshone woman who helped guide the explorers over the Continental Divide, is said by some to have died at Fort Manuel in present-day South Dakota, in December 1812. According to other accounts, she lived many years among the Oklahoma Comanche, dying in 1884 on the Wind River reservation in Wyoming Territory.

Returning west as the first mountain man, John Colter roamed the Montana country and discovered the area that became Yellowstone National Park, although his exact route is a matter of controversy. In 1808, he and fellow expedition veteran John Potts were attacked by Blackfeet, who killed Potts but allowed Colter to run—after stripping him of clothes and moccasins. Eleven days later, the emaciated Colter staggered into Fort Raymond on the Yellowstone River, 250 miles distant.

Washington Irving wrote that William Clark's slave York "was taken with the cholera in Tennessee & died," but some claim York found contentment and respect among the Crow Indians in the Rocky Mountains.

The list goes on: Nathaniel Pryor, George Gibson, and George Shannon battled Indians, with Shannon losing his leg; John Ordway grew prosperous but lost everything in the New Madrid earthquake of 1811, apparently dying in poverty at age forty-two; George Drouillard, hunter, scout, and interpreter par excellence, cleared himself of murder charges only to meet death at the hands of the Blackfeet; the complex William Clark, capable of so much good will and fair-mindedness toward Indians, could never muster the same kind of compassion for his slaves; Jean-Baptiste Charbonneau, Sacagawea's son, spent several years in Europe, later returning west to mingle with the likes of Jim Beckwourth and Jim Bridger.

The amazing Patrick Gass, appointed sergeant at the death of Charles Floyd, published the first expedition journal in 1807 and fought in the War of 1812—losing his left eye during the war. As a sixty-year-old bachelor he took a twenty-year-old bride and fathered six children, surviving his wife by several years. He reportedly volunteered to serve in the Union Army when he was past ninety, and he was almost one hundred years old in 1869—and the final survivor of the expedition—when Central Pacific executive Leland Stanford raised a silver-headed hammer and drove a golden spike into the ground at Promontory Point, in present-day Utah. The territory of unscalable peaks and endless deserts—almost entirely unknown and unmapped by Euro-Americans at the beginning of the century—was now officially linked to the rest of the country with the completion of the transcontinental railroad. The story of what became of the corps after their exploration is thus the story of the American West.

One of the more amazing aspects of this story is the way the lives of expedition veterans interweave in the decades following their exploration of the West. Lewis and Clark, of course, were appointed to key government posts and worked together in St. Louis, maintaining the same friendly relationship they had enjoyed on the expedition. Several members of the corps returned west as trappers, often working in the same outfit. Some saw fellow expedition members killed by Indians. Toussaint Charbonneau and Sacagawea saw veterans at the Mandan villages in present-day North Dakota and in St. Louis. Their son, Jean-Baptiste, lived for several years with or near William Clark. As a judge in both Kentucky and Missouri, George Shannon likely saw former compatriots in both locations. In the War of 1812, Alexander Willard rode north along the Mississippi in an attempt to warn Nathaniel Pryor of an Indian threat.

In all of this, the lives of the expedition members continually criss-cross back and forth, making the story of the expedition itself that much more meaningful.

Rather than offering a series of mini-biographies, this book concentrates on fascinating events: the death of Meriwether Lewis; George Drouillard's murder trial; the New Madrid earthquakes; the rift between William Clark and York; John Collins's death at the hands of the Arikara. These chapters fall in chronological order.

In trying to be as accurate as possible, I have based my narrative on primary documents—everything from letters and journals to deeds, promissory notes, and court transcripts. Source information is listed in the Notes section. To find these documents I have searched several key archives in the United States and checked a multitude of records such as census reports, town records, manuscript collections, land transactions, probate proceedings, arrest warrants, and family genealogies. I have transcribed excerpts from original documents exactly as the authors wrote them.

My quoting of dialogue is taken directly from primary sources—none is created out of whole cloth. I label speculation as such, but even speculation is based on accounts from contemporaries of Lewis and Clark.

For certain members of the expedition there is a wealth of material— Lewis, Clark, Sacagawea, York, and Colter come to mind. But even with these individuals tantalizing mysteries remain. Some members of the corps seem to have vanished into thin air—Silas Goodrich, Hugh McNeal, Hugh Hall. Despite checking countless card catalogs, indexes, electronic databases, and Internet search tools, I have found just a few bits and pieces. Luckily, most of the thirty-three individuals fall somewhere in between—enough pieces of the jigsaw can be connected to offer a reasonably complete picture of what happened to them.

Of course, a single primary document is never absolute proof of anything— the person who wrote that document could have made a false statement, either intentionally or unintentionally. Still, when a certain event is confirmed through a number of independent sources, the weight begins to add up. I believe that historical "mysteries" can generally be solved through careful, thorough research. In all cases, I have tried to be honest about what we know and don't know. For me, the search has been compelling every step along the way. I hope the same is true for you.

CHAPTER ONE

"We Descended with Great Velocity"
The Triumphant Return of the
Lewis and Clark Expedition

The thirty-three members of the Lewis and Clark Expedition picked up speed as they headed home. On their journey west, which had begun near St. Louis in May of 1804, they had rowed, pushed, and pulled their boats upstream on the Missouri River, laboring to make ten miles a day. Now, in the summer of 1806, the wayworn explorers were running the Missouri from its Montana headwaters back to St. Louis, riding with the current in their pirogue—a huge hollowed-out log equipped with rudder and sails—and dugout canoes, stroking deep with their paddles, sometimes making seventy-five or eighty miles a day. As William Clark noted, they were eager to get home.

Although they had not discovered Thomas Jefferson's hoped-for northwest passage, a continuous waterway stretching from the Mississippi River to the Pacific Ocean—indeed, none existed to be discovered—Lewis and Clark's Corps of Discovery had mapped thousands of miles of uncharted territory, found the source of the Missouri River, crossed the Continental Divide, and reached the Pacific.

This was a military mission, and the original company consisted of two officers, three sergeants, and twenty-three privates, ranging in age from eighteen to thirty-four. Most were from Virginia, Pennsylvania, or New England, and many of them had migrated to Kentucky. All were skilled woodsmen, with expert hunters, gunsmiths, scouts, and boatmen among them. Because of the length and dangerous nature of the venture, Lewis and Clark, bachelors themselves, had (for the most part) recruited unmarried men. The group also included William Clark's slave, York, probably around thirty years old. In many ways, York's service on the expedition symbolizes the sad history of slavery in the United States: he had responsibilities similar to the others and performed them well, but he received no pay and was not included in the official roster.

Lewis and Clark also enlisted civilian employees, and by the time they departed the Mandan villages, where they had spent the winter of 1804–5, and headed west, the surprisingly diverse party included a uniquely skilled hunter and interpreter who was half-Shawnee, two other men who were half Omaha, a French-Canadian trader close to forty years old, a young Shoshone woman still in her teens, and a two-month-old baby boy.

Now on their return journey, they were "extreamly anxious to get on," wrote William Clark, "to get to their Country and friends."[1] But tracing the course of the 2,464-mile Missouri—the longest river in North America—was hardly a straight shot from what is now southwestern Montana to St. Louis. Though Lewis and Clark knew perfectly well that St. Louis lay to the southeast, they had to patiently follow the meandering Missouri northeast, across present-day Montana and into North Dakota, for the river offered the fastest, safest route back—in fact, the sole known route. (The group had used horses at various times, but they were now going exclusively by boat.) Then, on 14 August 1806, after traveling from sunrise to sunset the previous day— and making eighty-six miles—the party came in sight of a familiar group of earthen lodges lining a bluff, near present-day Stanton, North Dakota.

These were the five villages of the Mandan and Hidatsa Indians, who had befriended the expedition during the harsh winter of 1804–5, when the Missouri had frozen, the temperature plummeting to forty-five degrees below zero. The Indians were prosperous farmers and traders and had welcomed the Corps of Discovery and encouraged them to build a winter fort nearby. "Our wish is to be at peace with all," the Mandan chief Sheheke-shote, called Big White by the explorers (though his name actually means "Coyote"), had told them. "If we eat you Shall eat, if we Starve you must Starve also." The genuine hospitality of Sheheke and the other chiefs had eased Lewis and Clark's apprehension over the size of the Mandan and Hidatsa villages— their combined population of four and a half thousand was greater than either St. Louis or Washington and included fifteen hundred warriors, more than enough to massacre several corps of discovery.[2]

As the expedition returned to the villages after an absence of a year and a half, a crowd of Indians gathered on the shore to meet them. The explorers fired several shots as a greeting and paddled to the bank. The friendly Indians were outfitted in dress common among many Great Plains tribes—the men in buckskin leggings, breechcloths (later called loincloths), buffalo robes draped over their shoulders, and moccasins; the women in leather skirts, robes, and moccasins; and young children virtually naked when weather allowed. The Indians were "extreamly pleased to See us," wrote Clark. Then, in a touching scene that symbolizes William Clark's long friendship with American Indians, a Hidatsa chief named Black Moccasin began weeping when he saw Clark, who asked through an interpreter what was wrong.

The chief lamented that his son had gone to war with the Blackfeet and had been killed. The personable Clark comforted the chief. That day and the next he gathered with a number of chiefs in one of the earthen lodges that could house an extended Mandan family, their possessions, and their livestock. By now well versed in proper protocol, Clark waited to be seated—and he determined the status of various chiefs by their position in the circle. He also noticed some were missing fingers, which they had cut off to honor deceased relatives. Next he waited for a buffalo robe to be draped over his shoulders. Then he waited for the calumet, or peace pipe, holding it without disturbing the decorative feathers, smoking for the proper interval, and passing it on respectfully, all of which pleased the chiefs. When it was his turn to speak, Clark did so through an interpreter, inviting the chiefs to visit "their great father" in the east, Thomas Jefferson, and "hear his own Councils and receive his Gifts from his own hands."[3]

The chiefs wanted to see Jefferson; they were intrigued by Clark's promise that such a visit could hasten construction of a trading post; but they feared their enemies to the south, the Lakota, whom Clark had called "the vilest miscreants of the savage race" after the tribe had threatened the explorers on their westward journey in 1804. An eloquent Hidatsa chief expressed the thoughts of many of those present. He "wished to go down and See his great father very much," reported Clark in his journal, but "the Scioux [Lakota] were in the road and would most certainly kill him or any others who Should go down they were bad people and would not listen to any thing which was told them."[4]

On 16 August, after considerable persuasion by Clark, Sheheke, the principal chief of the lower Mandan village, agreed to go east to meet Jefferson. He had one condition: his wife and son, as well as interpreter René Jusseaume and his Mandan wife and two sons, must go as well. Jusseaume was an independent French-Canadian trader and interpreter who had lived for several years among the Mandan. Clark agreed.

While Sheheke sat in a circle with the men and smoked a pipe, the women cried. When he told Clark he was ready to depart, an even greater wail arose, with the other chiefs pleading with Clark to protect Sheheke.

Those who thought they were bidding a final farewell to the chief were mistaken, but Lewis and Clark, confident Sheheke would return in short order, were also wide of the mark. No one could have guessed that Sheheke's homecoming was more than three years in the future, nor that taking him east would help trigger a chain of events ultimately leading to Meriwether Lewis's lonely death in the backwoods of Tennessee.

In a portent of that future, Lewis was largely inactive during the reunion with the Mandan and Hidatsa because he was recovering from a gunshot wound, the only such injury suffered during the entire expedition. On 11 August, as Lewis and the one-eyed—and nearsighted—fiddler and boatman Pierre Cruzatte were hunting elk, Cruzatte had taken aim and fired at a brown patch in the willows. "Damn you!" yelled Lewis an instant later, "you have shot me." The ball had hit him in the backside, probably knocking him down; "the stroke was very severe," he wrote. Though he was in a good deal of pain and possibly in shock, Lewis kept his wits. After calling for Cruzatte several times and hearing no reply, he feared he had been shot by Indians. Mustering his strength, he scrambled for the river and "called the men to their arms to which they flew in an instant."[5]

Sergeant Patrick Gass and three others scouted for Indians while Lewis and fifteen other men readied their rifles and braced for an assault. (Clark and twelve others were downriver; Lewis met up with them the next day.) Gass found no Indians but returned with the befuddled Cruzatte, who claimed to know nothing of Lewis's wound, although Lewis was convinced that Cruzatte knew exactly what had happened. Gass helped Lewis dress the wound by packing it with rolls of lint. Luckily, the ball had hit no bones, passing through Lewis's left buttock an inch below his hip joint—otherwise, he might well have been doomed. Still, Lewis endured considerable pain and had fainted when Clark changed the dressing.[6]

Meriwether Lewis had begun preparations for the expedition in the spring of 1803. In June he had written to his old friend William Clark: "If therefore there is anything under those circumstances, in this enterprise, which would induce you to participate with me in it's fatiegues, it's dangers and it's honors, believe me there is no man on earth with whom I should feel equal pleasure in sharing them as with yourself."

When Clark received the letter in Kentucky a month later, he immediately replied: "I will chearfully join you," he wrote. "This is an undertaking fraited with many difficulties, but My friend I do assure you that no man lives whith whome I would perfur to undertake Such a Trip &c. as your self."[7]

Thus began one of the most illustrious partnerships in United States history. Though Lewis was technically the superior officer, he and Clark had the kind of friendship and mutual respect that allowed them to jointly command a strategic three-year mission, a rare—if not singular—accomplishment in military history.

Each of them recruited men—Lewis in the east and Clark in Kentucky. By 26 October 1803 they had combined their forces. On 14 May of the next year they departed, averaging fifteen miles a day as they made their way up the Missouri. They spent that winter near the Mandan villages, heading up-river again in April 1805. By mid-August they had reached the headwaters of the Missouri. They crossed the Continental Divide into present-day Idaho, hit an early winter, and nearly starved and froze in the Bitterroot Mountains.

Surviving with the help of Indians, they followed the Clearwater River, then the Snake, then the Columbia, rejoicing when they spotted the "emence Ocian" in November. Again, they made winter camp, this time enduring rain rather than snow, and grew so tired of eating fish that they killed dogs for fresh meat. Then, in March of 1806, they headed east, retracing their route back to the Continental Divide, where they split into five groups to explore present-day Montana. Through it all, the two captains had made one good decision after another—they had also enjoyed their share of good luck. At a cost of less than forty thousand dollars, they had successfully completed their three-year mission.

On the cool, clear morning of Sunday, 17 August 1806, after seeing the northern lights during the night, the men rose early and packed their supplies, eager to get started on the last leg of their long journey—the sixteen-hundred-mile homestretch run to St. Louis, which they would accomplish in five weeks. As they loaded their pirogue and canoes, the explorers watched one of their compatriots equip a separate canoe, one returning to the hinterlands the party had just left. After two and a half years away from civilization, John Colter was going back to the Montana country to trap beaver.

The free spirit Colter was an expert woodsman who had adapted readily to wilderness life but not nearly so quickly to military discipline. In the spring of 1804, across the river from St. Louis, while the men waited impatiently to get started—and while Lewis and Clark were away from camp—Colter had loaded his gun and threatened to kill Sergeant John Ordway. The captains court-martialed Colter and could have disciplined him in a variety of ways. But after Colter begged forgiveness and promised to mend his ways, Lewis and Clark let the matter go. After the group left St. Louis in May, the captains no longer tolerated insubordination, ordering some offenders whipped and others expelled from the permanent party.

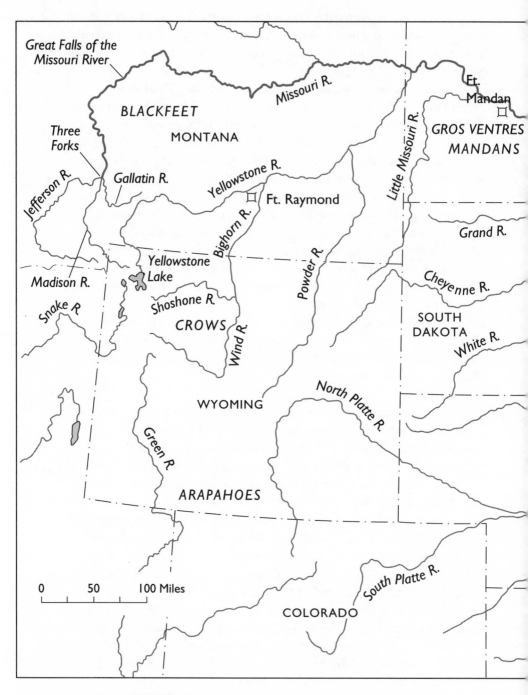

Great Falls of the
Missouri River

Missouri R.

Ft.
Mandan

BLACKFEET

MONTANA

GROS VENTRES
MANDANS

Three
Forks

Little Missouri R.

Jefferson R.

Gallatin R.

Yellowstone R.

Grand R.

Bighorn R.

Ft. Raymond

Madison R.

Yellowstone
Lake

Powder R.

Cheyenne R.

Snake R

Shoshone R.

CROWS

Wind R.

SOUTH
DAKOTA

White R.

WYOMING

North Platte R.

Green R.

ARAPAHOES

0   50   100 Miles

South Platte R.

COLORADO

Lewis and Clark's West

The Missouri River Region

(Map by Bill Nelson, based on an original from *Manuel Lisa and the Opening of the Missouri Fur Trade,*
by Richard Oglesby, © 1963 by the University of Oklahoma Press, Norman)

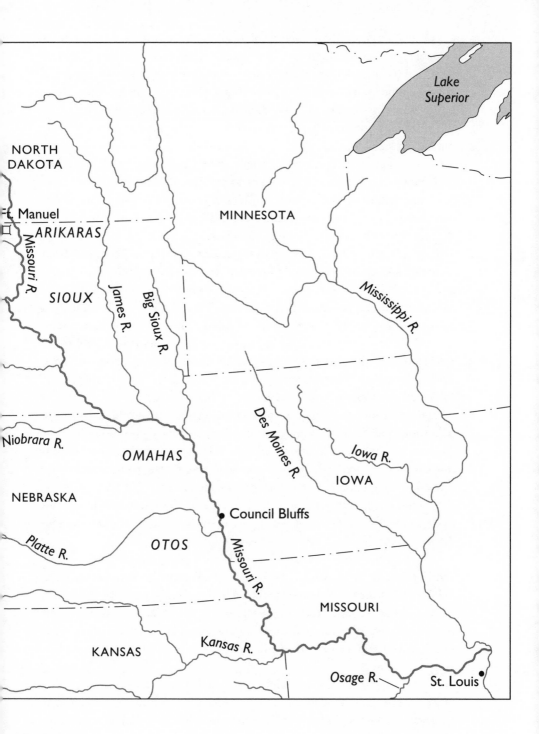

Colter did more than stay out of trouble: he became one of the most valuable members of the party. The captains relied on him to search for lost men, to scout ahead of the main group—not worrying when he was gone for days at a time—and to hunt. "Sent our hunters out early this morning," read one journal entry by Lewis. "Colter killed a deer and brought it in by 10 A. M. the other hunters except Drewyer [George Drouillard] returned early without having killed anything."[8]

On 29 July 1806, northeast of what is now Great Falls, Montana, Lewis had sent Colter, Joseph and Reubin Field, and John Collins "with orderes to hunt, and kill meat for the party and obtain as many Elkskins as are necessary to cover our canoes and furnish us with shelters from the rain." When the four men rejoined the group two weeks later (west of the modern site of Williston, North Dakota), they were surprised to learn that Lewis had been wounded and doubly surprised to see two new faces among the men. Trappers Joseph Dickson and Forrest Hancock, heading upstream on the Missouri, had met Lewis earlier that same day. These were the first white men the party had seen in almost a year and a half. The two had been trapping since 1804, and their luck had not been good: they had been robbed by Lakota Indians the previous winter and Dickson had been wounded. They were nevertheless "determined to Stay . . . untill they make a fortune," as John Ordway recorded, and they invited Colter to join them.[9]

The three men knew they could sell beaver pelts, called "plews," for $4 to $6 apiece in St. Louis. The average plew weighed one or two pounds. After trapping beaver in one location, they would bury the pelts in a "cache" and move on to the next area. If they could survive, if they could avoid being robbed by Indians, and if their caches remained intact—big "ifs" indeed— they could conceivably return to St. Louis with several hundred plews and make as much as a thousand dollars per man. By contrast, Colter was due $179.33 1/3 for his three years of service to Lewis and Clark.

More than anyone else on the expedition, Colter had the blood of adventure flowing in his veins—he is rightly called the first mountain man. While most of the others longed to return home as fast as possible, Colter was ready to go west again, ready to live without the most basic comforts for another two years. With no qualms at the prospect of spending his third—and fourth—winter in a row in the wild, Colter went to Clark and requested an early discharge.

On 15 August 1806, Clark wrote that he and Lewis were "disposed to be of Service to any one of our party who had performed their duty as well as Colter had done," and allowed Colter to leave. Clark gave Colter a good supply of powder, lead, knives, hatchets, and powder horns. Some of the men pitched in with other implements they could spare. Then the group looked on—some of them possibly with envy, for Clark had stipulated that no one else could join the trapping party—as Colter climbed in a small canoe with Dickson and Hancock, nodded goodbye, and plunged back into the wilderness. Though Colter's departure meant he would miss the thrill of the expedition's homecoming, the future was about to bring him one of the most incredible adventures in the history of the West.

After Colter's departure, William Clark turned back to the thousand details of his command, essentially doubled by Lewis's convalescence. Guns were the first priority—the men needed to check their arms and ammunition, which meant everything from flints and powder canisters to wiping cloths and ramrods. Second, and virtually as important to him and Lewis as the arms, he made sure the nearly one million words that he, Lewis, and several others had recorded in the expedition journals were safely packed. Next, scientific equipment—sextants, quadrants, compasses, chronometers, surveying tools—that allowed the group to take celestial observations, calculate their position, record their progress. All this reflected Thomas Jefferson's masterful planning of the expedition. Medical supplies included lances and flannel, opium and essence of peppermint. Zoological artifacts such as prairie dogs, buffalo horns, and skeletons of bighorn sheep had been preserved for the world of science—and for the eminently curious Thomas Jefferson. Finally, Clark likely consulted with the three sergeants to make sure the men themselves were all accounted for and that the more mundane items were packed—corn given to them by the Mandan; axes, knives, hatchets, ropes, cooking pans and utensils; and medals, flags, and beads as gifts for native tribes. Though each man had begun the journey with extra clothing, that had long since given out—they had now resorted to sewing clothes from deer and elk skin.

Clark inspected the boats, made sure they were not overloaded, and ordered two canoes lashed together to provide a more secure voyage for Sheheke, Jusseaume, and their families; he spoke to the Mandan through one interpreter and to the Hidatsa through another, assuring them of his good will, continually laying groundwork for friendly relations in the future. He also took time to bid farewell to interpreter Charbonneau and to the best-known member of the expedition after the two captains themselves, Sacagawea.

A Shoshone born south of present-day Salmon, Idaho, Sacagawea was only sixteen when she joined Lewis and Clark. Four years earlier, she and a friend had been kidnapped by a Hidatsa raiding party near the Three Forks, the sources of the Missouri River, and carried back to the Hidatsa's territory in the northern Dakota country. (The friend escaped, and in one of the most memorable scenes of the expedition, she and Sacagawea were unexpectedly reunited.) About 1804, four years after they had taken Sacagawea captive, the Hidatsa apparently sold her to a French-Canadian trader and interpreter by the name of Toussaint Charbonneau. More than twenty years Sacagawea's senior, he had lived among the Indians for several years. Lewis later described Charbonneau as a "man of no particular merit," who "was useful as an interpreter only."[10] Clark, however, had a higher opinion of him and employed Charbonneau after the expedition.

When they reached the Mandan and Hidatsa villages in the fall of 1804, Lewis and Clark were concerned about being able to communicate with Indians as they traveled west. After discovering that the French-speaking Charbonneau spoke Hidatsa and that his young wife Sacagawea spoke both Hidatsa and Shoshone, they hired Charbonneau as an interpreter—with the understanding that Sacagawea would accompany him. Neither Lewis nor Clark spoke French, but at least three men in the party could translate Charbonneau's French into English.

Sacagawea was pregnant when Lewis and Clark arrived at the Mandan villages, and she gave birth to a baby boy named Jean-Baptiste on 11 February 1805. Less than two months later, she and Charbonneau headed west with the explorers—with Sacagawea carrying Baptiste on her back. One of the more amazing aspects of an expedition brimming with astounding events is Sacagawea's safely taking her baby to the Pacific coast and back, through hostile Indian territory, up and down snow-covered mountains—surviving sickness, treacherous rapids, bitter cold, and near starvation.

One episode in particular had epitomized Sacagawea's mettle. On the journey west, she and Charbonneau and others were riding in a sail-equipped pirogue. A sudden squall capsized the vessel. Lewis and Clark both stood helpless on the shore—three hundred yards away—as the pirogue seemed certain to go under. The mission itself was in jeopardy because the pirogue contained the expedition's papers, instruments, books, and medicine. The captains fired their guns to get the attention of the crew and ordered them to cut the halyards and haul in the sail.

But the men could not hear over the wind, and the boat took in water for at least half a minute. Charbonneau cried to heaven for mercy, but Sacagawea had the presence of mind to save most of the articles that had been washed overboard, all the while preserving her papoose. Then Cruzatte righted the pirogue, and the men rowed to shore. Lewis wrote that Sacagawea had "equal fortitude and resolution, with any person onboard at the time of the accedent."[11]

Both captains came to admire Sacagawea, but Clark took a special interest in Charbonneau's family. Not long after departing the Mandan villages and heading west again, Clark wrote that he and Charbonneau walked along the shore, with Sacagawea following, and that "the Squar found & brought me a bush Something like the Current, which She Said bore a delicious froot and that great quantities grew on the Rocky Mountains." Walking with Charbonneau and Sacagawea became a habit for Clark. He, York, and Lewis also took their meals with the interpreter, his "squar," and their child and slept in the same tepee. One night Clark wrote that he "checked our interpreter for Strikeing his woman at their Dinner." Charbonneau apparently learned his lesson—though such chivalry was no doubt foreign to him—and apparently did not strike his wife again.[12]

During the journey to the coast and back to the Mandan villages, young Baptiste grew from a two-month-old infant to a walking, talking, curious, rambunctious nineteen-month-old toddler. Clark called him "my boy Pomp." One can imagine Clark playing with the boy, holding him on his knee in a pirogue, pointing out trout in the river. Clark also protected the boy and his mother. As the party made its way around the Great Falls of the Missouri, Clark was hiking with Charbonneau, Sacagawea, and Pomp. When a thunderstorm hit, the four of them took refuge in a ravine and found shelter under an overhanging rock. The sky blackened with thunderheads, the gale gathering strength, and "a torrent of rain and hail fell more violent than ever I Saw before," wrote Clark, alarmed at what might happen next. Then he heard what he feared—a flash flood roaring down the ravine, "with emence force tareing every thing before it takeing with it large rocks & mud." Clark clung to his musket and shot pouch with one hand and pushed Sacagawea and Pomp ahead of him with the other, trying to outrun the deluge—which would certainly sweep them to a ninety-foot falls in the river below. Then he saw Charbonneau on a bluff above them, reaching down, but so frightened he was immobile. Clark pushed the woman and her child up the incline as the torrent hit, engulfing him to the waist. "I Scrcely got out before it raised 10 feet deep," he wrote. Sacagawea, still recovering from a serious illness, was freezing and shivering, helpless to warm Pomp, whose clothes and cradleboard had disappeared in the flood. But thanks to Clark they were alive.[13]

Now, as Clark bade farewell to Charbonneau and Sacagawea, his genuine affection for them was evident. He offered to take them to the Illinois territory, but Charbonneau declined because he had no work prospects or acquaintances there. Next, Clark gave Charbonneau the blacksmith tools from the expedition. Then, wrote Clark, "I offered to take his little Son a butifull promising Child who is 19 months old." Charbonneau and Sacagawea "observed that in one year the boy would be Sufficiently old to leave his mother & he would then take him to me if I would be so friendly as to raise the Child for him in Such a manner as I thought proper, to which I agreed."[14]

Pomp did go to live with Clark when he was six years old. He eventually traveled to Europe and later returned west as a mountain man and scout. He guided John C. Frémont, Philip St. George Cooke, and others.

Clark saluted the well-wishers with a gunshot and "proceeded on," heading south, leaving the unique fellowship of the Mandan and Hidatsa for the "civilized" world. Getting to that world was not easy, even though the group was traveling downstream. On 23 August they stopped for three and a half hours because the wind was so strong and the water so rough they could not make any headway. The next day was the same story. "About noon the wind rose high from S. W. which detained us about three hours," Ordway noted succinctly. "Then procd. on though the work against us."

The nights were never easy—even a few hours of uninterrupted sleep was a rarity. The mosquitoes continually tormented them. The men had begun the voyage with mosquito nets, which they called "biers," but those were now full of holes, as were their blankets. "We were routed at day light by the mosquetoes," wrote John Ordway in a typical entry, often echoed by Lewis or Clark's "Musquitors very troublesom last night."[15] When it was not mosquitoes they had to contend with, there were tremendous midwestern thunderstorms. The group's tents had long since rotted or worn out; they tried to use tree limbs or elk skins for shelter. "Rained all last night," Clark wrote on 22 August, "every person and all our bedding wet." Nine days later he recorded a night of hard rain, violent wind, and "hard Claps of thunder and lightning." All hands left their bunks about midnight to keep the boats from being blown into the river. Even so, the wind snapped the cables of two small canoes, and when Privates Alexander Willard and Peter M. Weiser tried to save one canoe, they were blown across the river. Clark sent Ordway and six others to rescue them. The men all returned safely by 2:00 a.m. The weather did not let up until daylight, when the rugged men packed up the boats and proceeded downriver.

On 30 August, two weeks after leaving the Mandan villages, Clark was scanning the rolling grassland on the north side of the river with his telescope when he spotted several Indians on horseback at the top of a hill. He ordered the boats to the south shore and watched for other Indians. Within minutes, ninety warriors armed with muskets and bows and arrows came out of the wood on the northern side, just a few hundred yards downstream. The Indians fired their guns as a salute; the explorers fired two rounds of their own. Given the group's location (near the modern site of Yankton, South Dakota), the Indians could have been Yankton Sioux, Ponca, or Omaha, all friendly, and all likely to be wearing similar leggings and breechcloths. But "from their hostile appearance," wrote Clark, "we were apprehensive they were Tetons [Lakota]."

Excellent hunters and horsemen and fierce warriors, the Lakota were the most powerful tribe in the area, frequently attacking neighboring tribes. Also called Teton Sioux or Dakotas, they dwelled in tepees and subsisted largely through hunting buffalo. The Lakota were well known for robbing traders and demanding extravagant gifts. "On that nation," Thomas Jefferson had written Lewis, "we wish most particularly to make a friendly impression, because of their immense power."[16] The expedition had first encountered them on the journey west in September 1804, giving them medals, a United States flag, knives and other articles, and some tobacco. But it had soon become evident that the apparently friendly Lakota were simply waiting for an opportune moment to rob the corps of its valuable goods. As Clark stood on shore with a few companions, engaged in a suddenly tense negotiation, several Lakota seized the cable of one of the pirogues.

At that, Clark had drawn his sword. Lewis ordered the men to their arms. "The large Swivel loaded immediately with 16 Musquet Ball in it," wrote Ordway. "The 2 other Swivels loaded well with Buck Shot, Each of them manned." The other men trained their flintlocks on the Lakota warriors.

On the bank, some Indians drew arrows from their quivers, others cocked their guns. Clark was ready for a fight, and announced that his men were not squaws but warriors.

The Lakota chief Black Buffalo replied that they were also warriors, threatening, as Ordway recorded, to "follow us and kill and take the whole of us by degrees."

Clark countered that the expedition had been sent by the great father in the east, a man so powerful he could "have them all distroyed as it were in a moment." At that instant, Black Buffalo defused the situation by releasing the pirogue and asking if the women and children could see the party's boat. Clark agreed. A crisis had been averted, but the captains were determined not to trust this nation in the future.[17]

Now Clark watched as the throng on the opposite shore increased to two hundred, all well armed. Several Indians swam out to a sandbar, and Clark, still acting as sole commander while the hurting Lewis lay face-down in a boat, asked through interpreters what nation they represented. Lakota, came the reply. The captain, who had been so congenial to so many different tribes, did not mince words: "I also told them that I was informed that a part of all their bands were gorn to war against the Mandans & Menetarres [Hidatsa] &c, and that they would be well whiped as the Mandans & Menetarres & had a plenty of Guns Powder and ball, and we had given them a Cannon to defend themselves. and derected them to return from the Sand bar and inform their Chiefs what we had Said to them, and to keep away from the river or we Should kill every one of them."

Ignoring both threats and invitations to stop, Clark moved downstream. At the top of a nearby hill, Black Buffalo, the same chief who had released the pirogue almost two years earlier, struck the ground three times with his rifle, an action Sheheke understood well, for this was "a great oath among the Indians," pledging by the earth—one of the four supreme gods—to seek revenge. But Clark proceeded safely six miles downriver, where the group camped on a large sandbar. "Our encampment of this evening was a very disagreeable one, bleak exposed to the winds, and the Sand wet," wrote Clark. But they remained there because the Lakota could not stage an attack across the river. By the next night the group was seventy miles away from the dangerous Lakota.[18]

Navigating the muddy Missouri was constantly a headache and often a hazard. The immense, serpentine river wound southeast with so many bends and curves that traveling twenty miles on water sometimes equated to just a few miles on land. The boatmen fought wind and rain, suffocating dust, narrow channels, sandbars, whirlpools, shifting currents, runaway timber, and "sawyers"—half-submerged logs and branches stuck in the riverbed that could overturn or wreck the pirogue and canoes. Though the party had complained of the cold up in the region where the Mandan lived, they soon had the opposite problem, enduring weather Clark called "excessively worm and disagreeable."

But the natural forces so often against them also blessed them with unparalleled beauty. A delightful variety of fowl flew overhead—Carolina parakeets, pelicans, ducks, geese, hawks, and eagles. From their boats they saw swans, otter, beaver, turkey, wolves, black bear, elk, and deer. But nothing matched the buffalo. One day Clark made his way through the dry brown prairie grass that grew chest high and climbed a hill to admire the animals. "From this eminance I had a view of a greater number of buffalow than I had ever Seen before at one time," he wrote. "I must have Seen near 20,000 of those animals feeding on this plain."[19]

The pressures of the journey, which would have strained or ended most friendships, had strengthened the deep bond between the captains. In three years of working closely together, they had seldom disagreed and apparently never seriously argued. This incredible unity had rubbed off on the men, who worked extremely well together. Clark's affection for Lewis was apparent in his journal entry of 3 September, when he wrote, "I am happy to find that my worthy friend Capt L[ewis] is so well as to walk about with ease to himself."

That same day, in what is now the northeast corner of Nebraska, the men spotted two boats on the shore ahead of them. As they got closer, they could see fifteen or twenty trappers next to the boats. The expedition came ashore and was greeted warmly by a party whose leader was a Scot trader named James Aird. He invited Lewis and Clark into his tent, where it was warm and dry. The captains were famished for news, and this was their first chance to hear anything of the civilized world. (They had learned nothing from Dickson and Hancock, who had left St. Louis shortly after the expedition did in 1804.)

"Our first enquirey was after the President of our country and then our friends and the State of the politicks of our country," wrote Clark. Aird was glad to oblige, confirming their assumption that Thomas Jefferson had been reelected. But the next bit of news surprised them: on 11 July 1804, just two months after the expedition departed, vice-president Aaron Burr and Federalist leader Alexander Hamilton had faced off in a pistol duel in Weehawken, New Jersey. Hamilton had been wounded and died the next day. They also learned that General James Wilkinson was now governor of the Louisiana Territory, that two British ships had fired on a U.S. ship in the New York harbor, and that several Indians were in jail in St. Louis and others had been hanged for murder.

As they followed the river down the present northwestern border of the state of Missouri, Lewis and Clark met one group of trappers and traders after another, all making their way north. On 6 September they purchased a gallon of whiskey and "gave to each man of the party a dram which is the first Spiritious licquor which had been tasted by any of them Since the 4 of July 1805," wrote Clark. (Alcohol was still scarce among the native nations, but the multitude of traders who followed Lewis and Clark quickly changed all that.) Every two or three days there were more opportunities for a shot of whiskey—or more. One night they got all the liquor they could drink. Another night, 14 September, after savoring biscuits, cheese, and onion bestowed by a group of traders, the party "received a dram and Sung Songs untill 11oClock at night in the greatest harmoney," quipped Clark.

There was also more news from the east: soldier Zebulon Pike had explored the upper Mississippi River on orders from General Wilkinson and was now traversing the Great Plains in search of the origin of the Arkansas River. Pike's expeditions were of a scope similar to Lewis and Clark's, but he did not document them nearly as well as the captains did. He and his men were unsuccessful in their attempt to scale a fourteen-thousand-foot mountain in the Rockies that was later named Pikes Peak.

The most fascinating news concerned the Lewis and Clark team itself—rumors were running rampant that all the men had been killed or forced into slave labor in Spanish mines. The news bearers added, however, that "the President of the U. States had yet hopes of us."[20]

But there was also distressing news. On 12 September the party met the trader and interpreter Joseph Gravelines. Two years earlier, Gravelines had assisted Lewis and Clark by interpreting for them when they met with the Arikara Indians, near present-day Mobridge, South Dakota. At the captains' invitation, an Arikara chief had accompanied Gravelines back to Washington to meet Jefferson. Now, Gravelines was on his way to visit the Arikara, to personally deliver a letter from Jefferson to the tribe. From the letter Gravelines carried, Lewis learned the information he feared and had heard rumored in previous days: the chief "found nothing but kindness & good will wherever he passed," wrote Jefferson, but "was taken sick; every thing we could do to help him was done; but it pleased the great Spirit to take him from among us. We buried him among our own deceased friends & relatives, we shed many tears over his grave."[21]

Gravelines had gifts for the Arikara, who farmed and dwelt in earth lodges near the confluence of the Grand and Missouri Rivers. But the gifts would not appease them, and over the next year their anger at the chief's death reached a boiling point. Later, it also figured prominently in the downfall of Meriwether Lewis.

"The men ply their oares & we decended with great velocity," reported Clark in mid-September. They made fifty-two miles one day, seventy-two the next, sixty-eight the next, not stopping to hunt—though they were entirely out of provisions—and not stopping to eat during the day. They subsisted on pawpaws, a small yellow plum that was abundant along the banks. Several of the men later complained of sore eyes—probably an allergic reaction to handling and eating the pawpaws.[22]

On the morning of Saturday, 20 September, the men shouted cheers when they saw cows along the bank, a sure sign of civilization. Late that afternoon, they came in sight of La Charette, the first white settlement they had seen since May of 1804. "The men raised a Shout and Sprung upon their oares and we soon landed opposit to the Village," wrote Clark. Traders provided a "very agreeable supper," and the captains treated the men to two gallons of whiskey. The settlers were delighted at the expedition's safe return, said Clark, and "informed us that we were Supposed to have been lost long Since, and were entirely given out by every person."

The next day, after traveling almost fifty miles and passing many Indians paddling upstream in canoes, the party neared St. Charles, where the expedition had departed the civilized world on 21 May 1804. The men "plyed thear ores with great dexterity," observed Clark. While La Charette was an outpost with touches of civilization, St. Charles was a bona fide town, an established community—with shops, offices, mills, gardens, a church, a hundred homes, and five hundred citizens. What's more, it was a pleasant Sunday afternoon, and the corps saw quite a number of well-dressed gentlemen and ladies strolling arm-in-arm along the bank, a wondrous sight indeed for the bearded, grizzled, buckskin-clad nomads whose mission had lasted four times longer than Columbus's voyage to the New World. The men saluted the community by firing their guns; "we were met by great numbers of the inhabitants, we found them excessively polite," said Clark.

That evening there were no worries about mosquitoes or bad weather—the hospitable French citizens of St. Charles housed the party for the night. Throughout the town, in homes Lewis described as "small and but illy constructed," as a hard rain fell outside, the men of the Corps of Discovery sat near fires and told of their adventures while enjoying pork, biscuits, and beans, or stew and cornbread, or corned beef, carrots, and squash, with tea cake or bread pudding, topping off their meals with apple jack, whiskey, or rum.

The next morning, after taking the luxury to stay inside until the rain stopped, the party wished their St. Charles hosts well and proceeded downriver to Fort Bellefontaine, the first fort west of the Mississippi, which had been built while the expedition was in the West. They met and shared drinks with quite a number of friends at the fort, and they took Sheheke's group to the "publick Store" and bought them western clothes.

As the gentle Mississippi nudged them along, the men swung to their left, landing on the Illinois side of the river, at Camp Dubois, where they had wintered in 1803–4, preparing for the journey. Ordway noted that they stopped to visit a widow woman they had known that winter a world ago. The woman, whose name was not recorded, was running a plantation and getting along well. Then the men launched their canoes and pirogue for the final time, pushing hard for the buildings lining the shore on the opposite side of the wide river, the French-Spanish-British center of trade and government, the gateway to the West, St. Louis.

"About 12 oClock we arrived in Site of St. Louis fired three Rounds as we approached the Town and landed oppicit the center of the Town," wrote Ordway on 23 September. "The people gathred on the Shore and Huzzared three cheers. we unloaded the canoes and carried the baggage all up to a Store house in Town. drew out the canoes then the party all considerable much rejoiced that we have the Expedition Completed and now we look for boarding in Town and wait for our Settlement and then we entend to return to our native homes to See our parents once more as we have been So long from them.— finis."

CHAPTER TWO

"All the Red Men Are My Children"
Lewis and Sheheke's Visit to Thomas Jefferson

"A Letter from St. Louis (Upper Louisiana), dated Sept. 23, 1806, announces the arrival of Captains Lewis and Clark, from their expedition into the interior." Thus began a typical story that ran in newspapers from Frankfort, Kentucky, to Baltimore in the autumn of 1806. Lewis and Clark had returned to a home that would never be the same—they were national heroes. "I sleped but little last night," Clark wrote the day after arriving in St. Louis.

The long days of paddling rivers and hiking mountains had been replaced by a flurry of letter writing and festive receptions. Lewis wrote in an eighteen-hundred-word report to Thomas Jefferson: "It is with pleasure that I announce to you the safe arrival of myself and party . . . with our papers and baggage. In obedience to your orders we have penitrated the Continent of North America to the Pacific Ocean."[1] He went on to summarize the journey, the geography of the West, and possibilities for trade. Clark wrote one letter to relatives in Kentucky and another to his friend William Henry Harrison, governor of Indiana Territory. The captains were received by various members of the Chouteau family, which had founded St. Louis and the fur trade of the Missouri River. On Thursday, 26 September, William Christy, a longtime acquaintance of Clark's, honored Lewis and Clark and their men with a dinner and a ball.

So the men made their way through the muddy streets of St. Louis, that civilized, uncouth, eastern, western city, outpost of narrow, crowded streets overrun with boatmen, merchants, miners, hunters, trappers, gamblers, army officers, priests, bonneted women, and painted French girls. The population of fourteen hundred was largely French but also included Yankees, educated Virginians, southern slave owners and their slaves, free blacks, Spanish, Kentucky boatmen dubbed "Kaintucks," Creoles, and Indians. The streets were notoriously dirty, with flies buzzing around animal carcasses. The houses were made of stone or mud or in the French style of securing logs vertically rather than horizontally. One visitor remarked that the "French mode of building, and the white coat of lime applied to the mud or rough stone walls, gives them a beauty at a distance, which gives place to their native meanness when you inspect them from a nearer point of view."[2]

The social elite of St. Louis crowded into Christy's Inn to feast on a meal that the Frankfort *Western World* newspaper called a "splendid dinner." We don't know what the group drank—probably wine—but we luckily have a record of the toasts that were made. "To the president of the United States, Thomas Jefferson," rang out a voice, and all raised their glasses. "To his cabinet," someone else said, and they drank again. Then they toasted the expedition, the followers of Lewis and Clark, and the United States itself. They drank to the Louisiana Territory, to the memory of Christopher Columbus, to the federal constitution.

"To the memory of the illustrious Washington, Father of America," someone announced. "May his guardian spirit still watch over us and prove a terror to the engines of tyranny," and the group sipped in honor of the hero who had died seven years earlier. They drank to peace with all nations—without submission, of course—and to the country's commerce. One guest proclaimed, "To agriculture and industry." The twenty-nine explorers and a hall full of admirers raised their glasses. This was followed by a much more sentimental salute: "To our fathers who shed their blood and laid down their lives to purchase our independence." Next, "To the Missouri," and they drank again. They toasted the national council; then a gentleman in the crowd remembered the obvious: "To the fair daughters of Louisiana!" and the glasses tipped again.

The Lewis and Clark Expedition had undeniably left the wilderness of abstinence, where they went fourteen months without a drop of alcohol, and returned to the civilized world of wine, champagne, rum (and its hot variations of grog and toddies), whiskey, cider, beer (and its variations of porter, flip, and ale), and brandy. They were back in a society where men, women, and children chose alcoholic cider over water because it was much more sanitary. Back where inns were plentiful, most with casks of rum stacked in the corner. Back where sack (a kind of wine) was cheap and available to all classes. It is little wonder that, as Clark noted, expedition members who had been "perfectly weaned" from alcohol, and no longer cared about it, "relapsed into their old habits" after returning from the journey.

Deciding that seventeen toasts were sufficient, the captains thanked Mr. Christy and everyone else present. But that offered the perfect opportunity for another drink: "To Captains Lewis and Clark," rose the tribute, "their perilous services endear them to every American heart."[3]

By late October, Lewis, Clark, York, and expedition members John Ordway and François Labiche were traveling east with Sheheke, his wife, Yellow Corn, and his son, White Painted House, interpreter René Jusseaume and his Mandan wife and two sons, and a group of Osage Indians. They reached Louisville, Kentucky, in early November and were greeted by William Clark's elder brother George Rogers Clark, a Revolutionary War hero who had captured key forts in the Illinois country with a small company of men.

The townsfolk likely greeted the entourage with cheers, bonfires, and rifle shots, offering Sheheke and the others a delightful and unknown variety of meats, sauces, fruits, vegetables—and drink, with the endless toasts continuing. A toast offered at a reception two months later gives a good indication of how Sheheke's party was received: "The Red People of America—under an enlightened policy, gaining by steady steps the comforts of the civilized, without losing the virtues of the savage state."[4] After the feast, with the tables cleared away and fresh logs stacked in fireplaces at either end of the room, a reception line of well-dressed citizens was typically followed by dancing and more drinking.

By mid-November Lewis and the others—minus Clark—were on their way to Washington. After following the Mississippi and Ohio Rivers to Louisville, they now traveled overland, going east on the Wilderness Road, a swath that had been cut through the woods thirty years earlier by Daniel Boone. Boone's Trace, as some called it, was wide enough for one-way traffic and typically teemed with riders on horseback, freight wagons pulled by eight horses, farmers hauling produce, a good number of folks walking to the side of the path, and livestock, as handlers herded loud cattle, horses, hogs, and even turkeys along the rut-filled and often muddy road to eastern markets. Amid riders weaving around wagons, teamsters cursing at traffic jams, complaining cattle, and the pungent smell of fresh manure, Lewis led the group through the Cumberland Gap—where Kentucky, Tennessee, and Virginia meet—toward their great father in the east.

Clark had gone to Fincastle, Virginia, probably to give Lewis a moment alone in the Washington spotlight, and to visit the girl he hoped to someday marry. Clark, thirty-six, was courting a teenage girl, fifteen-year-old Judith

("Julia") Hancock; their difference in age was a common scenario in the early nineteenth century. Clark was acquainted with her father, the congressman and prominent Virginia landowner George Hancock. Clark had met Julia before the expedition, and during the voyage he had named the Judith River in Montana after her. George Hancock gave his blessing; William and Julia married in 1808 and eventually had five children.

Three days after Christmas in 1806, Lewis, Sheheke, Jusseaume, and the others arrived in the nation's capital. "Never did a similar event excite more joy through the United States," wrote one observer. "The humblest of its citizens had taken a lively interest in the issue of the journey and looked forward with impatience for the information it would furnish."[5]

Neither Jefferson nor Lewis left any details of their first meeting after the expedition's return, but it must have been a joyous reunion for both the thirty-two-year-old captain and his mentor, the president, who was twice as old. (Lewis's own father had died when he was five years old.) In 1801, shortly after taking office, Jefferson had selected the young army officer Lewis, a Virginia neighbor and acquaintance, to be his personal secretary. Over the following two years Lewis had become a close confidant. Now the two men undoubtedly talked for hours, with Jefferson asking about plants and seeds from the West, about zoological artifacts, wildlife, Indians, and the course of the Missouri River. Years later, Jefferson mentioned nonchalantly in a letter how he had got down on his hands and knees to study Clark's masterful maps.

Just as Clark had promised, Sheheke met the "great chief of the seventeen nations of America." Jefferson, who had sometimes sought justice for Indians and other times allowed ruthless campaigns against them, greeted him with genuine warmth. In the previous two years, quite a number of Indian chiefs had visited the president, and he had developed a standard speech. As Jusseaume translated, Jefferson recited: "My children . . . I take you by the hand of friendship and give you a hearty welcome to the seat of the government of the United States. . . . I thank the Great Spirit that he has protected you through the journey. . . . Your nation received [Captain Lewis] kindly, you have taken him by the hand and been friendly to him. My children, I thank you for the services you rendered him. . . . I have already told you that you and all the red men are my children, and I wish you to live in peace and friendship with one another as brethren of the same family ought to do. . . . If you will cease to make war on one another, if you will live in friendship with all mankind, you can employ all your time in providing food and clothing for yourselves and your families. Your men will not be destroyed in war, and your women and children will lie down to sleep in their cabins without fear of being surprised by their enemies and killed or carried away."[6]

In many ways the speech reflected Jefferson's complex attitude toward the native nations—his good will was not feigned, and he hoped to live in peace. He believed that Indians were on a "level with whites in the same uncultivated state," and he had no qualms about intermarriage between whites and Indians. At the same time, he wanted them to farm rather than hunt, with the clear implication that they would have to give up their land. Although he had urged Indiana governor William Henry Harrison and others to employ misleading and underhanded treaties to essentially steal land from American Indians, Jefferson thought the natives would benefit in the long run through integration into white society.[7]

So it was no surprise that Jefferson wanted his guests to enjoy the social life in Washington. Within a day or two of their arrival, Lewis took his visitors— including Sheheke and Jusseaume and their wives, five Osage Indians, and one Delaware—to the theater. During intermission, the Indians were persuaded to take the stage, with Sheheke sitting in an armchair while the others whooped and leaped about the stage in a war dance, complete with knives and tomahawks. "When they ran in," wrote a British diplomat, "the war whoop, or rather a frightful yell, was uttered by all. The drum still beating, the war whoop was repeated and renewed during their manoeuvres. . . . It is therefore I presume their song of joy and triumph." Senator William Plumer described Sheheke as "a *white Indian*, at least he is of a lighter complexion than many of our own people. He was dressed well, but had many ornaments on. Both his dress & ornaments were American."[8] (The Mandan were generally light-skinned and were even thought by some early explorers to be Welsh, a notion that had no basis in fact.)

The highlight of the trip came when Lewis and Sheheke attended an elaborate White House levee on New Year's Day. Jefferson, a generous host who appreciated good food and good wine, supplied plenty of both, with one guest recalling that the tables in the executive mansion were always "chock full." Another recalled sampling a variety of punches and French wines, turkey, duck, rolls of beef, eggs, the new foreign dish macaroni, and a full buffet of desserts—pastries, cakes, ice cream, and "a new kind of pudding, very porous and light, inside white as milk or curd, covered with cream sauce." Jefferson began dinner at 3:30 p.m., talking and drinking with his guests well into the evening.[9]

CHAPTER THREE

"They Appeared in Violent Rage"
Pryor and Shannon's Battle with the Arikara

On 18 May 1807, almost three years to the day after the expedition had begun, a contingent of soldiers checked their rifles and ammunition and boarded a keelboat in St. Louis to escort Sheheke and Jusseaume and their families back to the Mandan villages. Joining the soldiers was George Shannon, who had been hired as a hunter. His salary of $25 per month was a windfall—he had earned a grand total of $178.50 for three years of service on the expedition.

Shannon had joined Lewis and Clark in October 1803 at the age of eighteen.[1] His youth was sometimes painfully apparent: he had a habit of forgetting objects on the trail. He also became separated from the main party two different times. "We had the trumpet sounded and fired several guns," Lewis wrote on 6 August 1805, "but [Shannon] did not join us this evening. I am fearful he is lost again. this is the same man who was seperated from us 15 days as we came up the Missouri and subsisted 9 days of that time on grapes only."

The captains recognized, however, that Shannon was only partly at fault and that he kept his head in such situations. They later assigned him to deliver important messages and to search for lost horses. He proved himself to be particularly cool under pressure on a night when a wolf attacked a small group of scouts. The wolf had bit through Nathaniel Pryor's hand and lunged at Richard Windsor when Shannon dropped it with a sure musket shot.

Thomas Jefferson had handsomely rewarded Lewis and Clark for their successful mission. Each of them received 1,600 acres of land (worth at least two dollars an acre). The enlisted men each received 320 acres of land and back pay. In addition, Lewis received about four thousand dollars in pay and reimbursement and Clark about two thousand dollars, though Lewis had requested equal pay for the two of them. In February 1807 Jefferson went a step further by appointing Lewis governor of the Louisiana Territory and Clark its chief Indian agent. (Lewis's annual salary of two thousand dollars was comparable in spending power to a present-day governor's salary.) Both had thus assumed heavy, prestigious assignments, for the Louisiana Territory stretched north from the present-day Arkansas to Minnesota and diagonally from Arkansas to Montana, encompassing all of the Louisiana Purchase except what is now the state of Louisiana. Lewis's duties ranged from appointing justices of the peace to administering land sales and grants to overseeing road construction. Clark reported to Lewis and was responsible for negotiating treaties, settling disputes among Indian nations, and establishing trade policies. These were high-pressure assignments: both men faced frequent decisions that were likely to arouse controversy throughout the territory.

Clark was also appointed a brigadier general in the militia, and the War Department immediately ordered him to arrange for the safe escort of Sheheke and his family back to their nation. Returning Sheheke to the Mandan villages on the Missouri River thus became the first item of official business for both Lewis and Clark. The two men agreed with Jefferson and Secretary of War Henry Dearborn that Sheheke's safe return was a matter of national honor.

General Clark ordered Nathaniel Pryor to muster a detachment of soldiers to escort Sheheke. Pryor had served as one of three sergeants on the expedition. Lewis and Clark described him as "a man of character and ability" and helped him obtain an officer's commission in the First Infantry just a few months after the expedition.[2] As he was forming his company, Pryor naturally looked for men he already knew and trusted. He signed up Shannon and another expedition comrade, George Gibson, both of whom had served in Pryor's squad. Gibson had acted as an interpreter, probably using sign language, and he was also a first-rate hunter.

Pryor, Shannon, and Gibson had all been among the first group of recruits to the expedition, "the nine young men from Kentucky," described by Clark as "the best woodsmen & Hunters, of young men in this part of the Countrey."[3] These three men, who had traveled to the Pacific coast and back, who had journeyed through Hidatsa, Lakota, Yankton Sioux, and Crow territory without experiencing a single violent encounter with Indians, were about to see their luck change for the worse.

Clark anticipated trouble: "Ensign Pryors Party will consist of 48 men," he wrote to Dearborn, "which will be fully sufficient to pass any hostile band which he may probably meet with."[4] Clark had assumed too much, however, because only a third of these men were soldiers or former soldiers. The rest were laborers, and their lack of military training and discipline would prove disastrous.

In an effort to reduce costs, Dearborn had suggested that a party of fur traders travel with Pryor and receive exclusive trading rights with the Mandan in return. Auguste-Pierre Chouteau, a West Point graduate and Indian diplomat, jumped at the chance to obtain the rights. Chouteau brought with him a group that consisted mainly of boatmen and trappers, experienced with weapons to be sure, but not prepared for what lay ahead. Although Chouteau and his men accompanied Pryor—and were included in Clark's count of forty-eight men—they were not technically part of Pryor's military mission. It is possible that expedition veterans Joseph and Reubin Field, two more of the "nine young men," were part of Chouteau's group. According to Lewis, the Field brothers had been engaged "in all the most dangerous and difficult scenes of the voyage, in which they uniformly acquited themselves with much honor."[5]

Onto the scene stepped the imposing figure of Manuel Lisa, widely disliked and widely respected, an astute businessman whom Meriwether Lewis had called a scoundrel. Born of Spanish parents in New Orleans around 1772, the stocky Lisa had been a prominent fur trader since at least 1800. When Lewis and Clark returned in 1806, Lisa had almost immediately organized an effort to trap the upper Missouri River—which included the present states of North and South Dakota and Montana—the next spring. As his competitor Chouteau prepared boats and supplies to head up the river, Lisa did the same, acquiring two keelboats and hiring fifty men. Then, although the secretary of the territory, Frederick Bates, had instructed him to wait for Pryor and Chouteau, Lisa struck out on his own in April, wanting to make the Montana country before winter and also wanting a business edge. Although trading parties in the 1820s often included one hundred men or more, Lisa's company of fifty was good sized for 1807.

A prominent merchant like Lisa taking an interest in the fur trade surprised no one. Fur trading was perhaps the single greatest force behind the exploration and colonization of North America.[6] Beaver fur, used for posh hats and coats, was in particularly high demand. By 1800, a British trading firm, the Hudson's Bay Company, had been acquiring beaver pelts in the Great Lakes area for more than a century. The company's domain eventually included more than one-third of present-day Canada. For almost forty years Hudson's Bay competed with the North West Company, whose employees included such explorers as Alexander Mackenzie and David Thompson, until 1821, when the British government forced the two companies to merge.

The Louisiana Purchase and the Lewis and Clark Expedition had clearly made the Louisiana Territory the next great beaver market, and the leading businessmen positioning themselves to take advantage of that opportunity were Auguste and Jean-Pierre (commonly known as Pierre) Chouteau and Lisa. (Half-brothers Auguste and Pierre were the uncle and father, respectively, of Auguste-Pierre Chouteau, who accompanied Pryor up the Missouri.) Lisa and the Chouteaus eventually joined with William Clark, Pierre Menard, and others to form the St. Louis Missouri Fur Company. John Jacob Astor, a successful New York businessman born in Germany, became their chief competitor when he formed the American Fur Company and later the Pacific Fur Company.[7]

Fur trading was a complex, risky venture that frequently brought huge profits or huge losses. In 1832, Indian agent John Dougherty estimated that during the 1815–30 period, 25,000 beaver pelts had been sold each year and that the fur-trading business had made a total profit of $1,650,000. He also estimated that Indians had killed approximately 110 trappers and stolen $100,000 worth of furs and equipment.[8] Astor, who eventually monopolized the United States fur trade, was one of the few who amassed great wealth—he was worth $20 million when he died. Lisa's wealth was much more modest: he owned a lot and two houses worth $26,000 when he died in 1820.

By 1807 Lisa had married and purchased his first home in St. Louis. Although he never mastered French or English, he developed a fine sense of how to deal with both business associates and Indians. He also had a knack for choosing good men to work with. For his first trip up the Missouri, he had hired the hunter, scout, and interpreter par excellence George Drouillard, Lewis's right-hand man on the expedition. The son of a French-Canadian father and a Shawnee Indian mother, Drouillard was a civilian employee during the expedition. Lewis called him "a man of much merit" and, using the same language he had used to describe the Field brothers (and no one else), wrote that it was Drouillard's "fate also to have encountered, on various occasions, with either Captain Clark or myself, all the most dangerous and trying scenes of the voyage, in which he uniformly acquited himself with honor."[9]

By the time Lisa's first Missouri fur-trading venture concluded a year and a half later, the Spanish trader had made an indelible impact on the lives of at least six members of the Lewis and Clark Expedition.

Shannon's first voyage up the Missouri had been a once-in-a-lifetime adventure, with men intent on making discoveries and serving their country. The second, in the summer of 1807, was business, for the soldiers and more so for the traders, who were earning a living and showed little interest in discovery or patriotic ideals. Perhaps going upstream seemed even harder to Shannon this time.

A contemporary observer noted the difficulty of moving a keelboat upstream: "On each side [of the keelboat] was what was called a running board about eighteen inches wide with cleats nailed thereon to enable the men to have a foot-hold in forcing the boat up stream by long pike poles about twelve feet long with sharp iron sockets at one end and a flat button upon the other to be applied to their shoulder when in a stooping position, to force the boat up stream against the current."[10]

As he tracked and hunted deer, elk, and buffalo, Shannon was inclined to be cautious because he knew the dangers of frontier life in a most personal way: his father, the Revolutionary War veteran George Shannon Sr., had gone out hunting on a January morning in 1803, got caught in a blizzard, and froze to death. Shannon also knew what it meant to be lost. Just a few months into the expedition, after searching for horses that had strayed, he concluded that the party was ahead of him, so he rode his horse upstream for several days, trying to catch up. After running out of bullets, he killed a rabbit by firing a stick in place of a ball. He found grapes to eat but soon grew weak. Fearing he would never catch the boats, he started downstream, hoping for a trading boat. He was on the verge of killing his horse for food when he spotted the expedition's keelboat coming up the river. The group had been behind him the entire time.

Fighting heat, mosquitoes, sandbars, willows, and snags, Pryor and Chouteau's men labored upstream the entire summer, making twelve miles on a good day—sometimes pulling the barges from the shore, other times propelling them with oars or poles. As one observer in St. Louis wrote, "The men employed as hands upon these boats were none other than the hardiest race of men, of romantic nature, and athletes, for none other could perform such service, and withstand the exposure."[11] The men passed one river after another that flowed into the wide Missouri: the Gasconade, the Osage, the Kansas, the Platte. Shannon and his fellows passed the spot, near the site of Kansas City, Missouri, where the expedition first spotted bison, as well as the bluff marking Floyd's grave, near what became Sioux City, Iowa.

By late summer the keelboats reached Lakota country, making their way up the stretch of river where William Clark and the Lakota warriors had exchanged threats a year earlier, where Black Buffalo had vowed revenge by pounding the ground with his rifle. But if anything out of the ordinary happened this time, Pryor made no mention of it in his letters.

Making slightly better time than Lewis and Clark—understandable, since Pryor's party did not have to take regular compass readings, collect artifacts, or keep detailed journals—the group covered 1,430 miles in less than four months. At 9:00 a.m. on 9 September, they came in sight of the Arikara villages, unmistakably identified by a three-mile-long island near the mouth of the Grand River, just south of where the border between North Dakota and South Dakota now lies. Home to two thousand Indians, the island was a huge garden of beans, corn, and squash. The Indians fired their guns, and Pryor, through interpreter Pierre Dorian, asked what they wanted. "Put to shore," came the reply, "we will supply you with corn and oil." No doubt hoping to present the Arikara, commonly called Rees, with gifts and make his way peaceably upriver, as Lewis and Clark had done in October of 1804, Pryor ordered the boats to land.[12]

But Pryor soon learned that the Arikara and the Mandan were at war— the worst possible news for a party escorting a Mandan chief. Within minutes the bank was swarming with 650 armed Arikara warriors understandably still incensed at the death of their chief in Washington—though Gravelines had informed them of the death a year earlier—and eager to avenge the loss of two of their men recently killed by the Mandan. Then a captive Mandan woman came aboard Pryor's keelboat and told him a disturbing story about Manuel Lisa.

Lisa and his men had arrived some time before and were immediately threatened by the Arikara. Lisa, however, told them that Pryor would arrive soon with the Mandan chief, apparently implying that Pryor's party was a more attractive target. The Arikara knew that attacking Lisa would preclude ambushing Pryor because any survivors in Lisa's group would head downriver and warn Pryor. By this account, Lisa, a "master of the art of conciliating the good will of the Indians," had effectively sold out Pryor's party to save his own skin.[13] In a letter to Clark, Pryor stated the case metaphorically: "[Lisa's] failure [to wait for Pryor], has probably obliged him to divert the storm which threatened *his own boat*, by diverting the attention of the Ricaras to *ours*" (Pryor's emphasis). The Arikara then demanded a great quantity of powder and ball from Lisa and pillaged half his goods from him. They planned to kill him on his return. They further planned "to lose no time" in preparing to murder Sheheke and his escorts when they arrived.

Lisa later told a different story, reporting that he had ordered his boats to land after the Arikara fired on them. When a warrior brandished a knife, Lisa aimed his cannons at the large group of hostile Indians. But after the Indians came forward with peace pipes, Lisa held a council with them and gave them gifts. By his account, he did nothing to jeopardize Pryor's mission.

After hearing the disturbing report from the Mandan woman, Pryor ordered Sheheke and his family barricaded in the cabin of the keelboat and prepared his men for action. Shannon and the others checked the flints on their rifles; meanwhile, the Indians readied their own rifles and drove away the women and children. Still, Pryor managed to keep talking, presenting the Arikara chief Grey Eyes, who had been friendly to William Clark a year earlier, with a medal and thanking the tribe for befriending the expedition in 1804.

The Arikara made no reply but agreed to Pryor's moving the barges upstream. The interpreters Dorian and Jusseaume "went by land. The Indians followed in a body, using threats and menaces." At the upper village the warriors again amassed on the beach. "They appeared in violent rage," demanding that Pryor and Chouteau stay and trade with them. When Pryor refused to move his keelboat into a narrow channel, several Indians seized the cable of Chouteau's boat. Chouteau called out for help. "Make them an offer!" yelled Pryor. Chouteau responded by offering half his goods and a man to trade, but the Arikara were "determined on plunder and blood."

As the interpreters rejoined the party, the chief of the upper village, who wore a distinctive white bandage around his head, came on board Pryor's boat and "desired" to take Sheheke ashore. Pryor refused, and the chief "retired as hastily as he had entered," igniting a rapid-fire sequence of events: the Arikara demanded the arms of Chouteau and his men, which Chouteau refused; Grey Eyes threw his medal to the ground; another Indian struck down a trader with a rifle butt; "the Indians now raised a general Whoop" and fired their guns as they ran for cover from Pryor's cannons. One of Chouteau's men dropped, then another.

Pryor was well armed and returned fire with a "well directed volley" of swivels (thirty-inch cannons), blunderbusses (swivel-mounted buckshot rifles), and small arms. Shannon, Gibson, and the others fired their flintlocks and smoothly reloaded according to the complex procedure that was necessary at the time: bring the firelock down into priming position; open the priming pan, shake in powder, place the last three fingers on the hammer, and shut the pan; turn the rifle into loading position and place the butt down; raise the elbow square with the shoulder and shake powder into the barrel, then insert a square of linen and the ball; tap powder, linen, and ball into place with the starter; draw the ramrod and seize it backhanded in the center; pull the ramrod out entirely, turn it to the front, and place it in the barrel; push the ammunition to a specified point in the muzzle, withdraw the ramrod, and take aim. This procedure had become second nature among the trained soldiers; even so, it took at least fifteen seconds to fire a musket and reload it, long enough for an archer to shoot three arrows.

The chaotic din of gunfire, whistling arrows, whooping, military orders, and groans from the wounded—accompanied by a thick haze of musket and cannon smoke and the distinctive smell of black powder—endured for at least a quarter hour, with Pryor inflicting serious damage. Still, he was outnumbered more than ten to one and ordered a retreat as soon as possible. Shannon and the others continued reloading and firing as the boatmen maneuvered the barge through a tricky maze of sandbars. But Chouteau's nonmilitary group was rattled and confused and got stuck in the sandbars. They had to drag the boat under a volley of bullets from the willows sixty yards away. Pryor defended them, but this predicament "had nearly proven fatal to the whole party."

"We again floated in a narrow rapid current, and continued a retreating combat from both sides of the river for about one hour," wrote Pryor, who ran a gauntlet of Arikara warriors pursuing him on both sides of the narrow channel as he guided the boat downstream, past the upper villages, past the patchwork gardens of corn and squash, past the lower villages, at least three miles before he found safety in the vast river.

The sun was setting when the chief wearing the white bandage and forty of his men attempted to intercept the boats. One of Pryor's men aimed at the chief and fired: the chief fell and "appeared to expire in a moment on the Beach. His Partizans gathered about him and we saw no more of them," Pryor wrote.

Pryor finally had a chance to attend to his wounded men. He found that Shannon had taken a ball that broke his leg, Jusseaume was seriously wounded in both the thigh and the shoulder, and Gibson and one other man were also wounded. "Mr. Chouteau was far less fortunate," wrote Pryor. "He had one man killed on the Beach; one in a Perogue . . . one on board the Barge and another mortally wounded who died nine days afterwards. Six others of his men were badly wounded but have since recovered. This miscarriage is a most unhappy affair." One of the dead was possibly Joseph Field, whose expedition record shows he would have fought bravely.[14]

An expert hunter and woodsman, Field was about twenty-seven at the time of his death, possibly one year older than his brother and fellow expedition member Reubin Field. As far as we know, Joseph Field never married or had children. He was known to be alive on 26 June 1807, when his parents, Abraham and Betty Field, transferred a tract of land in Jefferson County, Kentucky, to him and Reubin. But four months later, on 20 October

1807, in another indenture, Abraham noted, "whereas my son Joseph hath departed this life intestate and his property hath come to me as his heir at law . . . I hereby convey unto the said Reubin Field . . . all my right . . . in the estate of the said Joseph."[15] It is thus quite possible that Joseph Field was one of those killed in the Arikara attack. In addition, we know he died a violent death because William Clark later listed him as "killed." He was the first expedition veteran to die after the return to St. Louis. As it turned out, it was more than six decades before the last survivor perished, and that man was nine years Joseph Field's senior.

Determined to carry out Clark's orders, Pryor proposed taking a three-day's journey over an unfrequented land route to reach the Mandan villages, but Sheheke believed it impossible with several wounded men, Pryor wrote, "together with the incumbrance of [his and Jusseaume's] wives and children." So the men continued downstream, taking Sheheke and Jusseaume and their families back to St. Louis. Jusseaume was permanently disabled, apparently by the wound in his thigh, but he continued to work as an interpreter. As late as 1834 he was still among the Mandan.

Although Pryor had failed in the mission to return Sheheke, he had proved his worth as a soldier by not losing a single man. "If my opinion were asked," he wrote to Clark, "'what number of men would be necessary to escort this unhappy chief to his nation,' I should be compelled to say, from my own knowledge of the association of the upper band of Sieux with the Ricaras that a force of less than 400 men ought not to attempt such an enterprize. And surely it is possible that even one thousand men might fail in the attempt."

The next attempt to return the "unhappy chief" did not come for another two years. During that time, Sheheke and his family lived at Fort Bellefontaine, near St. Louis. When this second attempt was made, it involved several hundred men, as Pryor had recommended. Because of a curious mix of circumstance, it also accelerated the decline of one of the men who ordered it, the governor of the Louisiana Territory, Meriwether Lewis. Such factors as the change of administrations in Washington, Lewis's personal financial situation, and the necessity of sending such a large group up the Missouri combined to make the return of Sheheke an extremely complicated matter. It turned out to be one of the key pressures weighing on Lewis in the last months of his life. It was a major factor in his decision to travel to Washington and also in the frenzied state of mind that resulted in his suicide on the way.

Riding with the current and using the sails whenever possible, the group made good time, but they were still a month away from expert medical help, a month that must have seemed interminable to Shannon, likely immobile, swarmed by mosquitoes, and pained by even the slightest rocking of the barge.

Gibson's wound, apparently through the fleshy part of his leg, was not life threatening, but Shannon's was because the ball had struck bone.[16] Pryor and his men did their best. They had medical supplies and knew the procedure for treating gunshot wounds: remove the ball if necessary and if possible; stop the bleeding through pressure and stitches; pack the wound with rolls of lint; periodically apply poultices of Peruvian bark, which was thought to restore proper blood flow. Even with minor wounds, infection was likely—since balls passed through unsterile clothing, and medical instruments and supplies were half-sterile at best. Shannon's serious wound could not heal by itself (as Lewis's wound had), and he and his caregivers could only watch as infection overtook his leg and gangrene set in.

The prominent St. Louis physician Bernard G. Farrar succinctly described the consequences in an 1816 statement: "I certify that I was called to visit George Shannon esqr. on the 31th of October 1807 and that I found one of his legs in a state of gangrene caused by a ball having passed through it, and that to save his life I was under the necessity of amputating the limb above the knee, the loss of which constitutes in my opinion the first grade of disability."[17] (Clark solicited this statement in a successful attempt to increase Shannon's pension from eight dollars a month to twelve dollars.)

Territorial secretary Frederick Bates wrote to Clark: "It has been impossible to avoid, making some *advances* prior to the final adjustment of several of the accounts: particularly to the unfortunate Shannon, whose life was, for a time despaired of but who is now, since the amputation of his leg, on the recovery." Ninety-five years later, George Shannon's youngest son, William Russell Shannon, wrote that his father's "amputated limb was burried at the old post [Fort Bellefontaine] on the bank of the [Missouri] river."[18]

Shannon's days of adventuring were over, but in the next three decades he made his name as a politician and jurist. He counted a surprising number of prominent men among his friends. He married and saw the beginnings of a fruitful posterity. He outlived most fellow expedition members. But in many ways his two trips down the Missouri, the first in glory and the second in defeat, foreshadowed his future: in Kentucky he would be elected to the state legislature but was later burned in effigy; the joy of his family life would be offset by the early death of his wife; he would be named U.S. attorney for the state of Missouri but was mysteriously not nominated for a second term. Shannon's eventful life was filled with peaks and valleys.

CHAPTER FOUR

"He Saw the Prairie Behind Him Covered with Indians in Full and Rapid Chase"
The Adventures of John Colter

Alone in his dugout canoe, John Colter skirted sandbars, wound his way around islands, and dodged sawyers, making good time as he navigated the Missouri. Colter knew from the flow of the river, the vegetation, and the temperature that it was midsummer, almost a year since he and his partners, Joseph Dickson and Forrest Hancock, had set off on their great trapping venture. The three of them had followed the Yellowstone River into present-day Montana, but they had not been trapping long when Colter and Hancock had a falling-out with Dickson. According to his friend Peter Cartwright, Dickson spent the winter alone while Colter and Hancock bartered for an Indian canoe and headed back down the Yellowstone. Dickson "dug his cave in the side of a steep hill, laid up his winter provisions, and took up his winter quarters all alone. In this perilous condition, his eyes became inflamed . . . from constant gazing on the almost perpetual snows around him, until . . . he could not see anything. Here he was utterly helpless and hopeless." Dickson prayed for help and was prompted to bathe his eyes in a bark poultice. In a short time his sight was restored, and "he fell to his knees to return thanks to God," living as a deeply religious man the rest of his life.[1]

Just where Colter and Hancock spent the winter of 1806–7 is not certain, but by the time the ice broke, they had parted ways. Hancock remained upriver, and Colter turned south and east for St. Louis, for the civilized society he had not seen for more than three years.

Now, in July of 1807, with Pryor and Shannon several hundred miles downstream—and their encounter with the Arikara still two months in the future—Colter passed the Arikara villages himself. According to Thomas James, who met Colter in 1809 and heard of his adventures firsthand, Colter's "character was that of a true American backwoodsman. He was about thirty-five years of age, five feet ten inches in height, and wore an open, ingenuous, and pleasing countenance of the Daniel Boone stamp. Nature had formed him, like Boone, for hardy endurance of fatigue, privations, and perils."[2]

Pelicans and eagles flew overhead as Colter passed the bluff where the Corps of Discovery had buried Sergeant Floyd three years earlier, near the site of present-day Sioux City, Iowa. The third day out from Floyd's grave, as he approached the mouth of the Platte River, he made out a keelboat and a group of trappers. Someone on shore fired off a shot as a sign of welcome. The faces on the bank turned out to belong to men he knew—George Drouillard, Peter Weiser, John Potts, Richard Windsor, and Jean-Baptiste Lepage, all veterans of the Lewis and Clark Expedition with Colter and all five now under the command of Manuel Lisa.[3]

Learning that Colter was a Lewis and Clark man who had trapped the Montana country for several months, Lisa offered him a job—apparently "free trapper" status in exchange for his services as a hunter and guide. This meant Colter could trap when and where he wanted, with full rights to his pelts and skins. (Most of Lisa's employees, by contrast, had signed contracts binding them to Lisa's company for three years and requiring them to turn over half of whatever furs they took.)[4] Knowing that he had a land grant and several hundred dollars' back pay waiting for him in St. Louis, and well aware that heading back up the river would mean wintering in the wild for a fourth consecutive year, Colter gave his answer: yes.

Among the group of trappers was one who looked much too old to be on a trapping expedition: Edward Robinson. Indeed, Robinson, an early settler of Kentucky and probably a friend of Daniel Boone's, was sixty-two years old. He had fought his share of Indian battles, and one of his foes, probably a Shawnee warrior, had scalped him. He had "since been obliged to wear a handkerchief on his head to protect the part." Robinson was apparently accompanied by two friends, fellow Kentuckians John Hoback and Jacob Reznor. These three men, dubbed the "doomed trio" by a modern historian, frequently crossed paths with Lewis and Clark veterans before being massacred by Shoshones in the rugged Idaho wilderness in 1814.[5]

Colter very possibly heard talk of what had happened two months earlier. In May of 1807, when the group reached the mouth of the Osage River, in what is now central Missouri, an enlistee by the name of Antoine Bissonnet had deserted and fled—even though he had signed on for a three-year term. Apparently anxious to maintain militarylike discipline on a fur-trading mission fraught with peril, Lisa had ordered Drouillard to go after Bissonnet and bring him back, "dead or alive." Sometime later, Drouillard returned, already sorrowful over having shot Bissonnet, and asked his fellows to help him carry the wounded man into camp. They apparently did what they could, even sending someone in a canoe to accompany Bissonnet back to St. Charles for medical help, but Bissonnet died on the way. Drouillard regretted what had happened, but Lisa did not, even haranguing Bissonnet as he lay mortally wounded.[6] Now the question loomed—would Drouillard face charges when he returned to St. Louis?

Ironically, Lisa had replaced Bissonnet with a trapper destined to become the most notorious mountain man in the history of the fur trade, Edward Rose. Said to be the son of a white trader and a woman of Indian and African-American blood, Rose had made a reputation as a New Orleans brawler and pirate while still in his teens. As one acquaintance put it, "his visage most conspicuously displayed the marks of turmoil and strife," with a large scar in the middle of his forehead. But "the most honorable mark he bore, and the one by which he became subsequently well known to all Indians between the Missouri and Rocky Mountains, was one made by the meeting of the upper and lower jaws of a 'big' Chillicothean, about two thirds of an inch from the tip of his noes, and resulting in the total loss of the part thus separated."[7]

It would have been easy for Colter to regret his decision to join Lisa's party when it hit a rash of problems: food ran low; a recruit by the name of Bouche held up the group by taking an unauthorized hunting trip; the keelboat was damaged. Then Lisa and his men encountered the hostile Arikara Indians. Lisa ordered the men to their arms, narrowly avoiding violence (and, according to the Mandan woman on the scene, diverting the wrath of the Arikara to Pryor's party, which arrived a month later). Within weeks, Lisa combined tough talk with gifts to avoid conflicts with the Mandan and the Assiniboin, even though his group was vastly outnumbered.[8]

The forty-odd men followed the Yellowstone River to the mouth of the Bighorn River (near the present site of Bighorn, Montana), arriving late in the fall, with Colter's former partner, Forrest Hancock, now a member of the group. This was prime beaver country, with a good supply of timber, and the men immediately began constructing a fort, calling it Fort Raymond, after Lisa's son. With winter coming on fast, Lisa charged four emissaries to scout the region and befriend the native nations, particularly the Crows. The four scouts he chose were Edward Rose, Peter Weiser, George Drouillard, and John Colter.

Captain Reuben Holmes, a later acquaintance of Edward Rose, said that "Rose, by this time, had given some proofs of his reckless bravery, and of a strong and vigorous constitution. . . . Accordingly, Rose among a few others, was selected to spend the winter with the Crow Indians, and was, accordingly, also supplied with such articles of trade as were considered best calculated to promote the interests of the expedition."[9] Rose's exact location during the winter is unknown, but he had a passion for Indian life, undoubtedly taking up Crow dress and the Crow language from the moment he arrived. The Indians were impressed by the large, powerful, fierce-looking Rose, and they called him Nez Coupe, or Cut Nose.

Peter Weiser, who had served as an Indian diplomat during the Lewis and Clark Expedition, apparently went west, following William Clark's 1806 route (in the opposite direction) along the Yellowstone River. He may have met the band of Crows that dwelled north of the Yellowstone River and told them about Fort Raymond. Near present-day Livingston, Weiser abandoned his canoe—and the river—hiking over Bozeman Pass and continuing overland until he reached a river that he probably knew was the Gallatin. He followed the Gallatin west a short distance to an expanse he had visited twice before, though never in winter. This was Three Forks, the headwaters of the Missouri, where the Jefferson, Madison, and Gallatin Rivers (all named by Lewis and Clark) united to form a single river.

Of all the strategic points along the Lewis and Clark trail, from Floyd's Bluff and Fort Mandan in the east to Lolo Pass and Fort Clatsop in the west, none was more significant in the lives of the corps than Three Forks. Here, around the age of twelve, Sacagawea had been kidnapped by Hidatsa raiders. Here, at the end of July 1805, with a cold autumn rapidly approaching, the two captains had correctly chosen the Jefferson as the river to follow, going west to the Continental Divide and the friendly villages of the Shoshone people. Here, within three years of Weiser's arrival, Potts and Drouillard met their deaths at the hands of Blackfoot warriors, and John Colter ran for his life in the most famous escape from Indians in the history of the West.

Searching for good beaver territory, and also heading away from Blackfoot country, Weiser ascended the Madison to the south. Reaching a plain near the present Idaho border, he left the river and crossed the Continental Divide, finding a picturesque frozen lake and a branch of the Snake River. Based on information from Weiser, Andrew Henry reached this spot three years later, establishing one of the first posts west of the divide and leaving his name everywhere—Henry's Fort, Henry's Lake, Henry's Fork.[10]

The third of Lisa's scouts who set out from Fort Raymond as winter 1807 approached, George Drouillard, had proved his skills on the Lewis and Clark

Expedition—from scouting and hunting to interpreting native languages to showing courage under fire. As a result, he had become a subpartner to Lisa and the official representative of Lisa's partners, William Morrison and Pierre Menard. Drouillard undertook two missions to the Crows, or Absaroke, going first to a tribe near the modern site of Billings where he probably met with Crow chiefs in one of their large lodges, which were framed in wood, covered by bushes, and decorated with skins. This was quite possibly the same group of Crows who had stolen several horses from William Clark's group as they made their way across the region of southern Montana in the summer of 1806. (Drouillard had been to the north, with Lewis.)

The French called the Crows "the handsome men." Clark had described them as "large portley men, Tall women well proportioned." The men wore hooded blankets made from buffalo hide and braided their hair on both sides of their heads. In full dress, they used glue and clay to stand their bangs straight up. The Crows spoke a language quite similar to that of the Hidatsa, and Lewis and Clark had correctly surmised that the two nations had once been part of the same Gros Ventre tribe. Using Hidatsa words he had picked up at Fort Mandan, as well as sign language, Drouillard invited the Crows to trade at Fort Raymond. Their cooperation was crucial to Lisa because they were adept beaver trappers, and they also acted as middlemen to facilitate trade with other nations.

Over the course of his two trips, Drouillard met with a number of Indians. It's also quite likely that he followed the Little Bighorn River across a wide plain and over a series of rolling hills, past the spot where, sixty-nine years later, three thousand native warriors annihilated 264 soldiers under the command of Lieutenant Colonel George Armstrong Custer.

Not surprisingly, Lisa chose another Corps of Discovery veteran, John Colter, as his fourth scout. An acquaintance wrote that "this man [Colter], with a pack of thirty pounds weight, his gun and some ammunition, went upwards of five hundred miles to the Crow nation; gave them information, and proceeded from thence to several other tribes."[11] Along with his flintlock rifle, powder horn, and lead, a typical trapper of the period carried a Spanish dagger, an eight-inch "scalping" knife, and a large tomahawk called a "Missouri war hatchet." In his "wallet" or "possibles sack" he carried extra flints, fishing hooks and line, needle and thread, pipe and tobacco, and a steel for striking fire. These mountain men replaced their western clothes with fringed buckskin pants and shirt, Indian-blanket "stockings," winter moccasins, wolf-skin hats, and buffalo-robe coats, waterproofing their leather outfits by wiping grease on them at every meal. They took along "bear paw" snowshoes with a hardwood frame and rawhide netting, like those used for centuries by the native nations of the Great Lakes region. Food rations included dried corn and pemmican—buffalo meat dried, pounded fine, and mixed with melted fat. They also carried such Indian presents as brilliant-colored handkerchiefs and beads, tobacco, "cheap looking glasses" (telescopes), earrings, and brass combs.

From Fort Raymond, Colter ascended the Bighorn River, following it south to its confluence with the Shoshone River, which he then followed west. As he approached the area near present-day Cody, Wyoming, Colter saw the Absaroka Range of the Rocky Mountains looming ahead of him. The river—later dubbed "Stinking River" by William Clark—began to smell of sulfur. Then, like a stranger in a strange land, the Lewis and Clark veteran wandered into what Captain Benjamin Bonneville later described as a "volcanic tract," with "gloomy terrors," "hidden fires, smoking pits, noxious streams and the all-pervading 'smell of brimstone.'"[12] Yellowstone National Park now lies fifty miles west of this region, which was also seen by Drouillard and was later nicknamed "Colter's Hell."

The hot springs in this alien landscape offered two luxuries of wilderness life—first, a soothing bath. Colter had already seen Indians amuse themselves this way at the Lolo Hot Springs. "After remaining in the hot bath as long as they could bear it ran and plunged themselves into the creek the water of which is now as cold as ice can make it," Lewis had written. "After remaining here a few minutes they returned again to the warm bath, repeating this transition several times but always ending with the warm bath." Second was an easily cooked meal. As one trapper later wrote, hot springs "are very serviceable to the hunter in preparing his dinner when hungry for here his kettle is always ready and boiling his meat being suspended in the water by a string is soon prepared for his meal without further trouble."[13]

Colter next followed the south fork of the Shoshone into the mountains, crossed Togwatee Pass—and the Continental Divide—and reached a spectacular valley near what is now Jackson, Wyoming. The valley was bordered on the west by a steep mountain range, with three distinct peaks, later called the Tetons. Colter crossed the frozen Snake River, the same waterway that had propelled him and the rest of the expedition into the Columbia River and the Oregon country (now Washington State) in October 1805.

Colter scaled a pass into what is now Idaho, following the Teton River north, near the modern location of Driggs, and then crossed back to the east to Jackson Lake. He traversed land that is currently part of Yellowstone Park, going north to "Lake Eustis" (now Yellowstone Lake). He then descended the lake's outlet, the Yellowstone River, about twenty-five miles to Tower Falls, where he hiked along the edge of the Absaroka Mountains to Clark's Fork

River. Traveling south, he may have passed through Colter's Hell a second time before following his original route back to Fort Raymond.[14]

By the spring of 1808, Colter had left on another journey to establish trade with friendly Indians, this time ascending the Yellowstone River, crossing Bozeman Pass, and following the Gallatin River to Three Forks (thus retracing Weiser's route). Sometime during this trek, Colter, who now spoke the Crow language reasonably well, fell in with a band of eight hundred Crows and Flatheads, including some he may have met the previous winter, or the winter before that—when he and Hancock trapped the Yellowstone. Colter was leading the Indians back to Fort Raymond when a band of fifteen hundred Blackfeet attacked. Colter fought alongside the Crows and Flatheads, some of whom were armed with flintlock rifles—as were some of the Blackfeet. Colter's friend Thomas James later reported that Colter was wounded in the leg but crawled to a small thicket and continued firing his musket. "The Black[feet] engaged at first with about five hundred Flatheads, who they attacked in great fury. The noise, shouts, and firing brought a reinforcement of Crows to the Flathead, who were fighting with great spirit and defending the ground manfully." The Blackfeet were eventually driven back, "but retired in perfect order and could hardly be said to have been defeated. The Flatheads are a noble race of men, brave, generous, and hospitable. They might be called the Spartans of Oregon. . . . Their desperate courage saved them from a general massacre."[15]

The bullet—or arrow—that struck Colter in the leg must have penetrated soft tissue, for he recovered with no ill effect and made it back to Fort Raymond. As Colter recuperated at the fort, he watched tensions rise. Lisa had threatened Etienne Brandt with a knife after Brandt was caught stealing supplies from a storeroom. Bouche, a troublemaker the entire trip, attempted an unsuccessful mutiny by spreading rumors that Lisa had given the men bad gunpowder. Edward Rose had finally returned from his long stay with the Crows, but to Lisa's astonishment Rose had given away a considerable amount of trade goods without requiring any beaver pelts in return.[16]

Then, probably in July of 1808, at the very moment Lisa was preparing to return to St. Louis, an argument broke out between him and Rose in the fort's counting room. Not one to hold his tongue, Lisa said something that enraged Rose, who "sprang, like a tiger," according to Reuben Holmes, upon the much smaller Lisa and quickly overpowered him. The noise brought expedition veteran John Potts into the room—just as Rose was about to kill Lisa. As Potts stepped in between the two men, Lisa ran out to the keelboat, showing no concern for the man who had just saved his life and who was now taking a beating in his place, "suffering severely by the interference."

"Rose saw the boat about moving slowly from the shore, as she swung around into the current; infuriated with passion, and almost blind with rage, he ran to a swivel pointed towards the river, and quickly directing its line of fire, 'touched it off' with his pipe," Holmes later wrote. The buckshot hit the cargo box of the boat, barely missing the crew members. As Rose madly attempted to reload the swivel, ten or fifteen men tackled him but "could barely restrain the effects of his ungovernable passion."[17]

Within days—and no doubt encouraged by the quorum of men who had subdued him—Rose packed up his supplies and returned to live with the Crows. Washington Irving, who described Rose as "a dogged, sullen, silent fellow, with a sinister aspect and more of the savage than the civilized man in his appearance," later wrote that Rose "had betaken himself to the wilderness, and associated himself with the Crows, whose predatory habits were congenial to his own, had married a woman of the tribe, and, in short, had identified himself with those vagrant savages."[18]

The man who had saved Lisa, thirty-two-year-old John Potts, had been born in Germany. It is unknown when he had come to America, but he joined the U.S. Army in 1800. His military record described him as having black hair, black eyes, and a fair complexion. He was a miller by occupation. Throughout his first year with Lisa, Potts had piled up one debt after another to keep himself in guns, ammunition, traps, beaver oil, kettles, and all the other supplies a trapper needed. He signed a note to Thomas Whitley for $44.25, another to Manuel Lisa and Company for $170.00, another of $14.00 to the company, and a joint note with Peter Weiser that totaled $420.50.[19] He had trapped the upper Missouri for a year, but his dreams of a plentiful beaver harvest had come to naught.

Colter, who had served with Potts in John Ordway's squad on the expedition, had experienced similar luck in two years of trapping. As the two men healed from their injuries, they decided to head back to Three Forks together and trap the beaver-rich region, despite Colter's recent encounter with the Blackfeet. Finally, with autumn coming on, Potts rented two horses from the company, and he and Colter said goodbye to Weiser and Lepage and set out.[20] (Drouillard and possibly Windsor had returned to St. Louis with Lisa.) Potts and Colter may have reasoned that the Blackfeet had migrated back to the north. After all, the Lewis and Clark team had twice traversed Three Forks—once in July of 1805 and again a year later—without seeing Blackfeet. With Lewis and Clark and then with Lisa, they had not experienced a single battle with native warriors, though such conflict had again and again seemed inevitable.

But this run of good luck did not last long. According to those who recorded Colter's story (regrettably, he himself did not), Colter and Potts reached Three Forks without incident but took nothing for granted—setting their traps at night, taking their catch early in the morning, and staying concealed during the day. One morning they were in their canoe, checking traps on the Jefferson River when they heard "a great noise, resembling the trampling of animals," in the account that John Bradbury wrote after he later heard the tale from Colter. Colter concluded that there was a great number of Blackfeet nearby and urged a retreat, but Potts insisted that the noise had come from a herd of buffalo. Moments later, several hundred Blackfoot warriors appeared on both sides of the river and beckoned the two men to come ashore. Retreat was now impossible.[21]

Hoping the Blackfeet wanted only to rob them, Colter and Potts dropped their traps into the shallow water, and Colter turned the canoe for the shore. A warrior waded into the water, stepped up to the canoe, and grabbed Potts's rifle, but Colter, "a remarkably strong man, immediately retook it, and handed it to Potts, who remained in the canoe, and on receiving it pushed off into the river," wrote Bradbury. Colter pleaded with him to come ashore, but Potts refused. Within seconds, a Blackfoot shot an arrow at Potts, striking him near the hip. "Colter, I am wounded," cried Potts.[22]

Colter urged him again to come ashore. "I am too much hurt to escape," yelled Potts. "If you can get away, do so. I will kill at least one of them." With that, he raised his rifle and shot one of the Indians dead, perhaps preferring certain death to the prospect of being tortured. "He was instantly pierced with arrows so numerous, that, to use the language of Colter, '*he was made a riddle of.*'"[23] Several of the Blackfeet then rushed into the river and pulled the canoe ashore, dragging Potts's body onto the bank and hacking it to pieces with knives and tomahawks. Potts was the second expedition veteran to die, and the second to die a violent death.

The Blackfeet stripped Colter naked and debated how to kill him, initially deciding to use him as target practice. Colter was convinced he would first be tortured. Then a chief pointed at the prairie and motioned with his hand, saying, "Go, go away." Colter walked tentatively out into the grass, believing he would be shot "as soon as he was out of the crowd and presented a fair mark to their guns," James wrote later in his account of Colter's ordeal. He continued to walk, but an old Indian urged him on with impatient signs and exclamations, obviously wanting him to run. He was a hundred yards away and still walking when he turned to see a group of Blackfeet throwing off their leggings and blankets, "as if for a race. Now he knew their object. He was to run a race, of which the prize was to be his own life and scalp."[24]

Colter bolted, charging over rocks and cactus in his bare feet, galloping across the plain toward the Madison River, running for his life. Behind him he heard a war whoop as several young Indians took up the chase with spears in hand. Known as a fast runner by his fellow trappers, Colter ran with a speed that surprised even himself. He had run about half of the five or six miles to the Madison when blood began gushing from his nostrils. "At every leap the red stream spurted before him, and his limbs were growing rapidly weaker and weaker."[25] He glanced back to see a solitary Blackfoot far ahead of the others.

The warrior rapidly closed the gap on the exhausted Colter, who called out in the Crow language for his life to be spared. But the Blackfoot seemed not to hear and raised his lance as he approached. Colter suddenly turned and faced his pursuer. The surprised Indian lunged forward, tripping as he threw his spear "with such violence as to break the handle and miss the object," wrote William H. Thomas, who interviewed Colter in 1809. With his opponent sprawled on the ground, Colter "became the assailant, turned on the Indian and put him to death with the broken spear."[26]

Still holding the spear head, Colter seized the Indian's blanket with his other hand and resumed his flight. His strength was renewed, and he felt, as he later told James, "as if he had not run a mile. A shout and yell arose from the pursuing army in his rear as from a legion of devils, and he saw the prairie behind him covered with Indians in full and rapid chase."[27]

But the Madison was not far away, and as Colter approached it he heard the pursuing Blackfeet raise another war whoop as they discovered the body of their comrade. Colter ran through a tangle of willows and plunged into the chilling river. As he floated downstream he saw a large mass of driftwood (some said a beaver dam) that had lodged against a small island. He dove and—after several tries—got his head above water inside the heap of timber. "Scarcely had he secured himself, when the Indians arrived on the river, screeching and yelling, as Colter expressed it, 'like so many devils.'"[28]

Now he waited. The Indians scoured the bank on both sides, even swimming out to the island and tromping on the driftwood above Colter's head. He watched them through the chinks, fearing they would spot him or set fire to his hiding place. Again they searched the banks; again they returned to the island, with Colter waiting the entire day in "horrible suspense," his body half in and half out of the cold water.[29] When night finally came and he heard no more of his enemies, he swam downstream a good distance and mustered the strength to go east over another prairie, traveling all night.

"Although happy in having escaped from the Indians, his situation was still dreadful; he was completely naked, under a burning sun; the soles of his feet were entirely filled with thorns of the prickly pear [cactus]; he was hungry, and had no means of killing game, although he saw abundance around him."[30] Colter knew he was a week and a half from Fort Raymond, but he luckily knew the way.

He crossed the Gallatin River and headed due east, for Bozeman Pass. He had been through the pass two or three times with his friends the Crows, and he knew the Blackfeet were likely to guard this sole outlet from the valley into the mountains. "To avoid the danger of a surprise, Colter ascended the almost perpendicular mountain before him, the tops and sides of which a great way down were covered with perpetual snow."[31] At the summit he sheltered and hid himself till nightfall, when he somehow made his way down the other side.

From Bozeman Pass he hiked twenty miles east to the Yellowstone River, which would take him back to Fort Raymond, just as the river had taken a much more comfortable William Clark and his party east in 1806. Now a mountain man in the ultimate sense, Colter walked—more likely limped—along the river night and day, digging up roots with his spear head for sustenance and drinking from the Yellowstone. He kept up a brutal pace, resting only occasionally and averaging twenty miles a day for an amazing eleven days.[32]

Expedition veterans Peter Weiser and Jean-Baptiste Lepage were among those present at Fort Raymond when a solitary figure staggered toward the stockade. "His beard was long, his face and whole body were thin and emaciated by hunger, and his limbs and feet swollen and sore," James later wrote. When the poor man was finally inside the compound, someone asked who he was. Colter, came the reply.[33]

John Colter had survived his race against the Blackfeet, and then the long march back to the safety of the fort. But he still wasn't through venturing to the upper Missouri River country, and there were still more encounters with the hostile Indians of this region to come in the remaining years of his life.

CHAPTER FIVE

"This Has Not Been Done Through Malice"
George Drouillard's Murder Trial

On Monday, 19 September 1808, probably a month or so after Colter's long run back to Fort Raymond, the crowd in the St. Louis district courtroom buzzed as the constable ushered a prisoner to the defense table. He was well known as Manuel Lisa's fur-trading associate and also as a key member of the Lewis and Clark Expedition—George Drouillard. The charge was murder.

It seems quite likely that Lisa was also in the courtroom. He and Drouillard had been arrested for Bissonnet's death when they returned from Montana, and Lisa had posted a five-thousand-dollar bail to gain their freedom. Lisa's trial was to follow Drouillard's.

Twelve men filed into the jury box. Among them was a young man using a crutch and trying to get accustomed to his peg leg—George Shannon. After spending several months recuperating at Fort Bellefontaine, the twenty-three-year-old Shannon had returned to "normal" life.[1] He of course knew Drouillard well—the man had been his mentor and companion when the two of them successfully fulfilled a mission to find Nez Percé guides to show the expedition the way over the rugged Bitterroot Mountains.

Drouillard must have been shocked to see Shannon hobbling on a peg leg. Though Shannon had been wounded a year earlier, Drouillard had been in the Montana wilderness the entire time, out of touch with civilization. His arrival in St. Louis a few weeks earlier had offered the first opportunity to learn of Shannon's fate.

Presiding were the Honorable Auguste Chouteau, associate justice, and the Honorable John C. B. Lucas, presiding justice. Attorney General John Scott spoke for the prosecution. His case was simple and straightforward: On 14 May 1807, at the mouth of the Osage River, Drouillard, "not having the fear of God before his eyes, but being moved and seduced by the instigation of the devil," had willfully and with "malice aforethought" taken the life of one Antoine Bissonnet; he was therefore guilty of murder.[2]

A reporter for the *Missouri Gazette* sat in the courtroom scribbling notes. "The facts were briefly these," he later wrote. "Mr. Manuel Lisa and [Drouillard] had embarked . . . on a trading and hunting voyage up to the sources of the Missouri river. They had enlisted the deceased as a hand for the term of three years; he had engaged to do duty, not only as a hunter, but expressly covenanted . . . to mount guard, to give them timely notice of everything that might prove injurious to their interests, and not to leave their service on any pretext whatever."

Scott called a man by the name of Antoine Dubreuil, who had been a voyager on Lisa's expedition, as his star witness. "On the day when we had to leave the River of Osages to continue our trip," testified Dubreuil, "Mr. Manuel Lisa ordered the crew to go on the open [river]; as soon as the boat started going the crew exclaimed that one man was missing. Manuel ordered to land and to go and search for 'Bazine' [Bissonnet]. And he told Mr. George Drouillard, 'George go and find this Bazine. Go after him and bring him dead or alive.'"

Scott asked what happened next.

"Some time after that I heard the report of a gun," answered Dubreuil. "About half an hour later Mr. George Drouillard came back and said that he shot 'Bazine' but he did not die. Mr. Drouillard said he was sorry for it, and he came back to bring some more men with him to take the wounded man to the camp."

Scott asked what Lisa had been doing during this time.

Dubreuil replied that Lisa "took a boat and two men and when he left he said 'If I meet him I will shoot him on first sight.'" Dubreuil added that "[Lisa] came back two or three hours afterwards and as soon as he landed George Drouillard announced to him that he had wounded the man. [Lisa] said, 'It is well done. He's a rascal who got what he deserved.' He went up to 'bazine' and spoke to him in an angry tone, blaming him for the condition in which he had put himself and which was purely his fault."

Dubreuil concluded by saying that Lisa had sent Bissonnet to St. Charles for medical treatment the next day. Five other voyagers backed up Dubreuil's testimony, adding that Bissonnet was asked why he had deserted. "He could give no reason—it was a misfortune for him," said one of these witnesses. He was also asked if anyone had mistreated him. No, Bissonnet had answered.

Did the final detail cast a pall over Drouillard? Bissonnet had been shot in the back, "near one of his shoulders," and the wounded man had died before reaching St. Charles.

Three prominent St. Louis attorneys spoke for the defense, none of them disputing the accounts of the boatmen. Edward Hempstead argued that murder was not even the proper charge—this was really a manslaughter case. There was no question of malice on the part of the prisoner. "Mr. Hempstead read a variety of law cases in point, to support this position.—He spoke about 45 minutes in a forcible and impressive manner," the newspaper reporter wrote.

An impassioned Rufus Easton argued the case for twice that long. He reminded the jury that Bissonnet had committed larceny by stealing blankets and other articles and hiding them in the trunk of a tree. This "clandestine manner of deserting" proved Bissonnet's felonious intent. The killing was therefore perfectly justified by both human and divine law. Easton quoted several statutes to prove the human side. For the divine side, he noted that he was supported by holy writ. Opening his Bible, he quoted the prophet Moses: "If a thief be found breaking up, and be smitten that he die, there shall no blood be shed for him" (Genesis 22:2). Easton next spoke at length on the importance of the fur trade and how the success of such expeditions depended on the fidelity of each and every member. But he saved his most persuasive point for last:

"[Easton] pourtrayed with the livliest animation," reported the *Gazette*, "the persevering and unshaken fidelity of the prisoner in ascending the Missouri with intrepid and brave Captains Lewis and Clark, over the snowy and rocky mountains to the Pacific ocean.

"That with them he braved the unparalleled hardships of a desert and howling wilderness and though brought to gnaw the foot of a dog, yet he scorned to desert." Easton, of course, did not mention that Lewis and Clark had dealt with a variety of discipline problems, including desertion, without having any of their men shot.

William Carr argued along similar lines: Drouillard had rightly developed military habits on the Lewis and Clark Expedition, where "implicit obedience" was the norm. Therefore, he "could not be charged with having a bad heart for fulfilling the commands of his superior in this instance." In fact, intoned Carr, "if anyone is to blame, it is Mr. Lisa, who ordered him to bring the deceased '*dead or alive.*'" Finally, Carr "reminded the Jury of the Punishment of Manslaughter, and besought them not to fix such infamous stigma upon so deserving a character.

"He spoke about an hour, with his usual elegance of style and beauty of thought and expression," according to the *Gazette*'s report.

In his concluding argument for the prosecution, the attorney general argued that Bissonnet had harmed no one by deserting and taking the few articles he did. The killing was committed through malice—it was murder in the "fullest and most strict sense of the term." Scott also cited a number of precedents to support his view. The newspaperman called his summation "ingenious."

Drouillard later confided in a letter to his sister: "You have without doubt learned of the misfortune which happened to me last spring on my way to the Upper Missouri. I admit that this misfortune was very fatal to us but at the same time, I would have you observe without trying to excuse myself, that this has not been done through malice, hatred or any evil intent. Thoughtlessness on my part and lack of reflection in this unhappy moment is the only cause of it, and moreover encouraged and urged on by my partner, Manuel Lisa, who we ought to consider in this affair as guilty as myself for without him the thing would never have taken place. The recollection of this unhappy affair throws me very often in the most profound reflections, and certainly I think it has caused a great deal of grief to my family for which I am very sorry and very much mortified. That I have not lost the affection of my old friends proves that they did not believe me capable of an action so terrible through malice and bad intent."[3]

Drouillard's "old friends" certainly included Lewis and Clark, two of the most prominent men in the territory. Lewis was in St. Louis during the trial and was dealing with serious Indian problems. Clark had left on an expedition to establish Fort Osage on 25 August and returned to St. Louis late in the evening of 22 September. Whether either of them made an appearance in the courtroom is unknown.[4]

The trial occupied the entire week, and on Friday, 23 September, Judge Lucas instructed the jury and sent them out to deliberate. Nothing is known of their discussion. They knew that Bissonnet had not harmed anyone and that he had been shot in the back. The prosecutor had made those stark facts perfectly clear. Still, the men of the jury were accustomed to living in the violent world that was inevitable on the edge of civilization. They knew it was perfectly legal for military officers to execute a deserter, and they may well have reasoned that Lisa's expedition had been much like a military mission, with each crew member bound to do his duty in order to guard against Indian attack. Perhaps Shannon himself spoke of the dangers of traveling up the Missouri, of the absolute necessity of obeying orders. Such arguments apparently proved quite persuasive, for, as the *Gazette* succinctly noted, "the Jury retired from the bar, and in about fifteen minutes returned a verdict of *Not Guilty*."

Manuel Lisa was perhaps eager to get back to the mountains of paper-work piling up in his office. He had also been indicted, but since Drouillard had been tried first, Lisa may have assumed that he would not be tried if Drouillard was found not guilty. For this reason, Lisa likely hired Drouillard's lawyers and may have even suggested that they shift attention from Drouillard to himself. If so, the strategy worked. "The principle [*sic*] being found not guilty, I will no further prosecute this cause," wrote Attorney General Scott.

Drouillard wrote to his sister that the trial had "absorbed all my savings that I had made in the upper Missouri." Because of this, he was unable to visit his family during the winter of 1808–9. But he made plans for a future visit: "I do not think I can return from the Upper Missouri before three years and just as soon as I return I shall be delighted to see you all. . . . My respects to our Mother who I embrace well, also all my brothers and sisters who I would like very much to see."[5] As Drouillard predicted, he left for the upper Missouri the next spring. He and Colter would make one final trip to the Three Forks of the Missouri.

CHAPTER SIX

"The Gloomy and Savage Wilderness"
The Mysterious Death of Meriwether Lewis

Reaching the end of a hard, dusk-to-dawn, forty-mile ride through the Tennessee wilderness, Meriwether Lewis pulled his horse off the trail known as the Natchez Trace and rode toward a log structure in a nearby clearing. The date was Tuesday, 10 October 1809. The inn called Grinder's Stand offered food and lodging to travelers on the trace. Surrounded by the stumps of poplars that had been felled to build it, Grinder's Stand was actually two cabins, each with a huge fireplace, linked by a fifteen-foot covered breezeway the settlers called a dogtrot. Priscilla Grinder, wife of the absent owner, watched as her visitor approached—a serious, distinguished man wearing a loose-fitting blue-and-white-striped cloak. Apparently in her mid-thirties, Mrs. Grinder lived with her husband and three children at the edge of the Chickasaw nation and had no close white neighbors.

Mrs. Grinder asked if Lewis had come alone. No, he answered, two servants would soon arrive. He carried his saddle into the cabin and asked for spirits; Mrs. Grinder obliged, probably with the corn whiskey so common on the frontier, but Lewis drank very little. The pleasant, warm October day was giving way to a tranquil autumn evening, the sun just setting.[1]

Before long the servants rode up the path. Lewis asked his personal valet, John Pernia (also spelled Pernier), a free mulatto, about his gunpowder, saying he was sure he had some in a canister. Pernia seemed reluctant to answer the question, giving no reply that Mrs. Grinder could discern. She felt that something wasn't right, a worry confirmed when Lewis began walking back and forth in front of one of the cabins, muttering to himself. As Mrs. Grinder later reported, "he would seem as if he were walking up to her; and would suddenly wheel round, and walk back as fast as he could."[2]

Pernia and the other servant (whose name is not known) unsaddled their horses and led them toward the stable, which was about two hundred yards distant. Mrs. Grinder fixed supper—turkey and turnip stew with cornbread was typical—but Lewis "had eaten only a few mouthfuls when he started up, speaking to himself in a violent manner," she later recalled. He calmed down and then grew agitated again, his face "flush as if it had come on him in a fit." Then Lewis pulled a chair outside the door, sat down, and lit his pipe. He stared out at the twilight.

"Madam," he said, "this is a very pleasant evening."

He puffed at the pipe for some time, the aroma of tobacco wafting into the cabin and along the breezeway. Just then he jumped up and paced the yard, carrying on the same confusing monologue as before. Then he sat again and smoked, apparently perfectly composed. He noted again what a sweet evening it was, "casting his eyes wistfully towards the west."

As he gazed westward, experiencing the last peaceful moments of a life that was to end ten hours later, did Meriwether Lewis relive scenes from what he called his and William Clark's "voyage to the Pacific Ocean"? Perhaps he remembered the fine night when he had turned thirty-one.

On that calm evening of Sunday, 18 August 1805, in a sagebrush-dotted vale just east of the Continental Divide, Lewis and his men bivouacked next to the meandering Beaverhead River. Earlier, after watching Clark and his detachment head west into present-day Idaho, they had packed their supplies for transport over the pass by horseback, but a hard rain from the southwest had halted their labor. When the rain subsided they feasted on fresh venison and set a net for the numerous trout visible in the clear Beaverhead.

Only then did the introspective Lewis finally have a chance to write in his journal, making one of his most famous entries, one that reveals much about the man: "This day I completed my thirty-first year, and conceived that I had in all human probability now existed about half the period which I am to remain in this Sublunary world. I reflected that I had as yet done but little, very little indeed, to further the happiness of the human race, or to advance the information of the succeeding generation. I viewed with regret the many hours I have spent in indolence . . . but since [those hours] are past and cannot be recalled, I dash from me the gloomy thought and resolved in the future . . . to live for *mankind*, as I have heretofore lived *for myself*."

Four years later to the day, on 18 August 1809, his thirty-fifth birthday, Lewis penned another crucial document, an indignant letter to Secretary of War

William Eustis. Whereas his journal entry had looked outward to mankind and to a hopeful future, one that Lewis expected to last another three decades or more, the letter to Eustis focused on Lewis's honor and on disputes over money, foreshadowing an end less than two months away. By 1809, Lewis by all rights should have been living prosperously, publishing books, and preparing for marriage. Instead, he was deep in debt, unpublished, and alone, with no prospects for marriage, battling a host of personal and political problems.

Although Thomas Jefferson had appointed him governor of Louisiana in February 1807, Lewis inexplicably lingered in the east for an entire year, not reaching St. Louis until March of 1808, incomprehensible for a person who had one of the most difficult jobs in the country. As governor, Lewis was commander in chief of the militia, responsible for defending the huge territory against Indian attack and against the British to the north, who continually incited the Indians. Lewis also had to deal with land sales and grants, trade licenses, military schools, road construction and maintenance, mining claims, exploration, and incorporation of towns. He administered the law and appointed and dismissed justices of the peace and sheriffs. The myriad of Indian-related issues included dealing with disputes among various tribes, negotiating treaties, and establishing trade policies. (At least in these areas Lewis had a competent subordinate he trusted—William Clark, who had been appointed to manage Indian affairs for the territory.) As if all this wasn't enough, a previous governor, General James Wilkinson, had accepted bribes and granted favors to allies, leaving St. Louis in a state of contention and corruption. Lewis tried his best to manage remotely, something that simply could not be accomplished. When he finally did arrive in St. Louis, his long absence had made the Herculean task of governing the territory virtually impossible.[3]

Once in St. Louis, he mismanaged his finances and fell into debt, piling up one expense after another: $3,000 for land purchases, with another $2,700 pledged; $225 to help establish a newspaper; $30 to print and distribute the prospectus (advertisement) for the expedition journals; $70 to a botanist for drawings; $100 for "calculation of celestial observations"—all this and more on a salary of $2,000 per year. Not surprisingly, during 1808 Lewis began drawing advances on his salary and borrowing from friends.[4]

Despite journal-related debt, Lewis made no progress in actually preparing the journals for publication. This was not for lack of planning. He completed a good deal of preliminary work, including signing with a publisher, John Conrad of Philadelphia, and arranging for drawings, scientific notations, and navigational corrections. Rather than publishing journal extracts verbatim, Lewis intended to edit, synthesize, and rewrite the raw entries to produce an original work (and he was the person best qualified to do so). Circulated in the spring of 1807, the prospectus promised three volumes, "containing from four to five hundred pages, each, printed on good paper." But after two years, Lewis had not written a single word of the new work. Perhaps the historical and economic motivation to publish the journals had become one more albatross hanging around his neck. "Govr. Lewis never furnished us with a line of the M.S.," the publisher later lamented to Thomas Jefferson, after Lewis's death, "nor indeed could we ever hear any thing from him respecting it tho frequent applications to that effect were made to him."[5]

(Magnifying Lewis's failure, expedition member Patrick Gass had published his journal, heavily edited and rewritten by his publisher, in 1807. Another edition appeared the next year. In addition, counterfeit versions of the journals, mixing fact with fiction and plagiarizing legitimate sources, reached bookstores by 1809.)[6]

Embarrassment over his failure to even make a start on the journals was probably a key reason Lewis had virtually stopped communicating with his longtime friend Thomas Jefferson. A troubled Jefferson had written to Lewis in July of 1808: "Since I parted with you in Albemarle in Sep. last I have never had a line from you, nor I believe has the Secretary of War. . . . We have no tidings yet of the forwardness of your printer. I hope the first part will not be delayed much longer." Things had changed since the expedition's return to St. Louis, when Lewis had made writing a long letter to Jefferson his first order of business. Now he wrote one or two impersonal letters a year.[7]

Though he had resolved to marry, Lewis failed in courtship. In various letters he mentioned several women that he saw socially, but a comment from his brother Reuben seems to typify Lewis's misfortunes in romance: "We . . . had the pleasure of seeing the accomplished and beautiful Miss Lettissia Breckenridge one of the most beautiful women I have ever seen, both as to form and features. But unfortunately for [Lewis] she left the neighborhood 2 days after our arrival so that he was disappointed in his design of addressing her."[8]

Territorial secretary Frederick Bates had taken to undermining Lewis at every turn. Appointed by Jefferson, Bates had been tending to his duties in St. Louis the entire year that Lewis had loitered in the east. Bates, who had previously served as a judge and land commissioner in the Michigan Territory, was initially suspicious of Lewis's qualifications to be governor, and as the two men clashed, that suspicion blossomed into loathing. In a letter to his brother Richard, Bates described Lewis as a man for whom he had "no personal regard" and "a great deal of political contempt"; he boasted that Lewis "has fallen from the public esteem" but is "well aware of my increasing popularity."[9]

But the perpetual problem of returning Sheheke to his Mandan home overshadowed everything else. In the spring of 1807, just six months after the expedition's return, Clark had ordered Pryor to escort Sheheke back to his villages up the Missouri River. After Pryor and Auguste-Pierre Chouteau and their men were attacked by the Arikara (with Shannon and Gibson both wounded and Joseph Field possibly killed), Sheheke had accompanied the group back to Missouri. "The Mandane Chief heretofore happy at the camp [Fort Bellefontaine], where I have always seen him at the Officers tables, and treated with every kind and hospitable indulgence now insists on being at St. Louis," Bates wrote to Clark (who was temporarily in Kentucky). "He is made to believe that he is the 'Brother' and not the 'Son' of the President. . . . I am indirectly told that P. Chouteau provides for him since his abrupt return from Belle Fontaine."[10]

Because the journey up the Missouri took several months, and because winter travel was impossible, only one attempt to return Sheheke could be made per year. For reasons that are not clear, no attempt was made in 1808. Lewis arrived in St. Louis in March of that year—perhaps the press of other business precluded raising the manpower and money necessary for the task. In July of 1808, however, Lewis heard from Thomas Jefferson: "The misfortune which attended the effort to send the Mandane chief home became known to us before you had reached St. Louis. We took no step on the occasion, counting on receiving your advice so soon as you should be in place. . . . The constant persuasion that something must be on it's way to us, has as constantly prevented our writing to you on the subject. The present letter, however is written to put an end at length to this mutual silence, and to ask from you a communication of what you think best to be done to get the chief & his family back. We consider the good faith, & the reputation of the nation as pledged to accomplish this." (This was the same letter in which Jefferson voiced his concern over Lewis's lack of progress in publishing the expedition journals.) A month later the long-suffering Jefferson reiterated the importance of returning Sheheke: "I am uneasy, hearing nothing from you about the Mandan chief, nor the measures for restoring him to his country. That is an object which presses on our justice & our honor."[11]

Such warnings prompted Lewis to action, and in February 1809 he contracted with Pierre Chouteau (on behalf on the St. Louis Missouri Fur Company) "to engage and raise One Hundred and Twenty five effective men (of whom Forty shall be Americans and expert Riflemen) . . . for the safe conveyance and delivery of the Mandan Chief, his Wife, and child, to the Mandan Nation."[12] Lewis's sincere attempts to honor Jefferson's commitments, however, were undercut when the new administration of James Madison took office early in 1809, at the very time when Lewis was putting together the final plan.

In August 1809, with Chouteau and his party well on their way up the Missouri, Lewis had received a curt note from Secretary of War William Eustis: "your bill of the 13th of May last drawn in favor of M. P. [Monsieur Pierre] Chouteau for five hundred dollars [related to the return of Sheheke] . . . has not been honored." Eustis then concluded with the ironic barb that the "President has been consulted and the observations herein contained have his approval." Lewis was thus plunged further into debt to help cover Chouteau's escort of Sheheke, something specifically requested and stressed by the previous president.

"I have never received a penny of public Money," the financially strapped and exasperated Lewis wrote to Eustis. "Those protested Bills . . . have effectually sunk my Credit; brought in all my private debts, amounting to about $4,000, which has compelled me, in order to do justice to my Creditors, to deposit with them, the landed property which I had purchased in this Country, as Security."

More than anything, Lewis felt deeply dishonored by Eustis's cavalier attitude, which implied that Lewis was incompetent or even disloyal. "Be assured Sir," responded the resentful Lewis, "that my Country can never make 'A Burr' of me—She may reduce me to Poverty; but she can never sever my Attachment from her."[13] (The play on words in "Burr" was a reference to former vice president Aaron Burr, who had been tried—but acquitted—of treason the previous year.)

Deluged by these troubles as the summer of 1809 faded, Lewis determined to redeem himself by traveling east to personally appeal Eustis's decision and also to begin publishing the expedition journals in Philadelphia. A successful trip could virtually resurrect his career. "I think all will be right and he will return with flying Colours to this Country," wrote Clark.

But Clark also acknowledged that the rejected vouchers had pushed Lewis to the breaking point: "I have not Spent Such a day as yesterday fer maney years, . . . [I] took my leave of Govr. Lewis who Set out to Philadelphia to write our Book, (but more perticulary to explain Some matter between him and the Govt. Several of his Bills have been protested and his Creditors all flocking in near the time of his Setting out distressed him much. which he expressed to me in Such terms as to Cause a Cempothy [sympathy] which is not yet off—I do not believe there was ever an honest er man in Louisiana nor one who had pureor motives than Govr. Lewis[)]."[14]

Clark also had business in Washington, so the two friends planned to see each other there. For now, as Lewis prepared to leave St. Louis in September 1809, they bade each other farewell with the same genuine affection that had always been present when they parted on the trail. During the expedition they had often taken separate paths in the face of extreme danger, so a trip to the civilized east could hardly have seemed risky. But this was their final farewell: in six weeks the brilliant Lewis, who had such boundless potential, would be dead.

On Monday, 4 September 1809, Lewis and his servant John Pernia loaded up Lewis's trunks at the living quarters he shared in St. Louis with Pierre Chouteau (he took his meals with Clark and his wife, Julia) and made their way through the muddy streets of the town to the docks. Lewis's faithful Newfoundland dog, Seaman, which had accompanied the corps to the Pacific and back, trotted at the governor's heels.[15] Lewis intended to travel down the Mississippi River to New Orleans, and from there to Washington by ship, so he and Pernia booked passage on a keelboat. Up to eighty feet long and usually about ten feet wide, keelboats featured pointed prows at either end, a mast and sail, a covered cabin, runways on each side of the cabin, and a sharp keel. With oars at bow and stern and a mate manning a rudder, keelboats were considerably more mobile than flatboats and could travel upriver as well as down. They were therefore plentiful at St. Louis, which was near the confluence of the Mississippi and Missouri Rivers.

"The appearance of St. Louis was not calculated to make a favorable impression upon the first visit," wrote one visitor a decade later, "with its long dirty and quick-sand beach, numbers of long empty keel boats tied to stakes driven in the sand, squads of idle boatmen passing to and fro, here and there numbers pitching quoits; others running footraces; rough and tumble fights; and shooting at a target was one of their occupations while in port."[16] No doubt, the prospect of living in such a world had deterred some of the young ladies whom Lewis courted.

Lewis and Pernia boarded a keelboat to descend the Mississippi—that much is certain. But whether Lewis was sick or healthy, agitated or calm, is not clear. Land commissioner Clement Penrose blamed Frederick Bates for the "mental derangement of the Governor." Thomas Jefferson echoed this opinion by claiming that Lewis departed in a "paroxysm" of depression, but Lewis's clear handwriting, his careful record of debts, and his granting three friends power of attorney hardly seem like the actions of a man out of control.[17]

Whether or not he was sick when he boarded the boat, Lewis's account book shows that he was concerned about his health—he had "pills of opium and tartar" and pills for "billious fever." Significantly, "billious fever" (as well as "ague" and "fever") was a contemporary name for malaria, then rampant throughout the Ohio and Mississippi River valleys. The still water, swamps, and marshes along the rivers were perfect breeding grounds for mosquitoes, which transmit the parasite that causes malaria. Lewis had apparently contracted malaria as early as November 1803, when he was "siezed with a violent ague which continued about four hours and as is usual was succeeded by a feever which however fortunately abated in some measure by sunrise the next morning."[18]

As governor of the territory, Lewis was free to pass his time in the cabin, but Pernia and the other passengers were expected to help man the boat, loaded to the brim with furs, wheat, flour, salt, iron, and bricks. With everyone aboard, a mate sounded the signal horn, and the craft merged into the current of the Mississippi, a thoroughfare of flatboats floating downstream and keelboats traveling in both directions. (The first steamboat on the Mississippi would not appear for another two years.) The flatboats, or "broadhorns," were huge, unwieldy rafts carrying humans, livestock, and forty or fifty tons of cargo. Keelboat crews were known to shout greetings to fellow keelboatmen but curses to the "Kaintucks" manning the broadhorns.

Whatever his health at the outset of the journey, Lewis had suffered a recurrence of malaria after a week on the hot, humid Mississippi. Severe attacks of fever were likely to occur every two or three days, accompanied by mental disturbances, headache, muscular pain, and nausea. Lewis had probably brought along a powdered form of Peruvian bark, the aspirin of its day, which was effective for treating malarial fever because the bark contains quinine.

Lewis and Pernia stopped two hundred miles south of St. Louis at New Madrid, a town of "about a hundred houses, much scattered, on a fine plain of two miles square," with "a church going to decay and no preacher." With a witness on hand, Lewis made out his last will and testament: "I bequeath all my estate, real and personal, to my Mother, Lucy Marks, after my private debts are paid, of which a statement will be found in a small minute book deposited with Pernia, my servant."[19]

With his fever periodically breaking and recurring, Lewis reportedly set off in good health, and he and Pernia resumed their voyage southward. A Mississippi traveler at about that same time recorded being "dreadfully tormented by mosquitoes and gnats, particularly at night, when moored to the bank. By day, while floating in the middle of the river, they were less troublesome."[20] Lewis and Pernia required mosquito nets to sleep. Even then, sleep did not come easily because a hundred boats might stop for the night at a bend in the Mississippi, and one could hear fiddle music, boisterous conversation, and bawling livestock well into the night.

Within a few days, Lewis was sick again, taken with fever when the keelboat passed a series of bluffs he knew well. At the end of a two-mile-long, forty-foot-high bluff, near the confluence of the Wolf and Mississippi rivers (near present-day Memphis, Tennessee) stood the cannons of Fort Pickering, the very outpost Lewis had commanded in 1797. He was apparently carried by stretcher up the makeshift staircase of 120 square logs leading to the fort. Uniformed sentinels with muskets and fixed bayonets allowed the party to pass, where they were ushered to the quarters of commanding officer Captain Gilbert C. Russell.

Three months later, in a letter to Thomas Jefferson, Russell reported: "[Lewis] came here on the 15th September last. . . . His situation I [thought] rendered it necessary that he should be [stopped] until he would recover, which I done, & in a short time by proper attention a change was perceptible and in about six days he was perfectly restored in every respect & able to travel."[21]

In a second letter to Jefferson, written three weeks later, Russell offered a different explanation: "The fact is which you may yet be ignorant of that his untimely death may be attributed soley to the free use he made of lequor which he acknowledged very candidly to me after his recovery & expressed a firm determination never to drink any more spirits or use snuff again both of which I deprived him of for several days & confined him to claret & a little white wine. But after leaving this place by some means or other his resolution left him."[22]

Although Russell claimed that Lewis was drinking to excess at Fort Pickering, Frederick Bates, who had worked closely with him for a year and a half—continually scrutinizing his behavior—never hinted that Lewis had a drinking problem in St. Louis. Russell's curious testimony takes yet another twist in a statement he made two years later, in November 1811. According to this account, Lewis arrived "in a state of mental derangement, which appeared to have been produced as much by indisposition as other causes. The Subscriber [Russell is referring to himself] being then the Commanding Officer of the Fort on discovering his situation, and learning from the Crew that he had made two attempts to kill himself, in one of which he had nearly succeeded, resolved at once to take possession of him and his papers, and detain them there untill he recovered, or some friend might arrive in whose hands he could depart in safety."[23]

Russell's failure to mention such crucial details to Thomas Jefferson is inexcusable, but his report of Lewis's suicide attempts is backed up by an independent (but third-hand) source. In a letter to his friend Frederick Bates, army officer James House wrote on 28 September 1809 that "Majr Stoddart [Lewis's friend Amos Stoddard] of the Army arrived here [Nashville] from Fort Adams [Fort Pickering], and informs me that . . . he saw a person, immediately from the Bluffs who informed him, that Governor Lewis had arrived there (sometime previous to his leaving it) in a State of mental derangement—that he had made several attempts to put an end to his own existence, which the patroon had prevented, and that Cap Russell, the commanding officer at the Bluffs had taken him into his own quarters where he was obliged to keep a strict watch over him to prevent his committing violence on himself."[24]

The day after his arrival at Fort Pickering, Lewis managed to write a letter to President James Madison (at the time when Russell claimed Lewis was still deranged): "Dear Sir, I arrived here yesterday about 2 Ock P.M. yesterday very much exhausted from the heat of the climate, but having taken medicine feel much better this morning. My apprehension from the heat of the lower country and my fear of the original papers relative to my voyage to the Pacific ocean falling into the hands of the British has induced me to change my rout and proceed by land through the state of Tennisee to the City of washington. . . . Provided my health permits no time shall be lost in reaching Washington."[25] The letter contains several erasures but hardly seems to have been written by a deranged man.

Still at Fort Pickering on Friday, 22 September, Lewis wrote his last known letter, to his friend Amos Stoddard: "I am now on my way to the City of Washington and had contemplated taking Fort Adams and Orlianes in my rout, but my indisposition has induced me to change my rout and shall now pass through Tennessee and Virginia. . . . I hope you will therefore pardon me for asking you to remit as soon as is convenient the sum of $200. which you have informed me you hold for me."[26] The letter is clear and coherent, with only a single syllable struck out, in handwriting indicating that Lewis was his normal self again.

Five days later, preparing to leave, Lewis signed a promissory note to Russell for $379.58, the total representing a $100 loan Russell had given him (in the form of a check), two horses, and a saddle. This is the last known Lewis document. As historian Vardis Fisher has pointed out, making these loans and accepting the note in return indicates that Russell believed Lewis was sane and that he would repay the amount in a few months. (Russell also indicated that Lewis had $120 in cash in addition to the $100 check.)

Lewis never learned that three days earlier, on 24 September, Pierre

Chouteau and his force of at least three hundred soldiers and Indians, including George Drouillard and possibly other expedition veterans, had safely delivered Sheheke and his family to the Mandan villages, where, as Chouteau said, they were "received with the Greatest demonstration of Joy."[27] As noted, payment for some of Lewis's expenses for Sheheke's return had been rejected by the administration in Washington, which had plunged Lewis further into debt. Clearing up this matter—and, from Lewis's perspective, clearing his good name—was one of the main reasons he went east. (Adding irony to irony, the War Department later paid the disputed bills to Lewis's estate—after his death.)

On Friday, 29 September, Lewis and Pernia rose early, had their horses newly shod, and packed their supplies. Typical travelers in this area carried several pounds of hard biscuit, six pounds of flour, twelve pounds of bacon, three pounds of rice, and a little coffee and sugar.[28] Then they departed on horseback for the Chickasaw Agency (150 miles to the southeast, near today's Houston, Mississippi) accompanied by Chickasaw agent James Neelly, his servant (apparently a black slave), an Indian interpreter, and several Chickasaw men wearing long feathers in their hair, tin breastplates in the shape of a crescent, and large tin earrings. They followed an Indian trail that was little more than a bridle path through the woods, across hills that were sometimes "instantly deluged with torrents of rain, accompanied by . . . tremendous thunder and lightning" and heavy gusts of wind.[29]

A few days after leaving Fort Pickering, the foursome arrived at the Chickasaw Agency, a few buildings used to conduct business with the Indians, who had exclusive rights to trade in the area. They stayed for two days because of Lewis's poor health. Neelly said Lewis "appeared at times deranged in mind." Pernia later reported his account to William Clark, who quoted Pernia in a letter, saying that Lewis "would frequently 'Conceipt [conceive] that he herd me Comeing on, and Said that he was certain [I would] over take him, that I had herd of his Situation and would Come to his releaf.'"[30]

Lewis was clearly not himself, because the notion that Clark—who had departed St. Louis on 21 September on an eastern, overland route—would somehow turn up in Mississippi was simply not rational. But in imagining alternate worlds for Meriwether Lewis, perhaps none is sweeter than the image of his best friend, "that esteemable man Capt. William Clark," suddenly appearing in a clearing on horseback and riding up to the outpost to greet him. Clark would have seen to it that Lewis received proper medical attention and arrived safely in Washington. But any vision of Clark—at that moment making his way through Kentucky and unaware of his friend's crisis—coming up the trail was merely a specter in Lewis's troubled mind.

Lewis, Pernia, Neelly, and Neelly's servant started for Nashville, Tennessee, on Friday, 6 October, following the Natchez Trace, an eight-foot-wide, five-hundred-mile-long trail that ran northeast from Natchez, on the lower Mississippi River, to Nashville through dense woods of Choctaw and Chickasaw Indian territory. The four men made thirty to forty miles a day for the next two days—not the kind of feat a sick or deranged man could likely accomplish—traveling through what is now northeastern Mississippi into the northwestern corner of Alabama.

Lewis carried a rifle, two pistols, a tomahawk, a dirk (a long straight-bladed dagger), and a silver watch, and he probably wore a *chapeau de bras,* or cocked hat, with a feather plume, that aroused admiration and offers of trade among the Chickasaw. He had also loaded one of the packhorses with two trunks containing one black broadcloth coat, two striped summer coats, five vests, a pair of black silk breeches, several other articles of clothing, and quite a number of books and papers. Among the papers were nine memorandum books and sixteen morocco-bound notebooks that contained the bulk of the expedition journals.[31]

The woods were thick with squirrels, skunks, rabbits, black bears—and, most important, white-tailed deer, providing venison whenever the men desired it. They saddled up at dawn and rode until darkness fell, making their way past moss-draped trees and around swamps crawling with mosquitoes, snakes, and alligators, with bald cypress trees rising from the stagnant pools. Yellow jackets harassed them the entire day, and they constantly watched for poison ivy. They also watched for robbers, some of whom worked in gangs and some of whom posed as ministers. Traveling together, however, and bearing arms brought the four men relative safety. The trace was also frequented by Kaintucks hiking and riding back to the Ohio River where they would once again board flatboats and float south.

On the third day of their journey, Lewis and his companions reached the Tennessee River, site of Colbert's Stand—an inn complete with sleeping quarters, kitchen, storehouse, and stables—and Colbert's Ferry. George Colbert and his brothers, sons of a British trader and his Chickasaw wife, controlled much of the territory and charged steep prices for both food and whiskey. One traveler reported that Colbert was "an artful designing man more for his own interest than that of his [Chickasaw] nation ... very shrewd, talented man and withal very wicked. He had two wives. . . . He and his brother had a large farm and about forty Negroes working. We bought some corn, pumpkins, and corn-blades, for which he charged us a very high price."[32]

Typical guests at Colbert's Stand sat—on chairs if they were lucky, for such luxuries were not always provided at frontier stops like this—in a filthy cabin and ate hominy grits or squirrel stew with crude wooden spoons. Some spat tobacco juice on the dirt floor, removing their plugs while they ate. All the boarders shared a single towel before retiring to dark rooms that offered shelter and beds as well as an abundance of rats and insects.

But Colbert's main business was the ferry. When Lewis and Neelly reached the Tennessee River and gazed out at the deep, swift, five-hundred-yard-wide tributary of the Ohio that was impossible to ford, they knew Colbert had them at his mercy. Building their own flatboat—by chopping down trees and tying the logs together with vines—was out of the question, so they paid Colbert, a dollar for each horse and rider and fifty cents for each packhorse, to ferry them across.

Following the winding trace up and down rises, over streams, and through thick forests that blocked out the sun for hours at a time, the four riders entered Tennessee, the sixteenth state in the Union and second on the western frontier (after Kentucky). At the opposite corner of the state, in the hinterlands of Jefferson County, an obscure, poor, twenty-three-year-old hunter and farmer by the name of David Crockett was then eking out a living for himself, his wife, and their two young sons.

On Tuesday, 10 October, south of where Collinwood, Tennessee, now lies, the travelers woke to find that two packhorses had gotten free during the night. "I remained behind to hunt [the horses]," Neelly explained in his letter to Jefferson, "& the Governor proceeded on with a promise to wait for me at the first houses he came to that was inhabited by white people."[33] Knowing full well that Lewis was "in very bad health" and "deranged in mind" (Neelly's own words) and most likely also knowing of Lewis's suicide attempts, Neelly, a government agent entrusted with Lewis's care, mysteriously chose to abandon him rather than ordering one of the servants to search for the horses. He was apparently never asked to account for this dereliction of duty.

So Lewis rode on alone, with the servants following some distance behind. Though he rode alone all day, Lewis likely passed wayfarers headed both north and south—the ever-present boatmen, Indian traders, soldiers, families seeking a new life in the West, and postal riders. At Toscomby's Stand, nothing more than a rundown cabin, a traveler could water and feed his horse. It was another twelve miles, some of it slow going through a muckish, reddish mire, to Young Factor's Stand and trading store, where corn whiskey was available. Then another ten miles to McLish's Stand, which like the others was run by Indians or half-breeds, for this was still Indian territory.

Lewis rode on and soon heard rippling water, coming around a bend to see the Buffalo River, no more than a foot deep and twenty yards wide. He may not have known the river's name, but he certainly knew it was a tributary of the Tennessee, which flowed into the Ohio, which flowed into the Mississippi. The great moments of his life had been linked with rivers— taking command of Fort Pickering on the Mississippi; crossing the Potomac on his way to serve as Jefferson's secretary; traveling the Ohio and gathering men and supplies for the expedition; spending the entire first year of the expedition on or near the Missouri; deciding not to risk the unnavigable white water of the Salmon; picking up speed on the Columbia as the splendid Pacific came into view—and now Meriwether Lewis was about to cross his last river.

After another two miles he saw a marker indicating that he was leaving Indian territory. A mile after that a rudimentary sign announced Grinder's Stand, the first establishment he had encountered that was run by whites. Here he would wait for the servants and for Neelly. As Lewis rode toward the stand, after having traversed 144 miles since leaving the Chickasaw Agency five days earlier, Mrs. Grinder saw him approaching. She could not know that—however briefly—she was about to be thrust out of obscurity into the harsh glare of history.

Eighteen months later another solitary rider approached the stand, this one coming from the north. The rider was Alexander Wilson, a noted ornithologist whom Lewis had asked to make drawings of new bird species found on the expedition. Traveling from Philadelphia to New Orleans, Wilson made a special stop at Grinder's Stand to see if he could discover what had happened to his friend Lewis in those final hours. Wilson was aware of Neelly's claim that Lewis had committed suicide, but he also knew Neelly had not been present when Lewis died. Wilson came for a firsthand interview with the key witness, Mrs. Grinder.

"In the same room where [Lewis] expired," Wilson later wrote in his detailed account of his interview with her, "I took down from Mrs. Grinder the particulars of that melancholy event, which affected me extremely." She told him how Lewis had sat in the chair smoking his pipe, commenting on what a glorious evening it was. She prepared a bed for him in the opposite cabin, but he said he would sleep on the floor. Then he asked his servant to bring bear skins and a buffalo robe. The servant retrieved the items and spread them out on the floor. "It now being dusk," Wilson continued, "the woman went off to the kitchen and the two men to the barn which stands about two hundred yards off."

Disturbed by Lewis's erratic behavior, Mrs. Grinder could not sleep. She sat listening to Lewis—fifteen feet away in the other cabin—pacing back and forth and talking loudly to himself, "like a lawyer." This continued for several hours, long after her three children had fallen asleep. Then she heard a pistol shot and something falling heavily to the floor.

"Oh, Lord!" Lewis cried out.

Then came another round of pistol fire, and soon she heard Lewis at her door.

"Oh, Madam," he moaned, "give me some water and heal my wounds."

Paralyzed with fear, Mrs. Grinder later claimed, she watched through a space between the logs as Lewis staggered backward and fell against a stump. "He crawled for some distance, and raised himself by the side of a tree, where he sat about a minute," according to Wilson's recounting. (Research by John D. Guice indicates that Mrs. Grinder embellished her story: "Historians will never know how much starlight there was, but we know there was no moonlight. Inside the cabin where he slept the stars were not shining, and in a heavily forested area it is not likely that Mrs. Grinder could have witnessed the actions of Lewis through the cracks of her log cabin with the door bolted shut.")[34]

Again he stumbled to the door; again she stood frozen on the other side. He groped in the dark for a bucket, attempting to spoon out water with a gourd. The bucket was empty, and the "cooling element was denied the dying man."

As Lewis lay suffering, Mrs. Grinder, a woman well accustomed to frontier life, who had seen her share of thieves and vagabonds, found herself unable to do anything but wait. One, then two interminable hours finally passed. Exactly what she heard and saw during that lapse she did not say, but at dawn she sent her two older children to the stable to get the servants.

Pernia and his companion came running, Wilson wrote, "and on going in they found him lying on the bed. He uncovered his side, and showed them where the bullet had entered; a piece of his forehead was blown off, and had exposed the brains, without having bled much." Lewis assured the servants that they had nothing to fear, and he begged them to take his rifle and "blow out his brains," promising he would give them all the money in his trunk. They watched helplessly as Lewis's life ebbed.[35] He said several times, "I am no coward, but I am so strong, so hard to die." He may have lost consciousness after an hour or so, and they listened to his labored breathing. After another hour, just as the sun was rising above the trees, the breathing stopped.

A week after Lewis died, Neelly offered a sketchy account of the explorer's final hours, in a letter to Thomas Jefferson: "[Lewis] reached the house of a Mr. Grinder about sun set, the man of the house being from home, and no person there but a woman who discovering the governor to be deranged, gave him up the house & slept herself in one near it. His servant and mine slept in the stable loft some distance from the other houses. The woman reports that about three o'Clock she heard two pistols fire off in the Governors Room: the servants being awakined by her, came in but too late to save him. He had shot himself in the head with one pistol & a little below the Breast with the other—when his servant came in he says; I have done the business my good Servant give me some water. He gave him water, he survived but a short time. I came up some time after, and & had him as decently Buried as I could in that place."[36]

Although he was not an eyewitness to Lewis's death, James Neelly found himself in the perfect position to forever close the case. He could have thoroughly—and separately—interviewed his own servant, Pernia, and Mrs. Grinder (and Mrs. Grinder's children or slaves, if any were present), transcribing their statements and having them sign affidavits. He could have given his own detailed statement of the nature of Lewis's wounds. He could have examined Lewis's pistols and written a report. One of the most important men in the country had just died a violent death, and as the sole government official on the scene, Neelly was duty-bound to produce comprehensive records. But just as he had failed Lewis by leaving him alone in a fragile state, Neelly failed Lewis a second time by summarizing matters that should have been treated in great detail, forever casting doubt as to how Meriwether Lewis actually died.

Predictably, rumors materialized almost immediately. On 20 October, two days after Neelly had written his letter to Jefferson—and in the same location—a Nashville newspaper reported that after serving supper and spirits to Lewis and his servants, "Mrs. Grinder retired to the kitchen with the children, and the servants (after the Governor went to bed, which he did in good order) went to a stable about three hundred yards distant to sleep— no one in the house with the governor—and some time before midnight Mrs. Grinder was alarmed by the firing of two pistols in the house—she called to the servants without effect—and at the appearance of daylight the servants came to the house when the Governor said he had now done for himself—they asked what and he said he had shot himself and would die, and requested them to bring him water, he then laying on the floor where he expired about 7 o'clock in the morning of the 11th—he had shot a ball that grazed the top of his head and another through his intestines, and cut his neck and arm and ham with a razor."[37]

Other newspapers rushed similar stories into print, and on 28 October, two weeks after Lewis's death, a heartsick William Clark wrote to his brother Jonathan: "when at Shelbyville [Kentucky] to day I Saw in a Frankfort paper called the Arguss a report published which givs me much Concern, it Says that Govr. Lewis killed himself by Cutting his Throat with a Knife, on his way between the Chickaw Saw Bluffs and nashville, I fear this report has too much truth, tho' hope it may have no foundation—my reasons for thinking it possible is founded on the letter which I recved from him at your house, in the letter he Says he had Some intintion of going thro' by land & his only objection was his papers." (This letter, which Lewis apparently wrote as he was making his way down the Mississippi, potentially offers important information on Lewis's state of mind, but it has not been located.) Clark then expressed the emotions of many, both present and future, when he said, "I fear O! I fear the waight of his mind has over come him, what will be the Consequence?"[38]

A week or so later, the rumors had reached the East Coast. At his Monticello home, retired president Thomas Jefferson, mentor and surrogate father to Lewis, heard and read reports of Lewis's death by early November. Like Clark, he agonized over such hearsay, hoping it was unfounded (just as rumors of the explorers' deaths during the expedition had been without basis). Then, on 21 November he received Neelly's letter: "It is with extreme pain," Neelly wrote, "that I have to inform you of the death of His Excellency Meriwether Lewis, Governor of upper Louisiana who died on the morning of the 11th Instant and I am sorry to say by suicide." Neelly backed up his suicide theory by informing Jefferson that Lewis had intimated that he wouldn't reach Washington alive: "Some days previous to the Governors death he requested of me in case any accident happened to him, to send his trunks with the papers therein to the President, but I think it very probable he meant to you [Jefferson]."[39]

Neelly's letter was possibly delivered by Lewis's valet, Pernia, who rode Lewis's horse into the northeast corner of Tennessee, through the Cumberland Gap, and into Virginia, arriving at Monticello sometime before 26 November. Jefferson interviewed Pernia, and what he learned—together with Neelly's letter—convinced him that Lewis had died by his own hand. (Pernia also claimed that Lewis had died owing him $240.) However, Jefferson, who left detailed written records of all kinds of odd and sundry events, unaccountably left no report of his historic meeting with Pernia. Jefferson then gave Pernia enough money to get to Washington and entrusted him to deliver a letter to President James Madison, which Pernia did.

Jefferson later sealed the suicide verdict by writing: "Governor Lewis had from early life been subject to hypocondriac affections. It was a constitutional disposition in all the nearer branches of the family of his name, & was more immediately inherited by him from his father. . . . He stopped at the house of a Mr. Grinder, who not being at home, his wife, alarmed at the symptoms of derangement she discovered, gave him up the house and retired to rest herself in an out-house, the governor's and Neeley's servants lodging in another. About three o'clock in the night he did the deed which plunged his friends into affliction, and deprived his country of one of her most valued citizens."[40]

In early December, William Clark arrived at Monticello. Completed just a few months earlier (though Jefferson had resided there for years), Monticello's Roman-style dome and Greek portico made it instantly recognizable. Visitors typically found the door open, stepped inside, and announced their arrival to a servant, soon to be greeted by Martha Randolph, Jefferson's daughter, and not long after that by Jefferson himself, dressed casually in "corduroy small clothes, grey worsted stockings, blue waistcoat, and a rather stiff homespun jacket badly made from the wool of his prized merino sheep."[41]

Jefferson, sixty-six, and Clark, thirty-nine, knew and loved Meriwether Lewis better than anyone other than Lewis's immediate family did, and they also had a genuine affection for each other, creating a bittersweet reunion. Jefferson must have given Clark a tour of his "Indian Hall," complete with Native American paintings, sculpture, clothing, utensils, weapons, and ornaments, several of which Clark recognized as expedition artifacts. The Mandan eagle-bone whistle and Sauk tobacco pouch had been collected on his and Lewis's first season on the Missouri.

Sadly, Jefferson's final letter to Lewis, which had been carried from Monticello to St. Louis by the English botanist John Bradbury, arrived several weeks after Lewis's death. Knowing that Lewis was preparing to journey east, Jefferson had written: "Your friends here are well, & have been long in expectation of seeing you. I shall hope in that case to possess a due portion of you at Monticello, where I am at length enjoying the never before known luxury of employing myself for my own gratification only. Present my friendly salutations to Genl. Clarke, and be assured yourself of my constant & unalterable affections."[42] Jefferson had no doubt hoped that any hard feelings Lewis might have been nursing over the mild chastisement he had received about his lack of correspondence could be mended with those kind words, but Lewis never read them.

Clark wrote that he spent the night at Monticello and that he and Jefferson "spoke much on the affairs of Gov. Lewis." Jefferson and Clark shared an enthusiasm for cartography, and Jefferson's library contained a series of maps and an Indian scene painted on a buffalo hide. We know the two men discussed the expedition journals, which Lewis had been carrying in one of his trunks when he died. (Fortunately, Neelly turned the journals over to a government official, Thomas Freeman, who took them to Washington. They were subsequently given to Clark.) Other visitors reported talking well into the evening with Jefferson, with a servant bringing tea, followed by wine and cheese. The same was probably true of Clark and Jefferson, with Lewis's death sadly punctuating their hours of fellowship.[43]

Jefferson and Clark both believed Lewis capable of suicide and both believed he had in fact killed himself.[44] Such a conclusion is quite consistent with the statements of the three key witnesses: John Pernia, James Neelly, and Priscilla Grinder. Ironically, however, these three individuals—and rumors about them—also helped fuel the controversy concerning Lewis's demise.

Pernia brought suspicion on himself by making a conspicuous effort to collect the money Lewis supposedly owed him—apparently seeking it from Lewis's family, Jefferson, Madison, and Clark. Since the $120 in cash that Lewis had been carrying did not turn up among his possessions when an official inventory was taken (a month and a half after his death), many considered Pernia the primary suspect to have murdered and robbed Lewis. Jefferson unwittingly added more fuel to the fire in 1810 when he wrote in a letter that Pernia had "followed his master's example" by committing suicide.[45] Some took this as a sign of Pernia's remorse.

Others thought Neelly guilty of foul play. After all, the two packhorses had mysteriously disappeared one day before Lewis's death, and Neelly had conveniently volunteered to search for them. Maybe Lewis's suicide was a botched murder and robbery by Neelly, who had actually been following close behind the entire day. Furthermore, Captain Russell, commander of Fort Pickering, claimed that during the journey along the trace, "this Agt [Neelly] being extremely fond of liquor, instead of preventing the Govr from drinking or putting him under restraint advised him to it & from every thing I can learn gave the man every chance to destroy himself."[46] (Russell never explained how he supposedly obtained such information, but he could have heard it from southbound travelers after they arrived at the fort.) Russell also claimed that Neelly had no money when he and Lewis left Fort Pickering, but in his letter to Jefferson, Neelly said he had given Pernia fifteen dollars.

Finally, Neelly, who informed Jefferson that he had Lewis's horse, rifle, pistols, and dirk, held on to them rather than turning them over to authorities. Two years after Lewis's death, his half-brother John Hastings Marks traveled to Tennessee for the specific purpose of retrieving these items from Neelly. Marks wrote to Reuben Lewis that, although Neelly was not home, Marks had obtained the horse and rifle from Neelly's wife. As for the pistols and dirk, Neelly reportedly carried them with him wherever he went. There is no record that he ever gave them back to the family. It is very difficult to see Neelly in a positive light.[47]

(Adding to the confusion, Neelly had been appointed to the post of Indian agent by General James Wilkinson, commander of the western army and a former governor of Upper Louisiana. Wilkinson had been spying for the Spanish for years and perhaps had reason to fear that Lewis was about to expose his treason. Wilkinson was certainly capable of ordering Lewis's murder, but there is no hard evidence that he did so.)[48]

Then there is Mrs. Grinder. Virtually nothing is known about her. Was she a person who was generally considered accurate and truthful? We don't know. It certainly seems that she was given to at least some exaggeration or embellishment, because it was probably too dark for her to have witnessed Lewis's actions outside her cabin. Unfortunately, she is the best witness, the only person who claimed to have heard the shots. This makes it all the more lamentable that Neelly was not more thorough in his investigation.

Mrs. Grinder hurt her own cause when she was interviewed by an unnamed schoolteacher in 1839, thirty years after Lewis's death, at a time when she was probably in her middle or late sixties. When a newspaper published an account of the interview in 1841, it contained shocking allegations. First, she said that "about dark two or three other men rode up and called for lodging. Mr. Lewis immediately drew a brace of pistols, stepped towards them and challenged them to a duel. They not liking this situation, rode on to the next house, five miles."[49]

Next, she said that Lewis and the two servants had all retired to the same cabin, not to different quarters. She also said she heard three shots and afterward saw Lewis crawling across the road on his hands and knees. Most shocking, she claimed that when the servants appeared, Pernia was wearing Lewis's clothes, claiming that Lewis had given them to him. When they discovered Lewis, he was wearing Pernia's clothes.

It is hard to know what to make of this bizarre tale. The account includes details not likely to be known by anyone but Mrs. Grinder, such as a statement she claimed Lewis had made saying, "If they do prove anything on me they will have to do it by letter," an apparent reference to the War Department. In addition, the account matches her earlier statements in a number of particulars.

On the other hand, the 1839 statement contains absurd details, such as Lewis's exclaiming, "O Lord! Congress relieve me!" after the first shot was fired. Perhaps Mrs. Grinder was slipping in and out of lucidity herself, getting some details right, getting others out of order, and inventing others.

Publication of the interview naturally kindled speculation that Lewis had been murdered. Be that as it may, the 1839 account was accompanied by triple difficulties: it lacked corroboration from other sources; it was far removed from the event in question; and the newspaper article was written by an anonymous author of unknown reliability.

By sharp contrast, Alexander Wilson's account of his interview with Mrs. Grinder in 1811 was largely corroborated by James Neelly's letter to Jefferson and by Pernia's statements to Jefferson and Clark; it was conducted within a year and a half of Lewis's death; and it was recorded by a person known to be careful in his statements. Wilson's diligent questioning of Mrs. Grinder and his thorough transcription of her statement (Neelly failed miserably in the latter) make his account the surest guide to what really happened in the early morning hours of 11 October 1809.

"He lies buried close by the common path, with a few loose rails thrown over his grave," concluded Wilson. "I gave Grinder money to put a post fence around it, to shelter it from the hogs and from the wolves; and he gave me his written promise that he would do it. I left this place in a very melancholy mood, which was not much allayed by the prospect of the gloomy and savage wilderness which I was just entering alone."

CHAPTER SEVEN

"I Give and Recommend My Soul"
The Deaths of George Gibson,
Jean-Baptiste Lepage, and John Shields

O n 26 October 1806, Thomas Jefferson had written to Lewis: "I received, my dear Sir, with unspeakable joy your letter of Sep. 23 announcing the return of yourself, Capt. Clarke & your party in good health to St. Louis."[1] Indeed, it had been "unspeakable" that thirty-three people, including an infant, had safely made the journey from Fort Mandan to the coast and back. (In the summer of 1805, Jefferson had learned of the death of Sergeant Floyd, which occurred before the group reached Fort Mandan.) The corps had been greatly blessed or incredibly lucky—or both. But the good fortune of the expedition—only one death in three years of service, from 1803 to 1806—suddenly reversed itself, with six veterans dying in the next three years, four of them in the last half of 1809. (As noted, Joseph Field had been killed in 1807 and John Potts in 1808, and Meriwether Lewis was one of those who died in 1809.)

In the spring of 1807, sometime after the members of the corps learned that they would be awarded land grants west of the Mississippi River, George Gibson and seven others signed a petition to Congress. "Many of your Petitioners are poor & earnestly solicit that whatever price their country may set upon their toilsome & perilous services may not be withheld from them," it read in part. "Your petitioners would beg leave to represent, that many of them have married since their return & are generally residents of the Territory of Louisiana or Indiana—where they have settled themselves; not doubting, but that it would be found equally expedient to lay off their lands within the limits of one of the said Territories, as within the boundaries of any more distant Country." They therefore requested that they receive land grants not requiring them to travel a great distance to obtain their titles.[2]

About the same time he signed the petition, Gibson also made arrangements to travel up the Missouri with George Shannon. The two of them had much in common: they were both among the "nine young men from Kentucky," they had joined the expedition at the same time, and they had both served in Sergeant Pryor's squad. During the expedition, they (along with Richard Windsor) had accompanied Pryor on a mission to take several head of horses across the eastern part of what is now Montana (Crow Indians stole the horses). For their second journey together, in June of 1807, Shannon and Gibson again accompanied Pryor on a special mission—this time to return Sheheke and his family to the Mandan villages. As noted, both were wounded on this trip, Gibson apparently in the fleshy part of his leg—we have no other details. By all indications, however, his wound was less serious than Shannon's.[3]

Like Shannon, Gibson recuperated at Fort Bellefontaine. But by the spring of 1808 (at a time when Shannon was still in the hospital), he was in the Indiana Territory and had married Maria Reagan (sometimes spelled Mariah), daughter of Jacob Reagan. On 21 March of that year, George and Maria sold a piece of land they had inherited from Maria's father for sixty dollars.[4]

By January 1809, Gibson's erstwhile companion Shannon had recovered and departed to attend school in Kentucky, but Gibson himself was back in St. Louis, so sick that he believed himself on the verge of death. "In the Name of god amen," wrote Gibson in his will, "I George Gibson . . . being Vary Sick and weak in Strength but in perfect Mind and Memory thanks be given unto god, Calling unto Mind the Mortality of My body and Knowing that it is appointed for all Men Once to die do Make and ordain this My Last will and Testament . . . I give and Recommend My Soul Into the Hande of almighty god that gave it, and my body I recommend to the earth to be buried. . . . Nothing Doubting but at the General Resurrection I Shall Receive the Same again by the all Mighty power of god." He left everything to Maria. As far as we know, the couple had no children.[5]

The nature of Gibson's illness is not known, but during the expedition Lewis had treated him for syphilis with mercury, a common treatment of the day.[6] It is therefore possible, but hardly certain, that Gibson was suffering from mercury poisoning. He may have lingered near death throughout the winter and spring of 1809. He had rendered fine service as an interpreter and hunter on the expedition, during which he had won a marksmanship competition, but nothing was more memorable than his fiddle playing, especially when he and Cruzatte had played together for the Indians. "Soon after we landed," Clark recorded near the confluence of the Snake and Columbia

Rivers, "Indians Came from the different Lodges . . . we Smoked with all of them, and two of our Party Peter Crusat & Gibson played on the *violin* which delighted them greatly."[7]

By 10 July 1809, George Gibson was dead. William Clark, who later confirmed that he had died a nonviolent death, may have been a visitor during these final months. (Clark was in St. Louis for most if not all of the period from January to July 1809, for his first child, Meriwether Lewis Clark, had been born on 10 January, and he wrote letters from St. Louis to his brother Jonathan on 2 January, 21 January, about 1 March, 28 May, and 22 July.) When Maria made her first court appearance to settle George's estate, the ever-considerate Clark accompanied her and cosigned a bond of one thousand dollars. She was apparently uneducated, for she signed her name with an *X*. George's will was somehow lost and was not discovered until 1826. By the time Maria appeared in court in December of that year, she was married to Richard Dunlavy.[8]

Like Toussaint Charbonneau, Jean-Baptiste Lepage was a French-Canadian trapper who had been living among the Mandan for some time when the expedition reached their territory, in what is now North Dakota. Lepage had made at least two impressive explorations on his own. Clark recorded that Lepage had ascended the Little Missouri River (apparently in 1803) in a canoe, concluding that the river was not navigable; "he was 45 days descending," wrote Clark. Lepage may have been the first white man to explore this river, going as far as present-day Montana or Wyoming in the process. Clark questioned him about the terrain, later reporting that "Lepage the Frenchm. who joined us at the Mandans & who had come down the L. Missouri says hills all up there are burnt as on Missi. No other volcanic appearance there." Lepage had apparently seen the Black Hills, in what is now South Dakota.[9] When the captains met Lepage in November 1804, they promptly hired him to replace John Newman, who had been expelled for mutinous conduct.

Born in Kaskaskia, Illinois, in 1761, Lepage was forty-three when he met the captains, making him the oldest member of the party. He had apparently lived in St. Louis before heading up the Missouri in 1803 (or earlier), marrying and fathering three or four children. (Nathaniel Pryor and John Shields had also married and had children before the expedition, but their families were living farther east, near Louisville, Kentucky.)

Within weeks of returning to his family in St. Louis following the expedition, in the fall of 1806, Lepage sold rights to his land warrant to John Ordway. Then, presumably after spending the winter with his family, he signed a note to Auguste Chouteau on 25 April 1807 for twenty-seven piastres and fifty sols, promising to repay the debt in deer skins and two and a half pounds of venison. Chouteau, one of the founders of St. Louis and a half-brother of Pierre Chouteau, was a prominent merchant and banker who could have been providing Lepage with supplies for Manuel Lisa's first trapping excursion up the Missouri. Expedition veterans George Drouillard, Richard Windsor, Peter Weiser, and John Potts were also part of the group. Lepage's X on the promissory note indicates that he was uneducated; trapping probably offered his best opportunity to support his family.[10]

The evidence strongly suggests that Lepage indeed joined Lisa's group, never returned to St. Louis, and died in the region that became Montana and North Dakota, in 1809. If so, he saw his wife, four sons, and one daughter for the final time when he bade them adieu at St. Louis in April 1807; and if so, then he was with Lisa's men when Bissonnet deserted and Drouillard shot him, was encamped at the mouth of the Platte when John Colter came down the river in a dugout canoe and joined the party, could have been one of those who wrestled an enraged Edward Rose to the ground while Lisa made his escape, and would have been present when the half-starved Colter amazingly returned to Fort Raymond.

Lepage apparently remained on the upper Missouri—possibly at his old home with the Mandan—because when Meriwether Lewis listed his debts before departing on his fatal trip east, he still owed Lepage more than one hundred dollars for expedition service. It seems that Lepage certainly would have collected his pay had he returned to St. Louis between 1807 and 1809. Moreover, a promissory note signed on 31 December 1809 (at Fort Raymond rather than St. Louis) to the estate of J. B. Lepage indicates that he had died in the area by this time. Finally, Lepage was in debt to Manuel Lisa for an undisclosed amount when he died, and Lisa was named one of the executors of the estate—further evidence that Lepage was in Lisa's employ when he died, at age forty-eight. Lepage was the first veteran of the expedition to leave his children fatherless behind him. Although, according to William Clark, Lepage did not die violently, he did die intestate, and several of his coats, shirts, and jackets were sold to help pay his debts. The total came to $16.25.[11] Neither Lepage nor his heirs ever received his expedition pay of $116.33.

Like Shannon and Gibson, John Shields had been one of the "nine young men from Kentucky," although he had actually been in his thirties—and the oldest of the original members—at the time. (Lepage, of course, was older but was not an original member of the group.) Shields had married Nancy White around 1790, and their daughter, Martha Jannette, had been born a year or two later. Nancy White is thought by some to have been the sister of Hugh Lawson White, the Tennessee senator who ran for president in 1836, losing to Martin Van Buren but carrying Tennessee and Georgia.[12]

When Shields joined the expedition in October 1803 he was apparently living in West Point, Hardin County, Kentucky, twenty miles down the Ohio River from Louisville. Joseph and Reubin Field lived in this area, so it is quite likely that Shields knew them. Although the captains generally recruited unmarried men, they made an exception for Shields, perhaps because he was a skillful blacksmith and gunsmith. William Clark apparently promised to see that Shields's wife and daughter were taken care of while John was on the expedition. Jonathan Clark, an elder brother of William, lived near Louisville and conducted a variety of business transactions for William while he was away. One item of business was providing a Mrs. Shields with four dollars and twenty-one bushels of corn.[13]

Recruiting Shields turned out to be an excellent decision. "The Guns of Sergt. Pryor & Drewyer were both out of order," Clark wrote at Fort Clatsop; "the first had a Cock screw broken which was replaced by a duplicate. . . . the Second repaired with a new lock. . . . but for the precaution taken in bringing on these extra locks, . . . in addition to the ingenuity of John Shields, most of our guns would at this moment have been entirely unfit for use." Lewis said that Shields worked extremely well with either wood or metal and that the corps had been "much indebted to the ingenuity of this man on many occasions."[14]

Shields's ingenuity proved particularly valuable at crucial moments. During the winter of 1804–5, when the corps needed food, the natives showed little interest in trading away part of their corn until they saw Shields's blacksmith work. Lewis wrote that they were "extravagantly fond of sheet iron of which they form arrow-points and manufacter into instruments for scraping and dressing their buffaloe robes."[15] The natives also took a strong liking to battle-axes that Shields made entirely of iron. As a result, Shields and his fellow blacksmith Alexander Willard received seven or eight gallons of corn for each four-inch square of iron or battle-ax they provided to the Indians.

A year later, in February 1806, the corps was camped at Fort Clatsop on the Pacific coast when Private William Bratton developed a strange illness— he felt sick and weak and his lower back hurt. By mid-April he could not walk. Lewis tried every remedy he could think of: Rush's pills (strong laxatives that were nicknamed "thunderclappers"), Peruvian bark (used for everything from malaria to pleurisy to snakebite), Scott's pills (apparently a milder laxative), and an external treatment of liniment and warm flannel. Nothing worked. By the last week of May, when the group had reached present-day

Idaho, Lewis wrote that Bratton "is so weak in the loins that he is scarcely able to walk, nor can he set upwright but with the greatest pain."

Then John Shields proposed a sweat bath, saying he had seen "men in a similar situation restored by violent sweats." Bratton said he wanted to try it, and the captains gave their permission. The men dug a round hole three feet in diameter and four feet deep. Then Shields called for kindling and started a fire in the center of the hole. When the fire died down, Shields scooped out the embers and constructed a makeshift seat and foot rest. The immobile Bratton was "stripped naked" and lowered to the seat. Then Shields covered the hole with willows and blankets and instructed Bratton to pour water on the bottom and sides of the hole. As the water sizzled on the hot rocks and earth, steam rose out of Bratton's lair. Meanwhile, Shields had prepared "a strong tea of horse mint," and he handed down one hot cup after another to Bratton, who was continuing to create "as much steam or vapor as he could possibly bear."[16]

After twenty minutes, Shields called for men to help Bratton out of his private steam room. At Shields's direction, they plunged Bratton into the cold Clearwater River, then lowered him again into the hole. Shields handed down more water and more hot tea as the steam rose. This time Bratton stayed for forty-five minutes. Then his comrades helped him out of the hole and wrapped him in blankets, allowing him to cool off gradually.

The next day, Bratton was cured. "Bratton feels himself much better and is walking about today and says he is nearly free from pain," wrote Lewis. Within days he was rapidly recovering his strength, and within a week and a half walking with "considerable ease." His health was fine the remaining three months of the expedition, and he must have agreed with Clark that "the party owes much to the injinuity of this man [Shields]."[17] So there is a strange irony in Shields's dying in 1809 (at age forty) and Bratton's living a productive life for another thirty-two years.

In his report on the members of the expedition, Lewis went out of his way to compliment Shields, just as he had the Field brothers and George Drouillard. (Charles Floyd and François Labiche were the only other members receiving similar positive notice.) "Has received the pay only of a private," Lewis wrote of Shields. "Nothing was more peculiarly useful to us, in various situations, than the skill and ingenuity of this man as an artist, in repairing our guns, accoutrements, &c. and should it be thought proper to allow him something as an artificier, he has well deserved it."[18] As far as we know, however, Shields did not receive anything beyond the $178.50 that was due him.

After the expedition, Shields reportedly trapped with his kinsman Daniel

Boone in present-day Missouri. (It is not certain what he did with his land warrant to 320 acres in Franklin County, Missouri. By 1822 it had been processed by the Franklin land office in payment for land.) Then John and Nancy Shields followed another Boone, Daniel's brother Squire, to the area of Corydon in Harrison County, Indiana Territory, settling there in 1807.[19] About this same time their daughter, Martha Jannette, married her cousin John Tipton, who later became a hero in the War of 1812, a general in the army, and a U.S. senator from Indiana.

John Shields had nine brothers and one sister, and several of his siblings eventually moved to Indiana. Over the two years following the expedition's return, Shields may have worked as a blacksmith and gunsmith, just as he had on the voyage. He may have farmed with his brothers William and Benjamin. He may have gone into business with his brother James, an entrepreneur. He may have worked with his brother David, who ran flatboats on the Ohio River.[20] The future must have looked good, and John and Nancy may have seen their first grandchild, but by December 1809 John Shields was dead.

He died a nonviolent death, although we don't know anything more about it. For whatever reason, Shields's property was sold. The most valuable item was a horse that went for $110; a plow sold for $6.75, a Bible for $.75, and an Indian basket for $.87. "A variety of Small articles for Dressing guns" brought $1.67.[21]

Not included in the inventory was a keepsake that Nancy Shields must have treasured, a gift that symbolized John's habitual concern for others. In April 1805, at Fort Mandan, William Clark had written a letter to his brother Jonathan and sent the letter and several packages with the contingent of soldiers who took the keelboat down the Missouri that spring. He mentioned five buffalo robes that were on their way to Jonathan. "The one marked *John Shields* is Sent by him to his wife," wrote Clark.[22]

We don't know how long Nancy lived, nor do we know what became of the buffalo robe her husband sent from the Mandan country.

CHAPTER EIGHT

"A Sincere and Undisguised Heart"
George Shannon's Early Career

Days after George Drouillard's trial ended, George Shannon left for Lexington, Kentucky, to enroll at Transylvania University. William Clark wrote to his brother Jonathan: "The Bearer of this letter is Mr. George Shannon [one or two words lost due to the seal tear] unfortunate fellow who lost his leg by a wound received in the action at the Ricaras, he is going to lexington to go to School, with the view of acquiring Some knowledge to fit him for an employment to get his liveing, he is Studious, and ambitious, and a man of impeachable [impeccable] Charector."[1] With interest possibly sparked by Drouillard's trial, Shannon eventually took up the study of law.

The oak, beech, hickory, and maple trees were bursting with autumn hues as Shannon rode his horse across the lush Bluegrass region of Kentucky late in October 1808. A contemporary wrote that the area "beggars description. Poetry cannot paint groves more beautiful, or fields more luxuriant. The country is neither hilly nor level; but gently waving."[2] Shannon had visited Jonathan Clark in Louisville, probably fielding friendly questions about the expedition, about his own welfare, and about William Clark and his wife, Julia, then several months pregnant with her first child. William had married Julia Hancock in January of 1808, and they arrived in St. Louis in June, about the time Shannon left the hospital. He had spent time in their home and probably viewed sixteen-year-old Julia as a younger sister. Now Shannon had headed east for Lexington to, as Clark put it, acquire some knowledge.

For a young man accustomed to the Ohio frontier and the western wilderness, Shannon would have found a startling contrast in the "Athens of the West." Lexington boasted spacious streets, scores of two- or three-story brick homes, an impressive county courthouse, quite a number of stores and just as many churches, several rope and bagging factories, a dancing school, and three newspapers. Two weeks before Shannon's arrival, a four-hundred-seat theater had opened on Spring Street. The Lexington Jockey Club met regularly at Postlethwait's Tavern to socialize, sip Kentucky whiskey, and place bets on local horse races.

But Shannon was perhaps most impressed by the number of books that one could buy or borrow. Bookstores and print shops did a steady business. The public library's fifteen hundred volumes were complemented by a similar number at Transylvania. Founded as a seminary, it had recently been organized into a university, offering instruction in natural and moral philosophy; literature and theology; mathematics, geography, and astronomy; and law and medicine. According to contemporary university records, "In the fields of Greek and Latin, the academy student had to be able to read selections from Erasmus, Caesar's *Commentaries,* Ovid's *Metamorphisis,* Vergil's *The Aeneid,* Horace, Cicero's *Select Orations,* and four books of Homer's *Iliad.*"[3]

As the sole teenager on the expedition, Shannon had always been the kid, the greenhorn, a surrogate son to men like Clark and Drouillard, both in their thirties. Now his role had been reversed: he was a man among the teenagers attending Transylvania, his peg leg making him that much more conspicuous. Word must have spread quickly that he had explored the West with Captains Lewis and Clark, that he had lost his leg in a battle with Arikara Indians. The students came from the privileged class, and they entered Transylvania with solid preparatory schooling, something that Shannon lacked. He had come from a literate family, however, and had been instructed at home. And though he also lacked social status, he brought with him recommendations from the governor of the Louisiana Territory, the brigadier general of the Louisiana militia, and quite possibly from Revolutionary War hero (and Transylvania University trustee) George Rogers Clark, William Clark's brother.[4]

Once he arrived, Shannon made friends with a fifteen-year-old classmate by the name of Stephen Austin, son of the prominent businessman and mine owner Moses Austin. Stephen was soft-spoken, introspective, and intelligent. Shannon also had a contemplative nature, as shown by two of his student essays that have survived, one on the subject of dreams and the other on benevolence. "Children dream very early," he notes in the first, writing in an unpretentious, legible hand. "But what ideas these are, that present themselves so early, to the young mind, I am at a loss to know. Are they ideas which he has brought with him from some other world. or has he received them since his arrival in this? what anyhow; is this active faculty in man which exhibets itself so early, and which I believe never sleps? what is its origin?" The second paper is a seven-page reply to the question, "Is man susceptible of disinterested benevolence?" Yes, answers Shannon, humans do act without self-interest. "Are not men often known to sacrifice interest to benevolence? Did the tear of pitty never flow from the eye of the way worn traveller, in some distant land, on beholding even the stranger in distress? And has he not divided with him the last pence in his purse to alleviate his misery?"[5]

Stephen Austin no doubt wrote similar papers, as did another friend and classmate, Robert Todd. Young Todd had an aptitude for mathematics, for calculating profits and losses, and he and Austin both took an interest in a Lexington belle by the name of Eliza Parker, from a prominent Lexington family. But it was Todd who eventually courted and married Eliza. Their daughter, Mary Todd, married Abraham Lincoln in 1842.

University regulations forbade gambling and drinking and further dictated that "no student shall frequent Taverns, nor places of licentious or unprofitable amusement." Still, Lexington offered frequent acceptable social events—recitals, plays, balls, and dances. "Lexington has some charms," wrote a young woman, "particularly its Gayety." She noted that sixty-seven "elegantly" dressed young women were present at one party (where there were presumably a similar number of young men), making it "too large to be agreeable."[6] Stephen Austin and Robert Todd loved such social functions; Austin took up a lifelong love of dancing. By all indications, however, George Shannon was too self-conscious about his missing leg—and possibly his age and social standing—to join in these parties.

Shannon and Austin and their fellows heard constant talk of a brilliant lawyer by the name of Henry Clay, eight years Shannon's senior. Licensed to practice law in Kentucky at the age of twenty-one, Clay had been named professor of law and politics at Transylvania seven years later, in 1805. The next year he had successfully defended Aaron Burr and been elected to the U.S. Senate—both in the same month. By the time Shannon and Austin arrived in Lexington, Clay had completed his first stint in the Senate (serving the brief remainder of John Adair's term after Adair resigned) and was now a state congressman (for the second time) and a trustee of the university. The students likely heard his articulate rhetoric firsthand (and likely heard tales of his drinking, cursing, and gambling third or fourth hand).

Two months after Shannon's arrival, Henry Clay and his political enemy Humphrey Marshall (both a brother-in-law and a cousin to Chief Justice John Marshall) crossed the Ohio River near Louisville—presumably to avoid polluting Kentucky soil—to fight a duel. Both were slightly wounded. Accounts of the duel must have generated a healthy buzz among the young men at Transylvania. Henry Clay's star continued to rise, and a year later he was once again elected to the U.S. Senate. Exactly when he and Shannon met for the first time is not certain, but Clay befriended Shannon sometime before the summer of 1810.[7]

Shannon stayed in touch with William Clark and received regular government checks from him. Clark had written to his brother Jonathan: "I Shall Continue to pay [Shannon] his Salerry untill ordered to the reverse by the Secty. of War, which will enable him to pay his board and Schooling." Thomas Jefferson's secretary of war, Henry Dearborn, apparently had no objection to this arrangement. But Dearborn's replacement, William Eustis, did have objections. In a letter to Clark, written a few weeks after he rejected Meriwether Lewis's vouchers, Eustis declared: "It is not proper that the pension of George Shannon should be paid out of the Funds for the Indian Department: every soldier who is disabled in the service of the United States is entitled to a pension; but he must take the course prescribed by Law, to enable him to receive it."[8]

Clark was traveling through Kentucky in October 1809 when the first newspaper accounts of Lewis's death appeared. Shannon probably read of a letter received by a Lexington resident. "The accounts are," read the letter, "that Governor Lewis arrived at a house very weak, from a recent illness at Natchez, and showed signs of mental derangement. After a stay of a few hours at the above house, he took his pistols and shot himself twice, and then cut his throat."[9]

Clark and his wife and their party arrived in Lexington on 30 October. By this time Clark had concluded that Lewis had indeed taken his own life. Clark paid Shannon his last check for forty dollars from the Indian Department but assured Shannon he would keep pushing for an approved pension—which would take another four years of cutting through red tape, with the captain all the while acting as the younger man's advocate. Just how Shannon covered his living expenses for the next several months is uncertain. He probably had help from Clark and others.

In the midst of the distressing news about Lewis there was also joy, for Shannon was probably able to see William and Julia Clark's first child—a nine-month-old boy named Meriwether Lewis Clark, called Lewis by his parents.[10]

George Shannon, Stephen Austin, and the other students at Transylvania held to a rigid schedule: study from sunrise to noon, with an hour's break at

8:00; study again in the afternoon from 2:00 to 5:30 (in summer) or from 1:30 to 4:00 and 5:00 to 8:00 (in winter). Each day began and ended with prayer. Each student was expected to attend Sunday services at a church of his choosing. At the end of each session, the trustees held oral examinations, focusing particularly on public speaking—a skill that served both Shannon and Austin well in later years.[11]

Interestingly, Shannon and Austin both left Transylvania in 1810, before completing the standard two-year program. In April 1810, Austin returned to Missouri, apparently because his father needed him to look after the family mining business.[12] Four years later, at the age of twenty, Austin was elected to the Missouri territorial legislature.

Just a few weeks after Austin left Transylvania, Shannon once again met with William Clark, now returning from the east to St. Louis. Clark had a surprising and thrilling mission in mind for Shannon: he was to travel to Philadelphia and assist in publishing the expedition journals. After Clark visited Thomas Jefferson in December 1809, he had gone on to Philadelphia, discussing the publication of the expedition journals with such prominent Philadelphians as John Conrad, Charles Willson Peale, Bernard McMahon, Benjamin Rush, Caspar Wistar, and Benjamin Smith Barton. One of these men apparently suggested Nicholas Biddle as the editor of the journals. Biddle, who had graduated from Princeton at age fifteen (and was actually a year younger than the twenty-five-year-old Shannon), was a "young Philadelphia lawyer possessed of rare literary ability." He had already served as secretary to the United States minister to France and as temporary secretary to James Monroe, United States minister to Great Britain.[13]

Biddle was not in Philadelphia at the time, but Clark wrote him from Virginia, inviting him to "Come to this place where I have my Books & memorandoms and stay with me a week or two. . . . I am at present with Col. Hancock my father in Lar who is now retired and plesently situated." When Biddle received the letter, he politely declined, writing to Clark that he had "neither health nor leisure to do sufficient justice to the fruits of your enterprize and ingenuity." A week later, however, Biddle reconsidered. "I will therefore very readily agree to do all that is in my power for the advancement of the work," he wrote. He also accepted Clark's invitation to visit Fincastle. Biddle arrived at the Hancock estate the third week in March 1810, and for the next three weeks, he and William Clark examined the journals and discussed the expedition at great length.

Biddle had never traveled west of the Susquehanna River, but he took to the journals as if he had been present at Fort Mandan, Fort Clatsop, and everywhere in between, displaying an unmatched enthusiasm for Lewis and

Clark's journey and everything associated with it. As he and Clark talked, Biddle took detailed notes (more than twenty thousand words' worth), covering the native method of catching horses, wildfires on the prairie, Sacagawea's reunion with her people, the natives' reaction to York, and a multitude of other topics. Biddle thus compiled a good deal of information not present in Lewis and Clark's original journals.[14]

Biddle needed assistance, Clark explained to Shannon, adding that his firsthand experience on the expedition and recent studies at Transylvania made him uniquely qualified for the job. Shannon accepted, just as Clark hoped—for he had already told Biddle about him. Clark immediately wrote to Biddle: "This will be handed to you by Mr. George Shannon the young man I spoke to you about, who was with me on the N.W. expedition; he has agreed to go to Philadelphia and give such information relitive to that Tour as may be in his power. This Young Gentleman possesses a sincere and undisguised heart, he is highly spoken of by all his acquaintance and much respected at the Lexington University where he has been for the last two years. Any advice and friendly attentions which you may show to this Young Man will be greatfully acknowledged by him, and Confur an additional obligation on me."[15]

Shannon made preparations to leave, and on 1 July 1810, Isaac Baker, a fellow Transylvania student, wrote to Stephen Austin that Shannon had left for Philadelphia on 12 June. He arrived in Philadelphia in August, and he and Biddle got to work, rising each morning at five o'clock and working on the project for much of the day. Biddle sometimes reported progress to Clark by alluding to incidents on the expedition: "To day I have sent you & ten men up into a bottom to look for wood to make canoes after the unhappy failure of your iron boat; so that you see how far I am."[16]

Biddle had a thousand questions, and Clark frequently referred him to Shannon: "Please to enquire of Mr. Shannon for the language of signs used by Indians, &c."; "I cant describe the Game among the Mandans mentioned in O[rd]ways journal if Shannon cant no one in this country can."; "Please to ask Mr. Shannon to describe the Buffalow Pathes to you."[17]

Biddle and Shannon labored together for months on end and got along well. When they weren't working together, Biddle was tending to his duties as a member of the Pennsylvania state legislature or devouring books on the American Indian—even ordering some volumes from France—and Shannon was studying law. Fortunately, Biddle had independent means to support them, for he had received nothing for his work on the journals. Then, in June of 1811, after the two men had worked on the journals for the better part of a year, Biddle wrote to Clark: "[I] by diligence have at length been able to get completely thro' the manuscripts and am now ready to put the work to the press as soon as Mr. Conrad wishes it." In his typical good humor—and in another allusion to the expedition—Biddle added, "I am obliged now to make an oration before the whole city on the fourth of July, which in our heats is more fatiguing than a elk hunt among the Shoshones."[18]

A week and a half later, Biddle added a note on Shannon: "The information [in your letters] was very valuable, & combined with what I have learnt from Mr. Shannon who I find very intelligent & sensible leaves me nothing to wish on the points I mentioned." Shannon then departed for Norristown, Pennsylvania, where he continued his law studies. In September, a letter arrived from Clark inviting Shannon to join him in a trading business. "If you should think proper to join in Trade the firm must be in the name of G. Shannon & Co," Clark wrote. He realized however, that Shannon might have already made plans for a law career and suggested, "On the Subject of Trade, do just as your feel an inclination join or let it alone. On that of Law do prosisely as your inclination leads you, you shall get every aid in my power in either deturmonation, or both if you should be enclined to embarke in both."[19]

Clark was right: Shannon had decided on law, and in January 1812 he requested Biddle's help in obtaining the position of "judge advocate, in this new Army which is to be raised." The appointment did not come, but Shannon was not discouraged—he made arrangements to return to Lexington, where his prospects looked good. Indeed, by the end of the year, the *Kentucky Gazette* had announced: "Mr. Shannon is appointed messenger for the Kentucky electors."[20]

About the time Shannon left Pennsylvania for Kentucky, in the summer of 1812, Clark got bad news from Biddle: for the past year, Biddle had been trying to get the journals printed. "Yet notwithstanding all my exertions the publication has been prevented from time to time till at last Mr. Conrad's difficulties have obliged him to surrender everything to his creditors & give up business."[21] With the printer bankrupt—and with the war against Britain and the native nations of the northwest intensifying—it was not clear when, or if, the journals would be printed.

Plates

Meriwether Lewis by Charles Willson Peale, from life, 1807
"He was early remarkable for intrepidity, liberality & hardihood,"
Jefferson wrote of Lewis, "at eight years of age going alone with
his dogs at midnight in the depth of winter, hunting wading
creeks when the banks were covered with ice & snow."
(Courtesy of Independence National Historical Park)

William Clark by Charles Willson Peale, from life, 1807–8
"[William] is a youth of solid and promising parts, and as brave as Caesar,"
a friend wrote to Clark's brother Jonathan.
(Courtesy of Independence National Historical Park)

Thomas Jefferson by Charles Willson Peale, from life, 1791–92
Jefferson directed Lewis to explore the Missouri River and find
"the most direct & practicable water communication across
this continent for the purposes of commerce."
(Courtesy of Independence National Historical Park)

"Great Falls of the Missouri," A. E. Mathews, *Pencil Sketches of Montana*, 1868
"Hearing a tremendious roaring above me I continued my rout . . . and was
again presented by one of the most beatifull objects in nature," wrote Lewis.
(Courtesy of the Montana Historical Society, Helena)

"Three Forks of the Missouri," A. E. Mathews, *Pencil Sketches of Montana*, 1868
George Drouillard and John Potts both lost their lives near this spot,
where Sacagawea had been taken captive around 1800.
(Courtesy of the Montana Historical Society, Helena)

York, Charles M. Russell, watercolor, 1909
"All the nation made a great deal of him," Ordway wrote of York.
"All flocked around him & examin^d him from top to toe."
(Courtesy of the Montana Historical Society, Helena)

"The Travellers Meeting with Minatarre Indians near Fort Clark,"
after Karl Bodmer, engraving with aquatint
Toussaint Charbonneau, right of center, is depicted making introductions for
Prince Maximilian of Wied in 1833.

(Courtesy of Joslyn Art Museum, Omaha, Nebraska, gift of Enron Art Foundation)

Buffalo and Elk on the Upper Missouri, Karl Bodmer, watercolor on paper, 1833
"So magnificent a Senerey in a Contry thus Situated far removed from
the Sivilised world and to be enjoyed by nothing but the Buffalo
Elk Deer & Bear," wrote Clark in July of 1804.
(Courtesy of Joslyn Art Museum, Omaha, Nebraska, gift of Enron Art Foundation)

Sheheke, or Big White, in a pastel by C.-B.-J.
Févret de Saint-Mémin
In January 1805, Sheheke described the
country west of the Mandan villages, "as far
as the high mountains, and on the South
Side of the [Yellowstone] River," informa-
tion Clark incorporated into his map.
(Courtesy of the American Philosophical Society)

Lewis and Clark Expedition, Charles M. Russell, oil on canvas, 1918
As Sacagawea is reunited with her childhood friend,
Charbonneau tells Clark what is happening.
(Courtesy of the Gilcrease Museum, Tulsa, Oklahoma)

Portrait of William Clark by Joseph H. Bush, ca. 1817
After the expedition, Clark became one of the most
prominent—and competent—Indian agents in the country.
(Courtesy of the Filson Historical Society, Louisville, Kentucky)

Mr. Shanons Octr. 28th 1809

Dear Brother

I proceeded on very well to Mr Smiths and arived there about an hour after dark, and this day have come on very well to this place – The Man boy is not well, tho' not worse than he was when you parted with us – When at Shelbyville to day I saw in a Frankfort paper called the Arguss a report published which gives me much Concern, it Says that Govr Lewis killed himself by Cutting his Throat with a knife, on his way between the Chickaw Saw Bluffs and Nashville, I fear this report has too much truth, tho' hope it may have no foundation – My reasons for thinking it possible is founded on the letter which I received from him at your house; in that letter he says he had some intention of going this by land & his only objection was his papers. The Boats I sent down with the pettres, under the Directions of Mr James McFarlane must have over taken the Govr. between New Madrid and the Chickasaw Bluffs, and if he was still disposed to go through, is it not probable that he might have intrusted his papers to McFarlane who is a particular

Original text of William Clark's letter of 28 October 1809 to Jonathan Clark

The letter, in which Clark discusses a report of Lewis's death, was discovered in Louisville in 1988. The Bodley family presented this letter and more than fifty others to the Filson Historical Society in 1990.

(Courtesy of the Filson Historical Society, Louisville, Kentucky)

Patrick Gass, the last survivor of the expedition
"I remember the old man with his staff would come to the Brewery . . .
& drink 2 glasses of beer and then take up his staff & go back home,"
wrote an acquaintance in West Virginia.
(Courtesy of Eugene Gass Painter)

Alexander Willard and his wife, Eleanor
They were married from 1807 until
Alexander's death in 1865.
(Courtesy of the Willard Family Association
of America, Inc.)

Colter's Race for Life, Charles M. Russell, pen and ink,
gouache, and graphite on paper, ca. 1922
"A tremendous yell let him know that the whole pack of bloodhounds
were off in full cry," wrote Washington Irving. "Colter flew
rather than ran; he was astonished at his own speed."
(Courtesy of Amon Carter Museum, Fort Worth, Texas [1961.129])

Lewis and Clark on the Lower Columbia, Charles M. Russell,
gouache, watercolor, and graphite, 1905
Sacagawea communicates with a Columbia River nation as Clark, York, and
others look on.
(Courtesy of Amon Carter Museum, Fort Worth, Texas [1961.195])

William Clark's list of expedition members

Clark drew up this list on the front cover of a cash book between 1825 and 1828.
This is a crucial source of information concerning the fate of the corps,
although York is not mentioned.

(Courtesy of the Everett D. Graff Collection, The Newberry Library, Chicago)

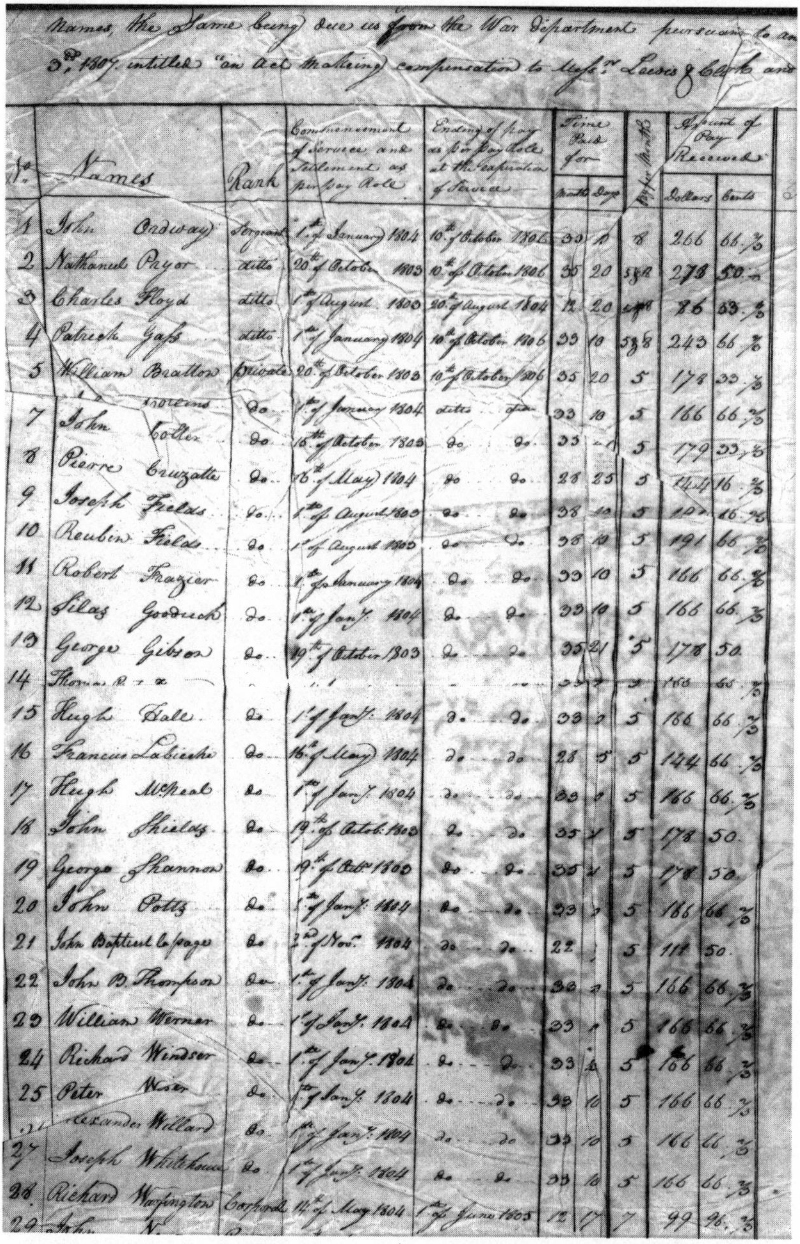

No	Names	Rank	Commencement of Service and Settlement as per pay Roll	Ending of pay as per pay Roll at the expiration of Service	Time Paid for Month	Days	[rate per Month]	Amount of Pay Received Dollars	Cents
1	John Ordway	Sergeant	1st January 1804	10th October 1806	33	10	8	266	66 ⅔
2	Nathaniel Pryor	ditto	20th October 1803	10th October 1806	35	20	5 8/12	278	50
3	Charles Floyd	ditto	1st August 1803	20th August 1804	12	20	5 6/12	86	33 ⅓
4	Patrick Gass	ditto	1st January 1804	10th October 1806	33	10	5 3/8	243	66 ⅔
5	William Bratton	Private	20th October 1803	10th October 1806	35	20	5	178	33 ⅓
7	John Collins	do	1st January 1804	ditto do	33	10	5	166	66 ⅔
8	Pierre Cruzatte	do	16th May 1804	do do	28	25	5	144	16 ⅔
9	Joseph Fields	do	1st August 1803	do do	38	10	5	191	66 ⅔
10	Reubin Fields	do	1st August 1803	do do	38	10	5	191	66 ⅔
11	Robert Frazier	do	1st January 1804	do do	33	10	5	166	66 ⅔
12	Silas Goodrich	do	1st Jany 1804	do do	33	10	5	166	66 ⅔
13	George Gibson	do	19th October 1803	do do	35	21	5	178	50
14	Thomas P. + x				33		5	166	66 ⅔
15	Hugh Hall	do	1st Jany 1804	do do	33	2	5	166	66 ⅔
16	Francis Labiche	do	16th May 1804	do do	28	5	5	144	66 ⅔
17	Hugh McNeal	do	1st Jany 1804	do do	33	1	5	166	66 ⅔
18	John Shields	do	19th Octob 1803	do do	35	1	5	178	50
19	George Shannon	do	19th Octo 1803	do do	35	1	5	178	50
20	John Potts	do	1st Jany 1804	do do	33	1	5	166	66 ⅔
21	John Baptiste Lepage	do	2d Nov 1804	do do	22		5	112	50
22	John B. Thompson	do	1st Jany 1804	do do	33	2	5	166	66 ⅔
23	William Werner	do	1st Jany 1804	do do	33	1	5	166	66 ⅔
24	Richard Windsor	do	1st Jany 1804	do do	33	4	5	166	66 ⅔
25	Peter Weiser	do	1st Jany 1804	do do	33	10	5	166	66 ⅔
26	Alexander Willard	do	1st Jany 1804	do do	33	10	5	166	66 ⅔
27	Joseph Whitehouse	do	1st Jany 1804	do do	33	10	5	166	66 ⅔
28	Richard Warfington	Corporal	14th May 1804	1st June 1805	12	17	7	99	96 ⅔
29	John N...								

Members of the Corps of Discovery

This document by William Clark lists the members of the corps,
their rank, dates of service, and pay.

(Courtesy of the Yale Collection of Western Americana, Beinecke Rare Book and
Manuscript Library, Yale University)

CHAPTER NINE

"He Must Have Fought in a Circle on Horseback"
George Drouillard's Death at the Hands of the Blackfeet

On 24 September 1809, 101 days after he had left St. Louis—and one year and one day after he had been found not guilty of murder—George Drouillard was with those who returned Sheheke to his people. One of the soldiers fired a shot as the keelboat approached the chief's village. A native returned the salute. Then a mate raised the Stars and Stripes, and the villagers crowded to the shore. "I then caused the mandan nation to be assembled," wrote Pierre Chouteau, who had commanded the flotilla of 350 men and thirteen keelboats, "as also the minnitari and ahwapaway nations of Indians, in Council, and presented to them the mandan chief, his wife and family, who were received with the Greatest demonstration of Joy, I explained to them the causes of his detention." Party member Thomas James added that the Mandan "were almost frantic with joy and eagerness to speak with him. . . . The natives made a jubilee and celebration for the return of Shehaka and neglected everything and everybody else. They hardly saw or took the least notice of their white visitors."[1]

Sheheke's brother quickly remedied this situation by inviting Chouteau's delegation to a celebration. "We found a plentiful supply of provisions," wrote the company surgeon, Dr. William Thomas. "The ladies had prepared a large stew of meat, corn, and vegetables, and our feast was seasoned by genuine hospitality. In the afternoon we prepared to visit the upper towns. An elegant horse was presented to their travelled chief, who had put on his full dress of uniform suit."[2]

After this moment of glory, Sheheke's status rapidly declined. Drouillard, who had been present when the Mandan chief consented to go east with Lewis and Clark, saw a reversal of the good feeling and devotion that had accompanied Sheheke's departure. Now several other chiefs eyed Sheheke suspiciously as he refused to share the gifts that had been sent "to be distributed among these nations." According to Chouteau, Sheheke "replied that the presents he had brought were not to be distributed, they were all his own, this seemed to occasion Jealousies and difficulties among all the tribes, and the more so as 'One Eye' the Great Chief of the minnetaries [Hidatsa] had in a quarrel a few days before murdered one of the principal men of the mandans."[3]

"On arriving at the Gros Ventre [Hidatsa] village," wrote Thomas James, "we found a hunter and trapper named Colter, who had been one of Lewis & Clark's men." Earlier that year, Colter had traveled from Fort Raymond (in present-day southeastern Montana) to the mouth of the Knife River (north of modern-day Bismarck). Here, Drouillard and several others listened as Colter told how he and Potts had been attacked at Three Forks a year earlier. Dr. Thomas was among those present. He returned to St. Louis a month and a half later (early in November 1809) and published the journal of his voyage in the *Missouri Gazette*, telling the story of Colter's run for the first time.[4]

Someone told Colter the party was headed to Fort Raymond to trap and then to Three Forks. They had the arms and force of men required to defend themselves. They had a good supply of traps. They planned to build a fort at Three Forks and reap a rich harvest of beaver pelts. Captain Clark and others had backed the enterprise. Next came the inevitable question: would Colter join them? It was October 1809 (Meriwether Lewis was then following the Natchez Trace toward Grinder's Stand), and this was the third time Colter had received such an invitation. The first had been when he met Dickson and Hancock in 1806; the second when he encountered Lisa and company near the mouth of the Platte River in 1807. A year earlier he had barely escaped with his life before enduring the harrowing run back to Fort Raymond. Now he was safe, only a month away from civilization, which he had not seen for more than five years. But his answer was yes—he would venture into Blackfoot country once again.

Drouillard, Colter, Reuben Lewis (Meriwether's brother), and a number of others spent the winter at Fort Raymond, at the confluence of the Bighorn and Yellowstone Rivers. To a man, they were eager to get to Three Forks, build their stockade, and commence trapping the rich beaver streams. So, in

March of 1810, well before the coming of spring, thirty-two men under the command of Pierre Menard loaded up their packhorses and headed west into the snow, following the icy Yellowstone River along the same route—but in the reverse direction—of Colter's run. Fittingly, Colter himself was the guide.[5]

The greenhorn trappers among the group had seen violent thunderstorms on the Missouri; they had endured severe hunger and had narrowly averted a battle among their own ranks. Now they were quickly initiated into additional realities. First came snow blindness. One man named Brown lost his sight the very day the group left Fort Raymond. "His eyes pained him so much that he implored us to put an end to his torment by shooting him," wrote James. "I watched him during that night for fear he would commit the act himself." James stayed close to Brown for the next three days, leading him by the hand when necessary, encouraging him even though he "moaned and groaned most piteously" and was convinced his eyeballs had burst. On the third day, Brown's vision slowly returned.

Next they experienced havoc and butchery. Two men had gone ahead with a Shoshone (Snake) chief, his two wives, and his son. They intended to hunt and prepare food for the group as it followed in their path. Two days out, the main party arrived at an Indian lodge, where they sensed and smelled death. "Stripped, and near by," wrote James, "we saw a woman and boy lying on the ground, with their heads split open, evidently by a tomahawk. These were the Snake's elder wife and son, he having saved himself and his younger wife by flight on horseback. Our two men who had started out in company with him were not molested. They told us that a party of Gros Ventres [Crows] had come upon them, committed these murders, and passed on, as if engaged in a lawful and praiseworthy business."

The image of death was followed by a Rocky Mountain blizzard. The men huddled inside their tents as the storm raged throughout the night, the snow flying horizontally and drifting in fifty-foot mounds. In the morning, they crawled out of the collapsed tents to see the heads and backs of their horses just above the snow. "We proceeded on with the greatest difficulty," said James. "The wind had heaped [the snow] up in many places to a prodigious height. . . . A horse occasionally stepped out of the beaten track and sank entirely out of sight in the snow. By night we had made about four miles for that day's travel." James and three others, who found themselves separated from the main group, forded the half-frozen Gallatin River and supped on a single piece of buffalo meat.

Next came snow blindness again, followed by near starvation: "We all now became blind, as [Brown] had been, from the reflection of the sun's rays on the snow. The hot tears trickled from the swollen eyes, nearly blistering the cheeks, and the eyeballs seemed bursting from our heads." Unable to hunt, James and his three companions had elected to slaughter a horse when one of them managed to kill a goose, which they used to make a soup that "stayed the gnawings of hunger," according to James. Their eyes improved and the next day they killed an elk. Well knowing "the dangers of gluttony after a fast," they ate in moderation. Later that day they found the main party. "They, like ourselves, had all been blind, and had suffered more severely than we from the same cause." The larger group had killed three dogs and two horses to stave off starvation.

As the men struggled through the snow toward Three Forks, Colter related his adventures of 1808. James recalled: "As we passed over the ground where Colter ran his race and listened to his story an indefinable fear crept over all. We felt awestruck by the nameless and numerous dangers that evidently beset us on every side. Even [James] Cheek's courage sank [he was a fearless man who the previous summer had nearly killed Lisa in a fit of anger], and his hitherto buoyant and cheerful spirit was depressed at hearing of the perils of the place. He spoke despondingly and his mind was uneasy, restless, and fearful. 'I am afraid,' said he, 'and I acknowledge it. I never felt fear before now but now I feel it.'"

Amazingly, Colter had returned to Three Forks not long after his escape from the Blackfeet, during the winter of 1808–9. On that visit, assuming the Indians "were all quiet in winter quarters," he hiked alone through the snow to retrieve the traps he had dropped in the river when he and Potts were attacked. He was camped near the Gallatin River when he heard something in the darkness. He doused his fire just as gunshots whistled around him. James recounted Colter's telling of this incident: "Again he fled for life, and the second time ascended the perpendicular mountain which he had gone up in his former flight, fearing now, as then, that the pass might be guarded by Indians. He reached the top before morning and resting for the day descended the next night, and then made his way with all possible speed to the fort. He said that at the time he promised God Almighty that he would never return to this region again if he were only permitted to escape once more with his life."

Colter had escaped once more, but he had not kept his vow, for now in 1810 he was returning yet again to the source of the Missouri River—for some reason the deadliest trapping spot in what would become the wide state of Montana—for the sixth time.

The party reached Three Forks on 3 April 1810 and immediately began constructing a fort. James and three others fashioned dugout canoes and headed downstream (north) toward Great Falls to trap. As James was leaving, Cheek bade him farewell. "It is the general opinion that you will be killed," said Cheek, "but I am afraid for myself as well as you. I know not the cause, but I have felt fear ever since I came to the Forks, and I never was afraid of anything before. . . . I may be dead when you return."[6]

Blackfoot warriors wore their hair long and loose around their shoulders, with a rectangular lock of hair falling down between their eyes. They wore no breechcloths but covered themselves in front with a criss-cross of skin leggings, leaving the buttocks uncovered. They used red and yellow lead paint on their faces. Hair feathers and necklaces of grizzly-bear claws were not uncommon. When needed, the universal buffalo robe completed their attire.

The Blackfeet, actually a confederation of three tribes, were roaming buffalo hunters who lived in tepees. They dyed their moccasins black (hence the name) and decorated them with a distinctive three-pronged beadwork representing their three nations—Blackfoot proper, Blood, and Piegan. They controlled an area ranging from the Saskatchewan River in the north (present-day southern Saskatchewan) to Three Forks in the south (southwestern Montana). Their enemies included the Assiniboin to the north, Flatheads and Shoshones to the west, and Crows to the southeast. Their arsenal of weapons included short, powerful bows, iron-tipped arrows and lances, scalping knives, and hatchet-shaped steel tomahawks and flintlock muskets, both of which were obtained from British traders of the North West Company.

On 12 April, nine days after the whole company of trappers had reached Three Forks, the Blackfeet attacked a small group of the men. "The party which was defeated consisted of eleven persons," wrote Menard, "and eight or nine of them were absent tending their traps when the savages pounced upon the camp. The two persons killed are James Cheeks [Cheek], and one Ayres. . . . Besides these two, there are missing young Hull who was of the same camp, and Freehearty and his man who were camped about two miles farther up. . . . In the camp where the first two men were killed we found a Blackfoot who had also been killed, and upon following their trail we saw that another had been dangerously wounded. Both of them, if the wounded man dies, came to their death at the hands of Cheeks, for he alone defended himself."[7]

On his return, James heard from one of the survivors that two men had run "up to Cheek and others and told them to catch their horses and escape. This Cheek refused to do, but, seizing his rifle and pistols, said he would stay and abide his fate. 'My time has come, but I will kill at least two of them, and then I don't care.' His gloomy forebodings were about to be fulfilled through his own recklessness and obstinacy. Ayers ran frantically about, paralyzed by fear and crying: 'O God, O God, what can I do?' Though a horse was within his reach he was disabled by terror from mounting and saving his life. Courage and cowardice met the same fate, though in very different manners. Hull stood coolly examining his rifle as if for battle. The enemy were coming swiftly toward them and Valle and his two companions started off, pursued by mounted Indians. The sharp reports of Cheek's rifle and pistols were soon heard doing the work of death upon the savages, and then a volley of musketry sent the poor fellow to his long home."[8]

Michael Immell, one of the eleven men in the trapping party, was out hunting when Cheek was killed, and Immell returned unaware of what had happened. He was alarmed to see the tent gone but then assumed the others had simply moved the camp. Then he heard something near the river and went to investigate. Making his way quietly into the willows, he scanned the opposite bank of the Jefferson River and saw quite a number of Indian lodges. He watched a Blackfoot woman walk down to the shore carrying a brass kettle, one he was certain belonged to him. Then he saw a white man tied to a tree but couldn't make out who it was. He checked his weapons, then crept silently back to the campsite, where he found Cheek's body lying face down, the scalp missing. One of the Blackfoot warriors had taken the scalp and Cheek's guns as trophies. When an Indian took a scalp, his wife would usually display the hair on a pole as the entire tribe danced and sang—celebrating their victory over the white men who had invaded Blackfoot territory and who supplied enemy Crows with goods and arms.[9]

Immell grabbed his traps and galloped his horse to the fort, arriving safely. Thirteen years later, he would once again encounter Blackfoot warriors in Montana, but he did not escape a second time. He, his partner Robert Jones, and five others were killed in what has since been called the Immell-Jones massacre.[10]

Colter had also been out trapping when the Blackfeet attacked. He was breathless and frantic when he reached the fort—which was little more than a bulwark of freshly hewn logs. He remarked on the deaths of Cheek and Ayres—and what must have been the worse fate of Hull, Freeharty, and Rucker (another trapper who had disappeared)—and recounted how he had promised God a year earlier to forever leave the region and how he had broken that promise. "Now," he said, throwing his hat on the ground, "if God will only forgive me this time and let me off I *will* leave the country day after tomorrow, and be damned if I ever come into it again."[11]

Convinced that Colter was serious this time, Pierre Menard and Reuben Lewis both wrote letters for him to deliver for them. Colter agreed to deliver

Menard's letter to his wife and Lewis's to his brother Meriwether. But what neither Colter nor Reuben knew—and what Reuben did not learn for at least another fifteen months—was that Meriwether Lewis had died at Grinder's Stand more than six months earlier.[12]

As he had promised, Colter left two days later and never returned. He and two others headed east, over territory Colter now knew perfectly well, and they were reportedly attacked by Blackfeet. They escaped by hiding in a thicket, eventually reaching Fort Raymond by traveling at night and "lying concealed in the daytime." A month later, Colter finally made it back to St. Louis, six years after he had departed with Lewis and Clark.[13]

Drouillard was undeterred. By early May he was trapping the Jefferson again, even venturing out alone. One day he returned to the main camp with six beaver pelts. James warned him of the danger. "I am too much of an Indian to be caught by Indians," replied Drouillard, who had been raised as a French-Canadian though his birth mother was a Shawnee. The next day he returned with additional pelts. "This is the way to catch beaver," he said.[14]

On the third day, Drouillard rose early and prepared his traps. James and the others urged him to wait for the protection of the whole party. Drouillard declined. Two Indian trappers, perhaps emboldened by Drouillard's cocksureness, left at the same time to hunt deer. The other men waited, but Drouillard did not return at his normal time. Nor did the hunters.

Finally a group of well-armed men mounted their horses and followed the Jefferson upstream to search for Drouillard. They had not followed the river far when they found the bodies of the two hunters—"pierced with lances, arrows, and bullets and lying near each other," said James. Knowing what must lie ahead, they mounted their horses and rode on, soon seeing what they feared but expected.[15]

"Farther on," wrote James, "about one hundred and fifty yards, [Drouillard] and his horse lay dead, the former mangled in a horrible manner; his head was cut off, his entrails torn out, and his body hacked to pieces." But Drouillard had gone down fighting: "We saw from the marks on the ground that he must have fought in a circle on horseback and probably killed some of his enemies, being a brave man and well armed with a rifle, pistol, knife and tomahawk." Indeed, the Blackfeet later reported that Drouillard had killed two of their number. "We pursued the trail of the Indians till night without overtaking them," concluded James, "and then returned, having buried our dead, with saddened hearts to the fort."[16]

Menard made it safely back to St. Louis, and the *Missouri Gazette*, basing the story on an interview with him, reported Drouillard's death. Six weeks after that, the same newspaper added a sad footnote to the life of Lewis's right-hand man, who never married or had children:

> All persons indebted to the estate of George Drouillard, deceased, are requested to make immediate payment, and those who have any claims against said estate will present their claims with lawful vouchers thereof to the subscriber.
>
> Manuel Lisa, Administrator
St. Louis, August 31th, 1810[17]

CHAPTER TEN

"Water as High as the Trees"
William Bratton and John Ordway
and the Great Earthquake

First came the noise—an unearthly, eerie, deafening, ear-splitting roar that jolted farmers and townspeople alike from their beds at 2:30 in the morning. "Inconceivably loud and terrific," said one; "equal to the loudest thunder, but more hollow and vibrating," said others. Violent shaking followed immediately, with the cacophony of crashing timber and collapsing bricks merging with the original roar, followed in turn by the ground itself rippling in waves.[1]

"We were awakened by a most tremendous noise," wrote one villager, "while the house danced about as if it would fall on our heads. I soon conjectured the cause of our troubles, and cried out it was an Earthquake, and for the family to leave the house; which we found very difficult to do, owing to its rolling and jostling about."[2]

Throughout the district of New Madrid, in what was soon to become the Territory of Missouri, the fifteen hundred inhabitants faced similar difficulties. But when they fled their damaged or demolished homes, they found a December chill, fog, and suffocating, blinding dust. Trees swayed as if in a tornado, though there was no wind; "all nature seemed running into chaos." The incessant noise persisted: moans from the injured, tumbling fireplaces, stampeding livestock, "the crash of falling trees, and the screaming of the wild fowl on the river." Then a smell as intense as the noise filled the air, a pungent, overpowering, sulfurlike stench.[3]

As families, farmhands, and merchants huddled in the darkness—or searched for missing loved ones—the ground quivered continually, one aftershock following another. "At half past 6 o'clock in the morning it cleared up," recounted a man whose name has been lost to history. "Believing the danger over I left home, to see what injury my neighbors had sustained. A few minutes after my departure there was another shock, extremely violent. I hurried home as fast as I could, but the agitation of the earth was so great that it was with much difficultly I kept my balance—*the motion of the earth was about twelve inches to and fro.* I cannot give you an accurate description of this moment; the earth seemed convulsed—the houses shook very much—chimmies falling in every direction. The loud, hoarse roaring which attended the earthquake, together with the cries, screams, and yells of the people, seems still ringing in my ears."[4]

The date was Monday, 15 December 1811. By 11 a.m. three major quakes had struck. The stunned residents of New Madrid had no way of knowing they had just witnessed three of the most powerful earthquakes ever to strike North America. Amazingly, two more major earthquakes hit by 7 February; all five quakes are believed to have measured between 8.0 and 8.8 on the Richter scale. Between five hundred and one thousand people likely perished in the quakes, most of them river travelers and Indians.[5]

Although several veterans of the expedition lived in the Missouri region and the surrounding territories and felt the earthquake, two were in the immediate vicinity: Private William Bratton and Sergeant John Ordway. Bratton was living and working on a keelboat that was in the vicinity of New Madrid at the time of the earthquake; for him, the quake turned out to be an interesting sidelight he could later tell his children and grandchildren about. Ordway, by contrast, lived in New Madrid and was among those who struggled to save his family during those chaotic hours of tumult and darkness. For him, the earthquake was catastrophic, spelling the immediate decline of a prosperous, happy life. He would not live to tell grandchildren about the great earthquake.

William Bratton is often remembered as the member of the corps who suffered serious health problems during the expedition—and for the courageous way he endured them. "Bratton . . . has had a tedious illness which he boar with much fortitude and firmness," wrote Lewis.[6] Fortunately, Bratton's severe back ailment was cured by John Shields's effective steam bath in May of 1806. In an irony that seems typical in the lives of Lewis and Clark's men, Bratton lived a long, healthy life, surviving—as far as is known—all but three or four of his fellow explorers.

One of the "nine young men from Kentucky," Bratton "was over six feet tall, square of build, very straight and erect, rather reserved, economical, of fine intelligence and the strictest morals."[7] He learned the blacksmith trade as a young man and assisted Shields with smithing duties during the expedition. Shields's concern for Bratton during the latter's illness indicates that the two of them grew close.

In a discharge written on 10 October 1806, Lewis spoke highly of Bratton: "I with cheerfullness declare that the ample support which he gave me under every necessary occation, and the fortitude with which he boar the fatugues and painfull sufferings incident to that long Voyage, entitled him to my highest confidence and sincere thanks."[8]

By 1811, Bratton had drawn on his experience with the corps to get into the keelboat business. In a letter written on 16 May 1811 and sent from Lexington to Natchez, a merchant by the name of James Weir mentioned a bill of lading for cargo "shipped by William Braton which I hope will arrive safe." Like a multitude of other boatmen, Bratton and his crew followed the Ohio River downstream from the Kentucky area to the Mississippi River and from there to Natchez. Historians have described the arduous journeys involved in the river trade of this time: "Flour, salt, iron, bricks, and barrel staves went west and south on the rivers. Molasses, sugar, coffee, lead, and hides came back upstream. A standard keelboat carried 300 barrels of freight, a back-breaking load to propel against the current."[9]

On Sunday, 15 December 1811, crews in the area had put in their normal strenuous day while continually watching for obstacles in the river and maneuvering around them, for hazards known as planters and sawyers could instantly sink their craft. Totally different from driftwood, planters and sawyers were trees that had been swept into the river during floods. The earth attached to their roots soon caused them to lodge in the river. Both were stationary, but sawyers were much more dangerous because their upper limbs bobbed up and down and side to side in the current, while planters remained still.

The day had been cold and clear; the boats were ordered to shore as soon as the sun set. The nights were long at this time of year, and boatmen typically idled about on the boat, socializing or gambling with the crews of other boats also stopped for the night. Those who went into the village of New Madrid—where an ill Meriwether Lewis had made out his will two years earlier—found little entertainment. The citizens were French Creoles, Americans, and Germans, and they were generally poor. They were known to charge high prices for dry goods, groceries, and liquor, higher still for "any common necessaries, such as milk, butter, fowls, eggs, &c."[10]

The naturalist John Bradbury was traveling the Mississippi by keelboat at the same time as Bratton, and he left a record of that night describing how he woke to the roar of the quake and a tremendous rocking that threatened to capsize the boat. Bewildered crew members ran about not knowing what to do. "Immediately the perpendicular banks, both above and below us," wrote Bradbury, "began to fall into the river in such vast masses, as nearly to sink our boat by the swell they occasioned." Bradbury was saved because his boat had been tied to a sloping bank. By daylight, he learned that three boats moored next to steep banks had been swamped, "and that all on board had perished."[11]

As trees along the shore toppled into the water, some crews lit fires and huddled around them, waiting for the dawn. By then there had been close to thirty aftershocks, but none as great as the initial "shake." The boats rocked crazily as the current of the river surged and eddied, spawning whirlpools, geysers, and tidal waves. The aftermath brought a scene unlike any the boatmen had ever witnessed: a swirling mass of foam and timber hardly recognizable as a river. Entire groves of cottonwood trees had been swept into the tide; new riverbanks had replaced old ones.

But nothing amazed the boat crews more than what happened an hour or two after the 7 February 1812 earthquake: they stared incredulously as the Mississippi began flowing upstream. This was not a momentary shift caused by an aftershock but a forceful current that rushed in the wrong direction for several hours. Finally, somewhere upstream, something gave, and the river righted its course. "Its accumulated waters came booming on, and o'er topping the barrier thus suddenly raised, carried everything before them with resistless power. Boats, then floating on its surface, shot down the declivity like an arrow from a bow, amid roaring billows and the wildest commotion," wrote one witness. Two sets of temporary waterfalls had also appeared— both upstream from New Madrid. One keelboat crew had been forced to cut loose from the bank when landslides threatened to bury them, and they rode the wild current downstream. "We were affrighted with the appearance of a dreadful rapid of falls in the river just below us," one of the men later wrote. "We were so far in the suck that it was impossible now to land—all hopes of surviving was now lost and certain destruction appeared to await us!" Luckily, they "passed the rapids without injury, keeping our bow foremost, both boats being still lashed together."[12]

Despite the peril, Bratton apparently made it safely downriver. His keelboat business, however, was soon interrupted by the War of 1812, and Bratton enlisted in the Kentucky militia in August of that year. In 1819 Bratton married Mary ("Polly") Maxwell, and the couple went on to have eight sons and two daughters. They spent most of their married life in Waynetown, Indiana, where Bratton was elected the first justice of the peace. He was prominent in both religion and education, and his descendants were among the founding members of the Wesley Church and Wesley Academy. Montgomery

County records show that he bought 160 acres of land in 1822 and another 200 acres a decade later. According to family accounts, William Bratton "was very saving and could not see anything wasted; that one time at a corn husking he was picking up the scattered grains of corn and some one made fun of him. He replied that he had seen the time he would have been very thankful for a few grains of corn. For the men of the Lewis and Clark expedition almost starved at times."[13]

William Bratton was sixty-three when he died in Waynetown, on 11 November 1841. An inscription on his tombstone reads: "Went in 1804 with Lewis and Clark to the Rocky Mountains."

John Ordway, who was born in New Hampshire in the area near the towns of Bow and Dunbarton around 1775, penned one of the most quoted expedition documents when he wrote to his parents: "I am well thank God, and in high Spirits. I am now on an expedition to the westward, with Capt. Lewis and Capt. Clark. . . . We are to ascend the Missouri River with a boat as far as navigable and then to go by land, to the western ocean, if nothing prevents, &c. . . . I am So happy as to be one of them pick'd Men from the armey."[14]

The journal Ordway kept is perhaps the surest indicator of his reliability: he was the only diarist to record an entry for every single day of the voyage, including such difficult periods as the Great Falls portage and the crossing of the Bitterroot Mountains. His faithful record-keeping was particularly valuable during the return trip, when the corps split into five separate groups to explore present-day Montana as carefully as possible. (As Stephen Ambrose has pointed out, the peril involved in splitting up was probably not justified, given the Indian war parties that were roaming the area.) Ordway's group carried out its duties in an efficient military manner, despite the absence of both captains. On 25 July, Ordway noted with pride: "hard rain comd. about noon and continued the remainder of the day, but did not Stop us from our urgent labours. halted as much as we were able to help the horses as the place So amazeing muddy & bad. in the evening we got to portage Creek and Camped. rained verry hard and we having no Shelter Some of the men and myself turned over a canoe & lay under it others Set up by the fires. the water run under us and the ground was covred with water."

After the expedition, Ordway assisted Lewis and Pierre Chouteau in accompanying Sheheke's delegation and a group of Osage Indians to Washington, D.C. He then stopped in New Hampshire, describing his grand adventure to friends and relatives and even inspiring a future explorer. John Ball, a member of Nathaniel Wyeth's expedition to the Pacific coast in 1832, wrote to his parents in 1833: "I have seen the country the description of which John Ordway gave you so interestingly when he returned from his tour with Lewis and Clark in 1806."[15]

By the fall of 1807, Ordway had married and taken up farming near New Madrid, in the "boot heel" of what became southeastern Missouri. While many expedition members bartered their land grants for quick cash, Ordway kept his and purchased additional land, and within a year he owned a thousand acres. He wrote his brother Stephen that he was breeding horses and cattle and that he had settled on the banks of the Mississippi, "where I have two plantations under good cultivation peach and apple orchards, good buildings &c &c." Ordway developed a genuine affection for the region and told his brothers and sisters "there is no better land in the world there is not one foot of waist [waste] land on all i own."[16] His description was convincing: by 1808 his brothers William and Daniel and his sister Sarah and their families had all joined him in Missouri. (John's brother Stephen and sisters Hannah and Polly remained in New England.)

John's wife, Gracey, apparently died around 1808. Her maiden name is not known, but she was also from New Hampshire. Late in 1807 she had been sick with "fever and ague." By 1809, John had married a widow named Elizabeth Johnson. She had two children from a previous marriage—David and Isidore Johnson.[17]

Ordway's activities during these years are well chronicled in public records: he frequently bought and sold land; he served briefly as constable in New Madrid; and he occasionally appeared in court, both as a plaintiff and as a defendant. By 1811, the year he turned thirty-six, John Ordway appeared to have a prosperous, steady future. In November he closed the last of several land transactions he conducted that year, carrying on business as usual.[18] But everything was about to change.

Like most others in the area, John Ordway probably lost virtually everything following the earthquakes. The surging waters of the Mississippi eventually covered much of the town of New Madrid, as well as tracts of farmland. In other areas, "hills had disappeared, and lakes were found in their stead." Huge amounts of timber were lost, with trees toppling, disappearing in rivers or lakes, or simply sinking into the earth—sometimes completely vanishing beneath the ground. Houses, outbuildings, and fences were all damaged or destroyed. Some structures in New Madrid appeared intact after the first quake, but not after the last in the series of quakes, on 7 February, the most powerful of the five. One witness reported that there "was scarcely a house left entire—some wholly prostrated, others unroofed and not a chimney standing."[19]

But nothing compared to the sand that flowed and exploded from everywhere: "sand blows" shot sand twenty-five feet in the air and left conical depressions almost as deep; liquid sand bubbled out of "sand volcanos" and "sand boils." Quicksand appeared out of nowhere. One witness wrote that in "all of the hard shocks the earth was horribly torn to pieces; the surface of hundreds of acres was from time to time covered over of various depths by the sand which issued from the fissures." Another described earth that was cracked in every direction and "circular holes in the earth from five or six to thirty feet in diameter . . . and surrounded with a circle of sand two or three feet deep, and a black substance like stone coal."[20]

Sand and water united in unimaginable scenarios: "The earth was observed to be rolling in waves of a few feet in height, with a visible depression between. By and by these swells burst, throwing up large volumes of water, sand and a species of charcoal." At other times, instantaneous geysers erupted. Ordway's sister-in-law Elizabeth Robison recorded an image that Ordway himself likely saw: "I lived on the Mississippi in the time of the earthquake which was a dreadful Sight to see the ground burst and threw out water as high as the trees and it threw down part of our houses so that it apeard like present distruction."[21]

A city of tents materialized northwest of the ruined town of New Madrid, with the bewildered residents struggling to feed themselves, stay warm and dry, and avoid disease amid the garbage heaps and open latrines. Then, by the first week of January, one family after another began to pick up and leave, until the 7 February quake brought on a mass exodus. "If we do not get away from here the ground is going to eat us alive," wrote one man. Another recalled how the multitude "fled in terror from their falling dwellings," a terror succinctly depicted by Colonel John Shaw:

> A young woman about seventeen years of age, named Betsy Masters, had been left by her parents and family, her leg having been broken below the knee by the falling of one of the weight-poles of the roof of the cabin; and, though a total stranger, I was the only person who would consent to return and see whether she still survived. Receiving a description of the locality of the place, I started, and found the poor girl upon a bed, as she had been left, with some water and corn bread within her reach. I cooked up some food for her, and made her condition as comfortable as circumstances would allow and returned the same day to the grand encampment.[22]

John Ordway's personal hardships were compounded by those of his relatives. In July of 1809 his brother William had run afoul of the law—he was charged with "selling spiritous liquors to Indians" and "trading with a slave in violation of the Laws of this territory." Just months after that, William died at age forty-four. The Ordways were still coping with William's troubles and death when Daniel died at age thirty-seven. (The cause of death is unknown in both cases.) John Ordway, who had two stepchildren and two children of his own—John Jr. and Hannah—now became surrogate father to at least nine nieces and nephews. One calamity followed another as the earthquakes struck, as Mary Scribner Ordway (William's widow) lost her second husband, Edward Matthews, and as Elizabeth Poor Ordway (Daniel's widow) saw her second husband, Kinsay Robison, drafted into the War of 1812, a war that further demolished the already ruined economy.[23]

By the time the spring of 1812 finally came, New Madrid was a ghost town. "This district, formerly so level, rich, and beautiful, had the most melancholy of all aspects of decay," wrote one witness. In May, George Shannon's friend Stephen Austin, now a mature eighteen years old, was hauling a load of lead and other goods down the Mississippi on a barge when he stopped at New Madrid, commenting in his diary on the "extraordinary convulsions" that had thrown a "hitherto fertile country into dessolation and plunging such of the unfortunate wretches who survive the ruin, into Misery and dispair. These emotions I experienced when on landing at N. Madrid the effects by the Earthquake were so prominently visible as well in the sunken and shattered situation of the Houses, as in the countenance of the fiew who remained to mourn over the ruins of the prosperity and past happiness."[24]

What became of John Ordway's family during this time is unknown. If Ordway wrote of the quake, that document has been lost. New Madrid records indicate that his buying and selling of land, so common in the three years before the earthquake, came to a halt after 1811. In the next six years his name appears in the public record just twice—in June of 1813, when he conveyed land in the amount of 300 arpents (a French unit of measure equal to about 85 percent of an acre) to his sister-in-law Mary Matthews, and in February 1816, when Frederick Bates extended Ordway's grant of 722 arpents (assigned to Ordway by Alexander Millikin).[25]

Then, on 5 February 1818, Elizabeth Ordway and her two children by John appeared in court to sign a document. "Know all men by these presents," it read, "that we Elizabeth Ordway widow of John Ordway, Deceased, John Ordway and Hannah Ordway the only heirs and legal representatives of John Ordway, Deceased, of the county of New Madrid and Territory of Missouri . . . do make ordain constitute & appoint James Brady of the County and Territory aforesaid our True and Lawful attorney." Elizabeth and her children each signed with an X.[26]

In this same document, Elizabeth and her children applied for compensation for losses suffered in the 1811–12 earthquakes. (In 1815, the U.S. Congress had passed a disaster relief act that allowed landowners from the region hit by the earthquakes to receive equal parcels of property elsewhere in Missouri.) They likely received little or nothing from this petition, however, because land sharks had moved in and bought as many claims as possible.[27]

The family troubles continued, and in November 1821, the New Madrid County Court ordered that "Betsy Ordway appear at the next Court to show cause why Isidore Johnson, David Johnson, Hannah Ordway, and John Ordway, her infant children, should not have a guardian appointed to take care of their estate." Three months later, John H. Walker was appointed guardian of Hannah and John Ordway. No other details are known. Elizabeth Ordway married for the third time in 1834, but she died a few years later. John Ordway Jr. died in 1836, having never married. The sole survivor, Hannah Ordway, married John Johnson and had a child, John Ordway's only grandchild. The child, however, died at a young age (it is not known whether the child was a boy or a girl), and Hannah herself died in 1839.[28]

The sparse record thus implies, although it hardly proves, that Sergeant John Ordway, Lewis and Clark's top soldier, never recovered from the New Madrid earthquake of 1811 and died in poverty at age forty-two, a sad end to an honorable life. He still owned land, to be sure, but much of it may have been rendered useless by the earthquake. The devastating impact of the earthquakes on the economy was followed by the War of 1812, which was in turn followed by "the year without a summer" in 1816, when survivors of the earthquake experienced snow or frost repeatedly throughout the months of May, June, July, and August.[29] Considering this series of catastrophes, it is quite conceivable that a man as prosperous before the earthquake as John Ordway could live on the edge of poverty afterward (and thus have little reason to be listed in the public record).

John Ordway, though, is best remembered not for his obscure demise but for the inestimable value of his faithful record of the expedition, a 100,000-word text that often depicts happy times that were apparently rare during his final years. The corps' second Christmas, for example, was described in typical Ordway fashion:

> Tuesday 25th Decr. 1804. cloudy. we fired the Swivels at day break & each man fired one round. our officers Gave the party a drink of Taffee. we had the Best to eat that could be had, &continued firing dancing & frolicking dureing the whole day. the Savages did not Trouble us as we had requested them not to come as it was a Great medicine day with us. we enjoyed a merry christmas dureing the day & evening untill nine oClock—all in peace and quietness.[30]

CHAPTER ELEVEN

"She Was a Good and the Best Woman in the Fort"
Sacagawea's Death

✦

In the spring of 1811, after a year and a half in civilized St. Louis, where the narrow streets outside his cramped quarters were continually bustling with comings and goings, Toussaint Charbonneau was preparing to head upriver, back to Mandan country, where he could see buffalo or elk from the door of his tepee. He bought fifty pounds of biscuit, or hardtack, from Auguste Chouteau. He sold a parcel of land (acquired the previous autumn) back to William Clark for one hundred dollars.[1] Then he signed on with Manuel Lisa, who was making his third consecutive biennial trip up the Missouri—he had gone in 1807 and in 1809 and was now going again.

Born in 1767 in Canada, Charbonneau had worked for the North West Company, a Canadian fur-trading concern and rival to the British Hudson's Bay Company, and had lived among the Hidatsa for several years when Lewis and Clark arrived in the fall of 1804. Charbonneau, of course, had taken Sacagawea, a Shoshone Indian, as his wife sometime before the captains' arrival. He is presumed to have bought her from the Hidatsa, who kidnapped her from the Three Forks area sometime around 1800. Lewis and Clark had gained different opinions of Charbonneau—Clark thought him more valuable than Lewis did—but there was no denying that Charbonneau's abilities as an interpreter and as a cook had come in very handy on the expedition.

The group going upriver with Lisa included an American journalist, Henry M. Brackenridge. Speaking of men like Charbonneau, Brackenridge wrote: "I have been acquainted with several who, on returning to the settlements, became in a very short time dissatisfied, and wandered away to these regions, as delightful to them, as are the regions of fancy to the poet."[2]

Brackenridge added a specific description of the forty-four-year-old Charbonneau and his twenty-three-year-old wife: "We have on board a Frenchman named Charbonet, with his wife, an Indian woman of the Snake [Shoshone] nation, both of whom accompanied Lewis and Clark to the Pacific, and were of great service. The woman, a good creature, of a mild and gentle disposition, was greatly attached to the whites, whose manners and airs she tries to imitate; but she had become sickly and longed to revisit her native country; her husband also, who had spent many years amongst the Indians, was become weary of civilized life."[3]

Lewis and Clark, of course, had left Charbonneau and Sacagawea—and their son, Baptiste—at the Hidatsa villages in August 1806. For the next three years, there is no contemporary record of the Charbonneaus. Since they had lived near the confluence of the Knife and Missouri Rivers—near present-day Stanton, North Dakota—before the expedition, it seems likely that they lived there afterward. If so, they would have been in the area when Pierre Chouteau's contingent of more than three hundred men successfully returned Sheheke to his home in September 1809. When part of Chouteau's group turned back for St. Louis, Charbonneau, Sacagawea, and four-year-old "Pomp" apparently elected to go with them. The group arrived in St. Louis late in the fall of 1809, just as news of Meriwether Lewis's death reached the city—and two months after William Clark had departed on a long trip east.

Then, on 28 December, at a log church on the banks of the Mississippi (at the site of the present Old Cathedral near the Gateway Arch), a Trappist monk by the name of Father Urbain Guillet officiated at the baptism of young Jean-Baptiste Charbonneau. Toussaint Charbonneau and Sacagawea were both present, as was Auguste Chouteau, standing in as godfather to the boy, and Chouteau's twelve-year-old daughter Eulalie.[4]

Possibly with help from Chouteau, the Charbonneau family remained in St. Louis and was there when William Clark returned on 7 July 1810.[5] In the fall, Charbonneau purchased land from Clark, apparently with the intention of remaining in St. Louis indefinitely. But by early spring 1811, he had changed his mind.

On 17 August 1805, near the Continental Divide (at the site of the modern-day Clark Canyon Reservoir, southwest of Dillon, Montana), Sacagawea had experienced two remarkable reunions with her native Shoshone tribe. "We soon drew near to the [Shoshone] camp," Nicholas Biddle later wrote, constructing a first-person narrative with help from George Shannon, "and just as we approached it a woman made her way through the crowd towards Sacajawea, and recognising each other, they embraced with the most tender affection. . . . They had been companions in childhood, in the war with the Minnetarees [Hidatsa] they had both been taken prisoners in the same battle, they had shared and softened the rigours of their captivity, till one of them had escaped from the Minnetarees, with scarce a hope of ever seeing her friend relieved from the hands of her enemies."

Following this unlikely reunion in 1805, the two captains arranged to meet with the Shoshone chief. After embraces, salutations, and the smoking of a pipe, Clark sent for Sacagawea to act as interpreter.

As Biddle recorded, "She came into the tent, sat down, and was beginning to interpret, when in the person of Cameahwait she recognized her brother: She instantly jumped up, and ran and embraced him, throwing over him her blanket and weeping profusely: The chief was himself moved, though not in the same degree. After some conversation between them she resumed her seat, and attempted to interpret for us, but her new situation seemed to overpower her, and she was frequently interrupted by her tears. After the council was finished the unfortunate woman learnt that all her family were dead except two brothers, one of whom was absent, and a son of her eldest sister, a small boy, who was immediately adopted by her."[6]

Following the council with the chief, the corps spent a few days in August 1805 with the friendly Shoshone people, who mended the soldiers' moccasins and provided horses, supplies, and guides. Cameahwait also presented Lewis with an elaborate robe or tippet made of more than a hundred ermine skins.[7] On the return journey in the ensuing spring and summer of 1806, Sacagawea did not meet her native tribe again because the corps split up and took a different route through their country. Sacagawea's brief visit to her family with the Lewis and Clark Expedition in 1805 proved to be the last time she saw them. When she did journey once again to this region, in 1811 with Manuel Lisa's trapping enterprise, hostile Blackfeet ensured that no trapping party of that year would venture near Three Forks. Decades later her brother Cameahwait was rumored to have been killed in a battle with the Hidatsa, the same nation that had kidnapped her and sold her to Charbonneau.[8]

Six years after Sacagawea's reunion with the Shoshone, she and Charbonneau apparently left their six-year-old son, Baptiste, with William Clark, who was in St. Louis at the time (he posted letters from St. Louis in March of 1811). They joined up with Manuel Lisa and his small group of twenty-five that departed St. Louis on 2 April 1811, extremely early in the season. Lisa was in a frantic rush to catch up with another party of trappers, one led by

Wilson Price Hunt. Joining with Hunt was crucial because a larger party offered much better protection against Indians. Hunt, a businessman hired by John Jacob Astor to lead an overland trapping expedition to the mouth of the Columbia River (while another group of Astorians was going by sea), had taken his group to the western part of what is now Missouri the previous October. Hunt himself and a few others had returned to St. Louis for the winter, but they had departed in March. With his characteristic zeal, Lisa believed he could catch Hunt's group before meeting the Lakota, who, Brackenridge noted, "of late had committed several murders and robberies on the whites, and manifested such a disposition that it was believed impossible for us to pass through their country [near present-day Yankton, South Dakota]."[9]

Brackenridge put Lisa in sharp focus when he wrote: "A man of a bold and daring character, with an energy and spirit of enterprise like that of Cortez or Pizarro. There is no one better acquainted with the Indian character and trade, and few are his equals in persevering indefatigable industry. Possessed of an ardent mind and of a frame capable of sustaining every hardship. It would have been difficult for the company to have found a person better qualified for this enterprise. . . . Unfortunately, however, from what cause I know not, the majority of the members of the company have not the confidence in Mr. Lisa which he so justly merits."[10]

Although Lisa's men indeed disliked him, they were convinced of the need to catch Hunt, and they cooperated—rowing, propelling, and pulling the boat upstream from dawn to dusk, and beyond dusk. When violent winds arose, Lisa took advantage of them by hoisting the sail. He seemed to always choose the fastest route around sandbars and islands. "As usual we set off to-day at day-break," wrote Brackenridge on 3 May. "Not a moment of our time is lost: we stop half an hour at breakfast; about the same length of time for dinner, and continue late at night." By careful questioning of anyone he met coming down the river, Lisa knew he was gaining on Hunt: by 25 April they had shortened the gap by a hundred miles.[11]

After a month of unremitting labor, some of the men began to grumble. "I overheard, with much chagrin," wrote Brackenridge, "some bitter complaints on the part of the men: 'We are not permitted a moment's repose; scarcely is time allowed us to eat, or to smoke our pipes. We can stand it no longer, human nature cannot bear it.'" Whether Charbonneau was among this group is not known; he was certainly a man accustomed to hard work. But in his year and a half with Lewis and Clark he had never heard mutinous talk among the men. With Lisa it would be much different. Brackenridge "endeavored to quiet their minds," encouraging them to "work cheerfully, and with confidence in Lisa, who would carry us through every difficulty."[12]

The crew did just that, pressing on despite sickness. On 15 May they endured a dangerous storm, with tremendous winds and air "darkened by clouds of sand, and we found ourselves at the upper end of the reach, in the midst of sawyers and planters, our situation dangerous in the extreme. Nothing but our great anxiety to force our voyage would have justified the running such a risk," Brackenridge wrote. The men were also impressed by Lisa's willingness to work just as hard as he asked them to: "While exerting ourselves to pass a difficult and dangerous rapid, Lisa who was at the head of the boat, with the grappling hook, fell overboard, and narrowly escaped being drowned." Moments later, Brackenridge himself fell overboard and was nearly swept away. He survived only by grasping the steering oar.[13]

When the group reached the Omaha villages, near modern Omaha, Nebraska, they learned that they were only four days behind Hunt. According to Brackenridge, "It was therefore deemed adviseable to despatch a messenger by land, who might overtake [Hunt] at the Poncas village, about two hundred miles further by water, and about three day's journey by land. For this purpose a half Indian was hired, and set off immediately in company with Charbonneau." The well-experienced messenger Charbonneau accomplished his mission—and would constantly take on similar assignments over the next two and a half decades. A week after he had set out, at daylight, Lisa's men "discovered a canoe descending with two men, who prove to be those sent by us, to Hunt. They [Charbonneau and his companion] bring us the pleasing information, that Hunt, in consequence of our request, has agreed to wait for us, at the Poncas village."[14]

Three days later, when Lisa's group reached the agreed-upon village, they were greeted with bad news: "In the evening, two men who proved to be deserters from the party of Hunt, came to us with very unwelcome intelligence. It seems that Hunt, was much astonished to find from our messengers that we were so near; but fearing to be passed, had sent us a feigned answer in order to conceal his real design, which was to make all possible haste to keep out of our reach. In order to affect this, he was now making every possible exertion." To their credit, said Brackenridge, Lisa's men took this setback as a challenge, "determining to strain every nerve, in order to overtake Hunt," sailing until past 11 p.m. for the next few days and making an incredible seventy-five miles in one twenty-four-hour period.[15]

Four days later, on 2 June, Lisa's party finally caught up with Hunt. Lisa's men were relieved, Hunt's men "suspicious that Lisa intended to betray them.—M'Clelland declared that he would shoot [Lisa] the moment he discovered any thing like it." Lisa, however, allayed these fears when he and Hunt held a council with twenty Arikara chiefs. (Though they had attacked

Pryor's party four years earlier, the Arikara were now eager to show their good will.) After smoking the pipe, Lisa "observed that he was come to trade amongst them and the Mandans, but that these persons, (pointing to Hunt and his comrades,) were going on a long journey to the great Salt lake, to the west, and he hoped would meet with favourable treatment; and that any injury offered them, he would consider as done to himself; that although distinct parties, yet as to the safety of either, they were but one."[16]

Among Hunt's men, Lisa and his crew saw three familiar faces—Edward Robinson, John Hoback, and Jacob Reznor. They had been with Menard when Drouillard was killed—and when Colter had left for the final time. After surviving a severe Idaho winter in 1810–11, the three Kentuckians had decided to go home. Then, when they met Hunt's group, they had changed their minds. Like Colter had done, they turned back west, back to the country they had longed to leave. Unlike Colter, however, they never made it back to their homes.[17]

Hunt's group also included another familiar trapper: Edward Rose. In spite of their past acrimony, Lisa and Rose were apparently civil with each other, for the next year Rose joined Lisa's 1812 expedition. Rose had lived with the Crows for more than two years, at one point leading Crow warriors into battle. The fearless Rose had reportedly killed five Hidatsa with his tomahawk. He was no longer known as "Cut Nose" but as "the Five Scalps."[18]

Lisa reached the Mandan villages in the fourth week of June. The two writers Bradbury and Brackenridge, who had struck up a friendship, paid a visit to Sheheke and his family. Sheheke came to the door of his lodge and said, "come in house." As they entered, Sheheke immediately asked for whiskey. They had brought no whiskey with them, but they presented him with silver ornaments, "with which he seemed much pleased," according to Bradbury. The three men then smoked a pipe before feasting on a meal of jerked buffalo meat, corn, and beans boiled together.[19]

Brackenridge described Sheheke as "very intelligent," adding that the chief and his wife "had returned home loaded with presents, but have since fallen into disrepute from the extravagant tales which they related as to what they had witnessed; for the Mandans treat with ridicule the idea of there being a greater or more numerous people than themselves. He is a man of a mild and gentle disposition—expressed a wish to come and live amongst the whites."[20]

Bradbury mentioned that he wished to buy some moccasins and was soon met by a group of Mandan women who offered many more than he could buy. "During our stay," he wrote, "She-he-ke pointed to a little boy in the lodge, whom we had not before noticed, and gave us to understand that his father was one of the party that accompanied Mr. Lewis, and also indicated the individual."[21]

Bradbury did not say which expedition member allegedly fathered the young boy, but members of the corps may have left behind illegitimate children. As the Lewis and Clark Expedition had made its way to the Pacific, it was not uncommon for various tribes to offer the men female companionship as a token of good will. Speaking of the Arikara, for example, Brackenridge noted that "it was a part of their hospitality, to offer the guest, who takes up his residence in their lodges, one of the females of the family as a bedfellow; sometimes even one of their wives, daughters, or sisters, but most usually a maid-servant, according to the estimation in which the guest is held, and to decline such offer is considered as treating the host with some disrespect; notwithstanding this, if it be remarked that these favours are uniformly declined, the guest rises much higher in his esteem."[22] Several of Lewis and Clark's men had accepted such offers. As for Lewis and Clark themselves, they apparently uniformly declined. (Aware of such customs, Lewis had packed medicine and instruments for treating venereal disease.)

Charbonneau and Sacagawea apparently spent the winter of 1811–12 at their old home near the Knife and Missouri Rivers, although their whereabouts is not known for certain. Lisa returned to St. Louis, where the St. Louis Missouri Fur Company held its last meeting on 23 January 1812, agreeing to let the company expire on 7 March. Lisa, William Clark, and others reorganized as the Missouri Fur Company, and Lisa prepared for another expedition. John Luttig, a clerk who kept a meticulous record of the voyage, joined the group on 8 May 1812, and Lisa arrived the next day.[23]

Luttig's entries included facts and figures but were also rich with warmth and detail. "This Morning we left our old she Cat at Camp," he wrote the last day of July; "at breakfast I missed her, and Mr. Manuel sent a Men for the Cat, he returned in the Evening with the Cat to our great satisfaction this Remark may seem ridiculous, but an Animal of this kind, is more valuable in this Country than a fine Horse. Mice are in great Abundance and the Company have lost [many goods] for want of Cats."[24]

Luttig could also write with a powerful, understated poignancy: "Mr. Manuels Negro Boy Charlo went out the Boat to get some grass or grasshoppers for a Prairie Dog which he had caught some days ago," read the entry for 25 July. "He fell down a precipe into the River, the Man who was steering the Mackina Boat saw it, and cried out to Mr [Reuben] Lewis (who was walking in the Rear of the Boats) to save the Boy but Mr Lewis unfortunately did not understand . . . when the Men came towards him, they went to find the Boy, alas he was gone, he must have been stunned by the fall or otherwise would have saved himself, the River was not 4 feet deep, he drowned at 5 oclock P.M. we searched for him some time but the Current had swept him off."[25]

On Sunday, 9 August 1812, Lisa's group reached a picturesque bluff twelve miles south of the Arikara villages (south of present-day Mobridge, South Dakota). The bluff was surrounded by several bottoms of good timber—the perfect spot to build a fort. By the next day, all hands were busy building a blacksmith shop and provision house. By 19 November Fort Manuel was completed. According to an 1838 newspaper account, Lisa had fortified the trading house "in the usual mode of stockade. At two of the angles he added bastions, and mounted a swivel [cannon] in each. . . . The fort was situated on a high riverbluff, which commanded an extensive view of the surrounding country."[26] This, it turned out, was Sacagawea's final home.

"Thursday the 19th clear and warm," wrote Luttig, "little Ice in the River at four oclock in the after noon hung the great Door of the Entrance of the fort, which ceremony was saluted by 7 Guns and 3 rounds of Musquetry, made the Tour—around the Fort and Baptized the same MANUEL in the Evening a good Supper and a cheerful glass of Whiskey was given to the Men, and a Dance at which all the Ladies then in Fort attended, concluded the Day."

Charbonneau and Sacagawea were present for this celebration, for they had arrived at the fort at the end of August, possibly traveling with Sheheke's party, which visited Lisa on 27 August.[27] Sacagawea had with her an infant daughter. The pleasant evening at the fort, with dancing and drink and a special meal, offered a moment of peace in an autumn that had grown increasingly violent. For Sacagawea, the autumn had also been a time of sickness. She had fought off many an illness in the time Charbonneau had known her, but this time was different.

Lisa's entourage included interpreters, boatmen, cooks, fishermen, hunters and trappers, blacksmiths and gunsmiths, carpenters and clerks, but no physicians. Sacagawea apparently had typhoid fever, one of a multitude of diseases that had been imported from Europe or Africa and were unknown to the native nations—along with smallpox, chicken pox, venereal disease, leprosy, yellow fever, diphtheria, tuberculosis, measles, scarlet fever, typhus, malaria, Malta fever, trichinosis, whooping cough, cholera, hookworm, mumps, and bubonic plague. The whites had developed various degrees of resistance, not by superior medicine but by past contact with these illnesses. American Indians were often helpless to fight the strange sicknesses. Symptoms of typhoid fever included chills, a high fever, vomiting, and diarrhea.

Charbonneau had to leave Sacagawea to the care of others, for he was much in demand because of his knowledge of the terrain and rivers, his ability with native tongues, and his proven skill as a negotiator. On 17 September, according to Luttig's journal, "the Wind blew heavy from the N.W., . . . Charbonneau who was on horse back came in full speed to the fort and cried out, *To Arms*, Lecomte is Killed . . . 10 armed Men went immediately after them but returned without Success." Two days later, "Charbonneau and Jessaume departed for to go to the Bigbellies [Gros Ventre], to try to get the [stolen] horses." Similar entries continued throughout the fall: on 3 October, "at night Charbonneau & Jessaume returned and brought with them 3 of the horses which had been stolen by the Mandans"; on 30 October, "Charbonneau and the 4 Warriors marched off to the Bigbellies"; on 15 November, "This Morning, Immel, Papin and Charbonneau left this [fort] for the Village, with the Bigbellies and 3 Rees [Arikara], to see into the Misconduct of those fellows and try to settle amicable."

Sacagawea's private collapse and inevitable death were matched by the collapse of the world of Fort Manuel. Ice in the river; infighting among the trappers; mounting distrust as the Cheyenne, Mandan, Gros Ventre, Sioux, and Arikara in the area bickered among themselves; occasional theft of tools and constant theft of horses by Indians; huge packs of howling wolves roaming the prairie; bone-chilling wind; the Arikara setting the grassland on fire because they did not get enough to eat at the fort; the frequent killing of Lisa's men—one on 17 September, three on 28 October, three on 30 November, one each on 12 and 16 December—all this spelled the inevitable death of the fort itself.

Saturday 3 October dawned clear and cold, with a white frost that brought a majesty to the plains. Every man remaining in the fort worked hard cutting pickets for the stockade. Then came news from the north, another portent of things to come from the Mandan village: "at Sunset 2 Mandans arrived with the sad news of the Big white [Sheheke] and Little Crow being killed by the Bigbellies and 3 Mandans wounded," Luttig wrote.[28]

Sheheke's death had come three years after his return to his homeland. Portraits of him show that he was in the prime of his life. He was a gentle soul who had gone east to visit Thomas Jefferson only after much persuading by William Clark. Nor was it unusual for Lewis and Clark to invite representatives of the native nations to visit the capital of the United States. In the case of Sheheke, however, his going east in 1806 triggered a chain of events that affected the lives of expedition veterans in ways no one could have predicted. It cast a pall over Nathaniel Pryor's post-expedition military career when his 1807 attempt to return the chief was cut short by an Arikara attack; in that same battle, George Gibson was wounded, George Shannon lost his leg, and Joseph Field possibly lost his life; returning Sheheke became a major concern for Meriwether Lewis, and the failure of the federal government to honor his expenses associated with that task turned out to be a key element in Lewis's financial woes and agitated frame of mind in the weeks preceding his death (indeed, the rejected vouchers were probably the principal reason Lewis undertook his fateful journey); and Charbonneau and Sacagawea's trip to St. Louis in the fall of 1809 was occasioned by Pierre Chouteau's successful return of Sheheke, as was George Drouillard's final voyage up the Missouri. Then there was Sheheke himself: the visit to the great father ironically transformed his status from that of a highly respected chief to a teller of tall tales and a laughingstock among his people.

Less than three months after noting Sheheke's death, John Luttig recorded a historic entry: "Sunday the 20th, clear and moderate, our hunter say Rees went out and Killed 20 . . . purchased a fine Dog of the Chajennes, this Evening the Wife of Charbonneau a Snake Squaw, died of a putrid fever she was a good and the best Women in the fort, aged about 25 years she left a fine infant girl."[29]

Thus came the end for Sacagawea, who died at a younger age than any other member of the expedition except Charles Floyd. Although she had longed to return to her homeland, she had never made it back to her Shoshone people after the unexpected reunion in 1805. We don't know how Charbonneau, or William Clark, or anyone else reacted to her death—only John Luttig. And although his brief notation described Sacagawea about as accurately as anyone could—wife of Charbonneau, a Shoshone (Snake) Indian, a woman of good reputation in her mid-twenties—his failure to mention her name led to inevitable controversy. More than a hundred years after Luttig recorded the death, some historians claimed that another of Charbonneau's wives had died at Fort Manuel and that Sacagawea had actually lived to be almost one hundred years old, dying in Wyoming in the 1880s. Subsequent to these claims, however, historian Dale Morgan discovered a key William Clark document that puts the matter to rest. Clark's list of expedition members, drawn up sometime between 1825 and 1828, confirmed Luttig's account by noting:

Se car ja we au   Dead[30]

On Wednesday 13 January 1813, three weeks after Sacagawea's death, as the sun was setting behind him, John C. Luttig watched from a stockade as a band of Indian hunters chased a bull buffalo onto the frozen Missouri River. "The poor Animal when he found he was pursued, fell several times, and at last tired could not gett up,—surrounded by many he awaited his fate patiently."

Within weeks, the thoughtful Luttig was using similar language to describe the desperate situation at Fort Manuel. With an Indian ambush appearing more and more imminent, Immell and four companions had mounted "swift horses" to scout the hills surrounding the fort. They had found the tracks of a war party that they estimated to be four hundred strong. Two miles west of the fort, this war party had met up with a group of sixty others. Luttig and his fellows watched as several dogs crossed the ice and headed into the woods where the Indians were apparently hiding.

On 5 February a young Indian living at the fort left on foot to hunt elk. In Luttig's account: "About 8 oclock P. M. we heard the Cry *to Arms* and two guns fired at the same time which proved to be out of the fort, opening the Door of the fort we found the above Young Men breathing his last, we found him shot in the Belly and Breast his hunt laid a little ways off . . . the Sioux were perpretators of this Act, he died 1 hour after, blew a hard gale all night."

About two weeks later, Charbonneau and another man returned from a mission to the Hidatsa. When Charbonneau had passed the Cheyenne camp, Luttig wrote, "they warned him to be cautious and take care of his Life . . . he arrived however without accident." The following day, Monday 22 February, at 1:45 in the afternoon, a trapper yelled, "To Arms! Archambeau is killed!"

Louis Archambeau, six years on the Missouri and described by Luttig as a very good man, had been on the opposite side of the river, hauling hay on a sleigh. As he approached the ice "he was shot and Killed Immediately." Lisa's men found themselves surrounded by Indians on all sides.

"We put ourselves immediately in Defence, and placed two swivels on the Bank of the River, but unfortunaly our Balls did not reach across," according to Luttig. The Indian warriors "took [Archambeau's] Scalp and cut him nearly to pieces, they marched off about 4 oclock, leaving us to lament the Death of fellow Citizen unrevenged, a party of our Men went across to bring the [corpse] which they found terrible mangled, they brought 29 Arrows which were sticking in his body and a good many more had been broken to pieces, his Head Broken the Brains scattered about his nose and ears cut off, his teeth Knocked out, and more terrible Deeds which I will not express with my Pen."

The men waited, posting guards throughout the night, keeping all of their dogs outside the fort to warn of intruders. Several days later, Luttig wrote: "Friday the 26th [of February] snowed last night and this Morning we are constant watching in our careful Situation, we hear and see nobody from all around us, and are like Prisoners in Deserts to expect every moment our fate." Four inches of snow fell on the last day of February. The next day was clear and cold, and "after dinner Charbonneau and Leclair set off for their Stations at the Bigbellies took some Powder and Ball to compleat his Equipoment, they were escorted by 5 of our Men, untill he would be out of Danger."

On Friday 5 March, Luttig made his final entry: "Snowstorm last night and continued snowing all this Day, the Mandans pursued their Route." Because of an attack—or the attack they knew would come—the small group of trappers abandoned Fort Manuel and fled south, seeking refuge at another trading post. On 20 May, Lisa paid Edward Rose $250 to guide a man to Reuben Lewis's camp on the Little Bighorn River and warn him of the Indian threat, and most likely to inform him that Fort Manuel had been burned to the ground.[31] Then Lisa's group returned to St. Louis, arriving late in May 1813.

John Luttig had survived. But he did not return to St. Louis alone—he had brought a small girl, Sacagawea's daughter, with him. There had been no word of Charbonneau since he had ridden off for the Gros Ventre camp at the end of February, and Luttig presumed him dead. On 11 August, Luttig appeared in the St. Louis probate court. Luttig had worked for William Clark before going up the Missouri in 1812 and was possibly representing Clark (who apparently was away from St. Louis temporarily) at the court. The document filed that day, regarding the disposition of Charbonneau and Sacagawea's children, Baptiste and Lisette, reads as follows:

"The court appoints John C. Luttig guardian to the infant children of Tousant Charbonneau deceased, to wit: Tousant Charbonneau, a boy about the age of ten years; and Lisette Charbonneau, a girl about one year old. The said infant children not being possessed of any property within the knowledge of the court, the said guardian is not required to give bond."[32]

Sometime later, Luttig's name was crossed out and replaced with the name of William Clark. Back in 1806, straining to write legibly as his pirogue rocked with the current of the Missouri, Clark had written a letter to Charbonneau as the returning corps passed the Arikara villages, expressing his fondness for "my boy Pomp," and offering to educate him and "treat him as my own child."[33] Now the red-headed captain was more than making good on his promise—he was adopting Pomp and his baby sister, both thought to be orphans.

CHAPTER TWELVE

"*The Crisis Is Fast Approaching*"
The Corps and the War of 1812

"I had arisen at a quarter after 4 o'clock," wrote General William Henry Harrison, "and the signal for calling out the men would have been given in two minutes." Harrison was reportedly in his tent talking with Adam Walker, a drummer of the Fourth U.S. Infantry, when the first shot rang out. Next came the scream of a wounded Indian, followed by a volley of arrows and musket balls from the line of Indians. "The attack . . . began on our left flank," Harrison wrote. "But a single gun was fired by the sentinels . . . which made not the least resistance, but abandoned their officer and fled into camps, and the first notice which the troops of that flank had of the danger, was from yells of the savages within a short distance of the line. . . . Such of [the soldiers] as were awake or easily awakened, seized their arms . . . others . . . had to contend with the enemy in the doors of their tents."[1]

The cold, drizzly day of 7 November 1811 had begun with a fight, the first battle in the War of 1812—the Battle of Tippecanoe. This battle had a direct impact on several members of the corps. Contrary to popular opinion, however, no expedition veterans were involved in the battle itself.[2] Harrison had expected the conflict, even welcomed it as a way of defeating the hostile Indians of the Wabash Valley in what was soon to become the state of Indiana. It was only the timing that surprised him—and his soldiers. They were nearly overwhelmed in the initial chaos of the early-morning battle. One sentinel reported such close combat that he fired his musket with the muzzle pressed against the chest of his attacker.

Harrison, the governor of the Indiana Territory and an expert at negotiating treaties that put the native nations at a disadvantage, had ridden into the valley on a distinctive gray horse. In the confusion that followed the attack, Harrison took a different horse, and Colonel Abram Owen mounted a gray horse, possibly Harrison's. Indians intent on killing Harrison shot and killed Owen instead (Owen's friends concluded that Harrison had deliberately switched horses). Even so, Harrison's horse was shot from under him before he got himself out of harm's way. When the fighting ended two hours later, Harrison had lost 62 killed and 126 wounded, and there were similar losses among the Indians. Harrison, however, took possession of Prophetstown (named after Tenskwatawa, the "Prophet," brother of the Shawnee Indian chief Tecumseh, who was not present at the battle) and claimed a victory. The hero status that Harrison achieved that day eventually propelled him to the White House.

William Clark, who was serving as both Indian agent for the Louisiana Territory and a general in the territorial militia, had seen the war coming long before the Battle of Tippecanoe. Well aware that Tecumseh and the Prophet were aligning themselves with the British and uniting native tribes throughout the region against white settlers, Clark had warned the War Department in July of 1810 that "the Post rider on his way from Vincennes to this place [St. Louis], was killed, and the mail lost." He further reported that 150 Indians were on a visit to the British agent and that many more were consulting with the Prophet. "On the night of the 20th of July," wrote Clark in his next letter, "four men who reside near the Missouri . . . who had been in pursuit of horses which had been stolen from them were killed in their camp and one wounded by the Indians." The chief of the Potawatomi Indians who lived in the area blamed the Prophet. By July of 1811, Clark was accurately predicting, "the crisis is fast approaching."[3]

Born in what is now Ohio in 1768 of a Creek mother and a Shawnee father, Tecumseh had been educated as a young man, taking a liking to both Shakespeare and the Bible. He fought with his people when Kentuckians pushed across the Ohio River into Indian territory. His father and two older brothers were both killed in the fighting, but Tecumseh became a leader. He gained a reputation for honesty and opposed the torture practiced by both Indians and whites.

"The white race is a wicked race," wrote Tecumseh. "Since the day when the white race had first come in contact with the red men, there had been a continual series of aggressions. Their hunting grounds were fast disappearing, and they were driving the red men farther and farther to the west. Such had been the fate of the Shawnees, and surely that would be the fate of . . . [all tribes] if the power of the whites was not forever crushed. The mere presence of the white man was a source of evil to the red man. His whiskey was destroying the bravery of their warriors, and his lust corrupting the virtue of their women. The only hope for the red man was a war of extermination against the paleface."[4]

Tecumseh called for the native nations to unite and resist aggression and underhanded treaties from the whites. Among those responding to his pleas were the Shawnee, Potawatomi, Kickapoo, Winnebago, Menominee, Ottawa, and Wyandot nations. At Prophetstown, Tecumseh's confederation rejected the 1809 Treaty of Fort Wayne (negotiated by Harrison), arguing that the chiefs who had signed the treaty had no authority to do so. Tecumseh and Harrison met several times, but Tecumseh accused Harrison of acting in bad faith. During a negotiation in 1810, when the two of them were sitting on a bench, Tecumseh had crowded Harrison right off his seat to illustrate how the Indians were being treated. Harrison thereafter called for the elimination of this "Indian menace" and blamed the British for Tecumseh's hostility.[5]

When Tecumseh appeared in Vincennes, the capital of the Indiana Territory, with three hundred warriors in the summer of 1811, he informed Harrison that he was on his way to meet with southern tribes and requested that white settlers stay out of the disputed region until the next spring, when the chief planned to appeal directly to President James Madison. It was clear there would be no hostilities while Tecumseh was absent. Weeks after the chief left, however, Harrison took advantage of his absence by marching twelve hundred men to Tippecanoe, where he successfully baited the Prophet, Tecumseh's less stable, medicine-man brother, into the battle.

At the time of the Battle of Tippecanoe, which was six weeks before the first New Madrid earthquake, Corps of Discovery veteran Nathaniel Pryor had mustered out of the army and obtained a license from William Clark to trade with the Winnebago Indians at a mine near present-day Galena, Illinois. Pryor built a trading post and living quarters and began operating a lead-smelting furnace. At Clark's request he also began gathering information on the activities of Tecumseh and the Prophet.

As late as Christmas Day 1811, Winnebagos in the area were "trading peaceably" with Pryor, unaware (as was Pryor) that twenty-five Winnebagos had been killed at Tippecanoe. Not part of Tecumseh's force, the Winnebagos had been returning from a visit to the British in Canada and had just happened to stop at Prophetstown the very night before the battle. In St. Louis, William Clark had received news of the hostilities and sent former expedition member Alexander Willard, employed as a government courier, to warn Pryor. But Willard was too late.

At noon on New Year's Day 1812, eight armed Winnebagos in war paint barged into Pryor's post and took him hostage. They held him and a fellow trader named George Hunt until sundown, when sixty others arrived, shooting Pryor's oxen and killing and scalping two of his men. The warriors were about to kill Hunt and Pryor when they were saved, as William Clark later wrote to the secretary of war, "by some Sock [Sauk] & Fox Squaws who lived with the young men declaring they were English men." The reprieve was only temporary, however. The Winnebagos placed Pryor and Hunt in a house, intending to burn it—with the captives inside—as soon as they plundered the post. They then began their rampage, burning the other buildings and destroying Pryor's equipment and goods. Although a sentinel had been posted, Pryor and Hunt somehow managed to sneak out of the house. With the trading post exploding in flames, they ran west, onto the frozen Mississippi River, soon pursued by enraged Winnebagos. They managed to escape a second time and made their way south, eventually learning that they had falsely been reported dead.[6]

For the second (but not the last) time, Pryor had survived a deadly Indian attack. The next year he reenlisted in the army, and he served as an officer under Andrew Jackson and fought in the Battle of New Orleans. He was discharged and ended his long military career on 15 June 1815.

Alexander Willard had been hired by Lewis as a government blacksmith for the Sauk and Fox Indians in 1808. When the Battle of Tippecanoe broke out, he was stationed on the west side of the Mississippi, across from present-day Nauvoo, Illinois. After receiving word of the battle from Clark, Willard rode north, only to find Pryor's post burned to the ground. Presuming that Pryor was dead, he continued north. "The views and intentions of those Bands of Indians whome we have suspected were hostily inclined, are no longer to be doubted," Clark wrote to the secretary of war in February 1812. "The Winnebagoes are Deturmined for War. . . . On the 8th [of this month] a party of that nation (some of whom were known) fired on my Express [Willard] about 40 miles above the Settlements, who was on his return from Prarie de Chien, the Mines & Fort Madison, on the 9th an American Family of women & children was killed on the bank of the Mississippi, a fiew minits before the Express passed the house."[7]

Several months after surviving the New Madrid earthquakes, on 15 August 1812, William Bratton had enlisted in the Kentucky volunteer militia as a private in Captain Paschal Hickman's Company of Riflemen, under Lieutenant Colonel John Allen. Late in 1812, about the time of Sacagawea's death, Colonel Allen marched his men north, to help control a section of Lake Erie (near the present southeast corner of Michigan). Early in January 1813, the bitter weather took its toll when the men were compelled to pull sleds because the horses were too malnourished to do so. The men themselves were reduced to half rations. On 17 January, Colonel Will Lewis with 550 men and Colonel Allen with 110 more—including Bratton—pushed on to save the residents of Frenchtown from British and Indian marauders. As Lewis and Allen and their men reached the Raisin River, they came under heavy fire from 200 Canadian soldiers and 400 Indians. They held the village, but they had lost 13 killed and 54 wounded by the next day.

On 20 January, General James Winchester reached Frenchtown with reinforcements numbering 300. Some of his troops camped behind a long line of eight-foot pickets, but some were unprotected. Convinced that the U.S. forces were vulnerable, British colonel Henry Proctor prepared for an attack, assembling a force of 500 soldiers and 600 Indians. Proctor and his well-armed men crossed the ice, bringing six three-pound cannons with them. At dawn on 22 January the British and Indians attacked and nearly overwhelmed one flank of Winchester's men. Several of the U.S. soldiers were captured, including General Winchester himself. After being forced to witness Indian atrocities, he sent an order for the 400 men behind the pickets to surrender. William Bratton was among them. When a group of Indians was assigned to guard Bratton and his fellow prisoners, they looted Frenchtown and killed thirty-three of the prisoners. "What shall I say or how begin," one of Bratton's fellow Kentuckians wrote to his brother: "My God, my God, hast thou forsaken us?"[8] The U.S. troops had lost 300 killed and 27 wounded, with close to 600 taken prisoner.

The details of Bratton's imprisonment are not known. The men undoubtedly suffered from cold and frostbite, dysentery, filthy conditions, unsanitary water, starvation, and quite possibly beatings and typhoid fever. Luckily, the back-and-forth nature of the war meant they were released in a matter of weeks. On 27 March 1813, by order of General William Henry Harrison, William Bratton was honorably discharged.[9] In the short space of a decade, he had taken his part in the Lewis and Clark Expedition, the New Madrid earthquakes, and the War of 1812. All this was later followed by a long marriage, children and grandchildren, and community service—all together, he lived a rich life indeed.

Rather than attack in large groups, the nations of the Missouri frontier aimed their wrath at unprotected individuals or families. A Cole party was massacred in present-day Missouri in 1810, a Cox family in Illinois Territory in June of 1811, and Mr. Price the same month. In March of 1813 a young man by the name of Pieper went searching for lost horses and disappeared. He was later found shot and scalped. "The Indians appear to be upon the frontier everywhere," wrote Ninian Edwards, governor of the Illinois Territory, on 26 March 1813. "I have raised, & have in active service, eight volunteer companies from the local militia; notwithstanding which, the savages have committed murders within bounds of every regiment of this territory." There were constant rumors about the British and the Indians gathering strength and moving close to St. Louis. "I expect we shall have to dig trenches around [St. Louis]," wrote one resident; "we have a few pieces of cannon which are to be mounted & 3 or 4 Spanish Blockhouses which will be put in Repair. It is said there are 500 men at Fort Massac intended for this place. I hope they may come on in time."[10]

On the upper Missouri, the Indians harassing Lisa's men were not acting on their own. On 21 February 1813 (two months after Sacagawea's death), Luttig wrote that Charbonneau had met with a local chief who informed him that "2 [British] Men from the N. W. Company had been with them, they came under pretext to trade dressd Buffaloe Skins . . . and began to harangue against the american traders . . . and that they the N. W. Company would furnish them with every thing without Pay if they would go to war, and rob and Kill the Americans."

William Clark, who had been reappointed brigadier general in September 1811, held a series of councils with Indian delegates in the spring of 1812, encouraging them not to join with Tecumseh. The Osages, the Shawnee, and others responded favorably. On 5 May, Clark left with several chiefs and warriors on a six-month goodwill tour to Washington.

When Clark visited Washington again the next spring, James Madison appointed him governor of the Missouri Territory (which had been established in June 1812); his official commission was dated 16 June 1813. He immediately ordered the construction of four heavily armed keelboats to patrol the Mississippi and Illinois Rivers. The fourth gunboat was completed in St. Louis under Clark's personal supervision. "My reasons for building one of the armed gunboats at this place," he wrote to the secretary of war, "was as well that the hostile Indians should hear of it, and magnify its size and importance (which I understand they have) as to have one of the boats built under my eye of such construction and size as to completely answer the service intended."[11]

Clark also continued his negotiations with the friendly Sauk and Fox Indians (several of whom had traveled with him to Washington) to move from their villages in the north to the south side of the Missouri River—removing them from the influence of hostile tribes and the British. In September 1813,

155 Sauk and Fox canoes arrived at Portage des Sioux (a peninsula near the confluence of the Mississippi and Missouri Rivers), for a final council with Clark. They were presented with substantial quantities of beef, pork, salt, and flour. Days later the Indians were migrating south, with Manuel Lisa and John Luttig both taking an active role in the councils.[12]

By May of 1814, Clark was confident enough to move up the Mississippi to Prairie du Chien (in present-day southwestern Wisconsin) and occupy the British post there. He headed up the river with his gunboats and approximately two hundred men; the small British force fled when they saw the boats moving upstream. Clark left two gunboats and a detail of men to fortify the post; then he returned triumphant to St. Louis. At a banquet at the Missouri Hotel, the toasts of "Our frontiers—It requires the patriotism of the West to say, 'They are ours'" and "Prairie du Chien—'The late expedition has cleansed it of British spies and traitors'" were reminiscent of the reception given Lewis and Clark when they returned to St. Louis in the fall of 1806.[13]

The celebration was short-lived. In July fifteen hundred Indians attacked the fort and drove away the gunboats. Two days later the United States forces surrendered. Then the relocated Sauk and Fox, whom Clark had supposedly appeased, began to show renewed signs of hostility. Clark's popularity steadily declined. Over the next several months, hostile tribes stepped up their hit-and-run tactics on the frontier, with the *Missouri Gazette* sometimes reporting such atrocities in detail:

> Mrs. Ramsey was attending the milking of her cows, and her pretty little children were amusing themselves feeding the poultry and assisting their mother. Mr. Ramsey, who you know has but one leg was near his wife at the moment the first shot was fired. He seen his wife fall and succeeded to lead her into the house, but as he reached the door he received a wound which prevented him to go to the relief of his children who were caught by the indians and cut to peices in the yard. Mr. and Mrs. Ramsey are dead, both were shot through the abdomen.[14]

The response of the *Missouri Gazette* to Indian atrocities seemed to typify the anger of the populace at large: "The BLOOD of our citizens cryed aloud for VENGEANCE. The general cry is let the north as well as the south be JACKSONIZED!!!" Clark's views were always much more moderate, however, and those views did not sit well with the majority of Missourians. When Clark, Auguste Chouteau, and others held a peace council with various tribes in the summer of 1815, they presented the Indians with thirty thousand dollars' worth of gifts, money that many believed should have gone to white victims of the war. A peace agreement was reached, but Clark's political career was clearly headed in the wrong direction. When Missouri attained statehood in

1820, Clark, the incumbent, ran against Alexander McNair. Clark's nephew, John O'Fallon, wrote that Clark's chances were fading: "They accuse Governor Clark of being friendly to the Indians, being stiff and reserved and unhospitable." When the final votes were counted, McNair's 6,576 had more than doubled Clark's 2,656.[15]

For the Corps of Discovery, the saddest note of the War of 1812 came not with Pryor's brush with death, Bratton's imprisonment, Patrick Gass's loss of his eye (detailed in Chapter 16), or Clark's political woes. It came with a quiet, nonviolent death in northern Missouri Territory that went unnoticed by the *Missouri Gazette*.

Captain Nathan Boone, son of the great explorer, had mustered a company of Mounted Rangers in the spring of 1812. They rode north, patrolled the northern frontier, and constructed blockhouse forts, lifting spirits throughout the region. The *Missouri Gazette* announced: "The new company of rangers now doing duty in the district of St. Charles are perhaps as fine a body of hardy woodsmen as ever took the field. They cover, by constant and rapid movements, the tract of country from Salt River on the Mississippi to the Missouri near Loutre."[16]

Besides Boone, the company included two lieutenants, an ensign, four sergeants, three corporals, and fifty privates. Among the privates, with names like John King, Robert Gray, and Alexander T. Chambers, was the intrepid John Colter. Now about thirty-seven, a decade or more older than most of his fellow privates, he had signed on the day the troop was organized—3 March 1812.

After his return to St. Louis in May of 1810, Colter had married a woman named Sally, and they had a son and named him Hiram. Colter met with William Clark and described his wanderings in the Wyoming region, with Clark incorporating the information into his maps. Colter also sued the estate of Meriwether Lewis for his expedition pay of $559.00—he settled several months later for $377.60.[17]

In the spring of 1811, as John Bradbury made his way up the Missouri with Hunt, he stopped near the French village of La Charette to visit with the seventy-seven-year-old Daniel Boone, who "had spent a considerable portion of his time alone in the back woods, and had lately returned from his spring hunt, with nearly sixty beaver skins." Boone presumably knew his neighbor and kindred spirit John Colter, for the next day Colter appeared. "He seemed to have a great inclination to accompany the expedition," wrote Bradbury, "but having been lately married, he reluctantly took leave of us."[18]

So it was not surprising that Colter had responded to Nathan Boone's call for troops. The company did its job well, and at a Fourth of July banquet the thankful citizens of St. Louis toasted Boone's men: "Our Frontiers—watched and protected by a hardy band of Spartan Warriors—the Rangers deserve well of their country."[19]

But Colter was not there for the celebration. Next to his name in the muster roll is the simple notation, "Died 7th May 1812." He must have been healthy when he joined in March but had apparently fallen ill in the interim. He was the only member of Boone's company to die. The cause of his death is not known, but Thomas James later heard that he died of jaundice. Of course, jaundice, a yellow coloring of the skin, is not a disease but a symptom that could indicate anything from a liver virus to gallstones to a tumor. After spending an amazing six full years in the wilderness, Colter had survived not quite two years in civilization.[20]

Colter's estate of $442.73 1/2 was liquidated the next year, bringing a net of $233.76 3/4 after his debts were paid. The sale bill shows that Hartley Sappington bought one pot and pothooks for $4.00, Zachariah Surlans one plow iron for $8.00, Enoch Greenstreete one coffee pot for $1.62 1/2, Mosias Maupin one bottle for $.50, and William Davis one colt for $16.50. Two books owned by John Colter were also auctioned, one for $1.75 and the other for $.86.[21]

CHAPTER THIRTEEN

"We Lost in All Fourteen Killed"
John Collins and Toussaint Charbonneau
Among the Mountain Men

E dward Rose galloped through the darkness, yelling to the trappers huddled on the beach that the Arikara had killed Stephens. Hearing that "war was declared in earnest," the half-sleeping men were instantly alert, checking their muskets and squinting through the rain toward the Arikara village. Someone climbed in a canoe and paddled out to the keelboat anchored in the Missouri River to warn William Henry Ashley, commander of the fur-trading expedition. "I was informed that the Indians had killed one of my men Aaron Stephens," wrote Ashley, "and in all probability would attack the boats in a few minutes; arrangments were made to receive them, my party consisted of ninety men, forty of whom were selected to accompany me to the Yellow Stone river by land, and were encamped on the sand beach in charge of the horses."[1]

Preparing for an attack that early morning of 2 June 1823 was arguably the most impressive group of mountain men ever assembled for a single excursion. Along with Rose were Jedediah Strong Smith, destined to join Lewis and Clark as one of the most important explorers in U.S. history; William L. Sublette, the first trader to take wagons to the northern Rockies; David E. Jackson, who later, as a partner with Smith and Sublette, purchased Ashley's company; Thomas "Broken Hand" Fitzpatrick, pioneer of the trail along the Platte River; James Clyman, prominent trapper and guide who saw virtually the entire West; and Hugh Glass, whose tale of solitary survival after a grizzly attack parallels the story of John Colter's run.[2] Joining them was Lewis and Clark veteran John Collins, one of the best hunters on the expedition.

When the corps returned to Missouri in 1806, Collins had immediately sold rights to his land warrant to George Drouillard (whose name was often spelled "Drewyer" in contemporary documents) for three hundred dollars. Then he and fellow corps member Pierre Cruzatte had apparently headed right back up the Missouri, trying to catch John McClellan's trapping party before bad weather set in. (McClellan had entered into secret negotiations with General James Wilkinson to establish trade relations with the Indians, something Wilkinson, as governor and superintendent of Indian affairs of the Louisiana Territory, was expressly forbidden to do.) Most of the men in McClellan's group, including McClellan himself and apparently Cruzatte, were eventually killed in what is now western Montana. Collins may have returned to St. Louis and informed William Clark of Cruzatte's fate.[3]

Now Collins had come up the Missouri again, this time with Ashley, a general in the Missouri militia and lieutenant governor of the state, who had recently entered the fur trade with Andrew Henry. On 30 May 1823, Ashley's group had reached the palisaded Indian villages across the river from present-day Mobridge, South Dakota. The nation poised for an assault was the Arikara, the same tribe that had attacked Pryor and Auguste-Pierre Chouteau's men sixteen years earlier—a battle in which George Shannon and George Gibson had both been wounded.

On the beach—which extended three hundred yards into the river—the twenty-four-year-old Smith, said to carry a gun in one hand and a Bible in the other, prepared his men for battle. Some, like Sublette and Jackson, followed instructions. Others ran about frantically, yelling for General Ashley to save them. Lightning flashed, followed by a deafening crack of thunder, and the men could see the Arikara towns—with their distinctive earthen lodges—silhouetted against the purple sky. The rain pelted the men's faces, the wind whipping and gusting, making it hard to hear anything at all.

Ashley sent back word for the men to stand their ground; at daylight he would go into the village and demand Stephens's body. (The previous night, Stephens, Rose, and others had visited the village without permission.) "We laid on our arms [expecting] an attack," wrote Clyman, "as [there] was a continual Hubbub in the village." Toward dawn the wind stilled; a friendly Indian drew near and said he would bring the body of the dead man in exchange for a horse. Again, a man paddled out to the keelboat to consult with Ashley.[4]

Collins, who had listed his residence as Frederick County, Maryland, was apparently a member of Captain Russell Bissell's company before signing on with Lewis and Clark on 1 January 1804. He had his share of problems over the next few months—stealing and slaughtering a local farmer's hog and being drunk on duty. Clark called him a "black gard," and he was flogged for misbehavior. Once the group left St. Louis in May, however, Collins mended his ways and proved his worth as a hunter. He also knew how to make beer from fermented camas roots.

After his second return from the West, Collins apparently married, had a son also named John, and settled in the Missouri Territory. Then, almost two decades after joining Lewis and Clark, Collins responded to a newspaper advertisement:

TO

Enterprising Young Men

The subscriber wishes to engage ONE HUNDRED MEN, to ascend the river Missouri to its source, there to be employed for one, two or three years.—For particulars enquire of Major Andrew Henry, near the Lead Mines, in the County of Washington, (who will ascend with, and command the party) or to the subscriber at St. Louis.

Wm. H. Ashley[5]

John Collins was hardly a young man. He was probably about the same age as Ashley, the forty-four-year-old organizer of the party. But Collins was an excellent hunter with unmatched credentials: he was a veteran of the Lewis and Clark Expedition who had seen the source of the Missouri first-hand. He knew the dangers of the Missouri but also knew how to survive.

Collins went with Ashley in either 1822 or 1823. The group that ascended in 1823 (eventually joining some who had gone upriver the previous year) saw one bad omen after another toward the end of May. As they came up the river, they learned that a few months earlier, traders at a post sixty miles downriver had given refuge to a Sioux woman who had escaped Arikara captivity. When several Arikara came after her, the traders had killed two of them, one the son of a chief. Then, as Ashley and his men came in sight of the Arikara villages on 30 May, the river was "lined with squaws packing up water thinking to have to stand a siege." On 31 May, Ashley successfully traded for nineteen horses—needed for his overland excursion to the Yellowstone—but the chiefs had demanded powder and ball, showing little interest in other trade goods. Then a friendly Indian warned of an attack and advised Ashley to swim the horses across the river. Ashley decided against it because the group had seen Indians on the opposite shore that day. To make matters worse, the two villages—which were separated by a ravine—were situated on a rise about thirty-five feet above the river, with each village "well picketed and in-trenched." Two-thirds of the seven hundred Arikara warriors were armed with British muskets, the others with bows and arrows.[6]

The notorious Edward Rose, who had trapped with at least eight differ-ent expedition members, had that same day warned Ashley of trouble and urged the general to moor the boats, with all the men aboard, on the oppo-site shore, but Ashley was apparently suspicious of Rose and turned a deaf ear to his sound advice.

Now, on 2 June, the friendly Indian who had offered to return Stephens's body in exchange for a horse waited patiently. The messenger sent to talk to Ashley finally returned in a canoe, saying that Ashley had agreed to give the Indian a horse. But the Indian, who would not come near enough to get the horse, simply shouted to them that "the Indians had put out [Stephens's] eyes, cut off his head, and otherwise mangled his body." From somewhere be-hind the picket line, an Indian called out to Rose—who had lived among the Arikara for some time—and warned him to take care for his life. Then came a single shot. The men crouched behind the horses, not sure where the shot had come from. As if the first shot had been a signal, "the Indians com-menced a heavy and well directed fire." The horses fell, one after another. "You will easely prceive," wrote Clyman, "that we had little else to do than to Stand on a [bare] sand barr and be shot at, at long range," with the Arikara taking full advantage of the "abundance of Powder and Ball" they had purchased from Ashley himself.[7]

With the horses all dead, wounded, or scattered, the men themselves began to fall. Smith, Sublette, Collins, and others lay behind fallen horses, fir-ing their rifles, reloading and firing again, straining to see in the half-dawn. But others were paralyzed, yelling for the boats to come ashore and take them on board. Ashley tried to do just that. "I ordered the anchor weighed and the boats put to shore," he wrote, "but the boatmen, with but very few exceptions were so panic struck that they could not be got to execute the order." He was only thirty yards from the beach, but his boatmen refused to move. Finally he persuaded some of his crew to take the two skiffs for a rescue.[8]

Glass and Fitzpatrick kept their heads, making a breastwork of the dead horses, firing their rifles and their pistols and reloading. Men around them continued to fall. A skiff came to shore and several men scrambled aboard, the overloaded craft almost sinking as it pushed off. Ashley and others fired from the keelboat, trying to cover the men in the skiff. The boatman rowing the second skiff was shot dead. A wounded man ran into the river and van-ished immediately.

Several Arikara rushed the camp and dragged off a wounded man. The first skiff returned, and another group of men reached it safely. They pushed off into the river, every man disappearing for cover inside the skiff. It caught the current and floated downstream. Three more men ran and jumped into the river. "Some swam to the boats," wrote Ashley. "Others were shot down in the edge of the water and immediately sunk, and others who appeared to be badly wounded sunk in attempting to swim. To describe my feelings at seeing these men destroyed, is out of my power."[9]

John Collins was one of those destroyed. He may have been scalped and then killed by the Arikara; he may have been shot on the beach; he may have drowned attempting to flee. He was the seventh—and, as far as is known—the last expedition veteran to die violently.

Clyman wrote: "I seeing no hopes of Skiffs or boats comeing ashore left my hiding place behind a dead hors, ran up stream a short distance to get the advantage of the current and concieving myself to be a tolerable strong swimer stuck the muzzle of my rifle in [my] belt the lock [over] my head with all my clothes on but not having made sufficien calculation for the strong current was carried passed the boat within a few feet of the same one Mr Thomas Eddie [saw me] but the shot coming thick he did not venture from behin the cargo Box and so could not reach me with a setting pole which [he] held in his hands."[10]

The few able-bodied men still on the beach fought on. Another band of warriors charged down from the picket line.

In 1880, a secondhand report claimed that "Sublette and Jackson after fighting bravely around the animals, until all were killed or dispersed, fought their way through the crowded ranks of Indians, leaped into the river, and under a hail of arrows and balls, swam to the boats." Jedediah Smith was with them, and their names in the future would be spoken as one—Smith, Jackson, and Sublette.[11]

Edward Rose, who had "taken his station behind a small bunch of willows," an acquaintance of his later wrote, "thought of nothing but the work in which he was engaged . . . until after he had been repeatedly called by some of his comrades, or by General Ashley himself, that he raised himself from the posture he had, Indian-like, assumed, and looked around him; he then saw, in himself, the sole occupant of the bar, the boats floating towards the other shore, and the Indians rushing from their village to take the scalps of those killed. . . . He plunged into the stream and swam for the boats, amid the pattering of a shower of balls on the water around him; he reached one of them, rifle in hand, in safety, and was the last man who did so."[12]

Meanwhile, Clyman was close to drowning. He tried to pull his musket free, but the lock caught in his belt. The current pulled him under as he tugged at the rifle with both hands. Finally he got it free and let it go. Still under water, he next unbuckled his belt and freed himself of the weight of his pistols. "Next let go my Ball Pouch and finally one Sleeve of my Hunting shirt which was buckskin and held an immence weight of water," he wrote.

As Clyman rose to the surface, he heard someone say, "Hold on, Clyman— I will soon relieve you." It was Reed Gibson, who had fled into the river and boarded an empty skiff. Gibson was just a few yards away, but Clyman was so exhausted that Gibson had to pull him into the boat. Clyman lay in the boat trying to catch his breath. Then he rose to take an oar when Gibson called, "Oh, God, I am shot." Clyman paddled with all his might, telling his friend the wound was not fatal. "A few more pulls and we will be out of reach," said Clyman. Gibson gave several more strokes, then complained of feeling faint and fell forward. Clyman paddled to shore only to discover several Indians swimming after them.

"Save yourself Clyman," said Gibson, "and pay no attention to me as I am a dead man, and they can get nothing of me but my scalp." Clyman considered charging the warriors and "braining them" with the oar. Then he realized there were too many of them and they were too near the shore. He looked for a place to hide, but there was only a "scant row of brush along the shore." He "concluded to take to the open Pararie and run for life."

Gibson had made it out of the skiff and stood by Clyman's side. "Run Clyman," he said, "but if you escape write to my friends in Virginia and tell them what has become of me." Nodding, Clyman ran for the prairie while Gibson hid in the brush. Clyman soon saw three Indians pursuing him. They were naked except for belts holding knives and tomahawks. They also carried bows and arrows. With a head start of 150 yards, Clyman ran across a broad prairie. He ran for thirty minutes, forty-five, an hour, with the three warriors still 150 yards behind him. Finally he came upon a hole surrounded by weeds and grass, and he dived in and hid himself. When he emerged from his den, his pursuers were four hundred yards away. Now he ran for the river, convinced he could never survive, "being at least Three Hundred miles from any assistanc unarmed and [unprovided] with any sort of means of precureing a subsistance not even a pocket Knife."

But he saw a wondrous sight when he reached the river: "here came the boats floating down the stream the [men] watcing along the shores saw me about as soon as I saw them the boat was laid in and I got aboard." He was amazed to hear that Gibson had also been rescued. "I immediately wen to the cabin [of the keelboat] where he lay but he did not recognize me being in the agonies of Death the shot having passed through his bowels I could not refrain from weeping over him who lost his lifee but saved mine he did not live but an hour or so and we buried him that evening."

Clyman added a sad last note: "before leaving the grave of my friend Gibson that [day and] before I had an oppertunity of writeing to his friends I forgot his post office and so never have writen."[13]

Twelve men, including John Collins, were killed in the battle; two others soon died of their wounds. "We lost in all fourteen killed and twelve wounded," wrote a trapper whose name has been lost to history. (Another wounded man died after this letter was written, bringing the total killed to fifteen.) Collins had thus joined the fraternity of his fellow corps members Pierre Cruzatte, George Drouillard, Joseph Field, John Potts, John B. Thompson, and Peter M. Weiser, all apparently killed by Indians after safely crossing the continent with Lewis and Clark. Ashley and his men were able to recover some of the bodies and bury them—whether Collins was among this group is not known. Back in St. Louis, Collins's family would not have learned of his death until at least 9 July, when the *Missouri Republican* printed a letter from Ashley in which he described the battle and listed the names of the dead and wounded.[14]

On 4 June, Ashley wrote a letter describing the attack to Major Benjamin O'Fallon, the government agent at Fort Atkinson (near present-day Omaha) and a nephew of William Clark. On 24 June, O'Fallon passed the news on in a letter to Clark, then serving in St. Louis as superintendent of Indian affairs. O'Fallon informed Clark that Colonel Henry Leavenworth (commander of the Sixth Regiment at Fort Atkinson) had left on 22 June to seek retribution on the Arikara. O'Fallon predicted that "those inhuman monsters will most probably be made to atone for what they have done by a great effusion of their blood." Clark echoed this sentiment when he wrote to Secretary of War John C. Calhoun on 4 July, "I have but little doubt of the success of our Troops in distroying the Arricara Towns & fortifications and the good effect the movement will have upon the other Tribes."[15]

Leavenworth and his 230 soldiers were joined by Joshua Pilcher, a partner in the Missouri Fur Company, and about 50 of his men, as well as Ashley and his party of about 70 trappers, and between 600 and 700 Sioux warriors who were more than ready to plunder the Arikara villages. Leavenworth dubbed this army "the Missouri Legion."

Among the legion was fifty-six-year-old Toussaint Charbonneau, hired as an interpreter. In the eleven years since Sacagawea's death, Charbonneau had found regular work as a guide and interpreter, his name becoming widely known for both good and ill. "Charbonneau & Jessaume Keep us in Constant uproar with their Histories and wish to make fear among the Engagees," John Luttig had written at Fort Manuel in 1812. "These two rascals ought to be hung for their perfidy, they . . . stir up the Indians and pretend to be friends to the white People at the same time but we find them to be our Enemies."[16]

On the other hand, such men as François-Antoine Lacrocque, a prominent Canadian trader, spoke quite highly of Charbonneau. Others seemed to agree, for Charbonneau made a good wage—sometimes four hundred dollars a year for his services.

Around 1814, Charbonneau and Edward Rose had successfully hatched a plan to purchase Arapaho women and girls held captive by the Shoshones (Sacagawea's nation) and take them to the trading posts on the upper Missouri, where they sold them to trappers. According to Rose's acquaintance Reuben Holmes, Charbonneau "conceived the singular plan" and communicated it to Rose, "who, glad of anything for a change, joyfully fell in with it."[17]

In 1816 Charbonneau joined a trading venture to the upper Arkansas River. He may have been with several men who were captured by the Spanish and imprisoned at Santa Fe. "We remained in prison (some of us in irons) forty-eight days," wrote Julius DeMun, one of the traders.[18]

As one who had worked with O'Fallon for years, Charbonneau probably knew what had recently befallen his former comrades Michael Immell and Robert Jones, news that O'Fallon relayed to William Clark early in July:

> I am at this moment interrupted by the arrival of an Express from the Military expedition, with a letter from Mr. Pilcher . . . in which he says, . . . "the [flower] of my business is gone, My Mountaineers have been defeated, and the Chiefs of the party both Slain—The party were attacked by three or four hundred Blackfoot Indians, in a position on the Yellow stone river, where Nothing but defeat Could be expected—
>
> "Jones & Immel and five Men were Killed. the former it is said fought desperately—Jones killed two Indians and in drawing his pistol to kill a third, he receiv'd two spears in his breast—Immel was in front, he killed an Indian, and was cut to pieces—I think we loose at least $15,000."[19]

Leavenworth had the full support of his superiors and more than a thousand men at his command, but his expedition faltered from the start. One of the boats wrecked going upriver—seven men were drowned. Then, when he got near the Arikara villages, on 9 August, he allowed the Sioux to charge ahead of his troops. The Arikara rode out to meet their old enemies, and a chaotic battle ensued. "When we arrived," wrote James Clyman, "the plain was covered with Indians which looked more like a swarm [of] bees than a battle field." Fearful that he would kill Sioux warrior allies, Leavenworth held his fire. The Arikara soon retreated to their picketed villages, with Leavenworth deciding it was too late in the day to resume the battle.[20]

Several Arikara lay dead on the plain, and as the sun set, a group of Sioux hacked up the bodies and triumphantly dragged body parts behind their horses. Clyman and the rest of Leavenworth's men had no rations—apparently due to Leavenworth's lack of planning—and they lay awake during the night listening to Indian women and children crying inside the villages, warriors on both sides yelling and firing their guns, mules braying, and dogs howling. As Clyman put it, all this, "intermingled with the stench of dead men and horses made the place the most disagreeable that immaginnation could fix Short of the bottomless pit."[21]

The next morning, Leavenworth staged an attack of sorts, but rifle fire seemed to have little effect on the Arikara behind the picket lines, and the cannon fire proved almost farcical—with the weapons aimed too high, the six-pound cannonballs sailed over the villages and splashed into the Missouri. The Sioux, apparently without food themselves, lost interest and meandered into the Arikara fields ripe with corn, squash, pumpkins, and beans. In an attempt to restore purpose to the mission, Leavenworth ordered an assault on the upper village. But, just when a junior officer was ready to carry out the order, Leavenworth reversed himself. Then he decided to attack the lower village, then reversed himself again. His men grew disgusted. Leavenworth sent word for the Sioux to return; instead, most of them vanished, taking with them six army mules and seven of Ashley's horses.

Seeing that a few Arikara had come out of their village, Leavenworth, Pilcher, and a few others, presumably including Charbonneau, went out to meet them. Leavenworth greeted the Arikara with a friendliness that shocked Pilcher. Leavenworth then attempted to smoke a pipe and negotiate an agreement on the spot. Pilcher objected, warning the Arikara they would have to deal with *him* at some point. Furthermore, it was not even clear that these Arikara had authority to speak for the nation. But Leavenworth demanded the return of Ashley's property, and the Arikara agreed.

That evening, Edward Rose warned Leavenworth of an Arikara retreat, just as he had warned Ashley of an attack. Again, Rose's warnings went unheeded: the next morning Leavenworth found the Arikara villages abandoned—save for an old woman, three or four dozen dogs, and a single rooster.[22]

Charbonneau and a few others were sent out to find the Arikara. They carried this message:

Ricaras
You see the pipe of peace which you gave to me in the hands of Mr. Charbonneau and the flag of the United States.
These will convince you that my heart is not bad—your Villages are in my possession. Come back and take them in peace and you will find evry thing

as you left them, you shall not be hurt if you do not obstruct the road or molest the Traders—If you do not come back there are some bad men and bad Indians who will burn your Villages. Come back and come quickly. Be assured that what I say is the truth.[23]

But Charbonneau and his fellow emissaries returned without finding any trace of the Arikara. On 15 August, as Leavenworth and his troops departed for the return journey back to Fort Aktinson, he "had the mortification to discover [the Arikara villages] to be on fire." He blamed this on members of the Missouri Fur Company, concluding that "those Indians will be excited to further hostilities."[24]

Joshua Pilcher denied the charges and placed the blame for the campaign's failure squarely on Leavenworth's shoulders. "You came to restore peace and tranquility," he wrote to Leavenworth, "[but] your operations have been such as to produce the contrary effect, and to impress the Indian tribes, with the greatest possible contempt for the American character. . . . you have by the imbecility of your conduct and operations, created and left impassable barriers."[25]

The retreat of the Arikara had an immediate impact on Toussaint Charbonneau. Within weeks he had taken employment with a French company of fur traders at Fort Kiowa (approximately sixty miles southeast of modern-day Pierre, South Dakota), a few days' travel downriver from the ruins of the Arikara villages. Many of Ashley's trappers arrived at the fort about the same time. With the whereabouts of several hundred well-armed Arikara warriors still unknown, no one wanted to travel upriver to Mandan country. In September, Ashley's partner Andrew Henry took a company of men, including Hugh Glass, and departed the fort, still trying to reach the Yellowstone River and trap there (Ashley's original objective when he had been attacked in June). Rather than going north on the Missouri, Henry went only to the Grand River (which flows into the Missouri near present-day Mobridge, South Dakota) and then headed west with pack horses.

A few weeks after Henry left, the French trader Joseph Brazeau asked Charbonneau to accompany five other men in a pirogue on a trading mission to the Mandan. They would be the first traders to attempt going up the Missouri since the Leavenworth debacle. According to a trader who talked to Charbonneau a few months later (and reported details in a letter apparently written to William Clark), he "was confident, and told [Brazeau], that his men would be killed by the Arickaras."[26] Just how Brazeau, who was not going himself, persuaded the cautious Charbonneau to join this group is unknown.

Early in October 1823, when the six men were making final preparations to leave, a lone figure limped into the fort: Hugh Glass. Known as a good hunter, Glass had been slightly ahead of the rest of Henry's men hunting for game when, in the words of James Hall (who published the first account of this episode two years after it occurred), "a white [grizzly] bear that had imbedded herself in the sand, arose within three yards of him, and before he could 'set his triggers,' or turn to retreat, he was seized by the throat, and raised from the ground. Casting him again upon the earth, his grim adversary tore out a mouthful of the cannibal food which had excited her appetite."

Despite his wounds, Glass attempted to escape; this time the bear "seized him again at the shoulder; she also lacerated his left arm very much, and inflicted a severe wound on the back of his head." In the meantime, the main body of trappers had run to Glass's rescue—seven or eight of them fired their muskets, "despatching the bear as she stood over her victim."

"Glass . . . had received several dangerous wounds, his whole body was bruised and mangled, and he lay weltering in his blood, in exquisite torment." With Glass's death considered a foregone conclusion—and with the hostile Arikara in the area—Henry offered two trappers a reward if they would stay with him until he died. A man named Fitzgerald and a nineteen-year-old greenhorn trapper by the name of Jim Bridger took the offer.

Fitzgerald and Bridger waited five days for Glass to die. Then, fearful of losing the main party and convinced Glass was on the verge of death, they departed, "taking his rifle, shot-pouch, &c. and leaving him no means of either making fire or procuring food." When they caught up with the others, days later, they reported Glass dead and buried.

"Meanwhile poor Glass, retaining a slight hold upon life, when he found himself abandoned, crawled with great difficulty to a spring which was within a few yards, where he lay ten days," Hall wrote. Slowing acquiring his strength, he began crawling toward Fort Kiowa, three hundred and fifty miles distant. He had traveled several days when he saw a buffalo calf torn to pieces by wolves. He waited till the wolves had eaten their fill, then drove them away. "With indefatigable industry he continued to crawl until he reached Fort Kiowa."[27]

Glass presumably rested at Fort Kiowa for a few days. Then someone informed him that Charbonneau and the others were about to head upriver. Though he still had not recovered from his wounds, he announced his plan to join them. As Hall put it, "The primary object of this voyage was declared to be the recovery of his arms, and vengeance on the recreant who had robbed and abandoned him in his hour of peril."[28]

So, about 10 October, the seven men boarded the pirogue and made their way up the Missouri. They found the Arikara towns still deserted. At least one of the men, Antoine Langevin (also known as Antoine Citoleux), shared Charbonneau's apprehension, for he made out his will on 15 October. Not long after that, three men in a canoe navigating their way downstream hailed Charbonneau and his mates but apparently did not stop. Incredibly, one of the three was John Fitzgerald, who, along with Bridger, had left Glass to perish. He even had Glass's musket with him in the canoe, but Glass did not recognize him.[29]

After a six-week journey, Glass, Charbonneau, and the others reached Mandan country. According to Charbonneau's acquaintance, when "they got within a day's march of [the Mandan] village, [Charbonneau] says, he got [out] and went by land, knowing there was less danger than by water." Luckily, Charbonneau was in his home territory, having lived among the Mandan and Hidatsa for several years. He found his way safely to a French stockade called Tilton's Fort, where he discovered that the Arikara were indeed in the area. He also learned that the day after he had left them, Langevin and his four companions—Peritan, Rozo, Superinart, and Charles Simons—had been killed by the Arikara, who stole their goods and sank their boat.[30]

Apparently following Charbonneau's lead, Glass had left Langevin and the others about the same time Charbonneau did. If they left together, they soon parted. Glass happened upon two Arikara women and fled. As Hall recorded, the women "were not long in rallying the warriors of the tribe, who immediately commenced the pursuit." Glass, still recovering from his injuries, "made but a feeble essay at flight . . . when two Mandan mounted warriors rushed forward and seized him." Glass expected to be turned over to the Arikara, but the Mandan instead "mounted him on a fleet horse" of his own and accompanied him to Tilton's Fort, where he found refuge.[31]

Glass soon departed west, to the Yellowstone country in what is now southern Montana; Charbonneau went southeast, to Lake Traverse, near the present-day South Dakota–Minnesota border. Whether Glass and Charbonneau ever met again is not known. After thirty-eight days of traveling alone through the snowy, trackless wilderness, Glass reached Fort Henry, near the mouth of the Bighorn River, where he met an astonished Jim Bridger.

"Young man," he reportedly said, "it is Glass . . . I swore an oath that I would be revenged on you. . . . For this meeting I have braved the dangers of a long journey. . . . But I cannot take your life; . . . you have nothing to fear from me; go,—you are free;—for your youth I forgive you."[32]

CHAPTER FOURTEEN

"Taken with the Cholera in Tennessee and Died"
The Sad Fate of York

From the moment of his birth, York was essentially the property of William Clark. He was born at the Clark plantation in Virginia a few years after William, and the two of them grew up with each other and played together as young boys. William Clark Kennerly, Clark's nephew, wrote that William "grew to be a sturdy lad, tramping the woods in search of small game, fishing in the Rappahannock, and in the long evenings listening to Brother George's tales of his daring campaigns of 1774 in the Dunmore Wars. On school holidays he rode about the countryside, always accompanied by his little Negro boy."[1]

In the custom of the day, it was common for the children of slave owners and the children of slaves to play together. It was also common for a young man's slave to become his body servant. So, as the Clark family moved from Virginia to Kentucky, William and York probably became regular companions, with York likely anticipating a role as a body servant. In the social strata of slaves, those who worked in the house held higher status than field hands.[2] They wore nicer clothes and endured a lighter workload than those who worked the fields, and they ate the same food as the masters. Further, they were privy to intimate family matters and accompanied the family on business and social trips. York apparently performed these services well—at the time of the expedition, he seems to have been Clark's only body servant. Clark's ownership of York became official in the summer of 1799, when Clark's father, John, died. His will stipulated that William was to receive eight slaves, among whom were "one Negroe man named York, Also old York, and his Wife Rose, and their two Children Nancy and Juba."[3] William Clark was about to turn twenty-nine at the time, York possibly twenty-six or twenty-seven. When Clark set out for his exploration of the West with Lewis, York went with him.

York had experienced a historic moment on the Pacific coast. The question was where to spend the winter, and the captains had called for a vote. One by one, the men voted, most of them wishing to cross over to the southern (Oregon) side of the Columbia River. Clark called off the names, and the twenty-ninth name he called was York's. Sixty years before the Thirteenth Amendment outlawed slavery, and 160 years before voting rights became a practical reality in the South, York voted for the Oregon side.

Clark next called the name "Janey," a nickname for Sacagawea. Sixty-four years before a territory or state would grant woman suffrage—fittingly it was the western territory of Wyoming—and 115 years before the Nineteenth Amendment granted women the vote nationally, Sacagawea cast the most original vote of the group, wishing for "a place where there is plenty of Potas"—wapatos, round roots about the size of a hen's egg that the Indians roasted.

Next the captains themselves voted, each of them for crossing to the other side, examining conditions there, and then making a decision.[4]

"In the Evening our Officers had the whole party assembled in order to consult which place would be the best, for us to take up our Winter Quarters at," wrote Joseph Whitehouse, a private with the expedition. John Ordway made a similar notation: "our officers conclude with the oppinion of the party to cross the River and look out a place for winters quarter." Patrick Gass offered more details: "At night, the party were consulted by the Commanding Officers, as to the place most proper for winter quarters; and the most of them were of opinion, that it would be best, in the first place, to go over to the south side of the river, and ascertain whether good hunting ground could be found there. Should that be the case, it would be a more eligible place than higher up the river, on account of getting salt, as that is a very scarce article with us."[5]

York continued to enjoy a measure of equality during the expedition, much more than he would ever see again after it. He went on hunting trips as often as Nathaniel Pryor or Robert Frazer, more often than Richard Windsor, John Thompson, Silas Goodrich, and several others. He collected food, scouted, and fished, much like any member of the corps. He took orders from the captains, but so did everyone else. On 26 October 1805, two years to the day after the corps had first traveled together as a group (leaving Clarksville,

Indiana Territory), Clark made a memorable entry: "In the evening 2 Chief and 15 men came over in a Single Canoe . . . one gave me a dressed Elk Skin, and gave us Som deer meet . . . we gave to each Chief a Meadel of the Small Size a red Silk handkerchief & a knife to the 1st a arm ban & a pin of Paint. . . . They deturmined to Stay with us all night, we had a fire made for them & one man played on the violin which pleased them much my Servant danced— . . . one man giged a *Salmon trout* which we had fried in a little Bears oil which a Chief gave us yesterday and I think the finest fish I ever tasted."

"York brought my horse, he is here but of verry little Service to me," wrote Clark to his brother in 1809; "insolent and Sulky, I gave him a Severe trouncing the other Day and he has much mended Sence Could he be hired for any thing at or near Louis ville, I think if he was hired there a while to a Severe master he would See the difference and do better."[6]

In many ways, this sad paragraph epitomizes Clark and York's deteriorating relationship after the expedition; it also reveals much about how the slave-holding culture perpetuated itself by denying slaves their full humanity. It is particularly poignant because William Clark is a sympathetic individual in so many ways. He treated his wife and children with love and tenderness. He habitually showed concern for his friends—as evidenced by his letters to or about Shannon and Pryor in the decades following the expedition. He was the kind of man who once rebuked Charbonneau for striking Sacagawea— an incident that makes his "trouncing" of York (who would have had no choice but to cower and take his beating without raising a hand in defense) all the more incomprehensible. William Clark was ahead of his time in his attitude toward the native nations, treating them with a compassion and empathy uncommon in the nineteenth-century United States. But regarding slavery he was very much a man of his time, imbued with a mentality that saw African-Americans as so inherently inferior to whites that it was best to sometimes treat them as children and other times treat them as animals.

Ironically, a letter from the happier times of the expedition holds the key to Clark and York's falling out. At Fort Mandan in April 1805, as the corps prepared to ascend the Missouri to its source, Clark had written to his brother Jonathan: "York tels me that he has put up in the 3d Box for his wife & Ben, as marked."[7] York was sending a buffalo robe to his wife, just as John Shields had done for his wife. The date of York's marriage and his wife's name and location are unknown, but she apparently lived in the Louisville area, probably near the Clark estate at Mulberry Hill, and was owned by someone other than Clark or his relatives. William Clark had apparently allowed York to marry his wife and spend time with her at a nearby plantation when his duties demanded or allowed such a visit.

After the corps returned in 1806, York was briefly reunited with his wife when he traveled with Lewis, Clark, and others to the Indiana Territory and Kentucky. Clark's nephew wrote: "York was in the quarters unpacking his Indian trophies to the 'oh's' and 'ah's' and prideful joy of his parents, Old York and Nancy, the cook. Cupid and Venus, George Rogers' faithful couple, leaving Old Henry at home to take care of their master, came over to Locust Grove to rejoice with them. Little work was done that first day, and candles burned late in the cabins as York recited his adventures with dramatic pose. He took much pleasure, too, in the fact of the buckskins' being abolished and in seeing his mater again in ruffled shirt, silken hose, and buckled pumps."[8]

If York's wife was present at this gathering, she probably also saw his Indian trophies about the same time. From all appearances, York and Clark were getting along well, with York still acting as body servant and showing appropriate concern for Clark's appearance. York's marriage had not driven a wedge between him and Clark, because the slave and his wife had adapted to the basic unfairness of the situation: they saw each other when possible, as long as it did not inconvenience their masters.

Even before the expedition, York had traveled a good deal with Clark. York and his wife knew that long separations were inevitable. Still, things changed radically when Clark was appointed Indian agent in 1807, for that meant a permanent move to St. Louis, with infrequent trips to Louisville. By July 1808—one month after it happened—several of Clark's slaves were apparently unhappy about the relocation to St. Louis.

"Indeed I have been obliged [to] whip almost all my people," wrote Clark, in another passage that makes the modern reader wince. "And they are now beginning to think that it is best to do better and not Cry hard when I am compelled to use the whip. they have been troublesome but are not all so now—"[9]

Within a few months, a frustrated Clark wrote to his brother: "I Shall Send york with nancy, and promit him to Stay a fiew weeks with his wife. he wishes to Stay there altogether and hire himself which I have refused. he prefurs being Sold to return[ing] here, he is Serviceable to me at this place [St. Louis], and I am deturmined not to Sell him, to gratify him, and have derected him to return in John H. Clarks Boat. . . . if any attempt is made by york to run off or refuse to provorm his duty as a Slave, I wish him Sent to New Orleans and Sold, or hired out to Some Severe master untill he thinks better of Such Conduct."[10]

Although Clark had tolerated York's relationship with his wife for some time, he had clearly lost his patience, never doubting that York's interests, indeed his relationship with his wife, were subordinate to Clark's needs, whether these might be serious or trivial.

By December 1808, two years after the corps' return, Clark wrote: "I did wish to do well by [York]—but as he has got Such a notion about freedom and his emence Services, that I do not expect he will be of much Service to me again; I do not think with him, that his Services has been So great (or my Situation would promit me to liberate him[)] . . . but I do not expect much from him as long as he has a wife in Kenty."[11] Within a few months after that, Clark was giving the unhappy York a severe trouncing.

Sometime in the next year, York got his wish to return to Louisville. He was hired out to a man there, a "severe" master. In a letter written from Louisville in the spring of 1811, Clark's nineteen-year-old nephew John O'Fallon wrote:

> Since I have been down which is about five weeks I have made frequent enquiries relative to the conduct of York since his living here and in justice to him must assert that all the information I have been able to gather contribute strongly to prove that his conduct is (has been) such as entitles him to credit— The term for which he was hired to Mr. Young yesterday expired but I believe agreable to request Mr. Fitzhugh [William Clark's brother-in-law] has again hired him to a Mr. Mitchell living about seven miles from this place— I believe your views for permitting him to live here in preference to St. Louis were that he might be with his wife—but I imagine now as there is a great probability that the owner of said wife will within a few months leave this quarter for Natches [Natchez] carrying with him the said wife your views on the score of York not [now?] being answered it will be needless to hire him out for a term equal to that for which he was last.
>
> I apprehend that he has been indifferently clothed if at all by Young as appearance satisfactorily prove—he appeared wretched under the fear that he has incurred your displeasure and which he despairs he'll ever remove—I am confident he sorely repent of whatever misconduct of his that might have led to such a breach and moreover has considerably amended and in fine deem it not unreasonable to recommend his situation to your consideration.[12]

To his credit, Clark had apparently granted York's wish to be hired out in Louisville so he could be near his wife. Clark seems to have done so at least partly out of disgust, however, with the alienation between him and York deepening as a result. Not only was York miserable about Clark's "displeasure," he was also about to lose his wife—and the children they may have had together (though this is not documented). Since there is no further mention of York's wife in the historical record, we can only assume that she indeed was taken by her owner to Natchez and that York never saw her again.

Nor was the rift between York and Clark mended. In December 1814, Clark wrote to his brother Edmund, "What have you done with . . . my negrow man York?" The next year, when William and his nephew John H. Clark formed a Louisville business to transport goods by wagon, York was the driver.[13] Now he was separated from a man he cared for and separated from his wife and family. His day-to-day work of endlessly loading and delivering goods must have been continually darkened by a sense of despair.

In 1832 the writer Washington Irving visited William Clark, then a widower for the second time (and not to remarry again). In his journal, Irving described Clark as a "fine healthy robust man—tall—about 50—perhaps more [he was actually sixty-two]—his hair, originally light, now grey—falling on his shoulders—frank—intelligent."

Irving and Clark ate a fine meal: "Dinner plentiful—good—but rustic— fried chicken, bacon and grouse, roast beef, roasted potatoes, tomatoes, excellent cakes, bread, butter, &c." In the course of their pleasant conversation, Clark discussed his slaves:

> His slaves—set them free—one he placed at a ferry—another on a farm, giving him land, horses, &c.—a third he gave a large waggon & team of 6 horses to ply between Nashville and Richmond. They all repented & wanted to come back.
>
> The waggoner was York, the hero of the Missouri expedition & adviser of the Indians. He could not get up early enough in the morning—his horses were ill kept—two died—the others grew poor. He sold them, was cheated——entered into service—fared ill. Damn this freedom, said York, I have never had a happy day since I got it. He determined to go back to his old master—set off for St. Louis, but was taken with the cholera in Tennessee & died. Some of the traders think they have met traces of York's crowd, on the Missouri.[14]

Irving did not say when York died—his notes give the impression that it was several years before the writer's meeting with Clark. But it seems that York was granted his freedom and that with Clark's help he started his own freight business. But freedom for former slaves was very much a mixed blessing—if it was any blessing at all. The slave-holding culture had a hard time abiding free African-Americans and frequently sabotaged their efforts. A man like York would likely be taken advantage of—or, as Irving noted— cheated. Seeking civil redress for such losses was a hopeless case—even freed slaves did not have the same standing in court as whites. Furthermore, a good many people would look on York with suspicion or refuse to do business with him.

Saddest of all, free African-Americans could be isolated from slaves. Slave owners often refused to allow their slaves to associate with free blacks, fearing discontent or even rebellion among their "boys." This meant that even if York had been able to find his wife—which was unlikely to begin with—he would probably not have been free to resume a marital relationship with her.

In 1839 a trapper by the name of Zenas Leonard published an account of his adventures "trapping for furs, trading with the Indians in the Rocky Mountains." Leonard wrote that in 1832 he journeyed to a Crow camp in what is now north-central Wyoming.

> In this village we found a negro man, who informed us that he first came to this country with Lewis and Clark—with whom he also returned to the State of Missouri, and in a few years returned again with a Mr. Mackinney, a trader on the Missouri river, and has remained here ever since—which is about ten or twelve years. He has acquired a correct knowledge of their manner of living, and speaks their language fluently. He has rose to be quite a considerable character, or chief, in their village; at least he assumes all the dignities of a chief, for he has four wives with whom he lives alternately. This is the custom of many of the chiefs.[15]

Leonard passed through the same Crow village two years later and again met the "old Negro," adding that "he has become thoroughly acquainted with their language, method of transacting their public and private business, and considered of great value by the Indians. He enjoys perfect peace and satisfaction, and has every thing that he desires at his own command."[16]

Not long after that, Leonard saw the black chief lead an assault against invading Blackfoot warriors: "he leaped from the rock on which he had been standing, and looking neither to the right nor to the left, made for the fort as fast as he could run. The Indians guessing his purpose, and inspired by his words and fearless example, followed close to his heels, and were in the fort dealing destruction to the right and left nearly as soon as the old man."[17]

Could this have been York? Some believe it may have been. York was the only African-American who "first came to this country with Lewis and Clark." Second, the time line seems to fit. York may have received his freedom around 1816. He could have moved to Nashville, tried his hand in the freight business, and failed by 1820. Then (assuming Clark heard a false report of his death), he could have gone west and lived among the Crows for "ten or twelve years" by 1832. Third, York was probably born around 1773 and would have been close to sixty in 1832—making him an "old man" at that time.

On the other hand, it would have been impossible for York to simply leave Tennessee, head up the Missouri, and begin living with the Crows. He would have needed to serve an "apprenticeship" in the fur industry, living and working with other trappers and becoming adept and savvy enough to gain the confidence of the Crows. (Nor did he have opportunity to learn the Crow language on the expedition.) There is no record of York's doing any of this—there is no specific mention of him at all in the voluminous annals of the fur trade. Furthermore, certain of Leonard's details aptly describe two men of African-American descent who did in fact live among the Crows: Edward Rose and James Beckwourth.

Rose, of course, had joined Lisa's party in 1807, traveling up the Missouri that year with six members of the corps, a fact that could have easily been transformed into "with Lewis and Clark"—either in Rose's telling or someone else's retelling. As for the other details, they fit Rose well: he had lived among the Crows for several years (although not consecutively from 1820–32); he was fluent in the Crow tongue; he was a Crow chief; and he was a fearless fighter who had sometimes incited the Crows to join him in battle by insulting them. Similarly, James Beckwourth—later a friend of Jean-Baptiste Charbonneau's—was of mixed blood (his mother was all or part African-American) and he lived and fought among the Crows for several years, including the 1832–34 period mentioned by Leonard.

According to Leonard, the old African-American said that "in a few years" after the Lewis and Clark Expedition, he "returned again with a Mr. Mackinney, a trader on the Missouri river." The publisher of Leonard's book clarifies that "Mackinney" should have been printed as "Mackenzie."[18] Although Beckwourth worked with trader Kenneth McKenzie in the 1820s, he did not meet him a "few" years after the Lewis and Clark Expedition—and he did not travel up the Missouri with him. For Edward Rose, however, the statement that he returned in a few years with a Mr. McKenzie is precisely true. In 1811, four years after first coming up the Missouri with Lisa's party, Rose again traveled up the river with a trading party. This time it was the overland Astorians, under the command of Wilson Price Hunt and Donald McKenzie. Not coincidentally, Hunt and McKenzie parted company with Rose when he joined his old friends the Crows.

Rose was in his fifties by 1832—old enough to be considered "an old man"—he had been with Lewis and Clark's men, and he was well-known for leading the Crows in battle. Leonard's description seems to fit him better than it does Beckwourth, who was probably born in the late 1790s and had no connection with Manuel Lisa's trapping ventures.

Indeed, during the winter of 1832–33, Rose was again—or still—in the area, trapping the Yellowstone River with the venerable Hugh Glass. These two former companions of Charbonneau were with another trapper as they made their way through what is now south-central Montana, territory they knew well. Then, as they crossed the frozen Yellowstone just a few miles below the mouth of the Bighorn River, a band of Arikara ambushed them.

The next summer, William Clark received a letter telling what happened next. "During the last winter," wrote Indian agent John F. A. Sanford, "a war party belonging to that [Arikara] nation came on the Yellowstone below the Big Horn where they fell in with three men belonging to A. [American] Fur Co. who they treacherously killed. . . . They scalped them and left part of the scalps of each tied to poles on the grounds of the murder. A large party of Crows went in pursuit of them the same evening or next day but could not overtake them. The names of the men killed are Rose, Menard & Glass."[19] So it was that Rose, "the celebrated outlaw," and Glass, known for "honor, integrity and fidelity," were forever united in death.

All this bears directly on the identity of the black Crow chief described by Leonard. Since Leonard reports seeing the man late in 1834, Edward Rose is ruled out because he and Glass were killed during the winter of 1832–33. Moreover, Leonard's reckoning of time seems reliable because he kept a journal during his travels and published his account in 1839. In addition, he reports seeing the old man after his journey to California with Joseph Walker, which definitely took place in 1833–34.

But rather than pointing to York, the evidence points to Beckwourth. The telling detail is this: in his autobiography, *The Life and Adventures of James P. Beckwourth*, Beckwourth takes credit for deeds actually accomplished by Rose. Beckwourth had plenty to brag about—for he had indeed lived and fought among the Crows and taken Indian wives—and when he spun tales combining his feats with those of Rose, he was entirely convincing (so much so that it is still not known whether certain events involved Rose or Beckwourth). In addition, by 1834, Beckwourth knew Rose could not contradict him because he himself had helped identify the bodies of Rose and Glass a year and a half earlier. So it does not seem at all surprising that Beckwourth may have told Leonard he had been with Lewis and Clark—or that Leonard saw "the Negro man" lead the Crows in battle. James Beckwourth had assumed an identity that was part himself, part Edward Rose, and part frontier exaggeration. This persona fits into Leonard's narrative quite nicely. As for Leonard's references to "an old man," Beckwourth had lived a hard life that could have made him look older than a man in his late thirties—with his detailed stories of the old days making him seem that much older. The man that Zenas

Leonard saw living so comfortably among the Crows, speaking their language, and leading them in battle was not York but almost certainly James Beckwourth.[20]

So York had not gone west a second time, to live out his days as a respected Crow chief. Rather, in an ending that symbolizes the tragedy of slavery itself, he had lost the companionship of William Clark, something he sincerely desired despite the hardships involved; he had lost the only home he had ever known (in Louisville); and he had lost his wife. Around 1822, somewhere in Tennessee, the same state where Meriwether Lewis had died alone, York apparently fell ill with chills, nausea, and diarrhea.[21] Did someone offer him shelter—or at least a dry stable where he could lie down? We don't know. We don't know if anyone was even with him when he died. We just know that cholera would have caused him to suffer from violent vomiting and excruciating muscular cramps, before it finally brought him his death.

CHAPTER FIFTEEN

"Men on Lewis & Clark's Trip"
William Clark's Accounting of Expedition Members

Throughout the 1820s, William Clark was immersed in Indian affairs, directing the work of several Indian agents and meeting with representatives of many different nations when they came to St. Louis. Sometime between 1825 and 1828, possibly to break the monotony of his never-ending government paperwork, Clark penned a historic document. Writing in a rather casual manner on the front cover of his cash book, Clark recalled the individuals who had accompanied him and Meriwether Lewis on their journey west:

Men on Lewis & Clarks Trip

Capt. Lewis   Dead
Odoway   Dead
N. Pryor   at Fort Smith
Rd. Windser   on Sangamah Ills.
G. Shannon   Lexington Ky.
R. Fields   near Louisville
Wm. Bratten   near Greenville Ohio
F. Labieche   St. Louis
R. Frazier   on Gasconade
Ch. Floyd   Dead
P. Gass   Dead
J. Collins   do.
J. Colter   do.
P. Cruzate   Killed
J. Fields   do.

Alr. Willard   Mo.
Geo. Drulard   Killed
Tous. Charbono   Mand[ans]
Se car ja we au   Dead
Tousant Charbon[o] in Werten-
    burgh, Gy. [Germany]

S. Goodrich   dead
G. Gibson   dead
T. P. Howard
H. Hall
H. McNeal   dead
J. Shields   do.
J. Potts   Killed
J. B. Le Page   dead
J. Thomson   Killed
Wm. Warner   Vir.
P. Wiser   Killed
[J.] Whitehouse
[R.] Warpenton
[J.] Newman[1]

Clark thus provided a wealth of information about the members of the Corps of Discovery—although he also left a number of unanswered questions. The list implies three basic categories: Clark seems to have listed a location if he knew the person was still alive; he said "killed" or "dead" if he knew the person had died ("do." stands for "ditto"); and he simply listed the person's name if he had no information. (Therefore, I do not believe one can conclude that a person who is listed with no other information—such as Hugh Hall or Joseph Whitehouse—was necessarily still alive when Clark made the list—he simply did not know whether they were alive or not.) York is conspicuously absent from the list, another symbol of Clark's attitude toward the slave who had served him faithfully on the expedition.[2]

A mysterious trapping expedition to the northwest bears directly on the fate of two members of the corps. In August 1807, not quite one year after the corps returned to St. Louis, the famed Canadian adventurer David Thompson was exploring present-day British Columbia, Canada, when two Kootenai Indians informed him that "about 3 weeks ago the Americans to the number of 42 arrived to settle a military Post, at the confluences of the two most southern considerable Branches of the Columbia that they were preparing to make a small advance Post lower down on the River. 2 of those who were with Capt. Lewis were also with them of whom the poor Kootanaes related several dreadful stories."[3]

The forty-two white Americans (who had settled in what is now northwestern Montana, south of Flathead Lake) were apparently John McClellan and his men, who were attempting to gain a commercial foothold on the upper Missouri at the request of James Wilkinson. As Lewis and Clark were descending the Missouri in September 1806, they had "met a Captain Mc-Clellin late a Capt. of Artily of the U States Army assending in a large boat."[4] (John McClellan should not be confused with Robert McClellan, no relation, another trader met by Lewis and Clark as they were descending the Missouri.) McClellan likely spent the winter at Loisel's Fort (forty miles southeast of present-day Pierre, South Dakota), going on to the western Montana country in the spring and summer of 1807. Corps members could have joined McClellan only by heading up the Missouri immediately after their return to St. Louis. (After Colter left the group, it stayed intact all the way to St. Louis.) Traveling light in a canoe, they conceivably could have reached Loisel's Fort by the time winter set in.

If there were two Lewis and Clark veterans with McClellan, they were most likely Pierre Cruzatte, whom Clark listed as "killed," and John Collins, the only two men apparently unaccounted for in the next few years. Half French and half Omaha Indian, Cruzatte, a valuable boatman, had served the expedition well with occasional interpreting and regular fiddling. "In the evening Cruzatte gave us some music on the violin," reads a typical entry by Lewis, "and the men passed the evening in dancing singing &c and were extreemly cheerfull."[5]

But Cruzatte had ended the expedition on a sorry note when he accidentally wounded Meriwether Lewis. This in itself may have prompted him to seek anonymity by going west again, but he also had an unpaid debt hanging over his head. He owed a man by the name of Gregorie Sarpy three hundred dollars, and Sarpy filed suit within weeks of Cruzatte's return. But by 14 October 1806, when the court of common pleas ordered the sheriff of the district of St. Louis "to take Pierre Croussatte . . . and him safely keep," Cruzatte was likely already on his way up the river. Another summons was issued in March of 1807, and then another the same month, indicating that Cruzatte was nowhere to be found. In June, Sarpy was awarded $3.88 for court costs, but Cruzatte was still missing.[6] Then Cruzatte disappears from the public record—Sarpy had given up.

Some historians have suggested that either Joseph Field or John B. Thompson was the second corps veteran accompanying McClellan to the upper Missouri. Both of them, however, were apparently in St. Louis in the spring of 1807, because they signed a petition to Congress there sometime after 2 March.[7] If they were in St. Louis then, neither could have been in what is now northwestern Montana by July. In addition, Field was killed sometime after 26 June, and his parents got word of his death by 20 October, not likely if he had been with McClellan.

John Collins is a more likely candidate. Like Cruzatte, he had skills that would have been valuable to McClellan—in his case hunting and scouting. And, like Cruzatte, he disappears from the public record immediately after the return to St. Louis. (Unlike Cruzatte, however, Collins did not disappear from the record permanently.)

Bits and pieces of evidence indicate that McClellan and his men stayed in the Flathead Lake region, with their number steadily decreasing because of Indian attacks. (It is not clear why they did not attempt to return to St. Louis during this time.) By the fall of 1810 (just a few months after Drouillard had been killed on the Jefferson River), only twelve of the original forty-two men were still alive. Those twelve were attacked by Blackfoot Indians somewhere between Great Falls and Three Forks, and McClellan and eight others were killed. If John Collins did belong to the McClellan group, then he was one of the three survivors of this attack, because he was still alive in 1822 or 1823, when he went up the Missouri one last time, with William Henry Ashley. It could have been Collins who made it back to St. Louis at some point and informed William Clark of Cruzatte's death.[8]

Clark also listed John B. Thompson and Peter M. Weiser as killed. Both were possibly killed by Indians, but no document to that effect has ever been found. It was not uncommon for the death of a fur trader to go forgotten or unrecorded. When the veteran trader (and the man who succeeded William Clark as superintendent of Indian affairs) Joshua Pilcher attempted to compile a list of men who had been killed between 1815 and 1831, he added: "I doubt not that this exhibit falls far short of the actual number killed during the time alluded to. It is the result of a few hours' reflection, and I am well satisfied that many have escaped my memory, murders and robberies being occurrences so common on the country in question as to leave but little impression on the mind of those who are not immediately interested." (Pilcher's list of 111 men killed included 45 whose names were not known.)[9]

John B. Thompson had enlisted in the army in 1799 for a five-year term. He listed his occupation as a laborer and his residence as Northhampton (with no state mentioned). He must not have been much of a cook, for he was one of three men assigned that duty but the only one relieved. He was said to have been a surveyor at Vincennes, Indiana Territory, before the expedition, so it is possible he helped Lewis with navigation. Otherwise, Thompson seems to have performed his duties without drawing unusual praise or criticism. After the expedition, John B. Thompson was one of those who signed the petition to Congress in St. Louis in the spring of 1807. A John Thompson received a land bounty for serving in the Missouri militia in the War of

1812. The next record we have concerning him is from the summer of 1815, when a St. Louis newspaper notified anyone owing or having demands of the estate of John B. Thompson, deceased, to present their accounts to Peggy Thompson, apparently his widow. William Clark said that Thompson was "killed," but nothing else is known.[10]

More is known of Peter Weiser. He had been with Lisa in 1807, had helped build Fort Raymond, and had gone west, most likely by himself, to Three Forks, before ascending the Madison River and crossing the Continental Divide into present-day Idaho. Here he spent the winter alone. Born to a prominent Pennsylvania family, Weiser had no doubt known the comforts of civilization, the joys of family life. Now he may have lived day after day without seeing a single soul, lying alone in his crude shelter as darkness fell and the cold night came on, every sound of the wild magnified in his ears.[11]

Weiser had possibly followed the Snake River all the way to present-day western Idaho. When Clark drew up a map of this area—which was not explored by Lewis and Clark—he named a tributary of the Snake "Weiser's River," indicating that Weiser may have explored the area and reported back to him. When a town was established at the confluence of the Snake and Weiser Rivers, it was also named Weiser.

Weiser likely remained in the Montana country from 1807 to 1810. He was with Menard at Three Forks when Drouillard's remains were found. In the summer of 1810, he apparently accompanied Menard back to St. Louis, for in November of that year he filed suit against the estate of John Potts for $499.50, which Potts had owed him when he was killed.[12]

In his years of toil and risk in the fur trade, Weiser had apparently returned with little, if anything. Whether he received anything from Potts's estate is not known, but by the spring of 1812, Weiser was bankrupt. He ran an ad in the *Louisiana Gazette*. "My creditors are hereby notified," it read, "that . . . I shall apply to the hon Bernard Pratte . . . to be permitted to take the benefit of the several laws of this territory, concerning insolvent debtors. Peter Wiser. April 19th, 1812."[13]

The last known record for Peter Weiser is his War of 1812 service in the Mounted Militia of Missouri under Captain Charles Lucas. He was paid $7.81 per day for thirty days of service in the spring of 1813. Then, not surprisingly, he apparently headed west again. There was still a chance of making it big in the fur trade. There was still a chance of recapturing the unique freedom and satisfaction experienced on the expedition. But the record of him has been lost. We know only that he was killed sometime during the next fifteen years, possibly becoming one of those on Pilcher's list identified by the simple notation, "name not known."

When he made his list, William Clark was apparently unaware that Thomas P. Howard and Reubin Field had both died. Born in Massachusetts, Howard was twenty-two when he joined the army in 1801. He had blue eyes and fair hair. Early in the expedition, Clark made the curious comment that Howard never drank water. Later, at Fort Mandan, in February 1805, Howard returned to the fort after dark and climbed over the wall rather than asking the guard to open the gate. An Indian followed Howard's "pernicious example" and climbed over the wall himself, much to Lewis's dismay. Lewis gave the Indian a small piece of tobacco and warned him never to scale the wall again. He then ordered a court-martial for Howard, writing that "this man is an old soldier which still hightens this offince." The court-martial—which was the last one of the expedition—found Howard guilty and sentenced him to fifty lashes. Luckily for Howard, the punishment was suspended.[14]

In 1808, a Private Thomas Howard served as a boatman under Captain H. Stark and was stationed for a time at Fort Adams (near present-day Memphis, Tennessee). This may have been the Howard of the expedition. About this same time, the expedition Howard married a French woman named Genevieve Roy. They had two sons—Joseph and Louis. The boys were young when their father died, probably early in 1814. He was about thirty-five, and though he died in St. Louis, Clark was unaware of it. The death received no notice in the newspapers, and Clark was governor of the territory and deeply involved in the War of 1812. It is not surprising that Howard's death went unnoticed by him.

Although Thomas Howard's property was valued at only $293.00, Genevieve was entangled in legal proceedings over the estate for the next decade, always signing her name with an X. In 1826 the sheriff of St. Louis County was instructed to "bring her forthwith before the judge of our Probate Court" to answer "touching a certain contempt" for not settling the accounts of her late husband's estate.[15]

One year later, probably at around twenty years old, Thomas's son Joseph boarded a keelboat and headed up the Missouri, on a trapping expedition to the westward with William Ashley. He remained on the upper Missouri for much of the next twenty years.

The quiet Kentucky farming life lived by Reubin Field in the fifteen years after the expedition represented a stark contrast to the deadly encounter that he, his brother Joseph, George Drouillard, and Captain Lewis had had with the Blackfeet in Montana. Convinced Indians were chasing them, they had ridden long and hard for the Missouri River, riding all day and well into the night, passing immense herds of buffalo in the darkness. To a man, they agreed they would "sell their lives dearly" if the Blackfeet caught them.

Expert woodsmen, Reubin and Joseph Field had been the best hunters in the group—after Drouillard, that is. So it was no coincidence that they found themselves "engaged in all the most dangerous and difficult scenes of the voyage." Like Drouillard, they had shone under pressure, prompting Lewis to bestow his highest compliment: "they uniformly acquited themselves with much honor."[16]

Reubin Field's three Montana companions had all died violent deaths within a few years of the expedition—his brother Joseph in 1807, Lewis in 1809, and Drouillard in 1810. Reubin himself had hoped for a commission in the army—and Clark had recommended him for a lieutenancy in 1807. But no offer came.

In 1808 Reubin married Mary Myrtle. They are listed in the 1820 census for Jefferson County, Kentucky—they were both between twenty-six and forty-five years of age. No children are listed in the census. Reubin and Mary held four slaves: a female between fourteen and twenty-five, and three boys under fourteen years of age.[17]

Reubin may have been sick when he made out his will in April 1822. He left everything to his wife, Mary, while at the same time dealing with a worry that had been nagging at him for some time: "To wife Mary Field, forever, entire estate; should their marriage performed in Indiana in 1808 by one they thought was a minister of the Gospel named Smith, but later learned may not have been, be considered illegal, then he bequeathed to her as Mary Myrtle, her former name, said estate forever."[18]

In less than a year, Reubin Field was gone. He had joined his three friends Joseph, George, and Meriwether in death. He had also joined them in another way: none of the four men who fled the Blackfeet had left descendants.

Early in the expedition, Privates Joseph Whitehouse and Robert Frazer had experienced discipline problems that foreshadowed trouble after the journey. Whitehouse had fought with "F" (one of the Field brothers, Frazer, or Floyd), and Frazer had done "bad," committing an unspecified offense. Still, they both remained with the corps and changed their ways. Whitehouse was the camp tailor, and Frazer was a frequent member of dangerous missions. "The men at Camp has employed themselves this day in dressing Skins, to make cloathing for themselves," Whitehouse wrote at Three Forks. "I am employed makeing the chief part of the cloathing for the party."[19]

At Fort Mandan, Frazer was one of four men "rushed on by 106 Sioux who robbed them of 2 of their horses." But Frazer and his companions (Drou- illard, Goodrich, and Newman) had stood their ground, even demanding that the Indians return a tomahawk.[20] Whitehouse and Frazer also both kept jour- nals, although Frazer's was later lost.

After the expedition, Whitehouse and Frazer both reverted to old habits, frequently running afoul of the law. For Whitehouse, the problem was debt. A few days after the corps had arrived in St. Louis, Whitehouse sold the rights to his land warrant to George Drouillard for $280. A month later he signed a contract with Manuel Lisa, apparently receiving money or goods from Lisa that he was unable to repay. In November 1807 (while Lisa himself was at Fort Raymond with Colter, Drouillard, and others), Lisa's attorney Edward Hemp- stead filed a suit against Whitehouse for an unpaid debt of $150.25.[21]

Over the next few months Whitehouse was summoned or arrested sev- eral times for bad debts. "We command you," read a typical order to the sheriff, "to take the said Joseph Whitehouse if he be found within your baili- wick, and him safely keep, so that you have his body before the same judges on the said day of March [1807] to satisfy the said Manuel [Lisa] of the afore- said costs." A similar order was issued for $52.79 that Whitehouse owed Peter Smith.[22] Frazer's offenses, on the other hand, tended to be violent. An 1808 court document stated that Frazer assaulted Sheriff Jeremiah Conner "with fists, feet, and sticks, did beat, and illy treat, to the great damage of the said Jeremiah, to the evil example of all others." A year later he was accused of attacking an Indian on the streets of St. Louis and striking him several times, without any provocation. But the most serious charge came in 1812: "Robert Frazier is charged with murder."[23] No further record of the case has been found, but we do know that within two years (if not sooner) Frazer was a free man.

In December 1807, in the midst of his financial woes, Whitehouse re- enlisted in the army, apparently serving at Fort Osage (in present-day west- ern Missouri) until 1812, when he reenlisted again. He fought in battles in the Niagara Falls area in 1814. But trouble was still dogging him. In August 1813 his rank was reduced from corporal to private. He served in the Corps of Ar- tillery in 1816 and again reenlisted, but the final entry in his up-and-down military record shows that Whitehouse deserted on 1 February 1817.[24]

Further contemporary record of Whitehouse remains to be found. How- ever, Whitehouse family records (the name was later changed to White) indi- cate that Joseph married a woman named Mary and had a son named Al- fred Eldoris. In addition, in 1903, Lewis and Clark scholar Reuben Gold Thwaites wrote: "Whitehouse upon his death gave the manuscript [of his ex- pedition journal] to Canon de Vivaldi, an Italian priest; I think it was about

1860, although my information on this point is still a little foggy."[25] If Thwaites was correct, then Whitehouse was still alive in the 1850s.

So, despite his personal troubles, Whitehouse left a journal, a hefty record that is longer than those of Ordway or Gass (and, of course, Floyd). It is also the only journal contributed by a private. Frazer, by fascinating contrast, had lost his journal but turned his life around. In 1814, just two years after being charged with murder, he ran a notice in the *Missouri Gazette* that a black and white spotted cow had been found on his plantation. Two years after that he ran another ad: "Wanted. A Journeyman cabinet-maker in Florissant, by the subscriber, much indulgence will be given, &c. by Robt. Frazer, March 28 [1816]."[26]

His effort to make an honest living continued. By 1821, Frazer had taught himself to repair watches, and he announced that he would be opening a clock- and watch-making business. He typically charged about $2.50 to repair a watch. He also married and had children and settled in Franklin County, Missouri. (Clark had correctly noted his location—he was living near the Gasconade River.) He was about sixty-two when he died in late 1836 or early 1837. The inventory of his estate included livestock, a long list of tools, twelve books, and a box of newspapers. But what became of his expedition journal is a complete mystery. In October 1806 he had been the first member of the corps to announce plans to publish his journal. John R. McBride, who knew him in Franklin County during the 1820s and '30s, apparently read the journal, for he said that Frazer's record "was in many respects more interesting than that of his commanders." But Frazer's journal has vanished.[27]

When the corps met the Salish Indians (also called the Flatheads) in the western Montana country in September 1805, François Labiche (who had no formal education) played a key role in the complicated translation chain that was necessary to communicate with the Indians: the captains spoke to Labiche in English; he translated this into French for Charbonneau; Charbonneau repeated the message in Hidatsa to Sacagawea; she spoke in Shoshone to a Salish boy; and the boy rendered the message in Salishan to his people. Then the process was reversed. After the journey, Lewis recommended a bonus for Labiche because of his "very essential services as a French and English interpreter."

Labiche, who was reportedly half French and half Omaha, was also an expert boatman and hunter. Not surprisingly, he found work in the fur trade after the expedition. As late as 1827 he was hiring out his services as a "boatman, voyageur, and winterer" to the American Fur Company.[28] His home base was St. Louis (correctly noted by Clark), where he owned property and was listed in the 1821 city directory as a boatman. He married Genevieve Flore, and they had seven children. Fur-trading records show that he was still alive in the mid-1830s, when he was about sixty years old. He may have died shortly after that because he is not listed in the 1840 Missouri census.

William Clark had also correctly noted that William Werner was in Virginia. In fact, Werner (who generally spelled his name Warner) may have lived the most stable life of any member of the corps. He married around 1807 and returned to his home state of Virginia. For the next thirty years he farmed in Montgomery County, Virginia, possibly living in the same house. He and his wife (whose name is not known) had several children, including a son named William Jr. On 20 February 1826, William guaranteed surety for William Jr.'s marriage to Nancy Emmons.[29]

Werner was a good enough cook during the expedition that he kept the job permanently. In the spring of 1807, Lewis, who was in Washington at the time, advanced Werner $30.75 and lent him a horse. Perhaps Werner was already living in Montgomery County. He must have settled this debt satisfactorily because Lewis lent him another forty dollars in November of that year.[30]

How did Clark know that Werner was in Virginia in 1825–28? Clark's two wives, Julia Hancock (who died in 1820) and Harriet Kennerly Radford (whom Clark married in 1821) were cousins, and their families lived in Fincastle, Virginia, not far from Montgomery County. Clark made visits to Virginia throughout the decades following the expedition, and he could have heard reports of Werner or could have even seen him from time to time. William Werner possibly died around 1838, because he was known to be alive in December 1837 but is not listed in the 1840 census for Montgomery County.[31]

In June 1805, Richard Windsor and Meriwether Lewis had been hiking along the top of a bluff when Lewis slipped in the mud. He was about to fall "into the river down a craggy pricipice of about ninety feet" when he drove his espontoon (a weapon with a long wooden shaft and pointed steel head) into the side of the cliff and hung on for his life. He had barely reached a spot where he could stand with "tolerable safety" when he heard Windsor cry out: "God god Capt. what shall I do?" Lewis turned to see that Windsor had also slipped and was "lying prostrate on his belley"—clinging to the edge with his left arm and leg while his right arm and leg hung over the precipice. "I discovered his danger and the trepidation which he was in gave me still further concern for I expected every instant to see him loose his strength and slip off," wrote Lewis. Acting perfectly calm, Lewis instructed Windsor to take his knife with his right hand and dig a foothold for his right foot. Windsor followed the instructions to the letter and raised himself to his knees. Next Lewis told him to slip off his moccasins and crawl forward on his hands and knees, holding his knife in one hand and his gun in the other. This Windsor "happily effected and escaped."[32]

Hugh McNeal had also experienced a life-threatening adventure on the expedition. He had been scouting on horseback when he suddenly saw a grizzly bear only ten feet away. The horse reared and threw McNeal, who looked up to see the grizzly rise to its "hinder feet for battle." The quick-thinking McNeal swung his musket, hitting the bear in the head and breaking his rifle off at the breech. The stunned bear fell to the ground and began scratching his head with his foot. McNeal ran to a nearby willow tree and climbed it. For the rest of the day he watched the grizzly waiting and pacing below him. Finally, when it was almost dark, the bear gave up and lumbered off. McNeal caught his horse and made it back to camp. "These bear are a most tremendous animal," wrote Lewis; "it seems that the hand of providence has been most wonderfully in our favor with rispect to them, or some of us would long since have fallen a sacrifice to their farosity."[33]

Whether Windsor or McNeal ever related these harrowing adventures to their grandchildren—or even their children—is unknown. Windsor, of course, hired on with Manuel Lisa in 1807 and apparently spent two or three years on the upper Missouri. Whether he was present when Drouillard was killed is not known. But after living in Missouri for a time, he rejoined the army, serving until 1819. He may have been the Richard Windsor who served with the Rangers, U.S. Volunteers, under Captain James B. Moore, in the War of 1812. Clark said in his 1825–28 list that Windsor was in Illinois, but no record of him there has been found.

McNeal, who was reportedly born in Pennsylvania around 1776, performed his expedition duties well, whether it was carrying a flag, cooking up berries and flour, or skinning a deer, but he also faded into obscurity after the expedition. A Hugh McNeal served in the army until 1811. Whether this was the same man—and what happened to him afterward—is not known. Clark simply said he was dead by 1825–28 (with the clear implication that his death was nonviolent).

Windsor and McNeal each left a memorable tale of adventure—and a host of unanswered questions.[34]

Silas Goodrich and Hugh Hall share Hugh McNeal's distinction of being the most obscure members of the corps. The best information on them comes from the expedition itself. Goodrich was the expert fisherman, at times offering welcome relief from a steady diet of buffalo, elk, and deer. In a typical entry, Clark wrote that Goodrich "caught two verry fat Cat fish." Hall had been born in Pennsylvania around 1772; he was 5 feet 8 3/4 inches tall, with fair hair, a sandy complexion, and gray eyes—and he could not swim. Interestingly, both Goodrich and Hall signed the 1807 petition asking Congress to locate their land warrants close to their homes.

In 1825–28, Clark said Goodrich was dead, meaning that he probably died before the age of fifty. He had reenlisted in the army after the expedition, but nothing else is known. Like George Gibson and Hugh McNeal, Silas Goodrich had been treated with mercury for syphilis during the expedition.[35] Whether mercury poisoning contributed to their deaths is not known. It seems worth noting, however, that all three men died by 1825–28 and all three died nonviolent deaths.

After the expedition, Hugh Hall apparently had some kind of difficulty with his land warrant. Sometime after March of 1807, he was listed among those who supposedly took possession of land in Indiana Territory belonging to the United States. He later assigned his warrant to another party. Hall was in St. Louis as late as 1809, because Meriwether Lewis lent him two dollars on 11 April.[36]

Clark listed Hugh Hall's name without giving any information, probably unaware that Hall had returned to his home state of Pennsylvania. In 1820 he was a farmer living alone in Washington County. He had apparently never married. Then he disappears from the public record, indicating that he died before the 1830 census.[37] On the expedition, and afterward, Hugh Hall was a quiet man, with a history not likely to surprise anyone. But Hall family history reveals a surprise indeed—the unassuming Hugh Hall offers a possible solution to an enduring expedition puzzle.

As Paul Russell Cutright has pointed out, the records indicate that seven of the enlisted men kept journals of the expedition. Although neither of the captains made an official list, the names of five eventually became apparent: Ordway, Floyd, Gass, Whitehouse, and Frazer. "Presumably Nathaniel Pryor, whose journal has yet to come to light, was another," Cutright wrote. "The author of the seventh remains a mystery."[38]

The author of the missing journal may have been Hugh Hall. John F. Hall (born in 1918) is a great-great-grandson of Charles Hall, who was apparently the brother of Hugh Hall. In a letter he wrote to Barbara Nell of the Lewis and Clark Trail Heritage Foundation in 1998, Hall told an amazing story. He said that when he was a young boy, his father took him to visit an elderly woman who was a relative of his, perhaps a great-aunt. "She said that she had a diary which Hugh Hall had kept," wrote Hall, "[and] if she approved of me, she would give it to me. . . . Apparently, I did pass muster because she gave that diary to my father to keep for me. . . . The pages were brown on the edges from age and the covers deteriorating. I can remember looking through it out of curiosity but not reading it, because I knew very little about the expedition or its importance, or for that matter, the importance of that diary." After John F. Hall was stricken with polio, the diary eventually passed to the hands of his widowed mother, who moved to the Los Angeles area. But "her home was burned to the ground in the big Bel-Aire fire and of course, the diary was consumed."[39]

Hugh Hall was apparently literate because he signed the 1807 petition to Congress. The possibility that he kept a journal on the expedition is intriguing, but the current historical record offers no definitive answer to this riddle.

Richard Windsor, Hugh McNeal, Silas Goodrich, Hugh Hall, and their companions voyaged on the great rivers of the nation—the Ohio, the Mississippi, the Missouri, the Snake, the Columbia; they gazed on the unspoiled western wilderness; they acted honorably among the native nations; they hunted buffalo and fled grizzlies, enduring bitter cold and near starvation on Jefferson's errand. For the most part, they were ordinary individuals caught up in an extraordinary event. But their very ordinariness makes them that much more sympathetic—they did their jobs well, with no significant prospect of future reward or fame—and it seems natural to want to know what became of them.

There is hope that future research will shed more and more light on the lives of the "obscure" members of the corps. For this reason, among others, recent scholarship on William Clark is quite encouraging. Although Lewis was clearly the moving force before the expedition, Clark was the one who ensured that the history of the journey was published, the last veteran to see Lewis alive, the one who pestered Congress about George Shannon's pension, the one who became Pomp's guardian. It was Clark who accompanied George Gibson's widow to a probate proceeding and cosigned a note, Clark who drew up the list of men on Lewis and Clark's trip. Buried in the thousands of letters he wrote, we are likely to find nuggets revealing details of what became of Thompson, Cruzatte, Howard, Labiche, Lepage, Hall, and the others.[40]

CHAPTER SIXTEEN

"*Active to the Last*"
The Final Decades of the Corps

The very day that David Crockett arrived in Nashville—16 April 1829—the governor of Tennessee resigned his office and confided to Crockett that he was departing for the Arkansas Territory, to dwell among the Cherokee. He knew the Cherokee people well, for he had lived among them for almost three years after running away from home at the age of fifteen.

A week earlier, the governor's eighteen-year-old bride, Eliza Allen, had left him, a breakup that quickly became public knowledge. Deeply hurt that his wife did not love him, he resigned, convinced it was the only suitable response to the disgrace he had suffered.

The forty-two-year-old Crockett had been on a campaign swing through western Tennessee in an effort to retain his seat in the United States Congress. It would be another six years before he would leave Tennessee and head southwest, to Texas. Crockett, who had reportedly killed 105 bears in six months, was the kind of campaigner who had once memorized an opponent's speech and recited it word for word. The governor—now former governor—was seven years younger than Crockett. Both of them had served under their fellow Tennessean Andrew Jackson in the War of 1812, though Crockett was now a political enemy of the general.

The former governor was an imposing figure, standing well over six feet tall, who had taught himself law, serving first as district attorney in Nashville and then as a two-term congressman. With his booming voice, penetrating eyes, and majestic bearing, he was bound to make his presence known whether in Washington or Arkansas. His name was Sam Houston.

A year and a half later, after making good on his promise to live with the Cherokee, who adopted him as one of their own, Houston wrote a letter to President Jackson, a foe of Henry Clay as well as Davy Crockett. Houston addressed the letter to General Jackson and wrote: "Sir. I have the honor to address you upon the subject of one of your old soldiers at the Battle of New Orleans, I allude to Capt. Nathaniel Pryor, who has for several years past resided in the Osages as a sub-agent by appointment of Gov. Clark, but without any permanent appointment from the Government." Recommending that Jackson appoint Pryor to a permanent post, Houston continued:

He was the first man who volunteered to accompany Lewis and Clark on their tour to the Pacific Ocean. He was then in the Army four or five years, resigned and at the commencement of the last war entered the Army again, and was a Captain in the 44th Regt. under you at New Orleans, and a *braver* man never fought under the wings of your Eagles. He has done more to tame and pacificate the dispositions of the Osages to the whites and surrounding tribes of Indians than all other men, and has done more in promoting the authority of the United States and compelling Osages to comply with the demands from Col. Arbuckle than any person could have supposed.

Capt. Pryor is a man of amiable character and disposition—of fine sense and strict honor—perfectly temperate in his habits,—unremitting in his attention to business. . . . He is poor, having been twice robbed by Indians of furs and merchandise some ten years since.

In another letter written the same day, Houston added: "when I see a *brave, honest, honorable and faithful servant of that country, which I once claimed as my own, in poverty with spirit half broken by neglect, I must be permitted to ask something in his behalf.*"[1]

Houston's pleadings summarize Pryor's career quite succinctly. He was the friend of some native nations but was victimized by others, never getting what was due him.

Pryor had married an Osage woman and lived among the Osage Indians for the entire decade of the 1820s, in a territory that was often violent and lawless. Speaking of Little Rock in the 1820s, Arkansas settler Hiram Whittington wrote: "Vice and immorality went hand in hand through our streets; the Sabbath was not kept; peaceable individuals were prevented from enjoying any rest by the midnight revels of your free-thinkers; virtuous females were insulted with impunity; justice had fled from our courts; every man carried arms, either for murdering his enemy or for his own defence; and murders were of every day occurrence. It was no very agreeable sight to see men in full health shot down in the streets like dogs. The murderer would have a mock trial, be acquitted and turned loose upon society, again to dip his hands in blood."[2]

It was in such an environment that Pryor became embroiled in a conflict between the Osages and the Cherokee. In 1821, at a government post on the Arkansas River, the men were informed that 350 Osage warriors "were on their way to kill and plunder the Cherrokees." A Captain Pryor was said to be urging the Osages to war and was also reportedly planning to lead them in destroying the post.[3]

In the coming days, a group of Osages did kill four Delaware Indians. But no attack was launched on the post, and no evidence was offered that Nathaniel Pryor had instigated anything. (Nor was it consistent with Pryor's past history to have encouraged robbery and plunder.) Still, reports of Pryor's purported involvement made their way to Secretary of War John C. Calhoun and possibly marred his reputation. As for his part, Pryor later said that in 1820 he had assisted a group of Osages in escaping from hostile Cherokee, thereby angering the Cherokee, who subsequently stole "about 150 weight of Beaver fur" from Pryor's post. Two years after that, some Cherokee stole Pryor's "large bright bay horse, with a star on his forehead, about 15 hands high," which he never recovered.[4]

The bad blood between Pryor and the Cherokee probably accounted for the rumors that were floated about him. But all that must have faded by the time Sam Houston arrived in the territory in 1829. Houston was an ally and confidant of the Cherokee—marrying a Cherokee and dressing like one (Calhoun had once criticized him for wearing full Cherokee dress when he represented them in Washington)—and would have known of any mistreatment by Pryor. Furthermore, Houston's letters must have carried weight, for less than three months after he wrote them Pryor received a permanent appointment as subagent for the Osage Indians. But Nathaniel Pryor's run of bad luck continued right to the end: he was dead one month later, dying in 1831 at about age fifty-nine, apparently from natural causes.[5]

George Shannon had married Ruth Price in Lexington on 18 September 1813. Over the next twelve years they had seven children. Although Clark suggested that he and Shannon start a trading business together, Shannon chose to practice law. He became friends with several of Lexington's leading citizens and was invited to speak at a remembrance of George Washington's birthday in 1814. The *Kentucky Gazette* wrote that the crowd was "addressed by

George Shannon in an eloquent and pertinent speech, commemorative of the virtues of Washington."

Shannon's most well known Lexington acquaintance, of course, was the flamboyant and influential Henry Clay, the "Western Star," who had been elected speaker of the U.S. House of Representatives in 1812. Clay pushed a special act through Congress in 1817 that increased Shannon's disability pension (which had finally been approved in 1814) from eight dollars a month to twelve dollars. Shannon also received a new land warrant with Clay's help, later selling the warrant to Clay himself. Shannon signed power of attorney over to Clay to enable him to accept Shannon's pension payments.[6]

Not surprisingly, Shannon ran for public office; he was elected to the Kentucky House in 1820, 1821, and 1822. Like most on the frontier, Shannon lived a precarious economic life, often owing money to or being owed by scores of individuals. He did well in 1822 and had $2,480 in assets besides his home and livestock. (He was also a slaveholder and owned six slaves.) But his finances steadily declined over the next few years.

Interestingly, four of Shannon's brothers also left their mark on U.S. history: Thomas Shannon was elected to the U.S. Congress; David served as a secretary to Andrew Jackson; James became a prominent Kentucky lawyer; and Wilson served as governor of both Ohio and the Kansas Territory.

In the mid-1820s, Shannon was appointed a circuit court judge. When he was selected to try Governor Joseph Desha's son for murder, he may well have foreseen the end of his Kentucky career. The governor's son had reportedly robbed and killed a man. Although the jury found the young man guilty and sentenced him to death, the defense argued that the jury had been tampered with and that the guilty verdict was not justified. Apparently agreeing with these arguments, Shannon set the verdict aside and ordered a new trial. The press accused Shannon of favoritism, and he was burned in effigy in Harrison and Bourbon counties. By 1828, Shannon, who had defaulted on the loan for his home, packed up his family and left Kentucky for good.[7]

Coming from the east this time, Shannon returned to St. Charles, Missouri, where the journey west had begun in 1804. Nearby was Fort Bellefontaine, where his amputated leg had been buried. Within a year, his career was again on the upswing: President Andrew Jackson appointed him U.S. district attorney for Missouri. In his most memorable case, however, Shannon argued for the defense.

In June of 1829, near today's Kirksville, in northeastern Missouri, a skirmish broke out between the Iowa chief Big Neck and his followers and a group of white settlers. "I saw an Indian load his gun," wrote one of the whites; "at length I heard a gun and I knew what the result would be, I ordered the man to light and fight." One of the Indians offered quite a different account: "When the party of whites arrived Big Neck stepped from his lodge unarmed . . . his hand extended . . . in token of friendship. While in this act, the Indians were fired upon."[8]

At the battle's conclusion, three whites and three Indians, including a child, were dead. When they were tracked down by a military unit, Big Neck and his companions agreed to travel to Huntsville for a trial. They were imprisoned in a Fayette jail where they were mistreated by white guards. Meanwhile, William Clark ordered a full investigation and urged the War Department to spare the Indians the death penalty if they were found guilty. When Big Neck and four others were brought to trial in March of 1830, George Shannon and two others took up their defense. "It was a period of deep excitement among the people of the upper country and of awful suspense," wrote Clark.[9]

At the trial, Shannon and his associates argued that Big Neck had misunderstood a treaty he signed in 1824. They also pointed out that various witnesses had given contradictory reports about who fired first. Without leaving their seats in the box, the jury delivered the verdict: "After examining all the witnesses and maturely considering the charges . . . , we find [the Indians] not guilty and they are at once discharged."

Though he was a free man, Big Neck went into mourning and blackened his face as a symbol of grief, convinced he had betrayed his people by selling tribal land in the 1824 treaty. "I have insulted the Great Spirit by selling the land and the bones of my fathers," he said; "it is right that I should mourn always." He never removed the black mark.[10]

Shannon's fortunes continued to improve. In September 1831, he headed a group of Jackson supporters proposing a convention to nominate a representative to Congress.[11] Shannon himself was one of those initially nominated, but he stepped aside in favor of William Ashley, who had tried so hard to save John Collins and his comrades that June morning in 1823. (Nor did Shannon run for or win election to the U.S. Senate, as is frequently claimed.)

In April 1833, the *Palmyra Courier* stated that it took "*great pleasure* in announcing George Shannon, Esq, as a candidate for Congress." Though his bid was unsuccessful, Shannon was a respected man, he was still in his forties, and he and his wife and seven children were comfortably settled in St. Charles. The future looked good.

But within months George's wife, Ruth, was sick with typhus. Symptoms typically included headache and skin rash, followed by pain in the joints and a high fever. Although some patients recovered from typhus, Ruth did not, dying on 12 September 1833. She was forty years old, and her three sons and four daughters ranged in age from eight to nineteen.

His wife's death signaled Shannon's decline. The next year his nomination for a second term as U.S. attorney was withdrawn, for unknown reasons. In June of 1835, he borrowed a thousand dollars, so he was apparently struggling again financially. Shannon was also said to be "quite fond of liquor." Rumor had it that he had once shot a ticking clock that was bothering him while he was drinking, although he paid the tavern owner for it the next day.[12]

In August 1836, five months after the Alamo fell, the fifty-one-year-old George Shannon traveled to Palmyra, Missouri, to defend a man accused of murder. He arrived there on 23 August in poor health and requested medical help. "He sustained his illness with a degree of moral courage and composure that has seldom been equaled," reported the *Palmyra Journal,* giving no specifics. "On the morning of Tuesday the 30th [of August], he sunk into the arms of death without the slightest emotion."

Four months later, Shannon's friend at Transylvania, the chronically ill Stephen Austin, only forty-three years old, succumbed to pneumonia in his beloved Texas. Sam Houston, who had routed General Antonio Lopez de Santa Anna at the Battle of San Jacinto in 1836—and who had subsequently defeated Austin to become president of Texas—instructed all government officials to wear black armbands in "respect to his high standing, undeviating moral rectitude, and as a mark of the nation's gratitude for his untiring zeal, and invaluable service."[13]

In 1808, two years removed from the expedition, William Clark married the young woman he had been courting, sixteen-year-old Julia Hancock, in Virginia. Clark returned to St. Louis with his wife, and their home became a social center of the city, especially after Julia's piano was shipped from the east. Clark eventually built a brick home on Main Street, with a large chamber doubling as a ballroom and an Indian museum. The *St. Louis Directory* reported in 1821: "The Council Chamber of Gov. William Clark, where he gives audience to the Chiefs of the various tribes of Indians who visit St. Louis, contains probably the most complete Museum of Indian curiosities, to be met with any where in the United States; and the governor is so polite as to permit its being visited by any person of respectability at any time."[14]

As a captain of the expedition, Clark took his responsibilities seriously, and he understood the importance of documenting the journey thoroughly and sharing the knowledge the corps had gained. When Clark first heard the rumors of Lewis's death in 1809, his first thought was for his friend, and his second thought was for the expedition journals—"what will become of his pap[e]rs?" Luckily, James Neely had sent the expedition journals to Washington. On 26 November, about six weeks after Lewis's death, Thomas Jefferson wrote to President James Madison: "I presume [Lewis's] papers may be opened & distributed . . . the Manuscript voyage &c. to Genl. Clarke, who is interested in it, and is believed to be now on his way to Washington."[15]

Madison apparently followed Jefferson's suggestion, for by 10 January 1810, Clark wrote to his brother Jonathan, "I have received my journals and maps."[16] By April he had turned the journals over to Nicholas Biddle, who proceeded to work with George Shannon on the expedition narrative for close to a year, but the bankruptcy of the publisher and the War of 1812 put publication on hold.

Then, early in 1814, when William Clark was hearing constant negative reports concerning the war, pleasant news came from the east: *The History of the Expedition Under the Command of Captains Lewis and Clark* had finally been published. The magnanimous Nicholas Biddle, who had donated all his time and was mentioned nowhere in the two-volume set—and didn't mind—wrote Clark with an announcement that the books "have been well thought of by the readers." Biddle then spoke of the recent death of his son, and added: "Let me hear from you often. Neither you nor I are great letter writers but I will always be happy to learn that you are well & your affairs prosperous."[17]

Six months later, Clark responded: "I do assure you that I was extreemly concerned for the loss you have met with in your familey, my own feelings enables me to know what those of a fond parent must be towards his child." Clark then discussed several details about the war, showing how preoccupied he was with that subject when he added this note: "I have borrowed a Copy of my Book which has reached this place but have not had time to read it as yet."[18]

As for the public reception, the publication of *The History of the Expedition* caused little stir. The expedition had ended more than seven years earlier; Patrick Gass's journal had been available much of that time; and the war seemed to be on everyone's mind. All these were factors. And William Clark, who had recorded more words on the expedition than anyone else, the man who taken custody of the journals and ensured that the history was published, received no royalties. But he had left future generations a rich treasure.

William Clark lived an extremely active public life, including a term as governor, and he and Julia had four sons and one daughter, naming their first child Meriwether Lewis Clark. In a letter to her brother, in 1814, Julia reported that she had given birth to a "fine little daughter" (Mary Margaret Clark) on New Year's Day; "she is really beautiful I wish you could see her."

Julia also wrote, "I am affraid we shall have some trouble in the spring with the indians."[19]

Three years earlier, when the Sauk and Fox leader Black Hawk threatened the area, Clark had sent Julia and the couple's two sons to Virginia, where they stayed at least two years. But Julia's health concerned him more than a possible Indian attack. His fears were confirmed when she was diagnosed with cancer in 1816. Three years later, William took her back to her family in Virginia. A visit to a warm springs did not help; nor did inhaling tar fumes. Clark had to return to Missouri and was tending to his duties in St. Louis in the summer of 1820 when he received word that twenty-eight-year-old Julia had died.[20]

Death was a constant in Clark's life. His best friend, Meriwether Lewis, had died in 1809, his brother Jonathan in 1811, his brother George Rogers in 1818. Even more trying must have been the death of his daughter, Mary Margaret, the beautiful baby that Julia had written her brother about. Little Mary was seven years old when she died on 15 October 1821. He was comforted by Harriet Kennerly Radford, a widow with three children (and a first cousin to Julia). He married her on 28 November 1821, a month and a half after Mary's death.

William and Harriet had two sons together, but the second, Edmund, died on 12 August 1827 at the age of ten months. That same day, Clark noted these details in his government record book: "*Edmond Clark* (my Infant Son) *died* at 8 1/2 A. M. (10 mo. 3 days old)."[21] A son from Clark's first marriage, John Julius, whom Harriet had taken as her own, was thirteen when he died on 5 September 1831. Even then, William Clark was not through grieving. That same year, on Christmas Day, 1831, Harriet died at age forty-three. "My spirits are low and my course indecisive," wrote Clark.[22] He never married again.

When Washington Irving visited Clark in 1832, the captain was sixty-two and had regained his optimism. "Fine nut trees, peach trees, grape vines, catalpas &c. &c. about the house," wrote Irving. "Look out over rich, level plain or prairie—green near at hand—blue line at the horizon. . . . Genl arrives on horseback with dogs—guns. His grandson on a calico poney hallowing & laughing—Genl on horseback—gun on his shoulder—cur—house dog—bullying setter."[23]

But all was not peaceful in 1832. In April, the Sauk warrior Black Hawk and about a thousand followers, including women and children, had crossed the Mississippi River in an attempt to resettle land in Illinois that the Indian nations had ceded to the United States decades earlier. "My reason teaches me that land cannot be sold," said Black Hawk. Clark, who had negotiated treaties relocating Indians to the western side of the Mississippi, reacted with anger, just as he had done when the Arikara attacked Ashley's party nine years earlier. "I hope the Indians will be forced to fight and receive a complete chastisement for their horrid crimes," he wrote to his son Meriwether Lewis Clark, known as Lewis.[24]

The chastisement came from General Henry Atkinson and a large number of troops, including the twenty-three-year-old Lewis Clark and the fifty-three-year-old Alexander Willard, who battled the Sauk and Fox throughout the summer. Then, in August, as Black Hawk and his people attempted to cross back over to the west bank of the Mississippi, near the mouth of the Bad Axe River, they were virtually annihilated as Atkinson's troops and their Sioux allies attacked men, women, and children, killing about three hundred of them.

Such suffering among the native nations was not untypical. And while William Clark's attitude toward them seemed to run the gamut from friendly to vindictive, he lived in a complex time. He was, by and large, a friend of the Indians, achieving a more favorable record than the great majority of his contemporaries. More than once he was accused of being *too* friendly to the Indians. He summarized his feelings on American Indians when he wrote to Thomas Jefferson in 1826: "It would afford me pleasure to be enabled to meliorate the condition of those unfortunate people placed under my charge, knowing as I do their wretchedness, and their rapid decline. It is to be lamented that this deplorable Situation of the Indians do not Receive more of the humain feelings of this Nation." Such concerns were shown to be well founded in 1833 when Secretary of War William Cass failed to provide smallpox vaccinations for part of the Arikara and all of the Mandan nations, even though Congress had instructed him to do so. When a smallpox epidemic broke out in 1837, the Mandan, who had befriended the corps so warmly that first winter, were virtually wiped out.[25]

William Clark was sixty-eight when he died at the home of his son Lewis on 1 September 1838, thirty-two years after the return of the expedition. "People lined the streets for blocks to watch the cortege led by a military band," wrote Clark's nephew. "Next came the St. Louis Greys in full uniform, followed by the Masonic fraternity, and the hearse drawn by four white horses in black plumes and trappings. . . . Last, before the carriages which held the family and friends, the General's horse was led by his servant, both in black. Clark's pistol, holster, and sword were laid on the saddle and his spurred boots were reversed in the stirrups. Following the carriages were many men on horseback; and, as we came within a half-mile or so of the burying ground, minute guns were fired from a cannon. So this great and good man, whose whole life had been given in selfless service to his country, was laid to rest."[26]

In 1839, one year after Clark's death, Indian agent Joshua Pilcher, who had been part of Leavenworth's Missouri Legion with Charbonneau, wrote: "On the 21st inst. Toussaint Charbonneau . . . arrived here from the Mandan villages, a distance of 1600 miles, and came into the office, tottering under the infirmities of 80 winters, without a dollar to support him, to ask what appeared to me to be nothing more than just, and I accordingly have paid his salary as Interpreter for the Mandan sub-agency, for the 1st & 2nd quarters of this year, with the understanding that his services are no longer required. This man has been a faithful servant of the Government—though in a humble capacity. . . . For the last fifteen years, he has been employed as the Government interpreter at the Mandans."[27] So Charbonneau survived Clark, who was three years his junior; it is not known when they last saw each other.

Although Pilcher and several others believed Charbonneau to be around eighty in the late 1830s, he actually turned seventy in 1837. During this time, he was frequently mentioned in the journals and letters of fellow trappers, just as he had been in the two decades following the expedition.

On 25 December 1834, F. A. Chardon, a trader in charge of Fort Clark (a post near the Mandan villages in present-day North Dakota), described a Christmas Eve feast held the previous evening: "We partook of a fine supper Prepared by Old Charbonneau, consisting of Meat pies, bread, fricassied pheasants Boiled tongues, roast beef—and Coffee."[28]

Two years after that, in 1836, when he was sixty-nine, the savvy Charbonneau showed himself to be alert and light on his feet: "One of the Young Sioux deliberately fired at a Gros Ventre boy," wrote trader David Mitchell. "Old Charbono, made a narrow escape two balls having passed through his hat."[29]

Charbonneau was still working on the upper Missouri when a smallpox epidemic struck the entire region in 1837. In present-day South Dakota, trader Jacob Halsey wrote: "Among the Indians it is raging with the greatest destruction imaginable at least 10 out of 12 die with it. I do not know how many Assiniboins have already died as they have long since given up counting but I presume at least 800 and of the Blackfeet at least 700."[30]

Conditions were just as bad at Fort Clark. "Two young Mandans shot themselves this Morning," Chardon wrote on 22 August 1837. "News from the Little Village, that the disease is getting worse and worse every day. . . . A

Ree that has the small pox, and thinking that he was going to die, approached near his wife, a young woman of 19—and struck her in the head with his tommahawk, with the intent to Kill her, that she might go with him in the Other World—she is badly wounded, a few Minutes after he cut his throat."[31]

On 31 August, Chardon added, "the Number of Deaths up to the Present is very near five hundred—The Mandan are all cut off, except 23 young and Old Men." A week after that, Charbonneau's Indian wife died, but the old trader was spared. A year later he took another wife, a fourteen-year-old Assiniboin girl he had apparently purchased from an enemy tribe, a situation highly reminiscent of his "marriage" to Sacagawea more than three decades earlier.[32]

We don't know when or where old Charbonneau died, but a legal document executed in 1843 named J. B. Charbonneau to receive $320 "from the estate of his deceased Father."[33] Charbonneau's friends the Mandan had virtually disappeared because of the smallpox epidemic—Charbonneau had to flee because, as a white man, he was blamed for the disease. Perhaps the old interpreter found refuge with another native nation and was able to die in the wilderness, his only true home.

A blacksmith who assisted John Shields during the journey, Private Alexander Willard married Eleanor McDonald six months after the return to St. Louis and settled in present-day Missouri. The couple had seven boys and five girls. Willard, who early in the expedition had been sentenced to one hundred lashes for falling asleep while on guard duty, kept in contact with Lewis and Clark and was advanced sixty-one dollars for a government blacksmithing assignment in 1808. A year later, Clark listed Willard as a blacksmith for the Shawnee and Delaware Indians. As noted, Willard served as a courier for Clark during the War of 1812 and barely escaped an Indian attack.

From the end of the expedition to the mid-1820s, Alexander Willard showed up frequently in Missouri records. In 1817 he announced that he had found a stolen horse. He paid taxes in St. Louis County in 1819 and 1823. He and Eleanor and their children were living in Franklin County, Missouri Territory, in 1820. They inherited one slave from Eleanor's father and sold another at auction in 1827. Shortly after that, Alexander and Eleanor moved north, to present-day Wisconsin, where they lived for approximately twenty-five years.

On 6 June 1836 (three months before George Shannon's death), someone ran to the door of Alexander and Eleanor Willard with tragic news: their son George Clark Willard had been shot and killed. Alexander, a veteran of the expedition and two wars and now in his fifties, had hoped to live out his life with Eleanor in relative peace, but it wasn't to be.

George Clark Willard, named after William Clark and about twenty-six at the time of his death, had become involved in a dispute between a neighboring woman and her husband, Lyndon McUmber. The couple had asked George to care for Mrs. McUmber's son by a previous marriage because they were, according a local resident, "utterly unable to provide for their family." The young Willard agreed, and the boy had been living with him and his wife, Aurelia, and their two infant sons since the previous fall. Then McUmber arrived at the house, determined to take his stepson again. George Willard was not home, but Aurelia spoke with McUmber while the boy ran and hid in a field. Within minutes George rode up to the house and, seeing McUmber, hurried inside and grabbed his gun. McUmber left, but George and Aurelia saw him walking toward the boy's hiding place. George mounted his horse and followed; McUmber turned, strode toward George, and swung a club, according to an account in the local newspaper, "striking him a tremendous blow on the left arm with the club." Consequently, "his gun was wrested from him by McU. who immediately ran off with it."

George armed himself with a stick and unwisely pursued McUmber. "Lay down the gun and go away," he demanded. "I won't harm you." McUmber refused. "Stand off, or I will shoot you," he said to George.

Again McUmber fled; again George pursued him. Seconds after the two of them disappeared over a ridge, "the report of the gun was heard, and McU. was seen running from the spot, on foot, where he had so basely fulfilled his impious threats." George was soon found "weltering in his blood" and died within minutes.

The killing had taken place two miles from Alexander and Eleanor Willard's home. Despite their heartbreak, they united with their family to see that justice was done, holding an inquisition in their own home. Alexander even delivered subpoenas to those called to testify, including his son Roland and his daughter-in-law Aurelia. In May of 1837, Lyndon McUmber (who had been recaptured after escaping from jail) was found guilty of manslaughter.[34]

In 1852, sixteen years after this tragedy, with the captains and most of the other expedition members long since gone, seventy-four-year-old Alexander Willard decided to journey west once again. Alexander, Eleanor, and some of their children and their families were heading to California. One pioneer who left Wisconsin the same year as Willard reported buying four good oxen and a wagon, 400 pounds of flour, 250 pounds of ham and side bacon, 200 pounds of corn meal, 100 pounds of hard biscuit, 100 pounds of crushed sugar, 100 pounds of vinegar pickles and sundries, 75 pounds of dried apples, 30 pounds of Rio coffee, rice, and white beans, 20 pounds of salt. When he added arms, ammunition, and clothing, the cost came to $598.50.[35]

The wagon train of forty-nine people (certainly an appropriate number for a group headed to the gold country of California) likely departed Platteville, Wisconsin, in April or May, going southwest and crossing the Mississippi River into Iowa, where they eventually picked up the Mormon trail and later the Oregon Trail. Although Lewis and Clark had followed the Missouri River across what is now North Dakota and Montana, the pioneers of the 1840s and '50s took the more southerly route of John C. Frémont, crossing the present states of Nebraska and Wyoming. As the group averaged about twelve miles a day across Iowa, Willard knew they would intersect the Lewis and Clark trail at only one point: Council Bluffs.

"Capt. Lewis and my Self walked in the Prarie on the top of the Bluff and observed the most butifull prospects imagionable," Clark had written, describing the area around Council Bluffs on 30 July 1804. "This Prarie is Covered with grass about 10 or 12 Inch high . . . under those high Lands next the river is butifull Bottom interspersed with Groves of timber, the River may be Seen for a great Distance both above & below meandering thro."

Forty-eight years later, the bluffs looked much the same. A traveler who saw the area the same summer as Willard noted "the handsomest Bluffs & Valleys I ever saw." He also wrote that the Missouri River, which Willard had likely not seen for a quarter century, was "very wide about 600 yds. & Sawyers coming down in every direction enough to capsize a Scow."[36] Willard himself had lost a rifle at this spot those many years before. Joseph Field had killed a badger nearby, and the group had feasted on turkey and geese as well as venison. They had seen swans swimming in a pond. Sergeant Floyd had been quite sick.

Alexander and Eleanor Willard made it safely to California, where they lived the final years of their fifty-eight-year marriage in tranquillity, with children, grandchildren, and great-grandchildren nearby. When Willard died in March of 1865, he was eighty-six years old.

In 1903, Lewis and Clark researcher Eva Emory Dye contacted Alexander Willard's son Lewis, who was then in his seventies. In response to a questionnaire, Lewis Willard offered several important facts about his father's history. Two of his answers are particularly interesting. In response to the question, "What did he say [about the Lewis and Clark Expedition]?" Willard replied, "He told of their hardships, of their being compelled to eat their dogs. He spoke of 'Loyd' and the negro man 'Yorke.' He did not speak much of Lewis but he was a personal friend of Gov. Clark and lived by him for years after the expedition was over." Alexander Willard's son then offered a tantalizing bit of information, which, like Hugh Hall's family history, provides a possible clue to the mystery of the missing expedition journal—or journals. In response to Dye's query, "Did he keep any journal or record of the journey with Lewis and Clark?" Lewis Willard replied, "Yes. But it was accidently destroyed, much to his regret."[37] No further details are known.

In 1846, six years before an aging Alexander Willard reached Council Bluffs, Brigham Young had led a flock of his beleaguered Latter-day Saints to the same spot. Mormon apostle Wilford Woodruff wrote in his journal: "I could stand and gaze to the east, west, north, and south and behold the Saints pouring out and gathering like clouds from the hills and dales, grove and prairie with their teams, wagons, flocks, and herds by hundreds and thousands as it were until it looked like the movements of a great nation."[38]

Within days, Brother Brigham, as he was known by the Saints, called for several hundred of his men to enlist in General Stephen W. Kearny's Army of the West and join the battle with Mexico. The request (or was it a command?) shocked his followers, who thought they had permanently left the United States and its injustices behind them. Official church minutes recorded the response: "Pres. Young asked who would volunteer to leave their families and go over the mountains; scores voted."[39]

On 16 July, 543 men, 33 women (most of whom served as laundresses), and 51 children headed southwest—on foot—arriving in Santa Fe in October. Colonel Philip St. George Cooke then reluctantly assumed command, writing that the Mormon Battalion was "enlisted too much by families; some were too old,—some feeble, some too young; it was embarrassed by many women; it was undisciplined; it was much worn by travelling on foot, and marching from Nauvoo, Illinois."[40]

Five days after leaving Santa Fe, Cooke met a guide hired by General Kearny to lead the group to California. The guide was half Shoshone and half French-Canadian. He was an expert hunter and scout who spoke some German, French, and Spanish—as well as a variety of Indian languages. "There was a quaint humor and shrewdness in his conversation," one man said, "so garbed with intelligence and perspicuity, that he at once insinuated himself into the good graces of listeners, and commanded their admiration and respect." Another said, "he wore his hair long—that hung down to his shoulders. It was said that [he] was the best man on foot on the plains or in the Rocky Mountains."[41] His name was Jean-Baptiste Charbonneau.

Baptiste joined Cooke on 24 October 1846. By 8 November, Baptiste and his fellow guides, veteran trappers Pauline Weaver and Antoine Leroux, were offering bleak predictions about the desert country ahead, where water was scarce and trails were nonexistent. Mexican soldiers were possibly nearby; if so, they were likely to attack. "It has now become obvious to all," wrote Cooke, "that we cannot go on so with any prospect of a successful or safe termination to the expedition." He sent a number of sick men back to Santa Fe, hoping to stretch rations as far as possible. "Solemn times for us," wrote Henry Standage, a Mormon private. "May the God of Heaven protect us all."[42]

Cooke's party included a number of wagons and could not follow the same route as General Kearny, who was ahead of Cooke and being guided by Kit Carson. Baptiste and his fellows knew of no route passable by wagon. "Where is water or our most advisable course?" Cooke wrote on 18 November. "Heaven knows! We are exploring an unknown country with wagons."[43]

A friendly Mexican trading party advised Cooke to swing south around a mountain range and then go north to pick up Kearny's trail along the Gila River. Baptiste, Weaver, and Leroux concurred. "What difference if this distance is doubled, it if is a better route?" wrote Cooke. "I shall strike the Gila all the same by either."[44]

On 22 November, Leroux signaled with white smoke that he had found water. After searching all day, Baptiste found his way to Leroux's location. Returning after dark, Baptiste was seen walking into camp carrying his saddle, his mule nowhere to be seen. When someone asked what had happened, he replied that he had come to a grassy area and stopped to let the mule eat. But the mule had kicked him and run out into the grass. Baptiste chased the stubborn animal for miles but could not catch it. Finally he had shot it to prevent it (and the saddle and pistols) from being taken by the Apache.[45]

The battalion reached the small water hole the next day, after traveling forty miles without any water at all. Baptiste next found a good route across a dry lake bed. A few days after that, the group scaled a mountain pass in what is now Arizona. "I discovered Charboneaux near the summit in pursuit of [grizzly] bears," wrote Cooke. "I saw three of them up among the rocks, whilst the bold hunter was gradually nearing them. Soon he fired, and in ten seconds again; then there was confused action, one bear falling down, the others rushing about with fierce cries, amid which the hunter's too could be distinguished; the mountain fairly echoed. I much feared he was lost, but soon, in his red shirt, he appeared on a rock; he had cried out in Spanish for more balls."[46]

Cooke skirted the present-day Mexican border before heading northwest to Tucson, even though a Mexican garrison was reportedly stationed there.

Luckily, the garrison had disbanded, and the battalion passed through safely. Four days before Christmas they reached the Gila River near the site of today's Florence, Arizona. He sent Baptiste and the others ahead with orders to watch for Mexican soldiers, but they saw none. "Will not this prove the best emigrant's road from Independence to California, by the route I came?" wrote Cooke. His prediction was accurate, for Cooke's Wagon Road, as it was soon called, became one of the key southwestern trails to California.[47]

Two days after the Mormon Battalion entered what is now California, on 11 January 1847, Cooke wrote: "I found on the high bank above the well, stuck on a pole, a note, 'No water, January 2—Charbonneaux.'"[48]

On 29 January the battalion reached the mission at San Diego, where they stayed for several weeks. The last mention of Baptiste came when Jesse Hunter, a Mormon captain, lost his wife, Lydia. She had had a high fever for at least a week, bearing a child in the midst of her illness. On 26 April she died at 10 p.m. Charbonneau was said to be quite thoughtful and considerate of Captain Hunter during this time.[49]

Though they had not had to fight, the Mormons had done everything asked of them. They had not liked Cooke, a man who surprised them when he wrote of their 2,030-mile trek: "History may be searched in vain for an equal march of infantry. Nine-tenths of it has been through a wilderness where nothing but savages and wild beasts are found, or deserts where, for want of water, there is no living creature. With crowbar and pick and ax in hand we have worked our way over mountains which seemed to defy aught save the wild goat, and hewed a passage through a chasm of living rock more narrow than our wagons. . . . Thus marching half naked and half fed, and living upon wild animals, we have discovered and made a road of great value to our country."[50]

In 1806, before returning to civilization, William Clark had volunteered to "raise" Baptiste Charbonneau, giving every indication that he would adopt the boy as his own son. The reality turned out to be something different—Clark is best described as the boy's guardian. He certainly supported Baptiste, but there is no sign that the boy ever lived in his home. In 1820, for example, the year Baptiste turned fifteen, Clark made a number of payments to the Reverend Francis Neil, a Roman Catholic priest who ran a boarding school. Clark also paid for such items as a history of Rome, a dictionary, paper, quill pens, a slate and pencils, shoes, socks, a hat, and four yards of cloth.[51]

James Haley White, who later became a prominent architect, arrived in St. Louis in 1819, at the age of fifteen. White was three months younger than

Baptiste and attended a school taught by the Reverend J. E. Welch, a Baptist minister, where he met the young Charbonneau. "He was a *Mestizo*," wrote White, and was "under the guardianship of Gov. William Clark." White also recalled that Clark "kept a large room adjoining his dwelling wherein was kept a large collection of Indian trinkets and relics collected during his expedition, and suspended over head was the bark canoe in which this boy Charbonneau was born. Often when I visited the museum with him, he pointed to the canoe calling it his cradle and telling its history."[52]

A few years later, on 21 June 1823, just three weeks after the Arikara had attacked Ashley's party, killing John Collins and several others, a German nobleman, Duke Paul Wilhelm Friedrich Herzog of Wurttemberg, reached a trading post at the site of present-day Kansas City. The twenty-five-year-old duke had come up the Missouri with the permission of William Clark. While he was at the post, Duke Paul met eighteen-year-old Baptiste Charbonneau and learned his history.

By 1 August, the duke had reached Fort Atkinson, near the modern site of Omaha. In a letter to Joshua Pilcher, Benjamin O'Fallon wrote: "His Royal highness the prince of Wirtemburg has arrived, puffing and blowing from a long and fatigueing [voyage] of about Eighty days in Messrs Choteaus & Co Boat and wants to continue up as high as the Grand Bend, to kill Buffaloe, Antalopes & other Animals not to be found about here—I consider him an inoffensive stranger, whom I feel every disposition to indulge so long as he discovers no disposition to ascend too high up this river."[53]

The man who eventually assisted and interpreted for the duke was Toussaint Charbonneau, fresh from his attempt to find the Arikara and shortly to head up the Missouri with Hugh Glass and the five doomed traders. Duke Paul and Charbonneau presumably discussed Baptiste, though this is not known for certain. Nor is it known how often the elder and younger Charbonneau saw each other, but one trader reported seeing them together at the Mandan villages when Baptiste was eleven or twelve (which would have been about 1816 or 1817). The same trader heard a rumor that Charbonneau Sr. had gambled away a horse belonging to his son.[54]

Late in the fall of 1823, when Duke Paul returned to St. Louis, Baptiste was with him. The two of them traveled to Europe, where Baptiste remained for six years. Although some later claimed that Baptiste received a classical education in Europe, this is pure speculation. If the experience of the Mexican Juan Alvarado, apparently a successor of sorts for the young Charbonneau, is any guide, Baptiste may have been baptized a Lutheran, accompanied the duke on various travels, and studied elementary geography, history, arithmetic, French, and Spanish.[55]

But the scant record of Baptiste in Europe is quite significant. Parish records at Bad Mergentheim show that a child by the name of Anton Fries was born on 20 February 1829 and died on 15 May the same year. The child's parents were "Johann Baptist Charbonnau of St. Louis 'called the American' in the service of Duke Paul of this place and Anastasia Katharina Fries, unmarried daughter of the late Georg Fries, a soldier here."[56]

When he returned from Europe, Baptiste promptly headed west to trap—with the Robidoux Fur Brigade in 1830, with Jim Meek in 1831, with Jim Bridger in 1832, with Kit Carson in the late 1830s. In 1830 the Robidoux group attempted to cross the Snake River Plain, going northwest from the present site of American Falls, Idaho, into lava fields and apparently into the area of volcanic cones and craters now known as Craters of the Moon National Monument.

"We entered on a tract of country evidently covered with the stratum of black rock which had evidently been in a fluid state, and had spread over the earth's surface to the extent of forty or fifty miles," wrote trapper J. H. Stevens. "[We] soon met with innumerable chasms, where it had cracked and yawned asunder at the time of cooling, to a depth often of fifty feet, over which we were compelled to leap our horses . . . but were finally brought to a full stop by a large chasm too wide to leap, and forced to return back to the plain. At this time we begun to feel almost insupportable thirst."[57]

After two days of searching, the group finally found water near the camp of a Hudson's Bay trapping company. But Baptiste had become separated from the main party while searching for water. One of Robidoux's traders told what happened next: "[Baptiste] states that he lost our trail, but reached the river Maladi [Malad River, in the southeast corner of present-day Idaho] after dark, where he discovered a village of Indians [actually the Hudson's Bay group]. Fearing that they were unfriendly, he resolved to retrace his steps, and find the main company. In pursuance of this plan, he filled a beaver skin with water, and set off on his lonely way. After eleven days' wandering, during which he suffered a good deal from hunger he attained his object, and reached the company."[58]

Baptiste met Nathaniel Wyeth in the mid-1830s and John C. Frémont several years after that. Frémont wrote of a memorable day at Baptiste's camp:

> Arrived at Chabonard's camp, on an island in the Platte. . . . Mr. Chabonard was in the service of Bent and St. Vrain's company, and he'd left their fort some forty or fifty miles above, in the spring, with boats laden with the furs of the last year's trade . . . finding it impossible to proceed, had taken up his summer's residence on this island, which he had named St. Helena. . . . the island here had a fine grove of very large cottonwoods, under whose

broad shade the tents were pitched . . . smoke was rising from the scattered fires, and the encampment had quite a patriarchal air. Mr. C. received us hospitably. One of the people was sent to gather mint, with the aid of which he concocted very good julep; and some boiled buffalo tongue, and coffee with the luxury of sugar, were soon set before us.[59]

Baptiste Charbonneau remained in California after his journey with the Mormon Battalion. For a time he served as *alcalde,* or magistrate, at the San Luis Rey Mission north of San Diego. Indians charged with various offenses came before him, and he apparently pronounced some harsh judgments, such as sentencing a Luiseno Indian by the name of Fulgencio to work off a debt of $51.37 at the rate of 12 1/2 cents per day. The Indians reportedly planned an insurrection to protest such treatment, and Baptiste was accused of being involved, a charge he denied. He soon resigned his position, however, with a clerk reporting his claim that "he has done his duty to the best of his ability but being 'a half-breed Indian of the U.S. is regarded by the people as favoring the Indians more than he should do.' "[60] (Some modern historians believe Baptiste resigned because of his concern for the Indians brought before him; others disagree.)

Baptiste went north and was in the Sacramento area in 1849 when Jim Beckwourth, the trapper and Crow chief apparently mistaken for York a decade and a half earlier, arrived with countless other gold seekers. "Here I found my old friend Chapineau house-keeping," wrote Beckwourth, "and staid with him until the rainy season set in." Similarly, another forty-niner recorded: "Tom Buckner's heart was gladdened by the appearance of other white men, not hostile, at his camp, in the person of J. B. Charbonneau, Jim Beckwourth, and Sam Mayers, all noted mountaineers."[61]

Baptiste was in the Sacramento area when Alexander Willard and his family arrived in 1852, although there is no record that the two ever met or knew of the other's presence. Baptiste is not known to have married or had children after returning from Europe in 1829. In 1861 he was clerking at the Orleans Hotel in Auburn. Five years later, he heard of a gold rush in the Montana Territory and joined with a party headed in that direction. They reached the Owyhee River in May of 1866. Baptiste probably crossed the frigid river astride his swimming horse. Soon he was sick with "mountain fever"—which probably meant pneumonia. His companions took him to Inskip Station, in southeastern Oregon, near the Idaho border. Both as an infant and as an adult he had spent a good deal of time in the Montana country, but he was not to see that territory again. He was sixty-one years old when he died, and he had survived all the members of the expedition, except one.

When William Clark drew up his list of expedition members, he noted that Patrick Gass was dead. He was mistaken. As Clark probably knew, Gass had served for three full years in the War of 1812, even though he had been blinded in one eye in the midst of that service. In Gass's own words:

> I inlisted with Captain Kingsley at Nashville in the Year 1812 in the 1st regmt. Infantry—in March 1813 moved to Fort Massack—thence to Belle-fontaine on the Missouri—then assisted in building a small fort on the Mississipi, called "Independance." In 1814 decended the Mississippi and acended the Ohio river to Pittsburgh, under the command of Col. Nichols—thence marched to Presque-isle—Fort Erie—Chipewa—and was in the battle at Lundays lane, under Captn. Symmes—after that battle returned to Fort Erie—where we were canonaded by the British for about seven weeks, and was finally marched to Sackets harbor, and discharged in June 1815, having obtained from the Surgen general a certificate of *total* disability on account of the loss of the sight of my left eye, whilst in service.[62]

Despite the loss of his eye early in the war, Gass carried on his military duties. As Gass himself noted, his unit ascended the Ohio River to Pittsburgh in 1814 and then went north. Near Niagara Falls in July 1814, Gass fought in the Battle of Lundy's Lane, where both British and American troops suffered heavy casualties. "The hand to hand fight over the guns is said to have been terrific," wrote Gass's biographer John Jacob, who interviewed Gass in the 1850s. "The dead were literally piled in heaps. Blue uniforms and red, promiscuously mingled in the ghastly piles. . . . It was indeed a scene of terrible slaughter." The Americans were outnumbered, but they fought to a standstill. Two weeks later, after the Americans had withdrawn to their former position at Fort Erie, the British were temporarily driven from the line. As Jacob recorded, "To each company was attached men whose duty it was to carry a supply of rat-tail files and a hammer with which to spike such cannon of the enemy as they should be so fortunate to capture." Sergeant Gass was dispatched to General Brown, "who was standing on a log, some yards from the spot to enquire whether he should destroy some 24 pounders. 'Destroy them, Sergeant,' said Brown, 'we don't know how long they'll be ours.'—Patrick says he slapped in the rat tail files and drove them home," disabling the British cannons by driving the files, or "spikes," into the vents. After surviving this battle, Gass passed the remainder of the war "without extraordinary incident," but one of his brothers was taken captive by the British and was never heard from again.[63]

Patrick Gass's discharge listed him as about five foot seven, with a dark complexion, gray eyes, and dark hair. His contemporary biographer added that

Gass was "somewhat low in stature, stoutly built, broad-chested and heavy-limbed, but lean, sprightly and quick of motion."[64]

Born in Pennsylvania in 1771, Gass was one of the oldest members of the corps. In the early 1790s he had battled Indians on the frontier. At age twenty-two he hired on as a flatboat hand, taking a load of lumber down the Ohio and then the Mississippi to New Orleans. From there he crossed over to Cuba, where he booked passage on a ship headed to Philadelphia. In the late 1790s, when it appeared that a war between the United States and France might erupt, he enlisted under General Alexander Hamilton. By the early 1800s, Gass and John Ordway were both with Captain Russell Bissell's company, First Infantry. They both signed on with Lewis and Clark on 1 January 1804. Gass was promoted to sergeant to replace Charles Floyd after the latter's death in August 1804.[65]

In the spring of 1807, just six months after the corps returned to St. Louis, David M'Keehan published Gass's journal of the expedition, and thrust Gass into a spotlight of international attention. Not only was this the first genuine account of Lewis and Clark's journey, it remained the only one until Biddle's version was published in 1814. It is quite likely that M'Keehan ghost-wrote parts of the published manuscript, but this cannot be confirmed because Gass's original document has vanished. Meriwether Lewis, who was making virtually no progress with his own account of the expedition, considered Gass's journal "unauthorized" and wrote in the *National Intelligencer* that its publication might "depreciate the worth of the work which I am myself preparing for publication." M'Keehan fired back a sarcastic barb that put words in Lewis's mouth: "I'll cry down those one-volume journals, and frighten the publishers; and no man, woman, or child shall read a word about *my* tour."[66]

M'Keehan reaped much more of a benefit from the publication than Gass. Although Gass received an initial payment and one hundred copies of the volume, M'Keehan retained the copyright. Gass likely received little or nothing from subsequent printings. (M'Keehan found himself in the same boat when other publishers reprinted Gass's journal without permission—and without paying M'Keehan anything.)[67]

William Clark apparently lost track of Gass after the War of 1812, perhaps hearing rumors that he had died. In actuality, Gass had wandered first to Ohio and then to what later became West Virginia, laboring at odd jobs—farming, running a ferry, hunting stray horses, manning a brewery. He remained a bachelor all these years, but that changed in Wellsburg, Virginia (now West Virginia), when he was in his late fifties.

"My father had learned the carpenter trade," his daughter Rachel Brierly later related, "and was working on a building that my Grandfather Hamilton was having erected, and while thus engaged fell in love with my mother, who was an only daughter and then a young woman in her teens. She reciprocated and the result was a runaway match for my grandparents objected seriously on account of the disparity of the ages of the lovers. They walked many miles over the hills to Squire Plummer, who married them."[68]

The "disparity of the ages" was this: when they married in March of 1831, Patrick was three months shy of sixty, and Maria Hamilton was twenty. But the worries of her parents turned out to be unfounded, for Patrick and Maria were a happy couple. He "immediately rented a house from a certain Crickett, who resided on the Crawford farm, in the vicinity of Wellsburg, and commenced house-keeping," according to John Jacob, his biographer.[69]

Eking out a living was difficult. "I am now nearly sixty years of age," Patrick had written in 1829, "having no real or personal property, except wearing appearl, and not able to procure, entirely, my subsistance by manual labor, being severely afflicted by rheumatic pains, the effect of severe and continued exertions in the service of my country, since I was capable of carrying arms until the close of the late war."[70]

Patrick and Maria Gass had seven children, one of whom died in infancy. "After various changes and removes, he finally purchased a piece of hill-side land on Pierce's Run, in Brooke county, and sat down with his increasing family to cultivate the soil," wrote Jacob.[71] But late in 1846 an outbreak of measles struck the community. All of the children were sick, then Maria, with fever and coldlike symptoms. The children recovered, but Maria did not. Perhaps the virus spread to her brain. She was thirty-six when she died on 15 February 1847.

At seventy-five, Gass was left with several young children, the youngest— Rachel Maria—only an infant. "With typical devotion," his grandson wrote, "he stayed on in the log cabin for several years until the older children had become self-reliant."[72] Then he went to live with a married daughter, Mrs. Annie Smith, wife of James Smith.

In the early 1850s, Gass petitioned Congress for an increase in his pension. The documents offer further insight into Gass and his life: "that he is left with a family of six children," reads an 1854 statement, "& has no pecuniary means whatever to procures for them what he most desires, a liberal, or at least, a substantial English Education. That two of his children died prior to the death of his wife, & the six still surviving are of tender years (the youngest not yet 8 years (eight) old,—Affidavit further states that George Shannon, brother to Hon. Wilson Shannon, M.C. from Ohio, was a member of the aforesaid Expedition under Capts. Lewis & Clarke. Affidavit further says that he has from time to time learned of the deaths and does not know of a single surviving member, save himself."[73]

Gass was obviously unaware that Alexander Willard and Jean-Baptiste Charbonneau were both still alive in 1854. But when Baptiste died in Oregon in May of 1866, Gass did become the sole remaining survivor of the expedition. Ironically, at thirty-two in 1803, he had been older than almost all the men—and thirty-four years older than Pomp. Lewis had died at thirty-five, Clark at sixty-eight. Patrick Gass lived until he was fourteen months short of one hundred.

His daughter Annie reported that "up until the very end, he was accustomed to walking the four miles to the town of Wellsburg for the mail; that on those walks he carried a hickory cane which he had made himself." "He was active to the last," added Gass's grandson. At his slow but steady pace, Gass walked not far from the Ohio River, the waterway that had carried Meriwether Lewis and several others west in the autumn of 1803, the first river that the entire group had traveled together. This was also the river where Gass's friends and neighbors had gathered on a Sabbath afternoon to see their elderly brother in the gospel baptized after confessing the Christian faith.[74]

During these last few years of his life, Patrick Gass wrote two letters that add to Lewis and Clark's official versions of the end of the expedition. Writing at the request of historian Lyman C. Draper (whose Draper Manuscripts have become one of the key document collections in the United States), Gass reported his two meetings with Daniel Boone: "In 1793 I seen Col. Dan Boone at Lewisville Ky. and again in 1806 at Boonsboro on the Mo. [Missouri River]"; "Col Boone in the spring of 1793 had been out on the Kentucky river among the Indians. In 1806 he had removed his family to Boonsboro on the northern Bank of the Mo [Missouri] above Jefferson City, if I mistake not. We were anxious to get home and did not stop long to converse with him."[75]

Fittingly, the Lewis and Clark team had stopped at the end of their journey to visit the great explorer of four decades earlier, Daniel Boone, who had led a party of five through the Cumberland Gap in 1769. None of the expedition journals mentioned this historic meeting. Although he was in his seventies at the time, Boone outlived close to half the members of the corps.

Gass also mentioned that in 1806 he "carried a letter from Capt. Clark . . . which I delivered to [George Rogers Clark] at the falls of the Ohio, and which he published. It contained an account of the heavy snows on the mountains." Gass thus made it clear that he was instrumental in announcing to the world the news of the corps' safe return, for he personally carried

William Clark's 23 September 1806 letter—actually written to another brother, Jonathan Clark, also in the Louisville area—to George Rogers Clark. One of the Clark brothers passed the letter on to the Frankfort, Kentucky, *Palladium,* which published it on 9 October 1806. As historian Donald Jackson notes, "The initial fame of the expedition rests largely upon this communication, which spread throughout the country as rapidly as the means of the day would allow."[76]

On 2 April 1870, five years after the end of the Civil War and almost a year after the driving of a golden spike that linked Lewis and Clark's West with the rest of the nation, Patrick Gass died, two months short of his ninety-ninth birthday. The expedition had ended.

Members of the Lewis and Clark Expedition

Compiled by Donna Masterson and Larry Morris

———————

1. **William Bratton** (1778–1841)

BORN: 27 July 1778 in Augusta County, Virginia.

PARENTS: George Bratton and Jane Elliott.

EXPEDITION SERVICE: From 20 October 1803 to 10 October 1806; pay, $178.33 1/3.

MARRIED: Mary (Polly) Maxwell on 25 November 1819 in Warren County, Kentucky.

CHILDREN: James M., George, John, William, Robert, Adam, Grizzella Ann, Eliza Jane, Marietta.

DIED: 11 November 1841 in Waynetown, Montgomery County, Indiana, at age sixty-three. Buried in a well-identified grave in the Old Pioneer Cemetery at the eastern edge of Waynetown (west of Crawfordsville), Indiana.

Sources: Heroes, 97–98; Jackson (3), 2:378; We Proceeded On (WPO) 28 (August 2002): 40; Wheeler (2), 94

2. **Jean-Baptiste Charbonneau** (1805–1866)

BORN: 11 February 1805 at Fort Mandan, in present-day North Dakota.

PARENTS: Toussaint Charbonneau and Sacagawea.

CHILDREN: Fathered a son, Anton Fries, in Germany; the child was born 20 February 1829 and died on 15 May the same year; the mother was Anastasia Katharina Fries.

DIED: 16 May 1866, at age sixty-one, at Danner's Station, Malheur County, Oregon, and is buried there.

OBITUARY:

> Death of a California Pioneer.—We are informed by Mr. Dana Perkins, that he has received a letter announcing the death of J. B. Charbonneau, who left this country some weeks ago, with two companions, for Montana Territory. The letter is from one of the party, who says Mr. C., was taken sick with mountain fever, on the Owyhee, and died after a short illness.
>
> Mr. Charbonneau was known to most of the pioneer citizens of this region of country, being himself one of the first adventurers (into the territory now known as Placer County) upon the discovery of gold; where he has remained with little intermission until his recent departure for the new gold field, Montana, which, strangely enough, was the land of his birth [he was actually born in what became North Dakota], whither he was returning in the evening of life, to spend the few remaining days that he felt was in store for him.
>
> Mr. Charbonneau was born in the western wilds, and grew up a hunter, trapper, and pioneer among that class of men of which Bridger, Beckwourth, and other noted trappers of the woods were the representatives. He was born in the country of the Crow Indians—his father being a Canadian Frenchman, and his mother a half breed of the Crow tribe. He had, however, better opportunities than most of the rough spirits, who followed the calling of trapper, as when a young man he went to Europe and spent several years, where he learned to speak, as well as write several languages. At the breaking out of the Mexican war he was on the frontiers, and upon the organization of the Mormon battalion he was engaged as a guide and came with them to California.
>
> Subsequently upon the discovery of gold, he, in company with Jim Beckworth, came upon the North Fork of the American river, and for a time it is said were mining partners.
>
> Our acquaintance with Charbonneau dates back to '52, when we found him a resident of this country, where he has continued to reside almost continuously since—having given up frontier life. The reported discoveries of gold in Montana, and the rapid peopleing of the Territory, excited the imagination of the old trapper, and he determined to return to the scenes of his youth.—Though strong of purpose, the weight of years was too much for the hardships of the trip undertaken, and he now sleeps alone by the bright waters of the Owyhee. . . .
>
> The old man, on departing for Montana, gave us a call, and said he was going to leave California, probably for good, as he was about returning to familiar scenes. We felt then as if we met him for the last time.
>
> Mr. Charbonneau was of pleasant manners, intelligent, well read in the topics of the day, and was generally esteemed in the community in which he lived, as a good meaning and inoffensive man. (*Placer Herald*, Auburn, California, 7 July 1866)

Sources: Furtwangler (2), 521; Meriwether Lewis journal entry, 11 February 1805; *Owyhee Avalanche*, Ruby City, Idaho, 2 June 1866

3. **Toussaint Charbonneau** (1767–ca. 1840)

BORN: 22 March 1767 in Boucherville, Quebec, Canada.
PARENTS: Jean-Baptiste Charbonneau and Marguerite Deniau.

MARRIED: Took Sacagawea as a wife after buying her from the Hidatsa; had other wives but no documented children by them.

CHILDREN: Jean-Baptiste, Lisette.

EXPEDITION SERVICE: From 7 April 1805 to 17 August 1806; pay, $409.16 2/3.

DIED: Between 26 August 1839 and 14 August 1843, between the ages of seventy-two and seventy-six.

Sources: FCA, 31–33; Joshua Pilcher to the Commissioner of Indian Affairs, 26 August 1839, Jackson (3), 2:648; Promissory note to Jean-Baptiste Charbonneau, 14 August 1843, Sublette Papers, Missouri Historical Society

4. **William Clark** (1770–1838)

BORN: 1 August 1770 in Caroline County, Virginia.

PARENTS: John Clark and Ann Rogers.

MILITARY RECORD: Lieutenant in the infantry, 7 March 1792; resigned, 1 July 1796. Second lieutenant, 26 March 1804; first lieutenant, 31 January 1806; resigned, 27 February 1807.

MARRIED: Julia Hancock in January 1808 in Fincastle, Botetourt County, Virginia. (She died 27 June 1820 at her father's estate, Fotheringay, in Montgomery County, Virginia.)

Harriet Kennerly Radford on 28 November 1821. (She died 25 December 1831 in St. Louis.)

CHILDREN: Meriwether Lewis, William Preston, Mary Margaret, George Rogers Hancock, John Julius (by Julia); Jefferson Kearny, Edmund (by Harriet).

DIED: 1 September 1838 in St. Louis, Missouri, at age sixty-eight; buried in Bellefontaine Cemetery.

OBITUARY:

It becomes our truly painful duty to announce the decease of one of the most highly respected and esteemed citizens of St. Louis, Governor William Clark, who for sometime past, has been complaining, and gave evidence of a rapid increase of his afflictions, and the ravages of old age. Lately his illness has greatly increased, and on Saturday night the first of the month, he breathed his last, at the residence of his son, Merriwether Lewis Clark Esq, of this City.

Though the event—from, the age and feeble health of the deceased—was not unlooked for, it will not be the less regretted. To see the great—the good—those whom all are constrained to love, as the benefactors of their country, and respected as their country's ornaments—whose names and whose histories are identified with all we know of the early history of our land—to such men falling around us will wring a sigh from every breast, and a tear from every eye.

The name of Governor Clark must ever occupy a prominent place on the pages of the history of this country. He arrived in St. Louis in the year 1803, and in company with his intrepid companion Merriwether Lewis and a small band of selected men, performed the first journey across the Rocky Mountains to the mouth of the Columbia river. The history of the pioneer trip of Lewis and Clark is familiar to every reader. After his return he served as Governor of the Territory of Missouri, and subsequently, Superintendant of Indian Affairs for the Western Division—which office he continued to hold until the day of his death. In this office, and in his intercourse with the Indians of the west, his services to the United States have been pre-eminently valuable. He well understood the Indian character, and his whole intercourse with them was such as won their highest esteem and their most unbounded confidence. His name is known by the most remote tribes, and his word was reverenced by them everywhere. They regarded him as a father, and his signature, which is known by every Indian, even in the most distant wilds of the far west, wherever shown, was respected.

Govr Clark was sixty eight years of age when he died, and was probably the oldest American settler residing in St. Louis. Through a long, eventful and useful life, he had filled the various stations of a citizen and an officer with such strict integrity, and in so affable and mild a manner, that at the day of his death, malice nor detraction had not a blot to fix upon the fair scroll which the history of his well-spent life leaves as a rich and inestimable legacy to his children, and the numerous friends who now mourn his death.

His remains will be interred to day, at the family burying ground, four miles from the City, at 10'Oclock A.M. from his sons residence.

The St. Louis Greys formed the escort with St. Louis Masonic Lodge No. 20 and the Western Academy of Natural Science in the cortege. (*Missouri Republican*, 3 September 1838)

Sources: Heitman, 1:306; Holmberg (1), xxix–xxx

5. John Collins (?–1823)

BORN: In Frederick County, Maryland.

EXPEDITION SERVICE: From 1 January 1804 to 10 October 1806; pay, $166.66 2/3.

MARRIED: Name of wife and date of marriage not known.

CHILDREN: John M. Collins.

DIED: Believed killed by the Arikara in present-day South Dakota, 2 June 1823.

Sources: Clarke (1), 45; Collins family genealogical records supplied by Rita Cleary; Jackson (3), 1:345

6. John Colter (ca. 1775–1812)

BORN: About 1775, reportedly in Virginia.

EXPEDITION SERVICE: From 15 October 1803 to 10 October 1806; pay, $178.33 1/3. (Lewis and Clark extended the official term of service even though Colter actually left the expedition on 16 August 1806.)

MILITARY RECORD: War of 1812 service from 3 March to 6 May 1812.

MARRIED: Sarah (Sally) around 1810 in present-day Missouri.

CHILDREN: Hiram.

DIED: 7 May 1812 near Sullen Springs, St. Louis County, Missouri Territory, apparently from illness at about age thirty-seven.

Estate probate proceedings began in St. Louis County in December 1813.

Sources: Carter (2), Louisiana-Missouri, 561–62; Clarke (1), 46–48; Colter-Frick (1), 140–47

7. **Pierre Cruzatte** (dates unknown)

BORN: To a French father and Omaha mother, probably near St. Louis.

EXPEDITION SERVICE: From 16 May 1804 to 10 October 1806; pay, $144.16 2/3.

DIED: Killed by 1825–28; exact cause and location of death unknown. May have been with the McClellan party.

No known marriages or children.

8. **George Drouillard** (1773–1810)

BORN: December 1773 near Detroit; given name was Pierre; baptized 27 September 1775, Roman Catholic Assumption Church in Sandwich (opposite Detroit).

PARENTS: Pierre Drouillard and Asoundechris Flat Head.

EXPEDITION SERVICE: Enlisted 11 November 1803; official service from 1 January 1804 to 10 October 1806; pay, $833.33 1/3.

DIED: Killed by Blackfeet, April 1810, near Three Forks, in present-day Gallatin County, Montana, at age thirty-six.

NEWSPAPER NOTICE REGARDING DEATH:

Early in May, George Druilard accompanied by some Delawares, who were in the employ of the company, went out to hunt, contrary to the wishes of the rest of the party, who were confident the Indians were in motion around them, and that from a hostile disposition they had already shown, it would be attended with danger, their presages were too true, he had not proceeded more than two miles from the camp before he was attacked by a party in ambush, by whom himself and two of his men were literally cut to pieces. It appears from circumstances that Druilard made a most obstinate resistance as he made a kind of breastwork of his horse, whom he made to turn in order to receive the enemy's fire, his bulwark of course soon failed, and he became the next victim of their fury. It is lamentable that although this happened within a short distance of relief, the firing was not heard so as to afford it, in consequence of a high wind which prevailed at the time. (*Louisiana Gazette,* 26 July 1810)

Estate probate proceedings began on 10 January 1814 in St. Louis; Manuel Lisa executor; File 80.

No known marriages or children.

Sources: Baptism records of Assumption Church; Jackson (3), 2:378; Skarsten (2), 18, 27; St. Louis and St. Louis County, Missouri, Probate Records, 4

9. **Joseph Field** (ca. 1780–1807)

> BORN: Around 1780 in Culpeper County, Virginia.

> PARENTS: Abraham Field and Betty.

> EXPEDITION SERVICE: From 1 August 1803 to 10 October 1806; pay, $191.66 2/3.

> DIED: Killed between 27 June and 20 October 1807, at about age twenty-seven; exact cause and location of death unknown.

> Did not marry or have children.

> *Sources:* Appleman, 16, 24–25; Clarke (1), 48–49; Holmberg (1), 93–94; Yater, 2–4

10. **Reubin Field** (ca. 1781–ca. 1822)

> BORN: Around 1781 in Culpeper County, Virginia.

> PARENTS: Abraham Field and Betty.

> EXPEDITION SERVICE: From 1 August 1803 to 10 October 1806; pay, $191.66 2/3.

> MARRIED: Mary Myrtle in 1808 in Indiana Territory.

> DIED: Between 22 April 1822 and 14 January 1823, in Jefferson County, Kentucky, at about age forty-one.

> Estate probate proceedings began in Jefferson County, Kentucky, on 14 January 1823.

> No known children.

> *Sources:* Appleman, 16, 24–25; Clarke (1), 48–49; Holmberg (1), 93–94; Yater, 2–4

11. **Charles Floyd** (1782–1804)

> BORN: In 1782 in Kentucky.

> PARENTS: Robert Clark Floyd and Lilyann.

> EXPEDITION SERVICE: From 1 August 1803 to 20 August 1804; pay, $86.33 1/3 (which was apparently given to his family).

> DIED: 20 August 1804 at Floyd's Bluff near present-day Sioux City, Iowa, at about age twenty-two.

> Did not marry or have children.

> *Sources:* Clarke (1), 39; Yater, 4–6

12. **Robert Frazer** (ca. 1775–ca. 1837)

> BORN: About 1775 in Augusta County, Virginia.

> EXPEDITION SERVICE: From 1 January 1804 to 10 October 1806; pay, $166.66 2/3.

MILITARY RECORD: May have served in the War of 1812.

MARRIED: Tabitha.

CHILDREN: Robert Russell H., Lewis C., and apparently others whose names are not known.

DIED: Between 29 July 1836 and 31 January 1837 in Franklin County, Missouri, at about age sixty-two; buried in unmarked grave.

Estate probate proceedings began in Franklin County, Missouri, 31 January 1837, Lewis C. Frazer administrator.

Sources: Clarke (1), 61; Colter-Frick (1), 247–61

13. **Patrick McLene Gass** (1771–1870)

BORN: 12 June 1771 in Chambersburg, Cumberland County, Pennsylvania.

PARENTS: Benjamin Gass and Mary McLene.

MILITARY RECORD: Height, 5 ft. 7 in.; hair, dark; complexion, dark; eyes, gray; occupation, carpenter. War of 1812 service from 25 August 1812 to 19 June 1815.

EXPEDITION SERVICE: From 1 January 1804 to 10 October 1806; pay, $243.66 2/3.

MARRIED: Maria Hamilton in March 1831. (She died on 15 February 1847.)

CHILDREN: Elizabeth, Benjamin F., William, Sarah Ann, Annie Jane, James Waugh, Rachel Maria.

DIED: 2 April 1870 in Wellsburg, Brooke County, West Virginia, at age ninety-eight.

Sources: Forrest, 219–22; Gass (1), 29; Jacob, 148–49, 170–93; Jackson (3), 2:649–53

14. **George Gibson** (?–1809)

BORN: In Mercer County, Pennsylvania.

EXPEDITION SERVICE: From 19 October 1803 to 10 October 1806; pay, $178.50.

MARRIED: Maria Reagan about 1808.

DIED: Apparently from an illness, between 14 January and 10 July 1809 in St. Louis, St. Louis County, now in Missouri.

Estate probate proceedings began on 10 July 1809 in St. Louis; Samuel L. White and Thomas O'Fallon executors; File 63.

No known children.

Sources: Clarke (1), 49; Jefferson County, Kentucky, Deed Records, 21 March 1808 (copy obtained at the Filson Historical Society); St. Louis and St. Louis County, Missouri, Probate Records, 3–4

15. **Silas Goodrich** (dates unknown)

BORN: Reportedly in Massachusetts, possibly on 3 June 1778.

PARENTS: Father may have been Ashbel Goodrich.

EXPEDITION SERVICE: From 1 January 1804 to 10 October 1806; pay, $166.66 2/3.

MARRIED: May have married Betsey and had eight children.

DIED: By 1825–28; cause and location of death unknown.

Sources: AF; Clarke (1), 50; Goodrich

16. **Hugh Hall** (ca. 1772–?)

BORN: About 1772 in Carlisle, Cumberland County, Pennsylvania.

PARENTS: Father may have been Thomas Hall.

MILITARY RECORD: Enlistment date, 13 December 1798; location, B. Canton; term, five years; age, twenty-six; height, 5 ft. 8 3/4 in.; rank, private; hair, fair; complexion, sandy; eyes, gray; occupation, not listed.

EXPEDITION SERVICE: From 1 January 1804 to 10 October 1806; pay, $166.66 2/3.

DIED: Apparently between 1820 and 1830.

No known marriages or children.

Sources: Appleby, 8; Company Book of Captains John Campbell and Robert Purdy, Moore (1), 21–24; Cumberland County, Pennsylvania, Tax Lists, 1768–70; Egle, 265; Washington County, Pennsylvania, Census, 1820

17. **Thomas Proctor Howard** (1779–1814)

BORN: In 1779 in Brimfield, Hampden County, Massachusetts.

MILITARY RECORD: Enlistment date, 1 September 1801; location, Hartford; term, five years; age, twenty-two; height, not given; rank, private; hair, fair; complexion, fair; eyes, blue; occupation, not listed.

EXPEDITION SERVICE: From 1 January 1804 to 10 October 1806; pay, $166.66 2/3.

MARRIED: Genevieve Roy.

CHILDREN: Joseph, Louis.

DIED: By 23 March 1814 in St. Louis, Missouri Territory, at about age thirty-five.

Estate probate proceedings began 31 October 1816 in St. Louis; Genevieve Howard, executor; File 126.

Sources: Clarke (1), 50; Company Book of Captains John Campbell and Robert Purdy, Moore (1), 20–24; St. Louis and St. Louis County, Missouri, Probate Records, 7

18. **François (William) Labiche** (dates unknown)

BORN: To a French father and Omaha mother.

EXPEDITION SERVICE: From 16 May 1804 to 10 October 1806; pay, $144.66 2/3.

MARRIED: Genevieve Flore about 1810. Reportedly had seven children baptized between 1811 and 1834.

DIED: Apparently in the late 1830s.

Sources: Clarke (1), 64; Fur Trade Ledgers, Missouri Historical Society; St. Louis Directory, 1821

19. **Jean-Baptiste Lepage** (1761–1809)

BORN: 20 August 1761 in Kaskaskia, present-day Illinois.

PARENTS: Prisque and Marie Michel Lepage.

EXPEDITION SERVICE: From 2 November 1804 to 10 October 1806; pay, $111.50.

MARRIED: Date of marriage and name of spouse unknown.

CHILDREN: Clement, Baptiste, Joseph, Claude, and one daughter whose name is not known.

DIED: During the latter half of 1809 at age forty-eight; location and cause of death unknown.

Estate probate proceedings began 25 July 1810 in St. Louis; Manuel Lisa, Charles Sanguinet, and Louis Labeaume executors; File 75.

Sources: Colter-Frick (1), 142; La Page family records; St. Louis and St. Louis County, Missouri, Probate Records, 4

20. **Meriwether Lewis** (1774–1809)

BORN: 18 August 1774 near Charlottesville, Albemarle County, Virginia.

PARENTS: William Lewis and Lucy Meriwether.

MILITARY RECORD: Commissioned an ensign, 1 May 1795; lieutenant, 3 March 1799; captain, 5 December 1800; resigned, 4 March 1807.

DIED: 11 October 1809 near Hohenwald (in present-day Lewis County), Tennessee, from suicide, age thirty-five. Buried at the same site.

Estate settled from October 1810 to 29 April 1813 in St. Louis; Edward Hempstead and Pierre Chouteau executors; File 77.

OBITUARY:
By last mail we received the melancholy account of the premature death of his Ex'y. Governor Lewis; he landed at the Chickasaw Bluffs much indisposed, and shortly after set out on his way to the Federal City via Nashville; about 40 miles east of the river Tennessee, the party stopped for the night and became much alarmed at the governor's behavior, he appeared in a state of extreme mental debility, and before he could be prevented, discharged the contents of

a brace of pistols in his head and breast, calling to his servant to give him a bason of water; he lived about two hours and died without much apparent pain. The governor has been of late very much afflicted with fever, which never failed of depriving him of his reason; to this we may ascribe the fatal catastrophe! Alas Lewis is no more—his bodily conflicts are over—his days have been numbered—the scene is closed for ever—He was no less conspicuous for his native affability, suavity of manners, and gentleness of disposition, than those domestic virtues which adorn the human character—a dutiful son, an effectionate brother, a kind and feeling friend.—Reader, picture to thyself, the poignant feelings of a fond and doting parent on being informed of the death of a son, whose general worth was highly appreciated by those who knew him.

Adieu! kind friend, thy own harmonious ways,
Have sculptur'd out thy monument of praise;
Yes: they'll survive till times remotest day,
Till drops the bust, and boastful tombs decay. (*Missouri Gazette*, 2 November 1809)

Did not marry or have children.

Sources: Dillon, 6, 274, 332–34; Heitman, 1:631; St. Louis and St. Louis County, Missouri, Probate Records, 4; see Thompson for information regarding claims that Lewis fathered an Indian son

21. **Hugh McNeal** (ca. 1776–unknown)

BORN: Reportedly in Pennsylvania around 1776.

PARENTS: May have been Robert McNeal and Jean.

EXPEDITION SERVICE: From 1 January 1804 to 10 October 1806; pay, $166.66 2/3.

DIED: By 1825–28; cause and location of death unknown.

No known marriages or children.

Sources: Ancestry World Tree; Clarke (1), 50–51; International Genealogical Index

22. **John Ordway** (ca. 1775–ca. 1817)

BORN: About 1775 in Dunbarton, Merrimack County, New Hampshire.

PARENTS: John Ordway and Hannah Morse.

EXPEDITION SERVICE: From 1 January 1804 to 10 October 1806; pay, $266.66 2/3.

MARRIED: Gracey around 1807. (She apparently died by 1809.)

Elizabeth Johnson (a widow) around 1809.

CHILDREN: Hannah and John (by Elizabeth).

DIED: Between February 1816 and 5 February 1818 in New Madrid, New Madrid County, Missouri Territory, at about age forty-two. Cause of death unknown.

Sources: Dye Collection, Oregon Historical Society; John Ordway documents, Meriwether Lewis Papers, Missouri Historical Society; Koetting and Koetting

23. **John Potts** (ca. 1776–1808)

BORN: About 1776 in Dillenburg, Hessen, Germany.

MILITARY RECORD: Enlistment date, 22 July 1800; location, Winchester; term, five years; age, twenty-four; height, not given; rank, private; hair, black; complexion, fair; eyes, black; occupation, miller.

EXPEDITION SERVICE: From 1 January 1804 to 10 October 1806; pay, $166.66 2/3.

DIED: Killed by Blackfeet in 1808 near Three Forks, in present-day Gallatin County, Montana, at about age thirty-two.

NEWSPAPER NOTICE CONCERNING DEATH:

WILL BE SOLD

On the 11th Nov. 1810. at 10 o'clock, A.M. of that day, for ready money at the Auction room of Patrick Lee in the town of St. Louis, A LAND WARRANT No. 22 for 320 acres, given to John Potts, deceased, pursuant to an act of Congress "making compensation to Messrs Lewis and Clark and their Companions."

Rufus Easton.
Administrator of John Potts, deceased.
November, 1st. 1810.

(*Louisiana Gazette*, November 1810)

Estate probate proceedings began 6 January 1810 in St. Louis; Rufus Easton, William Russell, and William Massy executors; File 69.

No known marriages or children.

Sources: Clarke (1), 51; Company Book of Captains John Campbell and Robert Purdy, Moore (1), 21–24; St. Louis and St. Louis County, Missouri, Probate Records, 4

24. **Nathaniel Pryor** (ca. 1772–1831)

BORN: About 1772 in Amherst County, Virginia.

PARENTS: John A. Pryor and Nancy Floyd.

EXPEDITION SERVICE: From 20 October 1803 to 10 October 1806; pay, $278.50.

MILITARY RECORD: Ensign in the infantry, 27 February 1807; second lieutenant, 3 May 1808; resigned, 1 April 1810. Served in the War of 1812 as a first lieutenant in the infantry, 30 August 1813, and captain, 1 October 1814. Honorably discharged, 15 June 1815.

MARRIED: Margaret Patton (or Patten) 17 March 1798. She may have died by 1803.

May have married Nancy S. Melton on 23 February 1811. A son, William Stokes Pryor, was reportedly born on 15 November 1811, and Nancy reportedly divorced Nathaniel in 1818.

Married an Osage woman apparently in the 1820s; three children.

CHILDREN: Jane B., James, Nancy, Robert L., Eliza, Nathaniel (by Margaret); Mary Jane, Angelique, Marie (by his third wife, an Osage woman whose name is not known).

DIED: 9 June 1831 in Arkansas Territory (near present-day Pryor, Mayes County, Oklahoma) at about age fifty-nine. Buried in Fairview Cemetery, east of Pryor. (The date of 9 June seems reliable because it was reported in a St. Louis newspaper just weeks after Pryor's death. Since the body was reinterred and the headstone is not the original, the date on the headstone—1 June—may be based on hearsay.)

NOTICE OF DEATH:

> DIED, On the morning of the 9th June last, Capt. N. PRYOR, Sub-Agent for the Osage Indians. (*St. Louis Beacon*, 21 July 1831)

Estate probate proceedings began in St. Louis in December 1831, Thomas Ingram Jr., administrator.

Sources: Heitman, 1:808; Prior; Nathaniel Pryor documents, Meriwether Lewis Papers, Missouri Historical Society

25. **Sacagawea** (ca. 1788–1812)

BORN: About 1788 in the area of present-day Lemhi County, Idaho.

Kidnapped by the Hidatsa and carried into what is now North Dakota around 1800. Subsequently sold to and became the wife of Toussaint Charbonneau.

CHILDREN: Jean-Baptiste and Lisette.

DIED: 20 December 1812 at Fort Manuel, near present-day Kenal, Corson County, South Dakota, at about age twenty-four.

Sources: Anderson (1) and (4); Drumm, 106–7

26. **George Shannon** (1785–1836)

BORN: In 1785 in Claysville, Washington County, Pennsylvania.

PARENTS: George Shannon and Jane Mulligan.

EXPEDITION SERVICE: From 19 October 1803 to 10 October 1806; pay, $178.50.

MARRIED: Ruth Snowden Price on 19 September 1813 in Lexington, Fayette County, Kentucky.

CHILDREN: Samuel Price, Mary Jane, Elizabeth Price, George Ross, Sarah Lavina, Anna Marie, William Russell.

DIED: 31 August 1836 in Palmyra, Marion County, Missouri, at about age fifty-one, of illness. Buried in unmarked grave in the Massie Cemetery, one mile north of Palmyra, Missouri.

NEWSPAPER ARTICLE REGARDING DEATH:

> [George Shannon] repaired to his room and obtained medical aid, but the fatal shift had been cast. He sustained his illness with a great deal of moral courage and composure that has seldom been equalled. On the morning of Tuesday [August] 30th, he sunk into the arms of death without the slightest emotion. (*Palmyra* [Missouri] *Journal,* October 1836)

Sources: Denton, 15–24; Dye Collection, Oregon Historical Society; Hagood; Holmberg (1), 152–53

27. **John Shields** (1769–1809)

BORN: In 1769 in Harrisonburg, Augusta County, Virginia.

PARENTS: Robert Shields and Nancy Stockton.

MARRIED: Nancy White about 1790.

CHILDREN: Janette Martha (or Martha Janette). She married her cousin John Tipton about 1807; they were divorced in July 1817.

EXPEDITION SERVICE: From 19 October 1803 to 10 October 1806; pay, $178.50.

DIED: In December 1809 near Corydon, Harrison County, Indiana Territory, at age forty; cause of death unknown, but death was apparently nonviolent; reportedly buried in unmarked grave in Little Flock Baptist Church cemetery, south of Corydon.

Estate probate proceedings began in January 1810 in Harrison County, Indiana; John Tipton (son-in-law) and Nancy Shields (widow) executors.

Sources: Harrison County, Indiana, Probate Files; Holmberg (1), 97–98; Shields family genealogical records; Yater, 7–8

28. **John B. Thompson** (?–ca. 1815)

BORN: Place and date of birth unknown.

MILITARY RECORD: Enlistment date, 20 February 1799; location, not listed; term, five years; age, not listed; height, not listed; rank, private; hair, complexion, and eyes, not listed; occupation, laborer; residence, Northhampton.

EXPEDITION SERVICE: From 1 January 1804 to 10 October 1806; pay, $166.66 2/3.

MARRIED: Peggy.

DIED: Killed by July 1815; exact cause and location of death unknown.

NEWSPAPER NOTICE CONCERNING DEATH:
All persons indebted to the estate of John B. Thompson, deceased, are notified to make payment and those having demands are requested to present their accounts.
Peggy Thompson
Administratix
Nathan Carpenter Administrator
July 20th, 1815 (*Missouri Gazette and Illinois Advertiser,* 29 July 1815)

Sources: Company Book of Amos Stoddard, Moore (1), 20–24; Clarke (1), 54

29. **Peter M. Weiser** (1781–?)

BORN: 3 October 1781 in Tulpehocken, Berks County, Pennsylvania.

PARENTS: John Philip Weiser and Barbara.

EXPEDITION SERVICE: From 1 January 1804 to 10 October 1806; pay, $166.66 2/3.

MILITARY RECORD: War of 1812 service from 22 April 1813 to 21 May 1813.

DIED: Killed by 1825–28; exact cause and location of death unknown.

No known marriages or children.

Sources: Clarke (1), 59, and (2); War of 1812, Missouri Soldiers, Missouri State Archives

30. **William Werner** (?–ca. 1839)

BORN: Possibly in Kentucky.

EXPEDITION SERVICE: From 1 January 1804 to 10 October 1806; pay, $166.66 2/3.

MARRIED: Around 1807; wife's name is not known.

CHILDREN: William Jr. and several others, whose names are not known.

DIED: Apparently about 1839 in Virginia.

Sources: Census and marriage records of Montgomery County, Virginia, 1810–30; Clarke (1), 54

31. **Joseph Whitehouse** (ca. 1776–?)

BORN: About 1776 in Fairfax County, Virginia.

PARENTS: James Whitehouse and Sarah.

MILITARY RECORD: Height, 5 ft. 10 in.; hair, light brown; complexion, fair; eyes, hazel; occupation, skin dresser. Reenlisted in the army in 1808 and again in 1812; served in the War of 1812. Reenlisted in 1816 but deserted from the army on 1 February 1817.

EXPEDITION SERVICE: From 1 January 1804 to 10 October 1806; pay, $166.66 2/3.

MARRIED: Date of marriage and last name of wife unknown; her first name was reportedly Mary.

CHILDREN: Alfred Eldoris.

DIED: Date and location of death unknown; may have died in the 1850s.

Sources: Cutright (1), 114, and (2), 146; Moulton (2), 2:525; Whitehouse/White family genealogical records

32. **Alexander Hamilton Willard** (1778–1865)

BORN: 24 August 1778 in Charlestown, Sullivan County, New Hampshire. (The plaque at Willard's grave lists a birth date of 24 August 1778, which is consistent with the enlistment record of Willard's being twenty-one years old in 1800. Other family records, however, give a birth date of July 1777, which is consistent with his obituary in the *Sacramento Union*.)

PARENTS: Jonathan Willard and Betty Caswell.

MILITARY RECORD: Enlistment date, 9 June 1800; location, Oxford, term, five years; age, twenty-one; height, 5 ft. 10 in.; rank, artificer; hair, brown; complexion, dark; eyes, dark; occupation, blacksmith; residence, Charlestown, New Hampshire.

EXPEDITION SERVICE: From 1 January 1804 to 10 October 1806; pay, $166.66 2/3.

MARRIED: Eleanor McDonald (4 July 1790–1 June 1868) on 14 February 1807 in present-day Missouri.

CHILDREN: Austin James, George Clark, Alexander Hamilton, Eliza Martha, Roland Rudolph, Christina D., Joel, Nancy Adeline, Narcissa C., Eleanor C., Lewis Augustus, Willis.

DIED: 6 March 1865 in Franklin Township, Sacramento County, California, at age eight-six. Buried in a well-identified grave in Franklin Cemetery, Georgetown (modern Franklin), Sacramento County, California.

OBITUARY:

> Alexander Willard, a native of New Hampshire, died at his residence on the lower Stockton road, in Sacramento county, Cal., on the [6th] of March, 1865, at the advanced age of eighty-eight years. He was perhaps the last survivor of the exploring party sent out by President Jefferson, under Captain Meriwether Lewis, for the purpose of discovering the course and the source of the Missouri river, upon the acquisition of [Louisiana]. He started with the company in the spring of 1804, returning with it in 1806, sharing the toils, dangers and hardships incident to such a perilous journey, [and] Is very favorably mentioned in the report of Lewis and Clark for his valuable services as a gunsmith and for his boldness, intrepidity [and] endurance during the trip. In 1798, when difficulty was apprehended with France, he was among the first to enlist in the army ordered raised by Congress under Washington, but the pacific settlement of that question relieved him from lengthened military service. He actively engaged in the Indian war prosecuted by Tecumseh in 1811, and was selected for his courage, perseverance and sagacity by Gen. Clark, to convey dispatches from St. Louis to Prairie Chien which service he ably and faithfully performed, with much suffering and many hairbreath escapes. He emigrated to this state in 1852. Mr. Willard left a widow aged seventy eight to whom he had been married fifty-eight years, four sons, and two daughters, in California, besides grand children and great-grand children. His remains were interred in the burying ground at Georgetown, in Sacramento county to which place they were followed by a large concourse of friends and neighbors, by whom he was respected and beloved in life. (*Sacramento Union*, 11 March 1865)

Sources: Descendants (1); Company Book of Amos Stoddard, Moore (1), 20–24

33. **Richard Windsor** (dates unknown)

BORN: Place and date of birth unknown.

EXPEDITION SERVICE: From 1 January 1804 to 10 October 1806; pay, $166.66 2/3.

DIED: Apparently after 1825–28.

No known marriages or children.

Source: Clarke (1), 59

34. **York** (ca. 1772–?)

BORN: About 1772 in Virginia.

PARENTS: "Old York" and possibly Rose.

EXPEDITION SERVICE: For the entire time William Clark was involved; received no pay.

MARRIED: Wife's name not known. No known children.

DIED: In Tennessee of cholera between 1816 and 1832.

Sources: Betts (including the epilogue by James Holmberg); John O'Fallon to William Clark, 13 May 1811, William Clark Papers, Missouri Historical Society; Kennerly, 12; McDermott (1), 82

Temporary Members of the Party

John Boley, E. Cann, Alexander Carson, Charles Caugee, Joseph Collin, John Dame, Jean-Baptiste DesChamps, Phillippe Degie, Pierre Dorian Sr., Joseph Gravelines, Charles Hebert, Jean-Baptiste La Jeunesse, La Liberte, Etienne Malboeuf, John Newman, Peter Pinaut, Paul Primeau, Moses B. Reed, François Rivet, John G. Robertson, Peter Roi ("Rokey" or "Ross"), Ebenezer Tuttle, Richard Warfington, Isaac White (Clarke [1], 37–72, 145–47; Moulton [1], 2:512–29).

Notes: Pay amounts were doubled by an act of Congress, 5 March 1807. The above list incorporates information from the genealogy files of the Lewis and Clark Trail Heritage Foundation (Lewis and Clark Interpretive Center Library, Great Falls, Montana), William Clark's 1807 roster of expedition members (Jackson [3], 2:378), and Clark's list titled "Men on Lewis & Clarks Trip," ca. 1825–28 (ibid., 2:638–39). I have followed Gary E. Moulton's conventions for the spelling of names. Some obituaries obviously contain errors.

The Death of Meriwether Lewis

DOCUMENTS

1. **James Neelly to Thomas Jefferson,** 18 October 1809

Nashville Tennesee 18th Octr. 1809

Sir,

It is with extreme pain that I have to inform you of the death of His Excellency Meriwether Lewis, Governor of upper Louisiana who died on the morning of the 11 Instant and I am sorry to say by Suicide.

I arrived at the Chickasaw Bluffs on or about the 18th of September, where I found the Governor (who had reached there two days before me from St. Louis) in very bad health. It appears that his first intention was to go around by water to the City of Washington; but his thinking a war with England probable, & that his valuable papers might be in danger of falling into the hands of the British, he was thereby induced to Change his route, and to come through the Chickasaw nation by land; I furnished him with a horse to pack his trunks &c. on, and a man to attend to them; having recovered his health in some digree at the Chickasaw Bluffs, we set out together. And on our arrival at the Chickasaw nation I discovered that he appeared at times deranged in mind. We rested there two days & came on. One days Journey after crossing Tennessee River & where we encamped we lost two of our horses. I remained behind to hunt them & the Governor proceeded on, with a promise to wait for me at the first houses he came to that was inhabited by white people; he reached the house of a Mr. Grinder about sun set, the man of the house being from home, and no person there but a woman who discovering the governor to be deranged, gave him up the house & slept herself in one near it. His servant and mine slept in the stable loft some distance from the other houses. The woman reports that about three o'Clock she heard two pistols fire off in the Governors Room: the servants being awakined by her, came in but too late to save him. He had shot himself in the head with one pistol & a little below the Breast with the other—when his servant came in he says; I have done the business my good Servant give me some water. He gave him water, he survived but a short time. I came up some time after, and & had him as decently Buried as I could in that place—if there is any thing wished by his friends to be done to his grave I will attend to their Instructions.

I have got in my possession his two trunks of papers (amongst which is said to be his travels to the pacific Ocean) and probably some Vouchers for expenditures of Public Money for a Bill which he said had been protested by the Secy. of War; and of which act to his death, he repeatedly complained. I have also in my Care his Rifle, Silver watch, Brace of Pistols, dirk & tomahawk; one of the Governors horses was lost in the wilderness which I will endeavor to regain, the other I have sent on by his servant who expressed a desire to go to the governors Mothers & to Montic[e]llo: I have furnished him with fifteen Dollars to Defray his expences to Charlottsville; Some days previous to the Governors death he requested of me in case any accident happened to him, to send his trunks with the papers therein to the President, but I think it very probable he meant to you. I wish to be informed what arrangements may be considered best in sending on his trunks &c. I have the honor to be with Great respect Yr. Ob. Sert.

James Neelly
U.S. agent to the Chickasaw Nation

The Governor left two of his trunks at the Chickasaw Bluffs in the care of Capt. Gilbert C. Russell, Commanding officer, & was to write to him from Nashville what to do with them.

Source: Jackson (3), 467–68

2. **Alexander Wilson,** Letter to a Friend, 18 May 1811

Next morning (Sunday) I rode six miles to a man's house, of the name of Grinder, where our poor friend Lewis perished.

In the same room where he expired, I took down from Mrs. Grinder the particulars of that melancholy event, which affected me extremely. The house or cabin is seventy-two miles from Nashville, and is the last white man's as you enter the Indian country. Governor Lewis, she said, came hither about sunset, alone, and inquired if he could stay for the night; and alighting, brought his saddle into the house. He was dressed in a loose gown, white, striped with blue. On being asked if he came alone, he replied that there were two servants behind, who would soon be up. He called for some spirits, and drank a very little. When the servants arrived, one of whom was a negro, he inquired for his powder, saying he was sure he had some in a cannister. The servant gave no distinct reply, and

Lewis, in the meanwhile, walked backwards and forwards before the door, talking to himself.

Sometimes, she said, he would seem as if he were walking up to her; and would suddenly wheel round, and walk back as fast as he could. Supper being ready he sat down, but had eaten only a few mouthfuls when he started up, speaking to himself in a violent manner. At these times, she says, she observed his face to flush as if it had come on him in a fit. He lighted his pipe, and, drawing a chair to the door, sat down, saying to Mrs. Grinder, in a kind tone of voice, Madam, this is a very pleasant evening. He smoked for some time, but quitted his seat and traversed the yard as before. He again sat down to his pipe, seemed again composed, and casting his eyes wistfully towards the west, observed what a sweet evening it was. Mrs. Grinder was preparing a bed for him, but he said he would sleep on the floor, and desired the servant to bring the bear skins and buffalo robe, which were immediately spread out for him; and, it now being dusk, the woman went off to the kitchen and the two men to the barn which stands about two hundred yards off.

The kitchen is only a few paces from the room where Lewis was, and the woman being considerably alarmed by the behavior of her guest could not sleep, but listened to him walking backwards and forwards, she thinks, for several hours, and talking aloud, as she said, "like a lawyer." She then heard the report of a pistol, and something fall heavily to the floor, and the words, "O Lord!" Immediately afterwards she heard another pistol, and in a few minutes she heard him at her door calling out, "O madam! give me some water and heal my wounds!"

The logs being open, and unplastered, she saw him stagger back and fall against a stump that stands between the kitchen and the room. He crawled for some distance, and raised himself by the side of a tree, where he sat about a minute. He once more got to the room; afterwards he came to the kitchen door, but did not speak; she then heard him scraping in the bucket with a gourd for water; but it appears that this cooling element was denied the dying man.

As soon as day broke, and not before, the terror of the woman having permitted him to remain for two hours in this most deplorable situation, she sent two of her children to the barn, her husband not being home, to bring the servants; and on going in they found him lying on the bed. He uncovered his side, and showed them where the bullet had entered; a piece of his forehead was blown off, and had exposed the brains, without having bled much.

He begged they would take his rifle and blow out his brains, and he would give them all the money he had in his trunk. He often said, "I am no coward; but I am so strong, so hard to die." He begged the servant not to be afraid of him, for that he would not hurt him. He expired in about two hours, or just as the sun rose above the trees.

He lies buried close by the common path, with a few loose rails thrown over his grave. I gave Grinder money to put a post fence around it, to shelter it from the hogs and from the wolves; and he gave me his written promise that he would do it. I left this place in a very melancholy mood, which was not much allayed by the prospect of the gloomy and savage wilderness which I was just entering alone.

> *Source:* Fisher, 147–49. Fisher uses the version of the letter (written to an unnamed friend) quoted in Wheeler (1), 64–66. I found a version in the Draper Manuscripts, 28CC78, State Historical Society of Wisconsin, which contains slight differences but nothing substantial. Dates given for the letter by nineteenth-century newspapers include 18 May 1810, 6 May 1811, 18 May 1811, and 28 May 1811.

3. **Recollections of Mrs. Grinder,** Recorded by an Unnamed Schoolteacher in 1839 and Printed in 1841

When I visited the grave in 1838 I could scarcely distinguish it from the common ground; it being grown over with shrubbery of different kinds, and no stone, no palings, no monument to tell whose grave it was. Grinder's old stand had long been collapsed to ashes. The field was grown up with bristles and briars, and it was lately a dreary, solitary looking place.

She said that Mr. Lewis was on his way to the city of Washington, accompanied by a Mr. Pyrna and a servant belonging to Major Neelly.

One evening, a little before sundown, Mr. Lewis called at her house and asked for lodgings. Mr. Grinder not being at home, she hesitated to take him in. Mr. Lewis informed her that two other men would be along presently, who also wished to spend the night at her house and as they were all civil men, he did not think there would be any impropriety in her giving them accommodations for the night. Accordingly she consented to let them stay. Mr. Lewis dismounted, fastened his horse, took a seat by the side of the house and appeared quite sociable. In a few minutes Mr. Pyrna and the servant rode up, and seeing Mr. Lewis, they also dismounted and put up their horses. About dark two or three other men rode up and called for lodging. Mr. Lewis immediately drew a brace of pistols, stepped towards them and challenged them to a duel. They not liking this situation, rode on to the next house, five miles. This alarmed Mrs. Grinder. Supper, however, was ready in a few minutes. Mr. Lewis ate but little. He would stop eating and sit as if in a deep study, and several times exclaimed, "If they do prove anything on me, they will have to do it by letter." Supper being over, and Mrs. Grinder seeing that Lewis was mentally deranged, requested Mr. Pyrna to get his pistols from him. Mr. P. replied, "He has no ammunition, and if he does any mischief it will be done to himself, and not to you, or anybody else." In a short time all retired to bed, the travellers in one room, as Mrs. G. thought, and she and her children in another. Two or three hours before day, Mrs. G. was alarmed by the report of a pistol, and quickly after two other reports in the room where the travellers were. At the report of the third, she heard some one fall and exclaim, "O Lord! Congress relieve me!" In a few minutes she heard some person at the door of the room where she lay. She inquired, "Who is there?" Mr. Lewis spoke, and said, "Dear Madam, be so good as to give me a little water." Being afraid to open the door, she did not give him any. Presently she heard him fall, and soon after, looking through a crack in the wall, she saw him scrambling across the road on his hands and knees.

After daylight, Mr. Pyrna and the servant made their appearance, and it appeared they had not slept in the house, but in the stable. Mr. P. had on the clothes Mr. L wore when they came to Mrs. Grinder's in the evening before, and Mr. L.'s gold watch in his pocket. Mrs. G. asked him what he was doing with Mr. L.'s clothes on. Mr. P. replied, "He gave them to me." Mr. P. and the servant then searched for Mr. L., found him and brought him to the house and though he had on a full suit of clothes, they were old and tattered, but not the same he had on the evening before; and though Mr. P. had said that Lewis had no ammunition, Mrs. G. found several balls, and a considerable quantity of powder scattered over the floor of the room occupied by Lewis; also, a canister with several rounds in it. When Mr. Lewis was brought to the house, he opened his shirt bosom, and said to Mrs. G., "Dear Madam, look at my wounds." She asked him what made him do so? He replied, "If I had not done it, somebody else would." He frequently asked for water, which was given to him. He was asked if he would have doctor sent for; he answered no. A messenger, however, went for one, but did not get him. He attempted to cut his throat, but was prevented. Some of the neighbors were called in. He frequently cried out, "O how hard it is to die. I am so strong!" He, however, soon expired. Major Neelly was sent for, and he and Mr. P. buried him and took possession of his effects. Mrs. G. heard that P. went to Mr. L.'s mother and that she accused him of murdering her son, that he finally cut his own throat, and thus put an end to his existence.

> Source: Chandler, 312–14. Chandler uses the version of the article from the Philadelphia *American,* 7 December 1841. I found virtually the same version in the Draper Manuscripts, 29CC56, State Historical Society of Wisconsin (from the New York *Dispatch,* 1 Feburary 1845).

MURDER OR SUICIDE?

Historians have generally argued one side or the other, with Coues, Wheeler, Thwaites, Bakeless, Fisher, Dillon, Chuinard, and Chandler arguing for murder; and Jackson, Cutright, Ambrose, Duncan, Burns, Moulton, and Holmberg making the case for suicide. (Recently, historians have clearly favored the suicide theory.)

(Of course, there are other possibilities. Thomas Danisi believes that Lewis's "'business' was a strange and tragic form of self-surgery [caused by malaria], not suicide" [Danisi, 15]. Dr. Reinert T. Ravenholt, an epidemiologist, has argued that the effects of syphilis drove Lewis to suicide ["Triumph Then Despair: The Tragic Death of Meriwether Lewis," *Epidemiology* 5 (May 1994): 366–79]. John Guice maintains that, "As do most advocates of suicide, Ravenholt starts with his conclusion and forces the evidence to fit it" [Guice (1), 12]).

Those convinced that Lewis was murdered ask the questions:

- Was it simply a coincidence that two horses turned up missing the day before Lewis died?
- If Neelly knew Lewis was unstable, why didn't he stay with Lewis and have one of the servants search for the horses?
- Where was Neelly during the night and when did he arrive at the stand?
- If Lewis was coherent enough to ask for water and discuss his wounds, why didn't he simply reload his pistols and try again?
- Was it simply a coincidence that Mr. Grinder happened to be gone?
- Would a woman used to living in the Tennessee wilderness and meeting all kinds of men (including thieves and bootleggers who frequented the Trace) really be afraid to give a dying man a drink of water?
- Was it simply a coincidence that the servants were sent off to sleep out of earshot?
- Why did Thomas Jefferson never record any details of his meeting with Pernia?
- Why did Neelly hurriedly bury the body and depart for Nashville instead of guarding the body and awaiting an official inquest?
- What became of the $120 in cash Lewis reportedly had? (It is not included in the inventory of Lewis's effects dated 23 November 1809.)

Despite any consistencies between the Neelly and Wilson accounts, these are difficult questions to answer. But those arguing for suicide have questions of their own:

- What about Lewis's suicide attempts while traveling on the Mississippi?
- Why were William Clark and Thomas Jefferson convinced that Lewis killed himself?
- If Lewis was attacked and shot, why didn't he say so?
- Who killed Lewis? If it was Mr. Grinder or Pernia or common thieves, why didn't Neelly detect evidence of that? If it was Neelly, why did Mrs. Grinder tell a suicide story to Wilson (after Neelly was long gone)?
- If Pernia was the assailant, why would he so foolishly cast suspicion on himself by changing into Lewis's clothes?
- If Lewis died by murder, how could an astute observer and friend of Lewis's like Alexander Wilson fail to turn up any clues?
- If Mrs. Grinder lied, why didn't Pernia or the other servant point that out to Neelly? (And why didn't Pernia point it out to Jefferson or Clark?)
- If General Wilkinson was involved in Lewis's death (via Neelly), why has no evidence of such a conspiracy ever been found?

Questions abound. Vardis Fisher echoed the opinion of many when he said: "Did he kill himself or was he murdered? It should be said at once in plain words that we do not know, and we can never know, unless evidence turns up of which today we have no knowledge" (Fisher, 19). I have a good deal of respect for Fisher's impressive research. However, I believe suicide is a much more likely scenario than murder. True, there are many unanswered questions—there are anomalies that any suicide theorist must contend with. That in itself, however, does not make a case for murder. There is a good deal of evidence for suicide (or at least self-inflicted wounds), and very little for murder.

Suggested Reading

I recommend the following: Chuinard (3), Cutright (3), Fisher, Guice (1) and (2), Phelps, and the February 2002 issue of *We Proceeded On* (much of which is devoted to Lewis's death). See the Bibliography for complete publication information. Each of these works in turn mentions other books and articles.

The Sacagawea Controversy

Seventy-two years after John Luttig recorded the death of Charbonneau's wife, on the Wind River Indian Reservation in what is now Wyoming (west of present-day Riverton), at a settlement not far from where John Colter had wandered during the memorable winter of 1807–8, an elderly Shoshone woman by the name of Porivo was laid to rest. Officiating at her burial, the Reverend John Roberts recorded:

"(Date) April 9, 1884, (Name) Bazil's mother (Shoshone), (Age) One hundred, (Residence) Shoshone agency, (Cause of death) Old age, (Place of burial) Burial ground, Shoshone agency, (Signature of clergyman) J. Roberts" (Wind River Reservation Church Register of Burials, no. 1, 114, cited in Hebard, 207).

About twenty years later, Grace Raymond Hebard and others became aware of reports that this Shoshone woman had been Sacagawea of the Lewis and Clark Expedition. Hebard, a professor of political economy at the University of Wyoming, researched this question for at least twenty-five years before publishing her book *Sacajawea, a Guide and Interpreter of the Lewis and Clark Expedition* (1933). During this same time, Dr. Charles A. Eastman, an official with the Bureau of Indian Affairs, also investigated the history of Porivo. Hebard and Eastman both concluded that Porivo was indeed Sacagawea and that her son Bat-tez (who died on the Wind River Reservation one year after Porivo) was Jean-Baptiste Charbonneau. As Dr. Eastman wrote to the commissioner of Indian affairs: "I report that Sacajawea after sixty years of wandering from her own tribe returns to her people at Fort Bridger and lived the remainder of her life with her sons in peace until she died on April 9, 1884, at Ft. Washikie, Wyoming, that is her final resting place" (Charles A. Eastman to the Commissioner of Indian Affairs, 2 March

1925, typescript, photocopy at the Lewis and Clark Trail Heritage Foundation Library [LCTHF], Great Falls, Montana).

Largely because of the efforts of Eastman and Hebard, markers identifying Porivo as Sacagawea and Bat-tez as Jean-Baptiste were erected at the reservation, while both government agencies and the public at large accepted this account of how Sacagawea's life had ended.

Hebard and Eastman based their conclusions on two groups of letters and affidavits, the first written around 1905 and the second around 1925. These documents appear to make a strong case that Porivo was indeed Sacagawea. Note these examples:

"This Indian woman not only told me that she was with Lewis and Clark on the expedition to the Pacific ocean, but that her son Baptiste was a little papoose whom she carried on her back from the Mandan villages across the shining mountains to the great lake, as she called the Pacific ocean" (Testimony of James I. Patten, 7 September 1926, cited in Hebard, 227).

"I am the son of Basil, grand-son of Porivo or Chief Woman. . . . I remember her telling that her first husband was a Frenchman. Also she used to tell with pride that somewhere she fed the white people with buffalo meat when they were very hungry" (Affidavit of Andrew Basil, 15 January 1925, typescript, photocopy at LCTHF).

"I first knew that she was with Lewis and Clark during the winter of that first year, 1871, when she spoke of being a guide for the Lewis and Clark expedition. . . . I never had any doubt but that she was the real Sacajawea of the Lewis and Clark expedition, nor did anyone who heard her of our small group. She told me that when she was coming back and was on the western side of the Rocky mountains, Mr. Clark wished to leave the main party of the expedition and come over on to the Yellowstone river. He requested Sacajawea to guide him down to the Yellowstone to its junction with the Missouri. . . . I remember very distinctly of her telling me where and when she was taken prisoner, and from her description of the place, I am almost sure it was on the Madison fork of the Missouri. . . . At this time of meeting and talking with Sacajawea, I had never read a book on the expedition, nor had I read any magazine articles on it" (Testimony of F. G. Burnett, 5 September, 1926, cited in Hebard, 230–32).

"I also saw Sacajawea wearing a beautiful medal around her neck, a little larger than the size of a dollar, which she said that army officers had given her" (Testimony of Grandma Herford, 29 November 1926, ibid., 249).

"The tradition was generally known by every Shoshone about Sacajawea and her life, that she led a large body of people in the early days to the waters of the west, and this tradition was a generally-accepted statement among her people. . . . I have no reason to doubt that she was the real Sacajawea of the Lewis and Clark expedition" (Testimony of Quantan Quay, 21 July 1919, ibid., 250).

Clearly, Porivo claimed to have been with Lewis and Clark. Moreover, she seemed to know details about the journey that her listeners did not supply on their own. Believing that such testimony "proves conclusively that the central figure of this volume was in reality the famous guide of the Lewis and Clark expedition" (Hebard, 215), Hebard postulated that the woman who went up the Missouri with Charbonneau in 1811 and died at Fort Manuel in 1812 was not Sacagawea but another of Charbonneau's wives. Sacagawea, according to Hebard, left Charbonneau, lived among the Comanche in what is now Oklahoma (in the 1840s), made her way to Fort Bridger in present-day Wyoming (in the 1860s), and finally settled with her Shoshone people at the Wind River Reservation (in the 1870s).

As Hebard points out, Charles Eastman "made a thorough and detailed search on behalf of the United States government for the grave of Sacajawea, and . . . declared that Sacajawea's last resting place was on the Shoshone Wind river reservation in Wyoming. This decision, as Dr. Eastman says, must be accepted on the basis not only of the tribal tradition, but of other evidence that corroborates that tradition so strikingly that its truth cannot be questioned" (ibid., 215–16).

Documents from the nineteenth century indicated that Sacagawea had died in 1812; documents from the twentieth indicated she died in 1884. Hebard and Eastman found the twentieth-century documents to be entirely convincing.

Some scholars did not take kindly to the "Wyoming" account of Sacagawea. "I have had a great deal of correspondence and some talk with Miss Hebard within the last ten years," wrote historian W. J. Ghent in 1933, "and I cannot do else than reject her theory utterly. There is no human possibility that the Indian woman who died at Fort Washakie in 1884 could have been the woman of the expedition. It is to me a terrible thing that this purely fantastic theory, without the slightest historical evidence in its favor, should be accepted by any one. That it is so accepted by a number of persons is only another illustration of the apparent futility of the effort to disentangle fact from myth in Western history" (W. J. Ghent to Eva Emery Dye, 12 April 1933, Dye Collection, Oregon Historical Society).

In 1955, after Grace Raymond Hebard and Charles A. Eastman had both died, historian Dale Morgan discovered William Clark's list of expedition members. Donald Jackson, the premier editor of nonexpedition Lewis and Clark documents, wrote, "the notation that Sacagawea was dead by 1825–28 is the most interesting piece of intelligence that Clark presents here, because it tends to contradict a popular belief" (Jackson [3], 2:639n.1).

Some argued that Clark had been wrong about Gass—claiming he was dead when Gass actually lived for another thirty-five years. But Jackson summed up the sentiments of many historians when he responded: "We are hardly justified in saying, 'If Clark is wrong about Gass, then perhaps he is also wrong about Sacagawea,' for the cases are different. Gass had gone back to Virginia and severed his contacts with the West, but Sacagawea, her husband Charbonneau, and her children were Clark's concern for many years after the expedition. He cared about them and felt a kind of responsibility for them. It is difficult to believe that he could have been wrong about Sacagawea's death" (ibid.).

Following in the tradition of Ghent and Jackson, a number of historians defended the "Fort Manuel" account of Sacagawea's death. Russell Reid, superintendent of the North Dakota State Historical Society, wrote: "It was not until about 25 years later that a serious attempt was made to identify the old Shoshone woman as Sakakawea. In order to support this theory much evidence has been collected in the forms of interviews, statements and affidavits. Most certainly no one has a right to question the motives nor the honesty of individuals who gave such testimony, but it should be pointed out that evidence of this kind is not always reliable. Far too often individuals are apt to confuse fact with fiction and stories they have heard with some of their own experience" (quoted in Anderson [4], 8). Similarly, Irving W. Anderson wrote, "I have found no official records embracing the period 1850–1884 which specifically identify the Wind River woman as Sacagawea" (Anderson [4], 8).

Anderson and others also pointed out that primary documents strongly supported the Fort Manuel theory. First of all, Charbonneau and Sacagawea were known to be in St. Louis in 1809–10. Second, as he made his way up the Missouri in the spring of 1811, Brackenridge specifically stated: "We had on board, a Frenchman named Charbonet and his Indian wife, who had accompanied Lewis and Clark to the Pacific" (Brackenridge, 152). Third, though he did not identify her by name, Luttig described Sacagawea perfectly when he wrote that "the wife of Charbonnea, a Snake Squaw, died of a putrid fever she was a good and the best women in the fort aged about 25 years" (Drumm, 106). Fourth, Clark adopted Charbonneau's children in the summer of 1813. Fifth, Clark himself said that Sacagawea was dead when he drew up his list sometime between 1825 and 1828. (Proponents of the Fort Manuel theory also argued that Jean-Baptiste's entire life had been well documented, including his death in Oregon in 1866. Therefore, Bat-tez could not have been Jean-Baptiste.)

As James P. Ronda summarizes, "Most scholars now accept Clark's note . . . and Luttig's note . . . as substantial evidence for Sacagawea's early death" (Ronda [1], 258–59).

Suggested Reading

To understand both the Fort Manuel theory and the Wyoming theory, read Anderson (1), (2), and (4), Crawford, Hebard, Howard, and Nelson. See the bibliography for complete publication information.

Notes

PROLOGUE

1. The great Canadian explorer Alexander Mackenzie (1764–1820) had already crossed the continent. In 1789 he followed the river that now bears his name north eleven hundred miles from Great Slave Lake (in the present-day Northwest Territories) to the Arctic Ocean. In 1792–93, he went southwest, reaching the Pacific Ocean north of Vancouver Island. (See DeVoto [2], 310–12, 348–55.) He published his journals in 1801, and Thomas Jefferson and Lewis and Clark were well aware of his travels. In 1536, the Spanish explorer Alvar Núñez Cabeza de Vaca had reached the Pacific north of present-day Mexico. Estevan, a "Moor" with Cabeza de Vaca, was probably the first black man to go overland to the Pacific, making York the second.

CHAPTER ONE: *"We Descended with Great Velocity"*

1. Clark's journal entry, 9 September 1806. Quotations from the journals of Lewis and Clark and the other men are all from Moulton (2). However, to assist readers in finding the quoted passages in any edition of the journals, I identify (either in the text or in an endnote) every quote by author and date.

2. Clark's journal entry, 1 November 1804. As Lewis and Clark made their way up the Missouri, news and rumors of their coming apparently spread throughout the area. Charles Le Raye, apparently in present-day Iowa or South Dakota, wrote: "On the 26th of August [1804], a report was spread among the Indians, that a party, an army, as they called it, of soldiers were coming up the Missouri" (Cutler, 202–3). Le Raye further reported that during the winter, large numbers of Indians assembled on

the Sioux River (he isn't clear on whether this is the Little or Big Sioux River) and decided to attack the soldiers at the Mandan and Hidatsa villages. By the time they were ready to attack, however (in the spring of 1805), they learned that the corps had already headed west. Scholars disagree as to the authenticity of Le Raye's journal. Doane Robinson thought it credible, but George E. Hyde and Bernard DeVoto did not. See DeVoto (2), 613.

To the north, in present-day Canada, Daniel W. Harmon, a trader with the North West Company, recorded on 24 November 1804:

> Some people have just arrived from Montagne a la Basse, with a letter from Mr. Chaboillez, who informs me, that two Captains, Clarke and Lewis, with one hundred and eighty soldiers, have arrived at the Mandan Village on the Missouri River . . . they hoisted the American flag, and informed the Natives that their object was not to trade, but merely to explore the country; and that as soon as the navigation shall open, they design to continue their route across the Rocky Mountain, and thence descend to the Pacific Ocean. They made the Natives a few small presents, and repaired their guns, axes, &c., gratis. Mr. Chaboillez writes, that they behave honourably toward his people, who are there to trade with the Natives. (Harmon, 101–2)

On 31 October 1804, Lewis and Clark had written a polite letter to Chaboillez and sent it by way of British trader Hugh McCracken; see Jackson (3), 1:213–14.

3. Clark's journal entries, 14 and 15 August 1806.

4. Clark's journal entry, 15 August 1806.

5. Lewis's journal entry, 11 August 1806.

6. See Ordway's journal entry, 14 August 1806; Clark's journal entry, 12 August 1806; and Lewis's journal entry, 11 August 1806.

7. Meriwether Lewis to William Clark, 19 June 1803, Jackson (3), 1:60; William Clark to Meriwether Lewis, 18 July 1803, ibid., 1:110–11.

8. Lewis's journal entry, 14 June 1806.

9. Ordway's journal entry, 12 August 1806.

10. Meriwether Lewis to Henry Dearborn, 15 January 1807, Jackson (3), 1:369.

11. Clark's journal entry, 14 May 1805; Lewis's journal entries, 14 and 16 May 1805.

12. Clark's journal entry, 30 April 1805; Clark's journal entry, 14 August 1805.

13. Clark's journal entry, 29 June 1805.

14. Clark's journal entry, 17 August 1806. Charbonneau also received his pay, settling with Clark for $500.33 1/3 for his service and a horse and a tepee that he had donated. (His official government pay was $409.16 2/3.) Sacagawea got nothing, not surprising considering the social climate of the times, but Clark later wrote to Charbonneau that Sacagawea, "who accompanied you that long dangerous and fatigueing rout to the Pacific Ocian and back diserved a greater reward . . . than we had in our power to give her at the Mandans" (Jackson [3], 1:315).

15. Ordway's journal entry, 5 September 1806; Clark's journal entry, 1 September 1806.

16. Thomas Jefferson to Meriwether Lewis, 22 January 1804, Jackson (3), 1:166.

17. Clark's and Ordway's journal entries, 25 September 1804.

18. Clark's journal entry, 30 August 1806.

19. Clark's journal entry, 29 August 1806.

20. Clark's journal entry, 17 September 1806. Note this example of how widespread the rumors were. On 22 February 1806, from a post in the Chickasaw nation (possibly in present-day Mississippi), Indian agent John McKee had written to General Wilkinson: "Has any news reached your capital from captains Lewis & Clark? it is rumored here that they have been killed. I hope sincerely there is nothing of it" (Graff Collection, Newberry Library).

21. Thomas Jefferson to "My friends & children of the Ricara nation," 11 April 1806, Jackson (3), 1:306.

22. Clark's journal entry, 19 September 1806. On pawpaws, see Rogers.

CHAPTER TWO: *"All the Red Men Are My Children"*

1. Meriwether Lewis to Thomas Jefferson, 23 September 1806, Jackson (3), 1:319–20.

2. Timothy Flint, *Recollections of the Last Ten Years,* 110, cited in Oglesby, 14.

3. Ronda (2), 19–20. William Clark's comment about certain men relapsing into old habits is quoted from Nicholas Biddle's notes, taken during a visit with Clark in Virginia about April 1810, Jackson (3), 2:544.

4. *National Intelligencer and Washington Advertiser,* 16 January 1807, cited in Foley and Rice, 6.

5. Dillon, 266.

6. Thomas Jefferson to the Wolf and People of the Mandan Nation, Washington, 30 December 1806. See also Jefferson to the Indian Delegation, 4 January 1806, Jackson (3), 1:280–83.

7. Lamar, 570.

8. Davis (1), 27–29; *William Plumer's Memorandum of Proceedings in the United States Senate, 1803–1807,* cited in Foley and Rice, 5; emphasis in original.

9. Wharton, 104–9.

CHAPTER THREE: *"They Appeared in Violent Rage"*

1. Some have given Shannon's birthdate as 1785, others as 1787. I was unable to find an original birth record. However, I have always favored the 1785 date because I believe it is much more likely that William Clark (in 1803) enlisted a youth of eighteen than one of sixteen. The 1785 date has been confirmed to my satisfaction because George Shannon's son W. R. Shannon gave 1785 as the year of his father's birth (W. R. Shannon to Eva Emery Dye, 8 December 1902, Dye Collection, Oregon Historical Society). The younger Shannon also confirmed that his father was born in Pennsylvania but did not mention the city or county.

2. Moulton (2), 2:514.

3. Jackson (3), 1:117.

4. Jackson (3), 2:414.

5. Ibid., 1:367.

6. Lamar, 412.

7. When the St. Louis Missouri Fur Company was founded, according to Hiram Martin Chittenden, "the members of the new company in the order in which their names appear in the record were Benjamin Wilkinson, Pierre Chouteau, Sr., Manuel Lisa, Auguste Chouteau, Jr., Reuben Lewis, William Clark, Sylvester Labadie, all of St. Louis; Pierre Menard and William Morrison, of Kaskaskia, Illinois; Andrew Henry of Louisiana, Missouri, and Dennis FitzHugh, of Louisville, Kentucky." On the other hand, "Mr. Astor was the [American Fur] company and the incorporation was merely 'a fiction to broaden and facilitate his operations'" (Chittenden, 1:138, 313). The various members of the Chouteau family are delineated in Chapter 6, note 12.

8. Reports, 32–39.

9. Meriwether Lewis to Henry Dearborn, 15 January 1807, Jackson (3), 1:368.

10. White (2), 5.

11. Ibid., 6.

12. Pryor's account is from his letter to William Clark, 16 October 1807, Jackson (3), 2:432–38. Quotes in this narrative are taken directly from Pryor's letter.

13. Chittenden, 1:116.

14. Of the expedition veterans accompanying Sheheke on this journey, only two have been positively identified: Nathaniel Pryor and George Shannon. Because George Gibson was an excellent hunter and scout and also an interpreter, as well as a close associate of Pryor and Shannon, I consider it quite likely that he was the member of the party identified only by the last name of Gibson. (Gibson is mentioned in a letter from Frederick Bates to Dennis Fitzhugh, 16 December 1807, in which Bates discusses advances made to the wounded men in Pryor's party [Marshall, 237].) The Field brothers are not identified by name, but James Holmberg has suggested that they could have been with Chouteau's party: "The time frame for Pryor's party to return down the Missouri from the Arikara villages fits. The Field family knew of Joseph's death by 20 October 1807. William Clark, in Louisville at the time, knew of Pryor's defeat by 24 October. The battle was 9 September, and the trip from those villages to St. Louis took about one month. If the party returned to St. Louis in early October, word could have been received in Louisville of Joseph's death by mid-October" (Holmberg [3], 95).

Although Harry M. Majors has suggested that Joseph Field may have accompanied the mysterious McClellan (or McClallen) party up the Missouri in the fall of 1806, I am convinced the documents indicate otherwise (Majors, 573). Sometime after 3 March 1807, eight members of the expedition signed a petition to the U.S. Congress, requesting that the men be allowed to receive their land grants in the territories east of the Mississippi, rather than in public lands west of the Mississippi (see Jackson [3], 2:378–80). (The petition's request was not granted.) The eight signatories were the Field brothers, John B. Thompson, Hugh Hall, Silas Goodrich, George Gibson, Alexander Willard, and Patrick Gass. A study of the document reveals distinctly different signatures, indicating that the men signed for themselves. (The similar signatures of the Field brothers are the only exception—it seems possible, but hardly certain, that the same person signed both names.) Anyone who was present to sign the petition could not have been with the McClellan party. On the other hand, the Field brothers and George Gibson could easily have signed the document in April and accompanied Pryor and Chouteau up the Missouri a month later. Because of this documentary evidence, as well as news of Joseph Field's death reaching Louisville by mid-October (highly unlikely if Joseph had been killed in the Montana country, where McClellan was during the summer of 1807), I believe that Holmberg's theory holds up quite well.

15. Appleman, 23.

16. In his letter to Clark, Pryor wrote: "My Hunter's leg was broken. One of the soldiers had a ball through the fleshy part of his leg—and a second was wounded in the hip and arm" (Nathaniel Pryor to William Clark, 16 October 1807, Jackson [3], 2:436). Historians have generally assumed that the hunter was Shannon. Frederick Bates may have been referring to the same three wounded men when he wrote to Clark's brother-in-law Judge Fitzhugh: "General Clark has desired me to draw on him at Louisville to meet the demands against the Indian Department, and informs me that they will be paid in his absence by yourself. I drew on the 7th in favor of Shannon for $300.. On the 12 in favor of Gibson for 200.. On the 14 in favor of Lorimier for 303.." (Frederick Bates to Dennis Fitzhugh, 16 December 1807, Marshall, 236−37). As for Pryor not mentioning the men by name, Jackson believes "the omission suggests that Pryor wrote Clark a personal account of the attack as well as this official one" (Jackson [3], 2:438n.6). If Pryor did write such a letter, he may have also discussed the Field brothers.

17. Statement of B. G. Farrar, 11 September 1816, Jackson (3), 2:620. An account published in 1880 claims that Shannon "ventured to walk upon [his wounded leg] before it was entirely well, and broke off the bone afresh, and to save his life the leg was amputated" (Caldwell [2], 187).

18. Frederick Bates to William Clark, December [no specific date given] 1807, Marshall, 248 (emphasis in original); W. R. Shannon to Eva Emery Dye, 8 December 1902, Dye Collection, Oregon Historical Society.

CHAPTER FOUR: *"He Saw the Prairie Behind Him Covered with Indians in Full and Rapid Chase"*

1. Cartwright, 254−57. Dickson reportedly arrived back in St. Louis in June or July of 1807, selling his furs for thousands of dollars. He and his wife, Susan, had nine children and lived in present-day Illinois and Wisconsin. Joseph worked as a farmer and trapper, donating much of his free time to religion and education. He died in

1844 at the age of sixty-nine. (See the articles by Frank H. Dickson, a great-great-grandson of Joseph, for more information.)

2. James (2), 56.

3. A number of documents show that these five Lewis and Clark veterans were part of Manuel Lisa's first trading venture up the Missouri, in 1807. For example, Drouillard's presence is clearly documented by the murder trial he faced in August 1808 (described in Chapter 5). Weiser and Potts both signed a promissory note to Manuel Lisa at Fort Raymond (Montana country) on 6 July 1808, which means they were also with this group, which spent the winter of 1807–8 at Fort Raymond (Manuel Lisa Collection, Missouri Historical Society). Richard Windsor's name is included in Pierre Menard's "List of Notes of the 'Men' on the Missouri Belonging in Part to Pierre Menard, 1808–1810" (Business Papers 1774–1825, Pierre Menard Papers, Illinois State Historical Library). The list, which identifies at least twenty men (some names are not legible), is obviously incomplete because it does not contain the names of Drouillard, Weiser, or Potts. (Burton Harris says there were forty-two men on Lisa's 1807 expedition, thirty-seven of whom were French Canadians [Harris, 60].) Since no trip up the Missouri took place in 1808, anyone working for Lisa in the Montana region by that time necessarily accompanied the 1807 group. Lepage's presence is a little more tenuous. On 31 December 1809, at Fort Raymond, Colter and Reuben Lewis signed a promissory note to the heirs of Lepage's estate, indicating that Lepage had died by that time and that he had trapped at Fort Raymond (see Colter-Frick [1], 98). Manuel Lisa was one of the executors of Lepage's estate (St. Louis Probate Records, 25 July 1810), another indication that Lepage was present. All this is consistent with Lepage's prior history—he joined the expedition at Fort Mandan and was already an experienced trapper and scout by 1804.

4. Richard Oglesby has speculated that Colter was offered "free trapper" status, and Colter's subsequent actions support such a theory (Oglesby, 46). For a typical fur hunter's contract, see Noy, 43–44.

5. Bradbury, 98. Robinson was definitely in the group because he is included in Pierre Menard's list mentioned above, in note 3. Richard Oglesby (*Manuel Lisa*, 45) and Robert M. Utley (*A Life*, 23) both speculate that Hoback and Reznor were also present. The phrase "doomed trio" is Utley's.

6. Skarsten (2), 271–79.

7. Holmes, 7. Rose had been living among the Osage Indians. He replaced the deserter Bissonnet near the mouth of the Osage River (Harris, 63). He may have been fleeing the law when he joined Lisa's party (Lamar, 987). According to Washington Irving, "Rose had formerly belonged to one of the gangs of pirates who infested the islands of the Mississippi, plundering boats as they went up and down the river, and who sometimes shifted the scene of their robberies to the shore, waylaying travelers as they returned by land from New Orleans with the products of their downward voyage, plundering them of their money and effects, and often perpetrating the most atrocious murders" (Chittenden, 2:676).

8. Oglesby, 47–51.

9. Holmes, 8.

10. At various times on the expedition, Weiser was assigned to obtain horses, salmon, and roots from Indians. Although my account of Weiser's journey is speculative, it is based on documents that indicate he did indeed follow the Madison. In a letter written in 1810, Reuben Lewis mentioned that "the rout by the middle fork on Madison's River is almost without mountains it is about 5 or 6 days travel to an illigable plan for a fort on that River where the Beavers from the account of Peter Wyzer, is as abundant as in our part of the country" (Oglesby, 95–96). In addition, when William Clark prepared a map of the region in 1809–11 (after consulting with Drouillard and Colter and possibly Weiser), he labeled a branch of the Snake River "Wiser's R." Some historians have suggested that Weiser accompanied Henry on the 1810–11 trip, but a November 1810 court document indicates that Weiser had returned to St. Louis by that time (Complaint of Peter Wiser against Rufus Easton, Missouri Historical Society).

11. Brackenridge, 91.

12. Washington Irving, *Adventures in the Far West*, cited in Mattes, 255–56.

13. Lewis's journal entry, 29 June 1806; Russell, 99.

14. Kubik, 12. Barbara Kubik based this composite of Colter's route on such sources as Saylor, Harris, Mattes, and Hiram Chittenden, *The Yellowstone National Park*. As she points out, the experts disagree on various aspects of Colter's journey, but "the 'composite' highlights the major points of Colter's route" (Kubik, 12). Mattes says: "Colter's precise route is subject to wide differences of opinion, largely revolving about the identification of 'Lake Biddle' and 'Lake Eustis' with Jackson Lake and Yellowstone Lake, respectively, and the true location of a certain 'Boiling Spring' and a 'Hot Spring Brimstone.' . . . While his route can only be conjectured, few have challenged the basic proposition that Colter did traverse, in some way, the Yellowstone Park area" (Mattes, 254). Kubik's map is similar—but not identical—to that of John Logan Allen, who agrees that Colter entered the area that is now Yellowstone Park, following the Yellowstone River north out of Yellowstone ("Eustis") Lake and then making his way east, back to the Shoshone River (Allen, 378). Neither Drouillard nor Colter left an account of his journey, but both apparently described their travels to William Clark, who drew maps of the area and traced the routes of both men. Clark was assisted by a map drawn by Drouillard, one that "showed the country around present-day Cody, Wyoming, with amazing detail" (ibid., 378n.57). Although he never saw the Yellowstone Park or Cody area himself, Clark had firsthand knowledge of Bozeman Pass and the Yellowstone River. Speaking of Clark's 1810 map, Paul E. Cohen wrote, "Its influence as the base map of the American West was not superseded until the final inputs of cartographic information from the Rocky Mountain fur trade and the explorations of John C. Fremont in the 1840s" (Cohen, 92)

15. James (2), 52–54. Colter's role in the battle (but not his wound) became known among those who followed him west. In 1819, more than two decades before James's account was published, Major Thomas Biddle wrote from Council Bluffs to Colonel Henry Atkinson: "This messenger [Colter] unfortunately fell in with a party of the

Crow nation, with whom he staid several days. While with them, they were attacked by their enemies the Blackfeet. Coulter, in self-defence, took part with the Crows. He distinguished himself very much in the combat; and the Blackfeet were defeated, having plainly observed a white man fighting in the ranks of their enemy. Coulter returned to the trading house" (Major Thomas Biddle to Colonel Henry Atkinson, 29 October 1819, ASP, Class II, Indian Affairs, vol. 2, 202). Biddle went on to mention Potts's death and Colter's escape.

16. Oglesby, 58–61.

17. Holmes, 9–10. Holmes's assertion that the buckshot harmlessly passed through the legs of a "long-legged man" before hitting the boat strains believability.

18. Chittenden, 2:676.

19. Potts documents, Meriwether Lewis Papers, Missouri Historical Society.

20. Potts signed a promissory note at Fort Raymond on 7 July 1808, so he and Colter left sometime after that.

21. Bradbury, 45n.18.

22. Ibid.

23. Ibid.; James (2), 57. John Potts's estate, which included his 320-acre land warrant, was probated on 6 January 1810 in St. Louis. He left no heirs, nor did he leave a will (St. Louis and St. Louis County, Missouri Probate Records, 1804–49). The paperwork dragged on for fifteen years, and "on the third Monday of December 1825, the Court ruled that the estate of John Potts was insolvent" (Colter-Frick [1], 269–71).

24. James (2), 58. James claims that the chief spoke to Colter in the Crow language (not explaining how the chief knew that Colter spoke Crow). Bradbury, on the other hand, accounts for the communication between Colter and the Blackfoot chief by noting that Colter "had in a considerable degree acquired the Blackfoot language, and was also well acquainted with Indian customs" (45–46).

25. Ibid., 59.

26. Jackson (2), 191–92.

27. James (2), 60.

28. Bradbury, 46–47n.18.

29. Ibid., 47n.18.

30. Ibid.

31. James (2), 61.

32. Bradbury says Colter's journey took "at least seven days"; Thomas says it took nine days; James says eleven. The latter figure sounds more reasonable to me because Colter had to travel approximately 220 miles, some of it over mountains or hills.

33. James (2), 62. My account synthesizes those of Thomas James (*Three Years Among the Indians and Mexicans*), John Bradbury (*Travels in the Interior of America*), and Dr. William H. Thomas (reprinted in Jackson, "Journey to the Mandans"), each of which has both strengths and weaknesses. James had the advantage of knowing Colter well and traversing the very route of the famous run with Colter himself. In addition, he heard Colter tell the story—presumably several times—in 1809, one year after Colter's escape. However, James did not publish his narrative until

1846. It is not known when he first recorded it. Bradbury, on the other hand, heard the story in 1810 (when Colter arrived in St. Louis) and published it in 1817 (apparently recording it in 1811). Bradbury's account implies he had one brief interview with Colter. Dr. Thomas was a surgeon who in the spring of 1809 accompanied Pierre Chouteau's party up the Missouri in the successful effort to return Sheheke to his home in present-day North Dakota (James was also in the party). Thomas met Colter in this region in September 1809 and published his account of Colter's run (in the *Missouri Gazette*) in December of the same year, making him both the first to record and the first to publish Colter's story. However, his account is by far the shortest. James's account is much more detailed than the other two, but one senses a certain embellishment. Bradbury's version includes a number of details without apparent embellishment, but he is nevertheless quite mistaken on certain points, such as claiming Joseph Dickson traveled from St. Louis to the headwaters of the Missouri by himself. Still, a reading of all three sources provides a reasonably coherent—and compelling—account of John Colter's remarkable adventure. Washington Irving, who never interviewed Colter, published his version of Colter's run in *Astoria*, in 1836, clearly drawing from Bradbury and giving proper credit.

CHAPTER FIVE: *"This Has Not Been Done Through Malice"*

1. Some have suggested that Shannon was involved in an expedition to explore saltpeter caves in the summer of 1808. As Donald Jackson states, "in a letter from [Meriwether] Lewis to Col. Thomas Hunt, 2 June 1808 (MoSHi), he asks the Colonel—commanding Cantonment Belle Fontaine—to shoe the horses of Lewis McFarlane and a Mr. Shannon who were going on the expedition" (Jackson [3], 2:473n.11). I don't believe this was George Shannon, however. It doesn't make sense that Lewis would send Shannon on an expedition just as Shannon was completing his convalescence from a leg amputation. As late as May of 1808, Lewis had apparently visited Shannon in the hospital, noting an expense of $68.27.5 for supplies for Shannon. It also seems strange that Lewis would mention McFarlane's first name but then refer to a man he knew well as "a Mr. Shannon." (Shannon was not an uncommon name in the Louisiana Territory at the time.) In addition, the saltpeter expedition was possibly still in progress when Drouillard's trial began. Jackson notes: "How long the exploration lasted I cannot say; but on 31 Oct. 1808 the factor at newly established Fort Madison paid Lewis McFarlane for his services as *patron* of a boat loaded with factory goods shipped to that post" (ibid.; emphasis in original).

2. My reconstruction of the trial is taken from the following documents: writs of habeas corpus for Manuel Lisa and George Drouillard, 8 August 1808, Lucas Papers, Missouri Historical Society (MHS); indictments for Lisa and Drouillard, 19 September 1808, Lucas Papers, MHS; summary of arguments and evidence, *United States v. G. Drouillard*, 19 September 1808, Lucas Papers, MHS; miscellaneous court documents, *U.S. v. George Drouillard*, 20 September 1808 and 23 September 1808, St. Louis

Court Files, MHS; "The United States vs. George Drouillard," *Missouri Gazette,* 12 October 1808; and the affidavit of Antoine Dubreuil, MHS, cited in Skarsten (2), 271–72 (translated from the French by Thomas Molnar). All quotations, including underlining, are reproduced verbatim. Although the trial is often thought to have taken place in its entirety on 23 September, the above documents show that the trial began on 19 September and ended on 23 September 1808. Lisa was definitely charged with murder; the trial transcript, however, makes it clear that Drouillard alone was tried.

3. George Drouillard to "My Dear Marie Louise," 23 May 1809, cited in Speck, 91–92, original in French. Drouillard's family lived near Detroit, where he was born in 1773. Drouillard's mother was a Shawnee named Asoundechris Flat Head. What became of her after George's birth is unknown; however, George's father, Pierre Drouillard, married Marie Angelique Decamps in 1776, and George was referring to her when he mentioned "our Mother." Marie Louise, who was five years younger than George, was technically his half-sister. (She died in 1855.) Pierre Drouillard was a British subject who served as an interpreter of the Huron language. As the letter shows, George Drouillard was an educated man (Skarsten [2], 18–19; Drouillard genealogy files, Lewis and Clark Trail Heritage Foundation).

4. The militia company of thirty-six dragoons who accompanied William Clark did not include any veterans from the expedition (Gregg [2], 49). Clark wrote one letter to his brother Jonathan (then living in Louisville, Kentucky) on 22 August 1808 and another on 1 October (before and after his expedition to the Osages). He did not mention Drouillard's trial in either one. Interestingly, the second letter was carried by George Shannon, then on his way to Lexington (Holmberg [3], 148–51). Nor did Meriwether Lewis mention Drouillard or Lisa in a letter he wrote to his friend Major William Preston on 25 July 1808 (Bentley, 171–74).

5. Speck, 92.

CHAPTER SIX: *"The Gloomy and Savage Wilderness"*

1. As Vardis Fisher points out, a number of historians "have accepted Mrs. Grinder's version of the death, though they haven't known where she came from, or her first name, or her age or the age of her husband, or her racial background. They haven't even known whether she could read or write her name. In short, they have known practically nothing about the quality of their witness" (Fisher, 121). Fisher researched the Grinders quite thoroughly (118–26), and I tend to follow his lead. The Grinders owned slaves at various times; whether any were present when Lewis died is uncertain. Fisher recounts the story of a slave named Malinda, supposedly present when Lewis died (160–70), but I believe this account is too far removed from the actual event—and passed on too many times—to be of value. Fisher based his tentative conclusions on careful study of Tennessee census records; still, with the evidence presently available, it is impossible to know how many people were present—or their

exact ages—at the stand when Lewis arrived. As for the name itself, Griner is considered the correct spelling, even though historians have traditionally used Grinder. Because the original sources virtually all have Grinder, I believe it is less confusing to follow that pattern. In the early 1800s, of course, it would not have been unusual for family members to spell their name differently at different times (see Chandler, 353n.18).

2. My account of Lewis's death is based on Alexander Wilson's letter of May 1811, which was published in Philadelphia in the *Port Folio* 7 (January 1812): 34–47. My quotations are taken directly from that document; see Appendix B for the complete letter. I have relied on Wilson's account because he was an impartial and careful observer who interviewed the key witness, Priscilla Grinder, within a year and a half of Lewis's death and immediately made a detailed record of the interview. Although James Neelly spoke with Mrs. Grinder directly after Lewis's death, his account (also reprinted in Appendix B) is problematic for at least two reasons. First, he summarizes items that Wilson covers in detail. Second, Neelly had possible motives for shading his report—he may have wanted to protect his position as U.S. agent to the Chickasaw nation and deflect criticism for his leaving Lewis alone. Of course, Mrs. Grinder had possible motives of her own for not being completely candid—she may have feared that she would be blamed for Lewis's death. That's exactly why Wilson's report has value—he had no ulterior motives. I also believe that a lie by either Mrs. Grinder or James Neelly would likely be revealed by the other's account (unless one assumes they were co-conspirators, which I take to be an untenable assumption). Pernia is another factor in the equation. Thomas Jefferson and William Clark both had a chance to interview him, and both of them apparently found his explanation acceptable. Therefore, despite the anomalies surrounding Lewis's death, I believe we can get at the truth through a careful look at the relevant documents.

3. For information on the state of affairs in St. Louis (which possibly involved a conspiracy among Aaron Burr, James Wilkinson, and others) while Lewis and Clark were on their journey, see Carter (1).

4. Ruth Colter-Frick argues that Lewis's financial problems were not as serious as they appeared: "it is clear that the governor of Upper Louisiana was a man of some means, even if he may have been short of cash" (Colter-Frick [2], 20).

5. The Conrad Prospectus, ca. 1 April 1807, Jackson (3), 2:394; C. and A. Conrad and Co. to Thomas Jefferson, 13 November 1809, ibid., 2:469.

6. See Beckham, 89–143, for information on the Gass journal and the counterfeit versions.

7. Thomas Jefferson to Meriwether Lewis, 17 July 1808, Jackson (3), 2:444–45. As Jackson says, "Lewis well deserved a scolding for his failure to write. From the time of his parting with Jefferson in the fall of 1807 to his death in the fall of 1809, he wrote him three, possibly four, letters. None of the surviving letters contains more than a perfunctory expression of the warm relationship that had once existed between the two men" (ibid., 2:445n.1).

8. Reuben Lewis to Mary Marks, 29 November 1807, cited in ibid., 2:721.

9. Frederick Bates to Richard Bates, 9 November 1809, Marshall, 108; Frederick Bates to Richard Bates, 14 July 1809, Marshall, 67–69. Bates was petty enough to re-hash a frivolous grievance *after* hearing of Lewis's death:

> Some time after this, there was a ball in St. Louis, I attended early, and was seated in conversation with some Gentlemen when the Governor entered. He drew his chair close to mine—There was a pause in the conversation—I availed myself of it—arose and walked to the opposite side of the room. The dances were now commencing.—*He* also rose—evidently in passion, retired into an adjoining room and sent a servant for General Clark, who refused to ask me out as he fore-saw that a Battle must have been the consequence of our meeting. He com-plained to the general that I had treated him with contempt & insult in the Ball-Room and that he could not suffer it to pass. He knew my resolutions not to speak to him except on business and he ought not to have thrust himself in my way. (Frederick Bates to Richard Bates, 9 November 1809, ibid., 109–10; emphasis in original)

Bates's resentment toward Lewis may have originated when Lewis was appointed Jefferson's secretary, a position Bates's father had hoped would be awarded to Bates's brother Tarleton. (Like the Lewis family, the Bateses were friends of Thomas Jeffer-son.) On 4 May 1801, Thomas F. Bates had written to his son Frederick: "A postscript to your letter, made by Tarleton 20th March, informs that a Capt. Lewis had received and accepted the appointment of private Secretary to the President, so that my golden dreams have been delusive" (Jackson [3], 1:134n).

10. Frederick Bates to William Clark, December 1807, Marshall, 250.

11. Thomas Jefferson to Meriwether Lewis, 17 July 1808, Jackson (3), 2:444, 445n.1.

12. Agreement for the Return of the Mandan Chief, ibid., 2:447. Pierre (Jean-Pierre) Chouteau (1758–1849), who signed this agreement, was an original partner in the Missouri Fur Company and half-brother to Auguste Chouteau (1749–1829). The Chouteau family had helped found St. Louis, and Auguste and Pierre were two of the most powerful men in the city. Pierre was the father of Auguste-Pierre Chouteau (1786–1838), a West Point graduate who had accompanied Nathaniel Pryor on the unsuccessful attempt to return Sheheke to the Mandan villages in 1807. Yet another Pierre Chouteau was Auguste-Pierre's younger brother Pierre, Jr., also known as Cadet (1789–1865). (See Lamar, 211–12.)

13. William Eustis to Meriwether Lewis, 15 July 1809, Jackson (3), 2:457; Meri-wether Lewis to William Eustis, 18 August 1809, ibid., 2:459–61.

14. William Clark to Jonathan Clark, 26 August 1809, Holmberg (3), 210. As Holmberg points out, it is not clear exactly when Lewis left St. Louis. Clark said it was 25 August, but Frederick Bates gave the date of 4 September (Frederick Bates to William Eustis, 28 September 1809, Marshall, 86). I favor Bates's account because it is more consistent with known dates of Lewis's journey downriver. It seems quite pos-sible that Clark wrote his letter thinking Lewis had left on 25 August, when in actual-

ity Lewis's trip was delayed for some reason. Bates was likely to keep an exact record of Lewis's comings and goings. In addition, Lewis reportedly attended a Governor's Council on 30 August, and Lewis's account book indicates he was still in St. Louis on 3 September (see Fisher, 77, 72–73).

15. Lewis had Seaman with him as early as September 1803, when Lewis was traveling from Pittsburgh to Louisville to meet Clark. "I made my dog take as many [squirrels] each day as I had occasion for," wrote Lewis on 11 September. "They wer fat and I thought them when fryed a pleasent food. . . . my dog was of the new-foundland breed very active strong and docile, he would take the squirrel in the water kill them and swiming bring them in his mouth to the boat." One researcher has suggested that Seaman "most likely had a black-and-white coat and was less bulky than the current breed, with longer legs and shorter hair" (Joyce Jensen, Letter to the editor, *We Proceeded On* 28 [May 2002]: 2). A book published five years after Lewis's death states that Seaman's collar was inscribed as follows: "The greatest traveller of my species. My name is SEAMAN, the dog of captain Meriwether Lewis, whom I accompanied to the Pacifick ocean through the interior of the continent of North America" (Timothy Alden, *A Collection of American Epigraphs and Inscriptions with Occasional Notes,* 5 vols. [New York: Privately printed, 1814], cited in Holmberg [2]). The author further states that Seaman was with Lewis when Lewis died.

16. White (2), 6.

17. Ambrose (2), 459; Thomas Jefferson to Paul Allen, 18 August 1813, Jackson (3), 2:592; Fisher, 73.

18. Fisher, 73; Lewis's journal entry, 13 November 1803. Historians debate whether Lewis had malaria and whether it caused him to commit suicide. For example, Thomas Danisi argues that Lewis indeed had malaria but that his self-inflicted wounds were "a strange and tragic form of self-surgery and not suicide" (Danisi, 15). The physician Ronald V. Loge, on the other hand, states that "the cardinal clinical features of malaria are recurring, physically disabling chills and fevers with a periodicity of 48 or 72 hours. Scrutiny of the Lewis and Clark journals fails to uncover any such pattern of illness in any member of the expedition" (Loge, 34). Eldon G. Chuinard, also a medical doctor, theorizes that Lewis had malaria but that he was murdered (Chuinard [3]).

19. *Cuming's Tour to the West,* Thwaites (2), 4:281; Dillon, 328. When Lewis and Clark returned from the expedition in September 1806, Lewis ended his long letter to Thomas Jefferson with thoughts of his mother, Lucy Meriwether Lewis Marks: "I am very anxious to learn the state of my friends in Albemarle particularly whether my mother is yet living" (Meriwether Lewis to Thomas Jefferson, Jackson [3], 1:324). Lucy Marks was described by Georgia governor George Gilmer as "sincere, truthful, industrious, and kind without limit" (Ambrose [2], 24); she survived her son Meriwether by twenty-eight years, dying at age eighty-five on 18 September 1837. (See Mary Newton Lewis for more information on the relationship between Lewis and his mother.)

John Ordway, the expedition's top soldier, lived in New Madrid. Whether he and Lewis saw each other at New Madrid is not known. If such a meeting did take place, Ordway was the last member of the corps to see Lewis alive.

20. *Cuming's Tour to the West*, Thwaites (2), 4:287.

21. Gilbert C. Russell to Thomas Jefferson, 4 January 1810, cited in Jackson (3), 2:574n.

22. Gilbert C. Russell to Thomas Jefferson, 31 January 1810, cited in ibid., 2:748. Russell also wrote to William Clark, but those letters are no longer extant. See Holmberg (3), 206–9.

23. Statement of Gilbert C. Russell, 26 November 1811, Jackson (3), 2:573.

24. James House to Frederick Bates, 28 September 1809, cited in Fisher, 87.

25. Meriwether Lewis to James Madison, 16 September 1809, Jackson (3), 2:464.

26. Meriwether Lewis to Amos Stoddard, 22 September 1809, ibid., 2:466.

27. Pierre Chouteau to William Eustis, 14 December 1809, ibid., 2:482.

28. Although we have no specific record of what Lewis and Pernia packed, such provisions were common for travelers in the area.

29. *Cuming's Tour to the West*, Thwaites (2), 4:313.

30. James Neelly to Thomas Jefferson, 18 October 1809, Jackson (3), 2:467; William Clark to Jonathan Clark, 26 November 1809, Holmberg (3), 228.

31. Memorandum of Lewis's Personal Effects [23 November 1809], Jackson (3), 2:470–72.

32. Chandler, 291.

33. James Neelly to Thomas Jefferson, 18 October 1809, Jackson (3), 2:467–68.

34. Guice (2), 23.

35. "As a surgeon," writes Eldon G. Chuinard, "I do not believe that Lewis could have sustained the second and fatal shot with the injury to his vital organs, and live for two hours and do all the moving about related by Mrs. Grinder" (Chuinard [3], part 3, 6).

36. James Neelly to Thomas Jefferson, 18 October 1809, Jackson (3), 2:467–68.

37. Fisher, 185–86.

38. William Clark to Jonathan Clark, 28 October 1809, Holmberg (3), 216–18. Clark wrote this letter at "Mr. Shannon's," and many historians have assumed Clark was visiting expedition veteran George Shannon, then attending Transylvania University in Lexington, Kentucky. Holmberg offers convincing evidence, however, that the Shannon in question was John Shannon, of Shelby County (ibid., 219). Clark did see George Shannon two days later in Lexington.

39. James Neelly to Thomas Jefferson, 18 October 1809, Jackson (3), 2:467–68.

40. Thomas Jefferson to Paul Allen, 18 August, 1813, ibid., 2:591–92. Jefferson, of course, had no firsthand knowledge of Lewis's death and was relying on Neelly and Pernia. In addition, his assumptions about Lewis's father cannot be documented. Strangely, Lewis's family did experience at least one case of serious mental illness, but it was on his mother's side rather than his father's. In 1819, ten years after Lewis's

death, a letter from a Mr. Harper to Meriwether's younger brother Reuben Lewis stated:

> Our neighborhood had been severely afflicted for some months past, among which your mother's family have had a large share, owing to the Doctor's [probably his half-brother, Dr. John Marks] situation; which has become to appearances hopeless; his insanity has assumed a dangerous appearance so that it has been found necessary to confine him. . . . You will now consider yourself the only prop of the family. Your mother yesterday requested that you might be immediately informed . . . and that you would hasten to their relief. Your mother's firmness is much weakened. Since writing above the Doctor has escaped from his friends and has not been heard of. (Drumm, 151)

Reuben Lewis promptly declined an appointment as agent for the Cherokees and returned to the family estate in Virginia, where he spent the remaining twenty-five years of his life. John Hastings Marks was the son of Lewis's mother and her second husband, Captain John Marks. Meriwether Lewis and Marks got along well, and Lewis had helped him launch a medical practice after the expedition. (I have not discovered what became of John Marks after he disappeared in 1819.) As for Meriwether's possible mental illness, Stephen Ambrose has suggested that Lewis was a manic-depressive and that after the expedition he also suffered from postpartum depression (Ambrose [2], 306–7, 430–31).

41. Adams, 225.

42. Thomas Jefferson to Meriwether Lewis, 16 August 1809, Jackson (3), 2:458.

43. Clark described his visit with Jefferson thus: "Soon after I got to Charlotsville saw Mr. Thos. Jefferson. He invited me to go and Stay at his house, &c. I went with him and remained all night, spoke much on the af[fair]s of Gov. Lewis &c. &c. &c." (Clark's 1809 Journal, ibid., 2:725). On 11 December, Jefferson wrote to C. and A. Conrad and Co.: "Genl. Clarke called on me a few days ago . . . and informed me that he had desired [Lewis's] trunks to be sent on to Washington under the care of Mr. Whiteside, the newly elected Senator from Tennessee. He is himself now gone on to Washington, where the papers may be immediately expected" (ibid., 2:479).

44. Clark's letter of 28 October 1809, cited above, clearly shows that Clark believed Lewis capable of suicide. As with virtually everything surrounding Lewis's death, however, even this is not cut and dried. According to Vardis Fisher, one of Clark's nieces said, "Uncle had a great love for Lewis, & he never spoke of him without the tears coming into his eyes. he never believed he committed suicide" (Fisher, 183).

45. Thomas Jefferson to Captain W. D. Meriwether, 21 August 1810, cited in Fisher, 248. Fisher investigated Pernia's possible suicide and concluded, "So far as anybody has been able to learn, it was only a rumor." Another rumor, which confuses York and Pernia (saying that Lewis's servant went on the expedition), reported that Pernia (or York) froze to death in 1880 or 1881 (Joe Dobbins to Eva Emery Dye, 21 January 1901, Dye Collection, Oregon Historical Society).

46. Gilbert C. Russell to Thomas Jefferson, 31 January 1810, cited in Fisher, 115–16. As of 1813, Russell was still trying to collect the money Lewis had owed him. He apparently received about $250 (of $379 due him) by 1816. (See Gilbert C. Russell to William D. Meriwether, 18 April 1813, Jackson [3], 2:732.)

47. Fisher, 136.

48. In *The Jefferson Conspiracies*, David Leon Chandler argues that General Wilkinson was the mastermind of a conspiracy to murder Lewis and that Thomas Jefferson was an accessory after the fact (supposedly because of his belief that Wilkinson's downfall would somehow lead to his own). Chandler, a Pulitzer Prize winner, did considerable research and produced a fascinating book, but he never actually presents any hard evidence to support his theory. I agree with John D. W. Guice that Chandler's theory is not credible (Guice [1], 11).

49. Fisher, 155. See Appendix B for the complete account.

CHAPTER SEVEN: *"I Give and Recommend My Soul"*

1. Thomas Jefferson to Meriwether Lewis, 26 October 1806, Jackson (3), 2:350.

2. Petition to the Senate and House, ibid., 2:379, written in the hand of Frederick Bates. The other signatories were John B. Thompson, Hugh Hall, Silas Goodrich, Alexander Willard, Patrick Gass, Reubin Field, and Joseph Field. Jackson makes no mention of Congress acting on this petition.

3. Concerning those wounded in Pryor's 1807 attempt to return Sheheke to the Mandan villages, Pryor wrote to William Clark: "My Hunter's leg was broken. One of the soldiers had a ball through the fleshy part of his leg—and a second was wounded in the hip and arm" (Nathaniel Pryor to William Clark, 16 October 1807, Jackson [3], 2:436). Correspondence from Frederick Bates apparently identifies these three as George Shannon, Gibson, and Lorimier (first name not known). Since Bates advanced $303 to Lorimier and $200 to Gibson, I assume Gibson had a less serious wound (Frederick Bates to Dennis Fitzhugh, 16 December 1807, Marshall, 236–37). As indicated earlier, the identification of George Gibson as the Gibson involved is likely but not certain.

4. Jefferson County, Kentucky, Deed Records, 21 March 1808. Maria was not present for the sale, and the judge sent representatives to interview her (apart from her husband) and ensure that she was freely selling the land.

5. George Gibson probate packet, St. Louis and St. Louis County, Missouri, Probate Records, 10 July 1810, File 63. Some of the language in Gibson's will was commonly used in wills of the period.

6. In his expedition journal entry of 27 January 1806, Lewis mentions treating Gibson the previous winter with mercury.

7. Clark's journal entry, 19 October 1805 (emphasis in original).

8. Holmberg (3), 189–205; Gibson probate packet. A note on George Gibson in the card catalog at the Missouri Historical Society reads as follows: "Died in St. Louis in 1809. His widow became Mrs. Cartmill, Mrs. Dunleavy and Mrs. Hayden."

9. Clark's journal entry, 12 April 1805; Nicholas Biddle notes, ca. April 1810, Jackson (3), 2:539; Clark's journal entry, 3 November 1804; Moulton (2), 3:227n.3.

10. Jackson (3), 2:382n.23. The note to Chouteau is located at the Missouri Historical Society and is written in French. Thanks to Elizabeth Watkins for her translation.

11. La Page family genealogy records provided by Jeffrey La Page; Lewis and Clark's settlement of account, 21 August 1809, Jackson (3), 2:462; Clark's list of expedition members, ca. 1825–28, ibid., 2:639; Fort Raymond promissory note dated 31 December 1809, cited in Colter-Frick (1), 155–56; Jean-Baptiste Lepage probate packet, St. Louis and St. Louis County, Missouri, Probate Records, 25 July 1810, File 75.

12. Shields family genealogy records provided by Richard B. Groharing; Yater, 7–8.

13. Holmberg (3), 97–98.

14. Clark's journal entry, 20 March 1806; Lewis's journal entry, 10 June 1805.

15. Lewis's journal entry, 6 February 1805.

16. The "horse mint" used to make tea was "probably nettle-leaved giant hyssop, horse-nettle, *Agastache urticifolia* (Benth.) Kuntze, which is common in the region" (Moulton [2], 7:285n.4).

17. Lewis's journal entry, 24 May 1806; Clark's journal entry, 8 April 1806. Concerning Bratton's recovery, author and physician Bruce C. Paton has written: "The primary problem, whatever the diagnosis, was in Bratton's lower back, within the spinal canal, or adjacent to the vertebral column, thus irritating the nerves going to the legs. Neither a malignant nor a benign tumor could have been cured in a sauna. . . . Many conditions cause lower back pain, but there are few problems that would go away spontaneously. After consulting with several orthopedic and neurosurgeons, the best conclusion is that Bratton had a herniated disc with muscle spasms. The heat relieved the spasms and the disc relocated spontaneously" (Paton, *Lewis and Clark: Doctors in the Wilderness*, 173–74).

18. Meriwether Lewis to Henry Dearborn, 15 January 1807, Jackson (3), 1:367.

19. Land records in Thomas Smith Letterbook, Western Historical Manuscript Collection, University of Missouri, Columbia. John Shields is listed in the 1807 census for the Indiana Territory.

20. Shields family genealogy records.

21. John Shields probate packet, 1 January 1810, Harrison County, Indiana.

22. Holmberg (3), 86.

CHAPTER EIGHT: *"A Sincere and Undisguised Heart"*

1. William Clark to Jonathan Clark, 1 October 1808, Holmberg (3), 151.

2. Amos Kendall to F. G. Flugel, 14 May 1814, cited in Remini, 17.

3. Minutes of the Board, 18 October 1799, cited in Wright (2), 35. "Between 1800 and 1830 the Transylvania Medical School was one of the three or four important institutions of its kind in the country. The university itself experienced its golden age during the decade 1817–27, when the New England Unitarian minister Horace Holley was president. Bickering, sectarianism, poverty, and anti-intellectualism, however,

wrecked the school. It never fulfilled its mission of becoming an important western public university" (Lamar, 1128).

4. George Rogers Clark (1752–1818) had lived in Kentucky for many years. Although a hero of the American Revolution, Clark had incurred debts in the northwest campaign that Virginia refused to honor. This led to his financial ruin and also contributed to his problems with alcoholism. William Clark was frequently involved in attempting to help him untangle his financial and legal difficulties. Ironically, George Rogers Clark suffered severe burns to his leg in a fire (during the period Shannon was attending Transylvania) and had to have the leg amputated. He suffered partial paralysis as a result (Holmberg [3], 24–25; Lamar, 220).

5. Manuscript by George Shannon on "Dreaming," 30 December 1809; manuscript by George Shannon on "Disinterested Benevolence," 20 November 1809; Meriwether Lewis Collection, Missouri Historical Society.

6. Cantrell, 39–40.

7. Shannon left Lexington in the summer of 1810 and traveled to Philadelphia. His mention of Henry Clay in an 1812 letter shows that he knew Clay by the time he left Kentucky (George Shannon to Nicholas Biddle, 5 February 1812, Jackson [3], 2:576).

8. William Clark to Jonathan Clark, 1 October 1808, Holmberg (3), 151; The Secretary of War to William Clark, 7 August 1809, Carter (2), *Territorial Papers of the United States, Louisiana-Missouri Territory*, 290.

9. Washington *National Intelligencer*, 15 November 1809, cited in Fisher, 184. As noted in Chapter 6, William Clark was traveling with his family and several others to Kentucky and Virginia and finally to Washington. They had left St. Louis on 21 September (Clark Journal, Jackson [3], 2:724).

10. Meriwether Lewis Clark was born 10 January 1809 in St. Louis. He graduated from West Point in 1830 and served as a major in the Mexican War. He sided with the South in the Civil War and served as a major of artillery and then a colonel. After the war he settled in Kentucky. He and his first wife, Abigail Prather Churchill, had seven children, several of whom went to live with relatives after Abigail's death in 1852. Lewis Clark's cousin John O'Fallon indicated that Lewis was self-indulgent and financially irresponsible. Lewis died of consumption on 28 October 1881. His son Meriwether Lewis Clark Jr. founded Churchill Downs and the Kentucky Derby before committing suicide in 1899 (Holmberg [3], 194–95).

11. Wright (2), 37.

12. Cantrell, 40. Austin received a certificate from Transylvania stating that he had "conducted himself in an exemplary & praiseworthy manner" at the university.

13. Cutright (1), 53–58.

14. William Clark to Nicholas Biddle, 20 February 1810, Jackson (3), 2:494; Nicholas Biddle to William Clark, 3 March 1810, ibid., 2:495; Nicholas Biddle to William Clark, 17 March 1810, ibid., 2:496; Cutright (1), 53, 59. Biddle's notes are reprinted in Jackson (3), 2:497–545.

15. William Clark to Nicholas Biddle, 22 May 1810, Jackson (3), 2:549.

16. Isaac L. Baker to Stephen Austin, 1 July 1810, Barker, vol. 2, part 1, 176; Nicholas Biddle to William Clark, 7 July 1810, Jackson (3), 2:551; Cutright (1), 60–61, which also notes that Biddle was referring to events of 10 July 1805, when Clark and ten others searched for large cottonwood trees near present-day Great Falls, Montana. Several weeks before Shannon left for Philadelphia, Robert Todd wrote to Austin: "I met George Shannon at Shelbyville and stayed a day or so with him" (Robert Todd to Stephen Austin, 17 May 1810, Barker, vol. 2, part 1, 172).

17. William Clark to Nicholas Biddle, 7 December 1810, Jackson (3), 2:563–64.

18. Nicholas Biddle to William Clark, 28 June 1811, ibid., 2:568–69.

19. Nicholas Biddle to William Clark, 8 July 1811, ibid., 2:569; William Clark to George Shannon, 8 August 1811, ibid., 2:570.

20. George Shannon to Nicholas Biddle, 23 January 1812, ibid., 2:575; *Kentucky Gazette* (Lexington, Ky.), 8 December 1812, 3, cited in Denton, 17.

21. Nicholas Biddle to William Clark, 4 July 1812, Jackson (3), 2:577.

CHAPTER NINE: *"He Must Have Fought in a Circle on Horseback"*

1. Pierre Chouteau to William Eustis, 14 December 1809, Jackson (3), 2:482; James (2), 26. During the winter of 1808–9, Chouteau, Manuel Lisa, William Morrison, Pierre Menard, Sylvestre Labbadie, William Clark, Reuben Lewis (Meriwether's brother), Andrew Henry, and others formed the St. Louis Missouri Fur Company. Meriwether Lewis contracted with the company to return Sheheke to his village. The initial fee of $7,000 may have been increased to $10,000. Some of Lewis's instructions to Chouteau are quite shocking to the modern reader. For example, Chouteau was to meet with an Arikara delegation and demand that they deliver the Indians who had killed members of his son's crew in 1807. If the chiefs could not determine who the guilty parties were, they were to "deliver an equivalent number with those murdered, from among such of their nation as were most active" in the battle, and "these murderers when Delivered will be shot in presence of the nation" (Meriwether Lewis to Pierre Chouteau, 8 June 1809, Jackson [3], 2:454). If the Arikara were uncooperative, Lewis advised Chouteau to encourage the Mandan and Hidatsa to attack them. To his credit, Chouteau met with the Arikara, reprimanded them, and demanded safe passage for Sheheke without shedding blood (Pierre Chouteau to William Eustis, 14 December 1809, ibid., 2:481–82).

2. Journal of Dr. Thomas, Jackson (2), 190–91.

3. Pierre Chouteau to William Eustis, 14 December 1809, Jackson (3), 2:482. James makes no mention of the conflict over the gifts, but Dr. Thomas confirms Chouteau's account: "It was expected by his people that he would be pretty liberal in the distribution of some of his valuables. However, their hopes were vain: Sheheken was as anxious to retain his property, as they were to receive it. Murmurs took the place of mirth, and on our departure from the village, his popularity was on the de-

cline" (Journal of Dr. Thomas, Jackson [2], 191). While Chouteau gives the generally accepted date of 24 September for Sheheke's reunion with his people, Thomas says it was 22 September.

4. James (2), 29; Journal of Dr. Thomas, Jackson (2), 191–92. Dr. Thomas's account was published in the *Missouri Gazette* in two parts, on 30 November and either 7 or 14 December 1809. (At the Missouri Historical Society, part of the 7 December issue and all of the 14 December issue are missing. Donald Jackson discovered that the second installment, which tells Colter's story, was reprinted in the 13 July 1810 issue of the Pittsburgh *Gazette*.) John Bradbury met Colter near Charette, in present-day Missouri, in May 1810 and published the best-known version of Colter's run in 1817 (Bradbury, 25–28). Washington Irving's retelling of Colter's adventure is based on Bradbury's version (Irving, 146–51). Thomas James spent several months with Colter in 1809–10 and heard of Colter's escape firsthand while visiting the site with him. James, however, did not publish his narrative (*Three Years Among the Indians and Mexicans*) until 1846.

Ruth Colter-Frick has theorized that John Colter and Meriwether Lewis were together in St. Louis in May 1809 (Colter-Frick [1], 70–71). This is based on the St. Louis court document *John Colter v. Estate of Meriwether Lewis, Dec'd*, which reads in part, "WHEREAS THE SAID MERIWETHER LEWIS ON THE FOURTH DAY OF MAY IN THE YEAR OF OUR LORD ONE THOUSAND EIGHT HUNDRED AND NINE AT THE DISTRICT AFORESAID WAS INDEBTED TO THE SAID JOHN IN THE SUM OF FIVE HUNDRED AND FIFTY NINE DOLLARS." I believe this is evidence that Lewis listed his debt to Colter (still unpaid for his expedition service) in a legal document, but I do not believe Colter was in St. Louis at the time. James and Thomas both make it clear that Colter was already at the Hidatsa village when they arrived. Furthermore, it is doubtful Colter could have left the northern Dakota region early enough in the spring to have arrived in St. Louis by the first week of May.

5. James gives the number of men on this venture as thirty-two (James [2], 45). Oglesby, however, believes the "figure must have been closer to eighty" (Oglesby, 93n.71).

6. James (2), 45–66.

7. Pierre Menard to Pierre Chouteau, 21 April 1810, Chittenden, 2:882.

8. James (2), 74.

9. Ewers, 139.

10. In May 1823, Immell and Jones and their companions were riding horses along a narrow, winding trail next to the Yellowstone River—and just a few miles from a friendly Crow camp—when a band of Blood Blackfeet "rushed on the whites with lance, battle-ax and scalping knife, and Immell and Jones fell among the first." Five other men were also killed (the names of four of them were apparently Berry, Plaude, Leblanc, and Lemerc), and four men escaped. The group lost horses, beaver pelts, traps, guns, and other supplies worth $15,500 (Morgan [1], 64; Reports, 35).

11. James (2), 65 (emphasis in original).

12. Reuben Lewis remained on the upper Missouri until 1813. Although he was later appointed agent to the Cherokees, he declined so that he could care for his mother and other family members in the wake of the mental illness of his half-brother, John Hastings Marks (above, Chapter 6, note 40). Reuben married his cousin, Mildred Dabney, in 1832, and he died twelve years later, leaving no descendants. He lived the last twenty-five years of his life at the family estate in Virginia (Drumm, 150–51).

13. James (2), 65. Bradbury later claimed that Colter traveled from the headwaters of the Missouri to St. Louis in thirty days (Bradbury, 44n.18). If accurate, this means Colter averaged eighty to ninety miles a day for the entire month.

14. James (2), 82.

15. Ibid.

16. Ibid., 83. "Months later the Bloods informed Alexander Henry that two of their men had been killed by the officer, or trader, from whom they looted 'fine cotton shirts, beaver traps, hats, knives, dirks, handkerchiefs, Russia sheeting tents, and a number of banknotes, some signed New Jersey and Trenton Banking Company'" (Harris, 150).

17. *Missouri Gazette*, 6 September 1810.

CHAPTER TEN: *"Water as High as the Trees"*

1. Penick, 4; Bagnall, 21–22, 25. The epicenter of the first series of earthquakes was actually sixty-five miles southwest of New Madrid, in present-day northeastern Arkansas near Blytheville (Penick, 6).

2. Penick, 32–33.

3. Ibid., 4; Bradbury, 204.

4. Penick, 33 (emphasis in original).

5. Bagnall, 21–22, 55; Stewart and Knox (1), 209; Stewart and Knox (2), 19. The New Madrid quake of 7 February 1812 is estimated at 8.8. The only North American earthquake of equal or greater magnitude is the one that struck Anchorage, Alaska, in 1964 and was measured at 8.8 or 8.9.

6. Lewis's journal entry, 8 June 1806.

7. Clarke (1), 44.

8. Jackson (3), 1:347–48. Bratton's daughter, Ella Fields, brought this document to historians' attention in 1901.

9. Draper Manuscripts, 21CC48; Lamar, 1126.

10. *Cuming's Sketches of a Tour to the Western Country, 1807–1809*, Thwaites (2), 4:281.

11. Bradbury, 204–6.

12. Penick, 68–70; Stewart and Knox (2), 19.

13. Montgomery, 64, 8, 10; Heroes, 98. Although some histories have claimed William Bratton lived in or near New Madrid at the time of the earthquake, his

grandson J. T. Fields helped clarify the situation: "In regard to Grandfather Bratton being near New Madrid at the time of the Earthquake, he was with a boating expedition as an employe, and never lived near there" (J. T. Fields to Eva Emery Dye, 18 November 1901, Dye Collection, Oregon Historical Society).

14. John Ordway to Honored Parence, 8 April 1804, Jackson (3), 1:176.

15. John Ball to his parents, 23 February 1833, in *Oregon Historical Society Quarterly* 3 (March 1902): 102. Ordway probably reached New Hampshire early in 1807 because a government record lists him as assisting Lewis from 11 October 1806 to 19 January 1807 (see Jackson [3], 1:325). There is no record of Ordway's discharge, although it presumably occurred after Sheheke and his party reached Washington. Wyeth, a Boston merchant trying to break into the fur trade, is memorably portrayed by Bernard DeVoto in *Across the Wide Missouri*.

16. John Ordway to Stephen Ordway, 15 November 1807, *Missouri Historical Review* 11 (July 1908): 282–83.

17. Before the expedition, John Ordway had written to his brother Stephen: "In May 1802 I received a letter from Betsey Cosby; She informed me that my friends & relatives are well also that she was about offering hirself a Sacrifice at the Shrine of Hymen which information I wish to have corroborated. . . . if She remains in a state of celibacy till my return I may perhaps join hands with hir yet" (John Ordway to Stephen Ordway, 5 September 1803, Jackson [3], 1:120). According to the Hebron, New Hampshire, town record, however, Betsey Crosby had married and died by 1806, before Ordway returned from the expedition. By November 1807, he had married Gracey. Although her maiden name is not known, Gracey was apparently from New Hampshire. Writing to Stephen—who remained in New Hampshire—John said, "Gracey sends hir love to all hir fathers family and yours not forgetting her grand marm nor any inquiring friends" (John Ordway to Stephen Ordway, 15 November 1807, 283). I found no further mention of Gracey and presume she died. A July 1809 document refers to Ordway's wife as Elizabeth; all subsequent documents call her Elizabeth or Betsey. A deposition filed with the United States General Land Office in 1848 states that Elizabeth Ordway had previously been married to David Johnson, father of David and Isidore Johnson (Deposition of John Johnson [no relation to David Johnson Sr.], widower of John Ordway's daughter, Hannah, copy in Ordway file, Lewis and Clark Trail Heritage Foundation Library, Great Falls, Montana). I believe Ordway met Elizabeth Johnson in the Missouri area because Martha Ordway Kibbler, a grand-niece of his, wrote that "the woman [John Ordway] married he found in the west" (Martha Ordway Kibbler to Eva Emery Day, 12 September 1902, Dye Collection, Oregon Historical Society).

18. New Madrid County, Missouri, Deed Records, 1805–1916, Books 3, 4, 5, 9, 10. From 1807 to 1810, John Ordway also conducted a good deal of business in the neighboring district of Cape Girardeau, where his brother William owned land. (Thanks to Jane Randol Jackson, director of the Cape Girardeau County Archive Center, for supplying information on these transactions.)

19. Penick, 83, 90, 41.

20. Bagnall, 28; Penick, 40.

21. Elizabeth Robison to Much Respected Brother and Sister Mother, 19 October 1817, Dye Collection, Oregon Historical Society. Probably because John Ordway and his brother Daniel both married women named Elizabeth—and because John and Daniel both died in Missouri and both left widows—some historians have mistakenly concluded that the author of this letter was John's widow. However, New Hampshire and Missouri records clearly show that Elizabeth Poor married Daniel Ordway in 1803, that he died by January 1811, and that Elizabeth married Kinsay Robison in March 1811, while John Ordway was still alive. The author of this letter is Elizabeth Poor Ordway Robison; the recipients were Stephen Ordway (John's older brother) and his wife Polly Mary Brown. Elizabeth added that after the earthquake, "to mend the matter my husband [Kinsay Robison] was drafted in time of the late war and went to Orleans and was gone six months but I have Grate Reason to be thankful that I have never wanted for anything to live on."

22. Stewart and Knox (1), 207; Penick, 42. Shaw reported that "Miss Masters eventually recovered" (Bagnall, 32).

23. Marshall, 127; Stephen Ordway, Letter for Petition of Administration, 7 January 1811, Grafton County, New Hampshire, Probate Records; Cape Girardeau County, Missouri, Deed Book C, 3 June 1813 and 17 November 1813; Elizabeth Robison to Much Respected Brother and Sister Mother, 19 October 1817. Showing a different side of his personality than what he revealed to Meriwether Lewis, Frederick Bates issued a posthumous pardon to William Ordway, who had been fined a total of fifty dollars for his offenses. "Whereas the said William Ordway, after the imposition of the said fines, departed this life, leaving a Wife and numerous family of infant, female children in indigent circumstances," wrote Bates, "Now therefore, be it known that I do hereby pardon the offences for which the said fines were imposed & require that all sheriffs or other collecting officers take one notice hereof."

24. Bagnall, 54; undated diary of Stephen F. Austin (apparently written 17–19 May 1812), Barker, 206–7. As Austin traveled down the Mississippi, he struck a sandbar and the barge sank in shallow water. He returned two months later and retrieved the cargo "with but little loss" (Cantrell, 48–49).

25. Cape Girardeau County, Missouri, Deed Book C, 3 June 1813; ASP, 3:330–31.

26. John Ordway documents, Meriwether Lewis Papers, Missouri Historical Society.

27. "According to Myron Fuller, 516 claim certificates were issued, but only 20 were used by original landowners" (Bagnall, 58). Bagnall also claims that William Clark was among those taking advantage of the situation by purchasing land titles via his agents.

28. New Madrid, 25–28; deposition of John Johnson.

29. Cold weather in many parts of North America during the summer of 1816 is generally attributed to the volcanic explosion of Mt. Tambora in Sumbawa, Indonesia, the previous year. Volcanic ash in the atmosphere radically affected the climate. See Stewart and Knox (1), 262.

30. Upon the expedition's return, John Ordway sold his expedition journal to Meriwether Lewis for three hundred dollars. After Lewis's death, William Clark later sent it to Nicholas Biddle, who used it as source material for his *History of the Lewis and Clark Expedition,* published in 1814. Ordway's journal was subsequently lost until 1913, when Biddle's grandsons found it among his papers. It was edited by Milo M. Quaife and published in 1916 by the Wisconsin Historical Society along with Lewis's Ohio River journal. See Moulton (2), 9:xvi–xvii, and Cutright (1), 70, 117, 128. The original Ordway journal is now housed at the American Philosophical Society, in Philadelphia. A recently discovered letter from Arthur Campbell to the Reverend Jedidiah Morse shows that Ordway initially considered publishing his journal on his own. See Oman, 7–10.

CHAPTER ELEVEN: *"She Was a Good and the Best Woman in the Fort"*

1. Drumm, 138. Charbonneau purchased the hardtack on 20 March 1811. The land sale occurred on 26 March.

2. Brackenridge, 152.

3. Ibid., 32.

4. Moore (2), 11. Bob Moore, the historian at the Jefferson National Expansion Memorial in St. Louis, made a significant contribution to Lewis and Clark scholarship when he discovered this baptism record. Although there is no record of Charbonneau and Sacagawea from August 1806, when Lewis and Clark left them at the Mandan villages, until the day of Pomp's baptism—28 December 1809—I agree with Moore, and Anderson (4), that Charbonneau and Sacagawea probably arrived in St. Louis for the first time in the fall of 1809. Grace Raymond Hebard theorizes that the Charbonneaus (as well as another Shoshone wife of Charbonneau's and her son) reached St. Louis in August 1806 and that Sacagawea and Pomp (and apparently the other wife and child) remained in St. Louis for the next four years, while Charbonneau was trapping in the southwest. Hebard reaches all these conclusions, however, with no supporting primary documents of any kind. (She does quote a 1925 statement from Dr. Charles Eastman, but this does not qualify as evidence [Hebard, 113].) Nor does she explain how the Charbonneaus could have possibly reached St. Louis ahead of the corps. As Anderson points out, "This is a truly remarkable accomplishment, considering that even the Lewis and Clark Expedition, which sailed from Mandan on an uninterrupted schedule, did not arrive in St. Louis until September 23, 1806!" (Anderson [4], 5). Although Hebard conducted a good deal of valuable research, this tendency to jump to conclusions consistently mars her work.

5. Clark pinpointed the date of his return in a letter to his brother Jonathan. In the same letter, he noted his disgust with Frederick Bates: "I find that Mr. Bates has disapproved of the proceeding[s] in the Indian departmt. and in addition to his Complaints against Govr. Lewis he has laid in Complaints against me to the government, the amount of which he has not Shewn me, but Sais he is ready to do it at any time I am at Some loss to determine how to act with this little animal whome I had mis-

taken as my friend, however I Shall learn a little before I act" (William Clark to Jonathan Clark, 16 July 1810, Holmberg [3], 248).

6. DeVoto (3), 202–3.

7. The artist C.-B.-J. Févret de Saint-Mémin later painted Lewis wearing this tippet.

8. Duncan and Burns (215) offer this information but do not quote a primary source. Similarly, Howard says that Cameahwait was killed in battle about 1840 but offers no source (Howard [1], 178).

9. Brackenridge, 31.

10. Ibid., 30.

11. Ibid., 70; Oglesby, 110.

12. Brackenridge, 72–73.

13. Ibid., 79–80, 93.

14. Ibid., 84, 90.

15. Ibid., 94–95.

16. Ibid., 111, 113. Lisa meant the Pacific Ocean when he mentioned "the great Salt lake to the west." Although Baron Lahontan (in the late 1600s) and Father Escalante (in the late 1700s) had both heard of the Great Salt Lake from Indians, neither had seen it. The Great Salt Lake, called "Pearl Shell Lake," was mentioned—without coordinates—on an 1802 government map, but Jim Bridger did not make his "discovery" of the salt lake until 1825 (see Alter, 57–62). Though Hunt may have heard of a large lake with brackish water, he clearly intended to follow the Missouri, Yellowstone, and Columbia Rivers to the Pacific Ocean. He ended up taking a more overland route than originally planned.

17. Bradbury, 98.

18. Holmes, 11–12.

19. Bradbury, 164.

20. Brackenridge, 137.

21. Bradbury, 164.

22. Brackenridge, 130–31.

23. Oglesby, 117, 126. Sacagawea's biographer, Harold P. Howard, assumes that Charbonneau (and possibly Sacagawea) spent the winter of 1811–12 in St. Louis because Charbonneau is included in Lisa's list of men for the 1812 expedition (Howard [1], 158). The list seems to indicate that all eighty-three men named were present when the two barges left St. Charles in May. However, a close look at Luttig's journal shows this is not true. On 4 June, for example, Luttig listed six men who had joined the party near Fort Osage. All are included in the list. Similarly, Edward Rose is presumed to have joined the group at the Arikara villages, and his name is included in the list. Therefore, it would not be contradictory for Charbonneau to be included even though he and Sacagawea may not have actually joined the group until August. (See Drumm, 157–58, for the list.)

24. Luttig's journal is reprinted in Drumm. Rather than multiply endnotes, I have included the date of each of his entries. John C. Luttig was apparently born and edu-

cated in Germany. He came to America, became a successful merchant, and arrived in St. Louis by 1809. He worked for William Clark as well as the Missouri Fur Company. In 1814 he settled in the Arkansas Territory and was named justice of the peace by Clark, then governor. Luttig died in July 1815 in Lawrence, Arkansas (Holmberg [3], 258). The fact that English was not Luttig's native language probably accounts for his contradictory style, seeming at times inept and at other times eloquent.

25. Probably because he was a slave, Charlo was not included in the official list of expedition members. However, George, apparently a free black, was included.

26. Cited in Anderson (2), 142.

27. "Thursday 27, clear and fresh," wrote Luttig, "the Big white mandan Chief arrived, with several of his Bravos and family, to pay a visit, he had a few Robes which he traded, and took some articles on Credit." I assume that Charbonneau and Sacagawea arrived at Fort Manuel with Sheheke because Luttig does not mention them prior to this time. Beginning on 17 September, Luttig makes frequent mention of Charbonneau.

28. Given the multiplicity and crossover of the names of native nations, it is sometimes quite difficult to know which tribe is being referred to. The Hidatsa, for example, were sometimes called the Minetarre, sometimes the Sioux, sometimes the Gros Ventre, and sometimes the Big Bellies. The Atsina were also called both the Gros Ventre ("Big Belly" in French) and the Big Bellies. Jim Holmberg suggests that Sheheke was killed by the Atsina (Gros Ventre of the Prairie) rather than the Hidatsa (Gros Ventre of the Missouri), since "the former were enemies and the latter were allies" of the Mandan (Holmberg [3], 117). Given what James Ronda calls the "always troubled state of Mandan–Hidatsa relations," however, I believe it is possible Sheheke had a run-in with the Hidatsa (Ronda [1], 88).

Concerning the date of Sheheke's death, some have claimed he died in 1832. This is based on a 7 January 1835 entry in trapper F. A. Chardon's journal, which reads: "Died this day three years, the Old Mandan Chief (The White Head) regretted by all Who Knew him" (Abel, 20). Annie Heloise Abel, the editor of Chardon's journal, believed this was a reference to Sheheke, whom the explorers called Big White. However, I don't know of Sheheke ever being called "The White Head." In addition, Chardon had no personal knowledge of Sheheke (nor does he make any claims about "The White Head" being associated with Lewis and Clark). Luttig's 1812 journal entry, on the other hand, specifically mentions "Big White" and says the report of his death came from the Mandan themselves. I therefore believe "The White Head" was a different person.

29. Drumm, 106. One expects Luttig to have said, "she was a good and the best Woman in the fort," which is how his words have generally been transcribed (and I have taken the license to use that phrase in the title of this chapter). A close look at the original journal, however, shows that Luttig wrote, "the best Women in the fort," which is how Stella M. Drumm transcribed the passage. (It is also consistent with Luttig's usage in other parts of his journal.)

30. Jackson (3), 2:638. See Appendix C for more information on the controversy concerning Sacagawea's death.

31. Anderson (2) offers an informative perspective on the fort, the question of Sacagawea's burial, and twentieth-century excavations at the site.

32. St. Louis Court Minute, 11 August 1813, cited in Anderson (4), 15. Sacagawea's daughter has almost universally been called "Lizette." However, as Anderson points out, the original manuscript clearly reads "Lisette." As Anderson notes, "Drumm inadvertantly altered it to 'z' and Hebard followed suit, as have most writers in citing the girl's name" (Anderson [2], 135n.12). No subsequent record of Lisette has been found. She may have been the Elizabeth Carboneau who married Joseph Vertifeuille in Missouri (see Howard [1], 162) or the Elizabeth Carbonau who married Chela Kanz in Kansas.

33. William Clark to Toussaint Charbonneau, 20 August 1806, Jackson (3), 1:315.

CHAPTER TWELVE: *"The Crisis Is Fast Approaching"*

1. Moyars, 4; Reid, 34.

2. Some sources claim that William Bratton was involved in the Battle of Tippecanoe, but, as explained in Chapter 10, he was working on a keelboat at the time and did not enlist until several months later, and he is not listed among the soldiers present at the battle (Reid, 52–64).

3. William Clark to the War Department, 20 July 1810, 12 September 1810, and 3 July 1811, U.S. War Department, Extracts of Letters About Indian Affairs, 1807–11, Ohio State Historical Society. In a letter to his brother Jonathan, Clark expressed similar sentiments: "Some time past an alarm was Stured up on the frontiers of Illinois—a Demand is made of the murderers & property by a party which is now in the Indian Country" (William Clark to Jonathan Clark, 17 August 1811, Holmberg [3], 259).

4. Steffen, 88.

5. Lamar, 1097.

6. Franklin Wharton to James Barbour, 28 February 1826, Jackson (3), 2:640–43; Nathaniel Pryor Papers, Meriwether Lewis Collection, Missouri Historical Society. Pryor later reported a loss of $5,216.75, including 30,000 pounds of lead, 300 pounds of beaver pelts, 4,000 muskrat skins, one yoke of oxen, five horses, one cart and harness, 300 pounds of powder, five pounds of vermillion, one whip saw, one cross-cut saw, two lead molds, four large salt kettles, one anvil, one bellows, two dozen shawls, six pieces of English calico—and the list goes on.

7. Carter (2), Louisiana-Missouri, 14:518–20.

8. Mahon, 129–31.

9. Heroes, 17, 95–99.

10. Gregg (1), 9, 187, 186.

11. William Clark to the Secretary of War, 12 September 1813, cited in ibid., 193.

12. Ibid., 198–99.

13. Gregg (1), 328–29; Steffen, 94–95.

14. *Missouri Gazette,* 27 May 1815, cited in Gregg (1), 343.

15. *Missouri Gazette,* 28 May 1814, cited in Steffen, 95; John O'Fallon to Dennis Fitzhugh, 18 August 1820, cited in Steffen, 127.

16. *Missouri Gazette,* 21 March 1812, cited in Gregg (1), 14.

17. Jackson (3), 2:567.

18. Bradbury, 43–46. Although Daniel Boone was sixty-nine when the Lewis and Clark Expedition began, and although he had many times barely escaped being killed by Indians, he survived several members of the corps, including Colter, dying at the age of eighty-six in 1820.

19. *Missouri Gazette,* 11 July 1812, cited in Gregg (1), 15.

20. Most historians, including Charles G. Clarke and Gary E. Moulton, have given Colter's death date as 1813. To the best of my knowledge, Fred R. Gowans was the first to correctly identify the date of Colter's death (in *Mountain Man and Grizzly*). He was followed by Ruth Colter-Frick, who offered information on Colter's service with Boone (*Courageous Colter and Companions*). Donna Masterson generously provided copies of Nathan Boone's muster roll and correspondence from the National Archives verifying Colter's death date. Masterson has pointed out that Colter's death was likely missed for so many years because the printed copy of Boone's muster roll (Carter [2], Louisiana-Missouri, 14:560–62) reads "John Cotter." The original document reads "Colter," but the scribe had crossed both the *l* and the *t*, making "Cotter" a reasonable conclusion.

21. John Colter papers, Meriwether Lewis Collection, Missouri Historical Society.

CHAPTER THIRTEEN: *"We Lost in All Fourteen Killed"*

1. Hasselstrom, 11; William H. Ashley to the *Missouri Republican,* 4 June 1823, Morgan (2), 26.

2. Jedediah Strong Smith, in a ten-year period of time, traveled from the Missouri River to the Pacific Coast, from the deserts of the southwest to the Canadian Rockies. He was the first man to go overland to California, the first to go up the West Coast to the Oregon country, the first to extensively travel the Great Basin (Chittenden 1:265).

A gentle, religious soul, Smith had a number of dealings with William Clark and at one point contributed Indian peace pipes made from green marble for Clark's museum. In July 1827, Smith wrote to Clark, still superintendent of Indian affairs, and told him of an amazing journey. From present-day Wyoming he had traveled south, past the Great Salt Lake, around the Wasatch Mountains, and along the Virgin River. He had then crossed the Mojave Desert, circled the area that now encompasses Los Angeles and San Diego, and headed north through what was to become central California. Turning east, he and his companions crossed the Sierra Nevadas and the Great Basin to the Great Salt Lake, where he retraced his path north. On his return journey, Smith had "stuck the S. W. corner of the Great Salt Lake, travelling over a country completely barren and destitute of game. We frequently travelled without water sometimes for two days over sandy deserts where there was no sign of vegetation. . . . we had but one horse and one mule remaining, which were so feeble & poor that they could scarce carry the little camp equipage which I had along; the balance of my horses I was compelled to eat as they gave out" (Jedediah S. Smith to William Clark, 12 July 1827, Morgan [1], 337).

By 1831, when he was still a young thirty-two years old, Smith had purchased a home in St. Louis and was ready to live a quiet life. But he could not resist going west again, this time traveling with a caravan to Santa Fe. He was scouting ahead, looking for water, when he confronted a Comanche hunting party. As his brother later learned from Spanish traders, Jedediah "went boldly up, with the hope of making peace with them, but found that his only chance was defence, he killed the head Chief. I do suppose that then they rushed upon him like so many blood-hounds; the Spaniards say the Indians numbered from fifteen to twenty. I have got [Jedediah's] gun and pistols, got from the Indians by the traders" (Morgan [1], 364).

3. See Majors for more information on the John McClellan expedition.

4. Hasselstrom, 11.

5. *Missouri Gazette & Public Advertiser*, 13 February 1822.

6. Anonymous Fort Kiowa letter, White (1), 157–58.

7. Anonymous letter, White (1), 158; Ashley to *Missouri Republican*, Morgan (2), 234; Hasselstrom, 12.

8. Ashley to *Missouri Republican*, Morgan (2), 26.

9. William H. Ashley to a Gentleman in Franklin, Missouri, 7 June 1823, ibid., 30.

10. Hasselstrom, 12.

11. Morgan (2), 234.

12. Holmes, 44.

13. Hasselstrom, 13–15. Although Clyman was unable to send a letter for Gibson, Hugh Glass did post a letter to the father of one of those killed, John Gardner (Morgan [2], 31).

Dr Sir,

My painfull duty it is to tell you of the deth of yr Son wh befell at the hands of the indians 2nd June in the early morning. He lived a little while after he was shot and asked me to inform you of his sad fate. We brought him to the ship where he soon died. Mr [Jedediah] Smith a young man of our company made a powerful prayr who moved us all greatly and I am persuaded John died in peace. His body we buried with others near this camp and marked the grave with a log. His things we will send to you. The savages are greatly treacherous. we traded with them as friends but after a great storm of rain and thunder they came at us before light and many were hurt. I myself was hit in the leg. Master Ashley is bound to stay in these parts till the traitors are rightly punished.

Yr Obt Svt
Hugh Glass

14. Anonymous letter, White (1), 159. Ashley wrote three letters in the days following the attack, and in each letter he listed the men who had been killed or wounded. Some names and spellings differed slightly in each of the three versions, one of which appears below, but he did list twelve men as killed each time. Gibson was the thirteenth. Ashley said that another wounded man later died, bringing the total to fourteen. Since another wounded man died in the hospital at Fort Atkinson, the final total was fifteen dead and nine wounded. The names of the last two fatalities are not known (Morgan [2], 30, 235).

KILLED

John Matthews,
John Collins,
Benjamin F. Sneed,
Thully Piper [elsewhere called Westley Peper],
James M'Daniel
Joseph S. Gardner [elsewhere called John],
George Flages [elsewhere called Flager and Fiager],
David Howard [elsewhere called Daniel],
Aaron Stephens,
James Penn, Jr.
John Miller,
Elliss Ogle.

WOUNDED

John Larrison,
Joseph Manso [elsewhere called Monse],
Reed Gibson, (since dead)
Joseph Thompson,
Robert Tucker,
James Davis [not included in Ashley's previous lists]
Aaron Ricketts [elsewhere called Abraham],
Jacob Miller
August Dufren,
Hugh Glass,
Daniel M'Clain [elsewhere called David McClane and Daniel McLlain]
Thilless, (black man.) [elsewhere called Willess]

Certain anomalies surrounding the history of John Collins have not yet been resolved. The Collins family favors the theory that he was not killed in the Arikara attack and that he married Lavinia Darby in St. Louis in 1829. I take this John M. Collins to be the son of the expedition member. (In July 1829, John M. Collins and his wife Lavinia Darby Collins won a settlement against Lavinia's father, John F. Darby. However, the court record offers no indication whether this was the Collins of the expedition—or his son. St. Louis Circuit Court Historical Records Project, Case 79.) And a document at the Missouri Historical Society signed by John Collins in 1832

(Meriwether Lewis Papers) could be this man. Such historians as Clarke and Moulton have agreed that the John Collins killed with Ashley was the Collins of the expedition, but I have not found a primary document confirming this. Contemporary documents, such as Ashley's letters and newspaper accounts, list his name and nothing more. Even Dale Morgan, the expert on Ashley, offers no comment on Collins's identity. In addition, when William Clark drew up his list of expedition members in 1825–28, he listed Collins as dead. One would expect him to say "killed," as he did with Drouillard, Potts, and others. Was this a slip of the pen or did Collins die a nonviolent death? I take it to be a slip of the pen and agree with Clarke and Moulton that the Collins of the corps was the same man killed by the Arikara. (In any case, Clark's list seems to me to offer good evidence that John M. Collins—who was still alive in 1829—was not on the expedition.) The following women married men named John Collins: Eliza Johnston in 1808, Jame Holeman in 1810, and Mary Bailey in 1811. A John Collins of St. Louis fought in the War of 1812, was wounded in the shoulder and jaw, received a land grant as compensation, and died sometime before 1818. Another John Collins married a woman named Betsey and had an estate probated in Jefferson County, Kentucky, in 1813. There is hope that future research will allow us to clearly distinguish among the various men named John Collins (there seems to be a multitude—in 1800 there were at least nine men by that name living in Kentucky). (It is worth noting, however, that John Collins was apparently illiterate when he returned from the expedition because he signed his name with an *X*.)

15. Morgan (2), 37, 46. As Indian agent, O'Fallon reported to Clark, but Leavenworth reported to Brigadier General Henry Atkinson, who was ultimately responsible to Secretary of War John C. Calhoun.

16. Drumm, 84.

17. Hafen (2), 58; Holmes, 20.

18. Hafen (2), 59. Hafen believes Charbonneau may have been one of those imprisoned, but Charbonneau's biographer, W. Dale Nelson, thinks it more likely that Charbonneau was sent to deliver lame horses before the group was imprisoned (Nelson, 75).

19. Benjamin O'Fallon, U.S. Indian Agent, Upper Missouri Agency, to William Clark, Superintendent of Indian Affairs at St. Louis, Fort Atkinson, 3 July 1823, Morgan (2), 44–45.

20. Morgan (2), 53.

21. Morgan (1), 70.

22. Ibid., 76.

23. Morgan (2), 56.

24. Report of Henry Leavenworth, Fort Atkinson, 20 October 1823, ibid.

25. Joshua Pilcher to Henry Leavenworth, 20 August 1823, ibid., 57–58.

26. Richard T. Holliday to William Clark [?], 16 February 1824, Morgan (2), 73.

27. LW, 216–17. This account was published in 1825, while Glass was still alive. Hall got his information from "an informant" at Fort Atkinson who had talked to Glass. (While Aubrey L. Haines attributes this account to Hall [Haines (1), 161], Dale

Morgan claims Alphonso Wetmore was the author [Morgan (1), 391].) Glass's adventure inspired the movie *Man in the Wilderness*, starring Richard Harris.

28. Ibid., 217.

29. Morgan (1), 99–100.

30. Holliday to Clark [?], Morgan (2), 73.

31. LW, 218.

32. Morgan (1), 102.

CHAPTER FOURTEEN: *"Taken with the Cholera in Tennessee and Died"*

1. Betts, 88–89. In the same passage, Kennerly said that as boys Clark and York played with young Meriwether Lewis. There is no document that supports this notion, and in Clark's own reminiscences he says that he and Lewis met for the first time in the army.

2. Ibid., 95.

3. Ibid., 85.

4. Clark's journal entry, 24 November 1805. See Moulton (2), 6:19n.1, for information on the wapato.

5. Journal entries of Whitehouse, Ordway, and Gass, respectively, for 24 November 1805.

6. William Clark to Jonathan Clark, 28 May 1809, Holmberg (3), 201.

7. William Clark to Jonathan Clark, April 1805, ibid., 86.

8. Betts, 110. Nancy was actually York's half-sister.

9. William Clark to Jonathan Clark, 21 July 1808, Holmberg (3), 144.

10. William Clark to Jonathan Clark, 9 November 1808, ibid., 160.

11. William Clark to Jonathan Clark, 10 December 1808, ibid., 183–84.

12. John O'Fallon to William Clark, 13 May 1811, William Clark Collection, Missouri Historical Society.

13. William Clark to Edmund Clark, 25 December 1814, Clark Family Papers, Filson Historical Society; William Clark and John H. Clark business agreement, 14 November 1815, John H. Clark Papers, cited in Betts, 167.

14. McDermott (3), 81–82. The phrase "traces of York's crowd" was probably a reference to children York had supposedly fathered on the expedition. Nicholas Biddle (apparently getting his information from Shannon) concluded that York did have sexual relations with some of the Indian women—just as several members of the corps did. Whether York fathered any children is purely speculative, as it is with the other members. (There were later legends that Lewis and Clark had both fathered children on the expedition.)

15. Leonard, 26.

16. Ibid., 74.

17. Ibid., 80.

18. Leonard, 29n.

19. John F. A. Sanford to William Clark, 26 July 1833, cited in Betts, 138. The Menard killed was not Pierre Menard.

20. Lamar, 987; Betts, 135–43. Betts argues that Beckwourth was simply too young to have been the man Leonard encountered.

21. Historian James Holmberg offers this insight on York's death: "When might York have died? In reflecting upon Clark's comments, I was struck by the feeling that they lacked an immediacy to them as recorded by Irving. Clark seems to be harkening back to events in the past rather than of recent memory. If that is the case, a time frame of perhaps six to twelve years or so prior to 1832 might be about the time that York died. Did he die during a period of about 1820 to 1826? Cholera was a known visitor to the upper South during this time. Dennis Fitzhugh [Clark's brother-in-law and business associate] died in 1822 of what was reported to be cholera. The answer of when York died might be out there somewhere or may never be known" (Holmberg, epilogue in Betts, 170–71).

CHAPTER FIFTEEN: *"Men on Lewis & Clark's Trip"*

1. Jackson (3), 2:638–40. Richard Warfington and John Newman were both temporary members of the party who returned to St. Louis in the spring of 1805. I have taken the license of adding an apostrophe to "Clarks" in my title for this chapter.

2. The question naturally comes up as to whether Clark meant to imply anything by listing Meriwether Lewis as "Dead." Would he have said "killed" if he believed Lewis had been murdered? We don't know. For at least two members, Clark listed inaccurate information. Patrick Gass, of course, was far from dead—he lived to be the last surviving expedition veteran. Reubin Field, on the other hand, had indeed lived near Louisville, but he had died in 1823. Since Clark had relatives in Louisville, it is surprising that he was apparently unaware of Field's death. The note that John Collins was dead also raises interesting questions, as discussed earlier.

3. Elliott, 43. Of course, the question remains, how did the Kootenai Indians know that the two men had been with Captain Lewis? Although Lewis and Clark knew of this nation, they had no contact with them, making it highly unlikely that the two Kootenai had personal knowledge of anyone from the expedition. If they heard this from someone else and then passed the information on to Thompson, he becomes a third-hand witness, and the information naturally becomes more suspect.

4. Clark's journal entry, 17 September 1806.

5. Lewis's journal entry, 9 June 1805.

6. Court of Common Pleas, District of St. Louis, 14 October 1806, 6 March 1807, 24 March 1807, 29 June 1807, Missouri Historical Society. The first document is dated 1806 but also the year of "our Independence the Thirty first," which would be 1807. When this document is taken in context with the other three, I believe the 1806 date is more likely.

7. This petition is discussed in some detail in Chapter 3, note 14.

8. Background information for this section is found in Majors, which offers a fascinating look at the mysterious McClellan expedition.

9. Reports, 29. John Collins is the only expedition member included in this list of men killed.

10. Company Book of Amos Stoddard, Moore (1), 20–24; Clarke (1), 54; *Missouri Gazette and Illinois Advertiser,* 29 July 1815. John Thompson was quite a common name in Missouri at this time. The John Thompson of the expedition was not the John W. Thompson who served as sheriff in St. Louis, nor was he the Captain John Thompson who served in the military or the one who trapped with William Sublette and others in the 1820s and '30s. The many other John Thompsons tend to merge into confusion, a problem that any genealogist is likely to appreciate. The reference in the *Gazette and Advertiser* was the only record I found of a John B. Thompson.

11. Simply guessing which day of the week it was must have been difficult, and Weiser may have felt like another trapper who wrote, "Extremely lonesome and low Spirited—I hardly know how to account for it, but I have always found Sunday to be the dullest and longest day in the week—that is—the Sundays spent in the Indian Country—I suppose it is because we are apt to contrast the scene with that of civilized life—when Kin and acquaintances all assemble at the sound of the *church going bell*. . . . That could I at this moment hear even the tinkling of a sheep bell—much less the Solemn toll of the church going bell, that the joyful Sound would repay Me for whole Months of privation" (*Chardon's Journal at Fort Clark,* cited in Maguire, 119; emphasis in original).

12. Complaint of Peter Wiser against Rufus Easton, administrator of the estate of John Potts, November 1810, Missouri Historical Society.

13. *Louisiana Gazette,* 2 May 1812.

14. Lewis's journal entry, 9 February 1805, and Moulton's accompanying note, Moulton (2), 3:290.

15. St. Louis and St. Louis County, Missouri, Probate Records, File 126. The summons of 20 March 1826 is the last document in the file.

16. Meriwether Lewis to Henry Dearborn, 15 January 1807, Jackson (3), 1:367.

17. Appleman, 33. Appleman's article contains a wealth of information on the Field family.

18. Kentucky, 294. There were two men in the Louisville area by the name of Reubin Field. On 22 September 1818 a notice in a Louisville newspaper read: "Seven slaves, the property of Reuben Field, deceased, will be sold at public auction on September 26th" (Crowder, 54). This man was reportedly a relative of the Reubin Field of the expedition.

19. Whitehouse's journal entry, 28 July 1805.

20. Clark's journal entries, 14 and 15 February 1804.

21. Jackson (3), 1:345; Joseph Whitehouse documents, Meriwether Lewis Papers, Missouri Historical Society. Whitehouse and Collins both sold their warrants to Drouillard, who sold them to Thomas Riddick and Alexander McNair, who in turn sold them to Frederick Bates. This buying and selling of warrants—which was quite

common among expedition veterans—created mountains of paperwork and mountains of confusion for subsequent generations. In the 1850s, long after most of the original claimants were dead, the federal land office was still trying to figure out who owned the rights to certain tracts of land. In 1853, William Gitt expressed the frustration of many when he wrote, "the scamps having subsequently assigned their claims, upon which the first action was had" (W. W. Gitt to Barton Bates, March 1853, Bates Papers, Missouri Historical Society).

22. Whitehouse documents, Meriwether Lewis Papers, Missouri Historical Society.

23. Colter-Frick (1), 248–52; Bartels, item 331. The assault charges were filed in St. Louis in 1809. The murder charge was recorded on 25 February 1812 in St. Charles County, Missouri.

24. Moulton (2), xv; Cutright (2), 146n.10.

25. Correspondence between the author and the White family, 2002; Cutright (1), 114. The history of Joseph Whitehouse thus provides fertile ground for future research. A check of United States census records, however, does not reveal a Joseph Whitehouse who lived in the same location from 1820 to 1850. Men by that name show up in Illinois, Indiana, Kentucky, Maine, Massachusetts, New Hampshire, New Jersey, New York, Ohio, Vermont, and Utah (but not in Whitehouse's home state of Virginia).

26. *Missouri Gazette,* 26 March 1814, 29 March 1816.

27. On his opening a business, *Independent Patriot* (Missouri) newspaper, 17 February 1812; on watch repair bills, Frazer documents, Meriwether Lewis Papers, Missouri Historical Society; on Frazer's life and death in Franklin County, Colter-Frick (1), 247–61; for the journal prospectus and quote from McBride, Jackson (3), 1:345–46.

28. Contract between François Labuche [Labiche] and P. Chouteau, 23 July 1827, Chouteau-Maffitt Papers, Missouri Historical Society. Labiche signed with an *X*. St. Louis tax records for the 1820s show that Labiche, like many others, sometimes had to sell property or land to pay delinquent taxes.

29. Montgomery County, Virginia, census records, 1810–30; Montgomery County Marriage Register, 1777–1853.

30. Jackson (3), 2:385. I saw a copy of the original November 1807 promissory note at the Jefferson National Expansion Monument Archives. Reuben Lewis was one of the witnesses. Clarke (1), 54, has speculated that Werner served as an Indian agent for Clark but offers no documentation.

31. A note in the card catalog for William Werner in the Missouri Historical Society reads as follows: "His warrant for land was later sold and purchaser located in Marion Co. Mo. In 1837, Dec 8, he made a quit claim deed to R. Dudley. In affidavit stated he was a resident of Montgomery Co.—Marion Co. Deed Recs." I have checked the listings of approximately ninety cemeteries in Montgomery County, Virginia, but have not found any listing for a William Warner (or Werner). However, a Montgomery County genealogist informs me that the inscriptions of many headstones from that era have faded and are now illegible.

32. Lewis's journal entry, 7 June 1805.

33. Lewis's journal entry, 15 July 1806.

34. From 1820 to 1840, the name Richard Windsor appears in census records of the District of Columbia, Kentucky, Missouri, New York, and Virginia (Illinois is conspicuously absent). A Hugh McNeil purchased public land in Illinois in 1818 (Section: NE; Sect: 24; Township: 03N; Range: 09W; Meridian: 4). According to one interesting but unsubstantiated theory, a man by the name of Daniel Snyder (born in upstate New York around 1780) got in trouble with the law and joined the army under the assumed name of Hugh McNeal. After the expedition, he returned to New York, discarded the McNeal alias—leaving others to think he was dead—married, and had children. With such names and dates available, this theory could probably be investigated and checked (I have not attempted to do so, although I did discover that Daniel Snyder was a very common name at the time). If it was true, however, one would expect Clark to have simply listed McNeal's name with no other information. Clark's note of "dead" next to McNeal's name indicates that Clark had reason to believe the man was dead. (See the McNeal file at the Lewis and Clark Trail Heritage Foundation Library for more information.)

35. Lewis's journal entry, 8 March 1806.

36. Carter (2), Indiana Territory, 571; Justus Post statement, 14 January 1817, Land Records, National Archives; Jackson (3), 1:371.

37. In the 1810, 1820, and 1830 census records for the United States, there are a total of twenty-three listings for Hugh Hall. I have checked all of them and eliminated all except the 1820 listing for Washington County, Pennsylvania. (I have also eliminated most of the thirty-one Hugh Hall listings for 1840 and 1850.) To date, I have not found a probate or cemetery record for Hugh Hall. He has proved to be extremely elusive. However, the 1820 Washington County listing fits for several reasons: Pennsylvania was Hall's home state, so it wouldn't seem strange for him to return there; the Washington County Hugh Hall was between forty and fifty—the correct age for the Hugh Hall of the expedition (who was twenty-six in 1798, and thus forty-eight in 1820); the Hugh Hall of Washington County could have still been alive in 1825–28, consistent with Clark's not reporting that Hugh Hall had died; and the Washington County Hugh Hall was unmarried and childless, which fits with the family tradition of John Hall's extended family. Thanks to John F. Hall for his support of this extensive research.

38. Cutright (1), 242.

39. John F. Hall to Barbara Nell, 6 February 1998, Lewis and Clark Trail Heritage Foundation Library.

40. Just as Jim Holmberg's *Dear Brother* offered information of great interest to students of the expedition, I suspect forthcoming works on William Clark by Jay Buckley and Landon Jones will do the same. Buckley's doctoral dissertation (University of Nebraska, 2001), *William Clark: Superintendent of Indian Affairs at St.Louis, 1813–1838*, is forthcoming from the University of Oklahoma Press, and, according to the editor of *Smithsonian* magazine, Jones's article on Clark (Jones [1]) offered "an early look" at a "definitive biography."

1. Sam Houston to Genl. Jackson, 15 December 1830, and Sam Houston to Gen. Jno. H. Eaton, 15 December 1830, typescript, Pryor documents, Meriwether Lewis Papers, Missouri Historical Society (emphasis in originals).

2. Hiram Abiff Whittington to Granville Whittington, 13 May 1830, Ross (2), 16.

3. Matthew Lyon to William Bradford, 10 April 1821, and Matthew Lyon to the Secretary of War [John C. Calhoun], 20 October 1821, Carter (2), Arkansas Territory, 330–33, 342–45.

4. Pryor documents, Meriwether Lewis Papers, Missouri Historical Society.

5. Ibid. Pryor was appointed subagent on 7 May 1831, one month before his death.

6. Denton, 19.

7. Information on Shannon's Kentucky years is drawn from Carolyn S. Denton's well-researched work.

8. Caldwell (1), 396, 398.

9. William Clark to William Eaton, 14 April 1830, cited in ibid., 408.

10. Ibid., 408.

11. The need to nominate a candidate had been precipitated by the death of Congressman Spencer Pettis. After Pettis made disparaging remarks about the U.S. Bank president (and friend of Shannon), Nicholas Biddle, Biddle's brother Thomas had challenged Pettis to a duel. On 27 August 1830 the men fought, mortally wounding each other in the first exchange. Pettis died the next day and Biddle three days afterward.

12. The thousand-dollar loan to Shannon was recorded on 6 June 1835, St. Charles County, Missouri Deed Records. Shannon's purported drinking is discussed in Shannon, 120.

13. Cantrell, 365.

14. Paxton, 1821.

15. William Clark to Jonathan Clark, 28 October 1809, Holmberg (3), 218; Thomas Jefferson to James Madison, 26 November 1809, Jackson (3), 2:475. Clark originally wrote "my paprs" in the letter to his brother, but he crossed out "my" and replaced it with "his."

16. William Clark to Jonathan Clark, 12 January 1810, Holmberg (3), 233.

17. Nicholas Biddle to William Clark, 23 March 1814, Jackson (3), 2:598–99.

18. William Clark to Nicholas Biddle, 16 September 1814, ibid., 2:600.

19. Julia Hancock Clark to George Hancock, 27 February 1814, William Clark Papers, Voorhis Memorial Collection, Missouri Historical Society.

20. Jackson (1), 40.

21. Barry, 32.

22. Jones (1), 106. As Landon Jones points out, this represented a "rare departure from [Clark's] usual stout optimism" (ibid.).

23. McDermott (3), 81. Washington Irving had mistaken one of William Clark's sons for his grandson.

24. Jones (1), 105.

25. Jackson (1), 40–42.

26. Kennerly, 91.

27. Jackson (3), 2:648.

28. Abel, 18.

29. Ibid., 386.

30. Ibid., 394–95.

31. Ibid., 131.

32. Ibid., 133, 135, 173.

33. Sublette Papers, Missouri Historical Society.

34. *Northwestern Gazette and Galena Advertiser,* 11 June, 2 July, and 20 August 1836; court minutes, Iowa County, Territory of Michigan, 1836–37. Thanks to Allee Olsen and Karen E. Willard for generously sharing their research on the death of George Clark Willard.

35. White (2), 84.

36. Turnbull, 161.

37. Lewis Willard to Eva Emory Dye, 25 February 1903, Dye Collection, Oregon Historical Society.

38. Journal of Wilford Woodruff, 30 June 1846, cited in Bennett, 39–40.

39. Bennett, 41.

40. Yurtinus, 1:189.

41. Sage, 206; statement of William M. Boggs, cited in Hafen (1), 217.

42. Nelson, 108.

43. Utley, 254.

44. Nelson, 111.

45. Nelson, 111; Hafen (1), 218–19.

46. Hafen (1), 219.

47. Nelson, 113; Utley, 254.

48. Anderson (3), 259.

49. Ricketts, 136. Interestingly, there is one other Mormon connection to Baptiste. In 1862, a man by the name of Jean-Baptiste was arrested in Salt Lake City for grave robbing. The man, who had lived in the area for around six years, reportedly robbed nearly three hundred graves, keeping the clothing and using the wood from the coffins as firewood. According to Kerry Ross Boren, author of the unpublished article "Jean Baptiste: The Ghoul of Great Salt Lake," the grave robber was branded, had his ears cut off, and was banished to an island in the Great Salt Lake. Rumors later spread that this was Jean-Baptiste Charbonneau. However, Charbonneau's residence in California in the early 1860s is well documented. Nor is there any evidence he ever traveled to the Utah Territory after it was settled or was guilty of such a crime. The grave robber was clearly a different person.

50. Yurtinus, 1:486.

51. Nelson, 76–77. As Nelson points out, it is not clear whether Clark used personal or government funds to pay these bills.

52. White (2), 11. Baptiste, of course, was born in February 1805—and the Missouri River was frozen over at the time. But he could have frequently traveled in such a canoe as a baby.

53. Benjamin O'Fallon to Joshua Pilcher, 1 August 1823, Morgan (2) 51.

54. Nelson, 77.

55. Furtwangler (2), 521. Rufus B. Sage, who met Baptiste in 1842, helped create the legend of his education when he wrote that Baptiste "had acquired a classic education and could converse quite fluently in German, Spanish, French, and English, as well as several Indian languages. His mind, also, was well stored with choice reading, and enriched by extensive travel and observation. Having visited most of the important places, both in England, France, and Germany, he knew how to turn his experience to good advantage" (Sage, 206). Baptiste had traveled to Europe and received some education, but Sage seems to have assumed too much. Confusion about the relationship between Duke Paul and Baptiste also arises over a passage in Paul's travel diary from the late 1840s. He saw a group of young Shoshone men employed at Sutter's Fort and wrote: "One of these Snake Indians was a very bright fellow and reminded me of the B. Charboneau who followed me to Europe in 1823 and whose mother was a Scho-sho-ne." But when Louis C. Butscher of the University of Wyoming translated the passage in the 1930s, he offered the following embellished version: "Among these latter [Shoshones] was a handsome youth who reminded me, on account of his startling likeness, of a lad from the same tribe whom I took to Europe with me from a fur-trading post at the mouth of the Kansas, in western Missouri in the fall of 1823, and who was my companion there on all my travels over Europe and northern Africa until 1829, when he returned with me to America in 1829. This latter was the son of a Shoshone woman who with her husband, a Canadian Frenchman, accompanied the Messrs. Lewis and Clarke on their expedition to the Pacific Coast in 1804–06, the one as guide and the other as interpreter. The boy was born on the return trip, and when still quite young, General William Clarke asked the mother's permission to take him to St. Louis in order that he might have him educated at the Catholic Brothers' Seminary" (Furtwangler [1], 307). Relying on Sage's conclusions and the embellished version of Paul's diary entry, Ann Hafen made certain assumptions about Baptiste's time in Europe that are now known to be unfounded (see Hafen [1], 210–12). Albert Furtwangler's research has cleared up a good deal of misinformation about Baptiste (see Furtwangler [1] and [2]).

56. Ibid.

57. Porter (1), 7–8.

58. Hafen (1), 212–13.

59. J. C. Frémont, *Report of the Exploring Expedition to the Rocky Mountains,* cited in Hafen (1), 215.

60. Nelson, 118; Furtwangler (1), 311–12.

61. Hafen (1), 220–21.

62. Patrick Gass to John H. Eaton, 12 March 1829, Jackson (3), 2:647. Although an 1851 statement claimed Gass lost his eye at the Battle of Lundy's Lane, "his medi-

cal certificate of 5 June 1815 states that he lost his left eye in Sept 1813 due to an injury sustained 'at Fort Independence on the Mississippi, Missouri Territory'" (ibid., 2:649–51). Gass was apparently assisting with the construction of the fort when he was injured by a fragment from a falling tree.

63. Jacob, 172–74; Smith, 26, 21.

64. Jackson (3), 2:648; Smith, 21.

65. Smith, 21; Jackson (3), 2:378, 1:366–70.

66. Beckham, 89–92.

67. Ibid., 89.

68. Gass (2), 20–21.

69. Jacob, 178.

70. Patrick Gass to John H. Eaton, 12 March 1829, Jackson (3), 2:647.

71. Jacob, 179.

72. Smith, 27.

73. Affidavit of Patrick Gass, 17 February 1854, Jackson (3), 2:652. The affidavit's reference to eight children (two who had died and six surviving) is not consistent with Gass family records, which list seven.

74. Taranik, 16; Earle R. Forrest to John Bakeless, 18 January 1948, Missouri Historical Society; Smith, 27.

75. Patrick Gass to Lyman C. Draper, 1 December 1866, Gass to Draper, 11 January 1867, cited in Holmberg (1), 15.

76. Ibid.; Jackson (3), 325–30.

Bibliography

Published Primary and Secondary Sources

Abel — Abel, Annie Heloise, ed. *Chardon's Journal at Fort Clark, 1834–1839.* Reprint, Lincoln: University of Nebraska Press, 1997.

Abrams — Abrams, Mrs. Rochonne. "Meriwether Lewis: Two Years with Jefferson, the Mentor." *Bulletin of the Missouri Historical Society* (July 1954): 3–18.

Adams — Adams, William Howard. *Monticello.* New York: Abbeville Press, 1983.

AHW — "Alexander Hamilton Willard, Patriot and Pioneer." *Golden Notes,* Sacramento County Historical Society, January 1959.

Allen — Allen, John Logan. *Passage Through the Garden: Lewis and Clark and the Image of the American Northwest.* Urbana: University of Illinois Press, 1975.

Alter — Alter, J. Cecil. *Jim Bridger.* Norman: University of Oklahoma Press, 1962.

Ambrose (1) — Ambrose, Stephen E. *Lewis and Clark: Voyage of Discovery.* National Geographic Society, 1998.

Ambrose (2) — ———. *Undaunted Courage: Meriwether Lewis, Thomas Jefferson, and the Opening of the American West.* New York: Simon and Schuster, 1996.

Anderson (1) — Anderson, Irving W. "A Charbonneau Family Portrait." Fort Clatsop Historical Association, 1988.

Anderson (2) — ———. "Fort Manuel: Its Historical Significance." *South Dakota History* 6 (Spring 1976): 131–51.

Anderson (3)   ———. "J. B. Charbonneau, Son of Sacagawea." *Oregon Historical Quarterly* (September 1970): 246–64.

Anderson (4)   ———. "Probing the Riddle of the Bird Woman." *Montana* 23 (1973): 2–17.

Anderson and Schroer   Anderson, Irving W., and Blanche Schroer. "Sacagawea: Her Name and Her Destiny." *We Proceeded On* 25 (November 1999): 6–9.

Appleby   Appleby, Aimee. *Listing of Inhabitants in 1778: Cumberland County, Pennsylvania.* Laughlintown, Pa.: Southwest Pennsylvania Genealogical Services, 1983.

Appleman   Appleman, Roy E. "Joseph and Reubin Field, Kentucky Frontiersmen of the Lewis and Clark Expedition." *The Filson Club History Quarterly* 49 (January 1975): 5–36.

ASP   *American State Papers.* 38 vols. Washington, D.C.: Gales & Seaton, 1834.

Bagnall   Bagnall, Norma Hayes. *On Shaky Ground: The New Madrid Earthquakes of 1811–1812.* Columbia: University of Missouri Press, 1996.

Bakeless   Bakeless, John. *Lewis and Clark: Partners in Discovery.* New York: William Morrow, 1947.

Baldwin   Baldwin, Leland D. *The Keelboat Age on Western Waters.* Pittsburgh: University of Pittsburgh Press, 1941.

Barker   Barker, Eugene C., ed. *The Austin Papers.* 2 vols. Washington, D.C.: Government Printing Office, 1924–28.

Barry   Barry, Louise, ed. "William Clark's Diary, May, 1826–February, 1831: Part One." *Kansas Historical Quarterly,* February 1948.

Bartels   Bartels, Carolyn M., comp. *St. Charles County, Missouri, Early Court Records, 1808–1815.* Shawnee Mission, Kan.: C. M. Bartels, n.d.

Beckham   Beckham, Stephen Dow, and Doug Erickson, Jeremy Skinner, and Paul Merchant. *The Literature of the Lewis and Clark Expedition: A Bibliography and Essays.* Portland: Lewis and Clark College, 2003.

Bennett   Bennett, Richard E. *We'll Find the Place: The Mormon Exodus, 1846–1848.* Salt Lake City: Deseret Book, 1997.

Bentley   Bentley, James R., ed. "Two Letters of Meriwether Lewis to Major William Preston." *The Filson Club Historical Quarterly* 44 (April 1970): 170–75.

Betts   Betts, Robert B. *In Search of York: The Slave Who Went to the Pacific with Lewis and Clark.* Boulder: University Press of Colorado, 1985, 2000.

Billon   Billon, Frederick L. *Annals of St. Louis in Its Territorial Days from 1804 to 1821.* St. Louis: Privately printed, 1888.

Botkin   Botkin, Daniel B. *Passages of Discovery: The American Rivers Guide to the Missouri River of Lewis and Clark.* New York: Berkley, 1999.

Brackenridge   Brackenridge, Henry M. *Views of Louisiana, Together with a Journal of a Voyage up the Missouri River in 1811*. In Thwaites (2), vol. 6.

Bradbury   Bradbury, John. *Travels in the Interior of America*. In Thwaites (2), vol. 5.

Bratton   *The Bratton Bulletin*, vol. 5, issue 1, October–December 1995.

Brown   Brown, Jo Ann. "George Drouillard and Fort Massac." *We Proceeded On* 25 (November 1999): 16–19.

BS   "A Bear Story—McNeal Escapes a Grizzly." *We Proceeded On* 5 (July 1979): 13.

Buckley   Buckley, Jay H. "The Price of Used Paper." *We Proceeded On* 27 (February 2001): 7–9.

Butler   Butler, John P. *Index: The Papers of the Continental Congress*. 5 vols. Washington, D.C.: National Archives and Records Service, General Services Administration, 1978.

Caldwell (1)   Caldwell, Dorothy J. "The Big Neck Affair: Tragedy and Farce on the Missouri Frontier." *Missouri Historical Review* 64 (July 1970): 391–412.

Caldwell (2)   Caldwell, J. A. *History of Belmont and Jefferson Counties, Ohio*. Wheeling, W.Va.: Historical Publishing, 1880.

Cantrell   Cantrell, Gregg. *Stephen F. Austin: Empresario of Texas*. New Haven: Yale University Press, 1999.

Carter (1)   Carter, Clarence E. "The Burr-Wilkinson Intrigue in St. Louis." *Bulletin of the Missouri Historical Society* 10 (July 1954): 447–64.

Carter (2)   ———, comp. and ed. *The Territorial Papers of the United States*. 25 vols. Washington, D.C.: Government Printing Office, 1943–60.

Carter (3)   Carter, Harvey L. "Jedediah Smith." In Hafen (3), 2:331–48.

Cartwright   Cartwright, Peter. *The Backwoods Preacher: Being the Autobiography of Peter Cartwright, the Oldest American Methodist Traveling Preacher*. London: Daldy, Isbister, 1878.

Catlin   Catlin, George. *Letters and Notes on the Manners, Customs and Conditions of the North American Indians*. London, 1841. Reprint, New York: Clarkson N. Potter, 1975.

Chandler   Chandler, David Leon. *The Jefferson Conspiracies*. New York: William Morrow, 1994.

Chittenden   Chittenden, Hiram M. *The American Fur Trade of the Far West*. 2 vols. New York: Press of the Pioneers, 1935. Reprint, Lincoln: University of Nebraska Press, 1986.

Chuinard (1)   Chuinard, Eldon G. "The Court-Martial of Ensign Meriwether Lewis." *We Proceeded On* 8 (November 1982): 12–15.

Chuinard (2)   ———. "Fincastle—and Santillane and William and Judith Clark." *We Proceeded On* 14 (February 1988): 10–15.

Chuinard (3) ———. "How Did Meriwether Lewis Die? It Was Murder." *We Proceeded On* 17 (August 1991): 4–12; 17 (November 1991): 4–10; 18 (January 1992): 4–9.

Chuinard (4) ———. *Only One Man Died: The Medical Aspects of the Lewis and Clark Expedition.* Fairfield, Washington: Ye Galleon Press, 1999.

CIS *CIS Index to U.S. Executive Branch Documents, 1789–1909; Guide to Documents Listed in Checklist of U.S. Public Documents, 1789–1909, Not Printed in the U.S. Serial Set.* Bethesda, Md.: Congressional Information Service, 1990–95.

CKP *Calendar of the Kentucky Papers of the Draper Collection of Manuscripts.* Madison: State Historical Society of Wisconsin, 1925.

Clarke (1) Clarke, Charles G. *Men of the Lewis and Clark Expedition.* Glendale, Calif.: Arthur H. Clark, 1970.

Clarke (2) ———. "Peter M. Weiser." In Hafen (3), 9:385–91.

Cleary Cleary, Rita. "Charbonneau Reconsidered." *We Proceeded On* 26 (February 2000): 18–23.

Clements Clements, Louis J. "Andrew Henry." In Hafen (3), 6:173–84.

Clyman Clyman, James. *James Clyman, American Frontiersman, 1792–1881.* Edited by Charles L. Camp. San Francisco: California Historical Society, 1928.

Cohen Cohen, Paul E. *Mapping the West: America's Westward Movement, 1524–1890.* New York: Rizzoli, 2002.

Colter-Frick (1) Colter-Frick, Ruth. *Courageous Colter and Companions.* Washington, Mo.: Privately printed, 1997.

Colter-Frick (2) ———. "Meriwether Lewis's Personal Finances." *We Proceeded On* 28 (February 2002): 16–20.

Coues (1) Coues, Elliott, ed. *Forty Years a Fur Trader on the Upper Missouri: The Personal Narrative of Charles Larpenteur, 1833–1872.* 2 vols. New York: Francis P. Harper, 1898.

Coues (2) ———. *The Journal of Jacob Fowler.* Lincoln: University of Nebraska Press, 1970.

Coues (3) ———. "Letters of William Clark and Nathaniel Pryor," *Annals of Iowa* 1 (April 1893): 613–20.

Crawford Crawford, Helen. "Sakakawea." *North Dakota Historical Quarterly* 1 (April 1927): 5–15.

Crowder Crowder, Lola Frazer. *Early Louisville, Kentucky, Newspaper Abstracts, 1806–1828.* Galveston: Frontier Press, 1995.

CTP *Calendar of the Tennessee and King's Mountain Papers of the Draper Collection of Manuscripts.* Madison: State Historical Society of Wisconsin, 1929.

Cutler   Cutler, Jervis. *A Topographical Description of the State of Ohio, Indiana Territory, and Louisiana. Comprehending the Ohio and Mississippi Rivers, and Their Principal Tributary Streams. By a Late Officer in the U.S. Army.* Boston: Published by Charles Williams. J. Belcher, printer, 1812.

Cutright (1)   Cutright, Paul Russell. *A History of the Lewis and Clark Journals.* Norman: University of Oklahoma Press, 1976.

Cutright (2)   ———. "The Journal of Private Joseph Whitehouse: A Soldier with Lewis and Clark." *Bulletin of the Missouri Historical Society* 27 (April 1972): 143–61.

Cutright (3)   ———. "Rest, Rest, Perturbed Spirit." *We Proceeded On* 12 (March 1986): 7–16.

Dale   Dale, Harrison C., ed. *The Ashley-Smith Explorations and the Discovery of a Central Route to the Pacific, 1822–1829.* Cleveland: Arthur H. Clark, 1918.

Danisi   Danisi, Thomas. "The 'Ague' Made Him Do It." *We Proceeded On* 28 (February 2002): 10–15.

Davis (1)   Davis, Richard Beale, ed. *Jeffersonian America: Notes on the United States of America Collected in the Years 1805–6–7 and '11–12 by Sir Augustus John Foster, Bart.* San Marino, Calif.: Huntington Library, 1954.

Davis (2)   Davis, William C. *Three Roads to the Alamo: The Lives and Fortunes of David Crockett, James Bowie, and William Barret Travis.* New York: Harper Collins, 1998.

Davis (3)   ———. *A Way Through the Wilderness: The Natchez Trace and the Civilization of the Southern Frontier.* New York: HarperCollins, 1995.

Day   Day, Donald Eugene. *A Life of Wilson Shannon, Governor of Ohio, Diplomat, Territorial Governor of Kansas.* Thesis, Ohio State University, 1978.

Denton   Denton, Carolyn S. "George Shannon of the Lewis and Clark Expedition: His Kentucky Years." In Yater and Denton, 15–24.

Descendants (1)   "Descendants of Alexander Hamilton Willard Sr." Compiled by Karen E. Willard. Privately printed, 2002.

Descendants (2)   "Descendants of Oliver Charbonneau." Privately printed, 14 November 2001.

DeVoto (1)   DeVoto, Bernard. *Across the Wide Missouri.* Boston: Houghton Mifflin, 1947. Reprint, New York: Mariner, 1998.

DeVoto (2)   ———. *The Course of Empire.* Boston: Houghton Mifflin, 1952. Reprint, 1980.

DeVoto (3)   ———. *The Journals of Lewis and Clark.* Boston: Houghton Mifflin, 1953. Reprint, 1981.

Dickson (1)   Dickson, Clair C. "Joseph Dickson: First on the Yellowstone." Privately printed, 1990.

Dickson (2)   Dickson, Frank H. "Hard on the Heels of Lewis and Clark." *Montana* 26 (January 1976): 14–25.

Dickson (3)   ———. "Joseph Dickson." In Hafen (3), 3:71–79.

Dillon   Dillon, Richard. *Meriwether Lewis: A Biography*. Santa Cruz, Calif.: Western Tanager, 1965, 1988.

DRA   "Did the Returning Astorians Use the South Pass? A Letter of Ramsay Crooks." *Oregon Historical Quarterly* 17 (1916): 47–51.

Drumm   Drumm, Stella M., ed. [John Luttig's] *Journal of a Fur-Trading Expedition on the Upper Missouri, 1812–1813*. St. Louis, 1920.

Duncan   Duncan, Dayton, and Ken Burns. *Lewis and Clark: An Illustrated*
and Burns   *History*. New York: Knopf, 1999.

Dunlap   Dunlap, William. *Diary*. Collections of the New York Historical Society. 2 vols. New York, 1930.

Egle   Egle, William Henry, ed. *Notes and Queries, Historical and Genealogical, Chiefly Relating to Interior Pennsylvania*. Baltimore: Genealogical Publishing, 1970.

Elliott   Elliott, Thompson Coit, ed. "'Narrative of the Expedition to the Kootanae and Flat Bow Indian Countries, on the Sources of the Columbia River,' by David Thompson." *The Quarterly of the Oregon Historical Society* 26 (March 1925): 23–49.

Ewers   Ewers, John C. *The Blackfeet: Raiders on the Northwestern Plains*. Norman: University of Oklahoma Press, 1958.

FCA   *French Canadian and Acadian Genealogical Review* 8 (1980).

Field   Field, Eugene A., and Lucie C. Field. "The Ancestry of Joseph and Reubin Field of the Lewis and Clark Expedition, the Corps of Discovery." Privately printed, n.d.

Fisher   Fisher, Vardis. *Suicide or Murder? The Strange Death of Governor Meriwether Lewis*. Chicago: Swallow, 1962.

Foley   Foley, William E., and Charles David Rice. "The Return of the
and Rice   Mandan Chief." *Montana* 29 (July 1979): 2–14.

Foote   Foote, Shelby. *The Civil War, A Narrative: Fort Sumter to Perryville*. New York: Vintage, 1958.

Forrest   Forrest, Earle E. "Patrick Gass, Carpenter of the Lewis and Clark Expedition." *Bulletin of the Missouri Historical Society* 4 (July 1948): 217–22.

Fulton   Fulton, Maurice Garland. *Diary and Letters of Josiah Gregg*. Norman: University of Oklahoma Press, 1944.

Furtwangler   Furtwangler, Albert. "Sacagawea's Son as a Symbol." *Oregon Histori-*
(1)   *cal Quarterly* 102 (Fall 2001): 290–315.

Furtwangler (2)	———. "Sacagawea's Son: New Evidence from Germany." *Oregon Historical Quarterly* 102 (Winter 2001): 518–523.
Gass (1)	"1860 Virginia Census Has Special Note About Gass." *We Proceeded On* 16 (February 1990): 29.
Gass (2)	"David B. Weaver Would Have Monument Erected to Memory of Patrick Gass: Sketch of the Life of the Famous Explorer." *We Proceeded On* 24 (August 1998): 20–23.
Ghent	Ghent, William. "Sketch of John Colter." *Annals of Wyoming* 10 (July 1938): 111–16.
Goodrich	*The Goodrich Family in America.* New York: A. J. & G. A. Goodrich, 1984.
Gowans	Gowans, Fred R. *Mountain Man and Grizzly.* Orem, Utah: Mountain Grizzly, 1992.
Grant	Grant, Bruce. *Concise Encyclopedia of the American Indian.* New York: Wings, 1958.
Gregg (1)	Gregg, Kate L. "The War of 1812 on the Missouri Frontier." *Missouri Historical Review* 33 (1938): 3–22, 184–202, 326–48.
Gregg (2)	———, ed. *Westward with Dragoons: The Journal of William Clark on His Expedition to Establish Fort Osage, August 25 to September 22, 1808.* Fulton, Mo.: Ovid Bell, 1937.
Grinnell	Grinnell, Calvin. "Another View of Sakakawea." *We Proceeded On* 25 (May 1999): 16–19.
Guice (1)	Guice, John D. W. "A Fatal Rendezvous: The Mysterious Death of Meriwether Lewis." *We Proceeded On* 24 (May 1998): 4–12.
Guice (2)	———. "Moonlight and Meriwether Lewis." *We Proceeded On* 28 (February 2002): 21–25.
Hafen (1)	Hafen, Ann W. "Jean Baptiste Charbonneau." In Hafen (3), 1:205–24.
Hafen (2)	Hafen, LeRoy R. "Toussaint Charbonneau." In Hafen (3), 9:53–62.
Hafen (3)	———, ed. *The Mountain Men and the Fur Trade of the Far West.* 10 vols. Glendale, Calif.: A. H. Clark, 1965–72.
Hagood	Hagood, J. Hurley, and Roberta R. Hagood. *George Shannon (Peg-leg): A Story of Courage Personified.* Hannibal, Mo.: Privately printed, 1988.
Haines (1)	Haines, Aubrey L. "Hugh Glass." In Hafen (3), 161–71.
Haines (2)	———. *Osborne Russell's Journal of a Trapper.* Portland: Oregon Historical Society, 1955. Reprint, Lincoln: University of Nebraska Press, 1965.
Hall	Hall, William K. *The Shane Manuscript Collection: A Genealogical Guide to the Kentucky and Ohio Papers.* Galveston: Frontier Press, 1990.
Hammond	Hammond, Priscilla, comp. *Vital Records of Bow, New Hampshire, 1710–1890.* Concord: Privately printed, 1942.

Hanson   Hanson, Charles E., Jr. "Expansion of the Fur Trade Following Lewis and Clark." Supplement to *We Proceeded On*, WPO Publication no. 4. Great Falls, Mont.: Lewis and Clark Trail Heritage Foundation, 1980.

Harmon   Harmon, Daniel Williams. *A Journal of Voyages and Travels in the Interior of North America, Extending from Montreal Nearly to the Pacific Ocean, a Distance of About 5,000 Miles, Including an Account of the Principal Occurrences, During a Residence of Nineteen Years, in Different Parts of the Country. By Daniel Williams Harmon, a Partner in the North West Company.* Andover: Flagg and Gould, 1820. Reprint, New York, 1903.

Harper   Harper, Josephine L. *Guide to the Draper Manuscripts.* Madison: State Historical Society of Wisconsin, 1983.

Harris   Harris, Burton. *John Colter: His Years in the Rocky Mountains.* Casper, Wyo.: Big Horn, 1965.

Hasselstrom   Hasselstrom, Linda M., ed. *Journal of a Mountain Man: James Clyman.* Missoula, Mont.: Mountain Press Publishing, 1984.

Hebard   Hebard, Grace Raymond. *Sacajawea, a Guide and Interpreter of the Lewis and Clark Expedition, with an Account of the Travels of Toussaint Charbonneau, and of Jean Baptiste, the Expedition Papoose.* Glendale, Calif.: Arthur H. Clark, 1933. Reprint, 1957.

Heitman   Heitman, Francis. *Historical Register and Dictionary of the United States Army from its Organization, September 28, 1789, to March 2, 1903.* 2 vols. Washington, D.C.: Government Printing Office, 1903. Reprint, Urbana: University of Illinois Press, 1965.

Heroes   *Heroes of 1812.* Written and published by the members of the Nebraska Society of United States Daughters of 1812, 1930.

Holcombe   Holcombe, R. I. *History of Marion County, Missouri.* St. Louis: E. F. Perkins, 1884. Reprint, Marceline, Mo.: Walsworth Publishing, 1979.

Holman   Holman, Albert. *Pioneering in the Northwest.* Sioux City, Iowa: Deitch & Lamar, 1924.

Holmberg (1)   Holmberg, James J. "Getting the Word Out." *We Proceeded On* 27 (August 2001): 12–17.

Holmberg (2)   ———. "Seaman's Fate?" *We Proceeded On* 27 (February 2000): 7–9.

Holmberg (3)   ———, ed. *Dear Brother: Letters of William Clark to Jonathan Clark.* New Haven: Yale University Press, 2002.

Holmes   Holmes, Reuben. "The Five Scalps." *Missouri Historical Society Glimpses of the Past* 5 (January–March 1938): 19–22.

Hopewell   Hopewell, Clifford. *Sam Houston: Man of Destiny.* Austin: Eakin, 1987.

Hosmer   Hosmer, James Kendell. *Gass's Journal of the Lewis and Clark Expedition, By Sergeant Patrick Gass.* Chicago: A. C. McClurg, 1904.

Houck   Houck, Louis. *A History of Missouri from the Earliest Explorations and Settlements Until the Admission of the State into the Union.* 3 vols. Chicago: R. R. Donnelley, 1908.

Howard (1)   Howard, Harold. *Sacajawea.* Norman: University of Oklahoma Press, 1971.

Howard (2)   Howard, Helen Addison. "The Mystery of Sacagawea's Death." *Pacific Northwest Quarterly* 58 (January 1967): 1–6.

Hunter   Hunter, John Dunn. *Manners and Customs of Several Indian Tribes Located West of the Mississippi.* Philadelphia: printed and published for the author, 1823.

Index   *Index to Volunteer Soldiers in Indian Wars and Disturbances.* Transcribed by Virgil D. White. Waynesboro, Tenn.: National Historical Publishing, 1994.

Irving   Irving, Washington. *Astoria.* 1836. Reprint, edited by Edgeley W. Todd. Norman: University of Oklahoma Press, 1964.

Jackson (1)   Jackson, Donald. *Among the Sleeping Giants.* Urbana: University of Illinois Press, 1987.

Jackson (2)   ———. "Journey to the Mandans, 1809; the Lost Narrative of Dr. Thomas." *Bulletin of the Missouri Historical Society* 20 (April 1964): 179–92.

Jackson (3)   ———, ed. *Letters of the Lewis and Clark Expedition with Related Documents.* 2 vols. Urbana: University of Illinois Press, 1963. Reprint, 1978.

Jacob   Jacob, John G. *The Life and Times of Patrick Gass, Now Sole Survivor of the Overland Expedition to the Pacific, Under Lewis and Clark, in 1804–5–6.* Wellsburg, Va., 1859.

James (1)   James, Edwin. *An Account of an Expedition from Pittsburgh to the Rocky Mountains, Performed in the Years 1819 and '20, by Order of the Hon. J. C. Calhoun, Sec'y of War: Under the Command of Major Stephen H. Long.* Philadelphia: H. C. Carey and I. Lea, 1823.

James (2)   James, Gen. Thomas. *Three Years Among the Indians and Mexicans.* Edited by Walter B. Douglas. St. Louis, 1916. Reprint, edited with an introduction by Milo Milton Quaife. New York: Citadel, 1966.

Jones (1)   Jones, Landon Y. "Iron Will." *Smithsonian,* August 2002, 96–107.

Jones (2)   ———, ed. *The Essential Lewis and Clark.* New York: Ecco, 2000.

Kennerly   Kennerly, William Clark. *Persimmon Hill: A Narrative of Old St. Louis and the Far West.* Norman: University of Oklahoma Press, 1948

Kentucky   *Early Kentucky Settlers: The Records of Jefferson County, Kentucky, from the Filson Club Historical Quarterly.* Baltimore: Genealogical Publishing, 1988.

Koetting and Koetting   Koetting, Jerome D., and Patricia G. Lowrey Koetting. *Descendants of James Lowry.* Privately printed, 1996.

Kubik   Kubik, Barbara. "John Colter: One of Lewis and Clark's Men." *We Proceeded On* 9 (May–June 1983): 10–14.

Kushner   Kushner, Howard. "The Suicide of Meriwether Lewis." *William and Mary Quarterly* 38 (July 1991): 464–81.

Lamar   Lamar, Howard R., ed. *The New Encyclopedia of the American West.* New Haven: Yale University Press, 1998.

Lange (1)   Lange, Robert E. "The Expedition's Brothers: Joseph and Reuben Field." *We Proceeded On* 4 (July 1978): 15–16

Lange (2)   ———. "George Drouillard: One of Lewis and Clark's Men." *We Proceeded On* 5 (May 1979): 14–16.

Lange (3)   ———. "John Shields: Lewis and Clark's Handy-Man: Gunsmith, Blacksmith, General Mechanic for the Expedition." *We Proceeded On* 5 (July 1979): 14–16.

Lange (4)   ———. "Poor Charbonneau! Was He as Incompetent as the Journals/Narratives Make Him Out to Be!" *We Proceeded On* 6: (May 1980): 14–17.

Lange (5)   ———. "Private George Shannon: The Expedition's Youngest Member." *We Proceeded On* 8 (July 1982): 10–15.

Lange (6)   ———. "William Bratton: One of Lewis and Clark's Men." *We Proceeded On* 7 (February 1981): 8–11.

Large (1)   Large, Arlen J. "Additions to the Party: How an Expedition Grew and Grew." *We Proceeded On* 16 (February 1990): 4–11.

Large (2)   ———. "The Clark-Sacagawea Affair: A Literary Evolution." *We Proceeded On* 14 (August 1988): 14–18.

Large (3)   ———. "Expedition Specialists: The Talented Helpers of Lewis and Clark." *We Proceeded On* 20 (February 1994): 4–10.

Larkin   Larkin, Jack. *The Reshaping of Everyday Life, 1790–1840.* New York: Harper and Row, 1988.

Lavender   Lavender, David S. *The Westward Vision: The Story of the Oregon Trail.* New York: McGraw-Hill, 1963.

Leonard   Leonard, Zenas. *Narrative of the Adventures of Zenas Leonard, a Native of Clearfield County, P.A. Who Spent Five Years in Trapping for Furs, Trading with the Indians, &c., &c., of the Rocky Mountains.* Clearfield, Pa.: D. W. Moore, 1839. Reprint, Ann Arbor: University Microfilms, 1966.

Lewis   Lewis, Mary Newton. "Meriwether Lewis: Devoted Son." *We Proceeded On* 16 (May 1990): 14–20.

Loge   Loge, Ronald V. "Meriwether Lewis and Malaria." *We Proceeded On* 28 (May 2002): 31–33.

LW   "Letters from the West. No. XIV. The Missouri Trapper." *The Port Folio,* Philadelphia, March 1825.

McDermott (1)   McDermott, John Francis, ed. *Tixier's Travels on the Osage Prairies.* Norman: University of Oklahoma Press, 1940.

McDermott (2)   ———. *Up the Missouri: The Journal of Edward Harris.* Norman: University of Oklahoma Press, 1951.

McDermott (3)   ———. *The Western Journals of Washington Irving.* Norman: University of Oklahoma Press, 1944.

McGirr   McGirr, Newman F. "Patrick Gass and His Journal of the Lewis and Clark Expedition." *West Virginia History* 3 (1942): 205–12.

Maguire   Maguire, James H., and Peter Wild and Donald A. Barclay. *A Rendezvous Reader: Tall, Tangled, and True Tales of the Mountain Men, 1805–1850.* Salt Lake City: University of Utah Press, 1997.

Mahon   Mahon, John K. *The War of 1812.* Gainesville: University of Florida Press, 1972.

Majors   Majors, Harry M. "John McClellan in the Montana Rockies, 1807: The First Americans After Lewis and Clark." *Northwest Discovery* 2 (November–December 1981): 554–630.

Malone   Malone, Dumas. *Jefferson and His Time,* vol. 5, *Jefferson the President, Second Term, 1805–1809.* Boston: Little, Brown, 1974.

Marshall   Marshall, Thomas Maitland, ed. *The Life and Papers of Frederick Bates.* St. Louis: Missouri Historical Society, 1926.

Mattes   Mattes, Merril J. "Behind the Legend of Colter's Hell: The Early Exploration of Yellowstone Park," *Mississippi Valley Historical Review* 36 (September 1949): 251–82.

Montgomery   *Montgomery County, Indiana, Original Entry Book, Dates 1821 & Later.* Kokomo, Ind.: Selby, 1990.

Moore (1)   Moore, Bob. "Company Books, and What They Tell Us About the Corps of Discovery." *We Proceeded On* 27 (August 2001): 18–24.

Moore (2)   ———. "Pompey's Baptism." *We Proceeded On* 26 (February 2000): 11–17.

Morgan (1)   Morgan, Dale. *Jedediah Smith and the Opening of the West.* Bobbs-Merrill, 1953. Reprint, Lincoln: University of Nebraska Press, 1964.

Morgan (2)   ———, ed. *The West of William H. Ashley.* Denver: Old West, 1964.

Morris (1)   Morris, Larry E. "Dependable John Ordway." *We Proceeded On* 27 (May 2001): 28–33.

Morris (2)   ———. "After the Expedition." *American History,* March 2003.

Moss   Moss, James Earl. "William Henry Ashley: A Jackson Man with Feet of Clay." *Missouri Historical Review* 61 (October 1966): 1–20.

Moulton (1)   Moulton, Gary. "New Documents of Meriwether Lewis." *We Proceeded On* 13 (November 1987): 4–7.

Moulton (2)   ————, ed. *The Journals of the Lewis and Clark Expedition*. 13 vols. Lincoln: University of Nebraska Press, 1986–97.

Moyars   Moyars, Karen Hall. *The Battle of Tippecanoe*. Lafayette, Ind.: Tippecanoe County Historical Association, 1999.

Narrative   "A Personal Narrative." [By Col. George Hunt] *Collections of the Pioneer Society of the State of Michigan* 8 (1907): 662–69.

Nasatir   Nasatir, A. P. *Before Lewis and Clark: Documents Illustrating the History of the Missouri, 1785–1804*, vol. 1. Lincoln: University of Nebraska Press, 1990.

Nelson   Nelson, W. Dale. *Interpreters with Lewis and Clark: The Story of Sacagawea and Toussaint Charbonneau*. Denton: University of North Texas Press, 2003.

New Madrid   *New Madrid County, Missouri Court Orders, 1816–1825*. Miami Beach, Fla.: T. L. C. Genealogy, 1990.

Noy   Noy, Gary. *Distant Horizon: Documents from the Nineteenth-Century American West*. Lincoln: University of Nebraska Press, 1999.

Nuttall   Nuttall, Thomas. *A Journal of Travels into the Arkansas Territory, During the Year 1819* . . . Philadelphia: Thos. H. Palmer, 1821.

Oglesby   Oglesby, Richard E. *Manuel Lisa and the Opening of the Missouri Fur Trade*. Norman: University of Oklahoma Press, 1963.

Oldenburg   Oldenburg, Joseph F. *A Genealogical Guide to the Burton Historical Collection*. Salt Lake City: Ancestry, 1988.

Oman   Oman, Kerry. "Serendipity." *We Proceeded On* 27 (November 2001): 7–10.

Osgood   Osgood, Ernest S., ed. *The Field Notes of Captain William Clark, 1803–1805*. New Haven: Yale University Press, 1964.

Ottoson   Ottoson, Dennis R. "Toussaint Charbonneau, A Most Durable Man." *South Dakota History* 6 (Spring 1976): 152–85.

PA   *Pennsylvania Archives*. 119 vols. Philadelphia, Harrisburg: J. Stevens, et al., 1852–1935.

Paxton   Paxton, John A. *The St. Louis Directory and Register*, 1821, 1836.

Penick   Penick, James Lal. *The New Madrid Earthquakes*, rev. ed. Columbia: University of Missouri Press, 1981.

Phelps   Phelps, Dawson A. "The Tragic Death of Meriwether Lewis." *William and Mary Quarterly* 13 (July 1956): 305–18.

Porter (1)   Porter, Clyde H. "Pioneer Portraits: Jean Baptiste Charbonneau." *Idaho Yesterdays* 5 (Fall 1961): 7–9.

Porter (2)   Porter, Kenneth W. "Roll of Overland Astorians, 1810–1812." *Oregon Historical Quarterly* 34 (1933).

Preston   *The Preston and Virginia Papers of the Draper Collection of Manuscripts.*
                 Madison: State Historical Society of Wisconsin, 1915.

Prior   *Family Connections,* Newsletter of the Prior Family Historical Society.
                 Published in Lincolnshire, England, by John Prior, September 1999.

Quaife (1)   Quaife, Milo M. "Notes and Documents: Some New-Found
                 Records of the Lewis and Clark Expedition." *Mississippi Valley His-*
                 torical Review 2 (June 1915): 106–17.

Quaife (2)   ———, ed. *The Journals of Captain Meriwether Lewis and Sergeant John*
                 Ordway. Madison: Historical Society of Wisconsin, 1916.

Ranck   Ranck, George Washington. *History of Lexington, Kentucky: Its Early*
                 Annals and Recent Progress. 1872. Reprint, Bowie, Md.: Heritage, 1989.

Reading   Reading, Mrs. James. "Jean Baptiste Charbonneau: The Wind
                 River Scout." *The Journal of San Diego History* 11 (March 1965): 28–33.

Reid   Reid, Richard J. *The Battle of Tippecanoe.* Fordsville, Ky.: Privately
                 printed, 1983.

Remini   Remini, Robert Vincent. *Henry Clay: Statesman for the Union.* New
                 York: W. W. Norton, 1991.

Reports   "Reports of the Fur Trade and Inland Trade to Mexico, 1831."
                 Missouri Historical Society Glimpses of the Past 9 (January–June 1942):
                 3–39.

Ricketts   Ricketts, Norma B. *The Mormon Battalion: U.S. Army of the West,*
                 1846–1848. Logan: Utah State University Press, 1996.

Robinson (1)   Robinson, Doane. "Official Correspondence of the Leavenworth
                 Expedition into South Dakota in 1823." *South Dakota Historical Collec-*
                 tions 1 (1902): 181–256.

Robinson (2)   ———. "Sac-a-jawe vs. Sa-kaka-wea." *South Dakota Historical Collec-*
                 tions 12 (1924): 71–81.

Rogers   Rogers, Ann. "Was It the PawPaws?" *We Proceeded On* 13 (February
                 1987): 17–18.

Rollins   Rollins, Philip A. *The Discovery of the Oregon Trail: Robert Stuart's Narra-*
                 tives of His Overland Trip Eastward from Astoria in 1812–1813. New
                 York: Charles Scriber's Sons, 1935.

Ronda (1)   Ronda, James P. *Lewis and Clark Among the Indians.* Lincoln: Univer-
                 sity of Nebraska Press, 1984.

Ronda (2)   ———. "St. Louis Welcomes and Toasts the Lewis and Clark Ex-
                 pedition." *We Proceeded On* 13 (February 1987): 19–20.

Ronda (3)   ———, ed. *The Voyages of Discovery: Essays on the Lewis and Clark Expe-*
                 dition. Helena: Montana Historical Society Press, 1988.

Ross (1)   Ross, Alexander. *The Fur Hunters of the Far West.* Edited by Kenneth
                 A. Spaulding. Norman: University of Oklahoma Press, 1956.

Ross (2)   Ross, Margaret Smith. *Letters of Hiram Abiff Whittington: An Arkansas Pioneer from Massachusetts, 1827–1834*. Little Rock, Ark.: Pulaski County Historical Society, 1956.

Russell   Russell, Carl P. *Firearms, Traps, and Tools of the Mountain Men*. New York: Knopf, 1967.

Ruxton   Ruxton, George Frederick Augustus. *Life in the Far West*. Glorieta, N.Mex.: Rio Grande, 1972.

Sage   Sage, Rufus B. *Rocky Mountain Life; or, Startling Scenes and Perilous Adventures in the Far West, During an Expedition of Three Years*. Boston: Wentworth, 1857.

Saylor   Saylor, David J. *Jackson Hole, Wyoming; in the Shadows of the Tetons*. Norman: University of Oklahoma Press, 1970.

Schaumann   Schaumann, Merri Lou Scribner. *Tax Lists—Cumberland County, Pennsylvania, 1768, 1769, 1770*. Carlisle, Pa.: Privately printed, 1972.

Schmidt (1) Schmidt, Thomas. *National Geographic Guide to the Lewis and Clark Trail*. Washington, D.C.: National Geographic Society, 2002.

Schmidt (2) Schmidt, Thomas, and Jeremy Schmidt. *The Saga of Lewis and Clark into the Uncharted West*. New York: Tehabi, 1999.

Shannon   "'Peg-Leg' Shannon." *Missouri Historical Review* 29 (January 1935): 115–21.

Shrum   Shrum, Edson E. *Pioneer Families of Scott County [Missouri]*. Scott County Historical Society, n.d.

Skarsten (1) Skarsten. M. O. "George Drouillard." In Hafen (3), 5:69–82.

Skarsten (2) ———. *George Drouillard, Hunter and Interpreter for Lewis and Clark*. Glendale, Calif.: Arthur H. Clark, 1964.

Smith   Smith, James S., and Kathryn Smith. "Sedulous Sergeant, Patrick Gass." *Montana* 5 (Summer 1955): 20–27.

Speck   Speck, Gordon. *Breeds and Half-Breeds*. New York: Clarkson Potter, 1969.

Stadler   Stadler, Frances H. "St. Louis in 1804." *We Proceeded On* 20 (February 1994): 11–16.

Steffen   Steffen, Jerome O. *William Clark: Jeffersonian Man on the Frontier*. Norman: University of Oklahoma Press, 1977.

Stewart and Stewart, David, and Ray Knox. *The Earthquake America Forgot*.
Knox (1)   Marble Hill, Mo.: Gutenberg-Richter, 1995.

Stewart   ———. *The Earthquake That Never Went Away*. Marble Hill, Mo.:
and Knox (2) Gutenberg-Richter, 1993.

Stoddard   Stoddard, Amos. *Sketches, Historical and Descriptive, of Louisiana*. Philadelphia: Matthew Carey, 1812.

Taranik   Taranik, Jeanette D. "The Patrick Gass Photographs and Portraits: A Sequel." *We Proceeded On* 6 (February 1980): 16–19.

Thompson   Thompson, Harry F. "Meriwether Lewis and His Son: The Claim of Joseph DeSomet Lewis and the Problem of History." *North Dakota History* 67 (2000): 24–37.

Thrapp   Thrapp, Dan L. *Encyclopedia of Frontier Biography*. Gendale, Calif.: Arthur H. Clark, 1988.

Thwaites (1)   Thwaites, Reuben Gold. "William Clark: Soldier, Explorer, Statesman." *Missouri Historical Society Collections* 2 (October 1906): 1–24.

Thwaites (2)   ———, ed. *Early Western Travels, 1748–1846*. 32 vols. Cleveland: A. H. Clark, 1904–7.

Turnbull   "T. Turnbull's Travels from the United States Across the Plains to California." *Proceedings of the State Historical Society of Wisconsin*. Madison: State Historical Society of Wisconsin, 1914, 151–225.

Utley   Utley, Robert M. *A Life Wild and Perilous: Mountain Men and the Paths to the Pacific*. New York: Owl, 1997.

Vinton   Vinton, Stallo. *John Colter, Discoverer of Yellowstone Park*. New York: E. Eberstadt, 1926.

Wagner   Wagner, Henry R. *The Plains and the Rockies: A Bibliography of Original Narratives of Travel and Adventure, 1800–1865*. Revised by Charles L. Camp. Fourth edition revised, enlarged, and edited by Robert H. Becker. San Francisco: John Howell, 1982.

War of 1812   *War of 1812 Pensioners, Missouri*. Wyandotte, Okla.: Gregath, 1983.

Wells   Wells, Merle W. "Jean Baptiste Charbonneau." *Idaho Yesterdays* 44 (Winter 2001): 12–14.

Wharton   Wharton, Anne Hollingsworth. *Social Life in the Early Republic*. Philadelphia: J. B. Lippincott, 1902.

Wheeler (1)   Wheeler, Olin D. *The Trail of Lewis and Clark, 1804–1904*. New York: G. P. Putnam's Sons, 1904.

Wheeler (2)   ———. *Wonderland 1900*.

White (1)   White, David A. *News of the Plains and Rockies, 1803–1865*. 8 vols. Spokane, Wash.: Arthur H. Clark, 1999.

White (2)   White, James Haley. "Early Days in St. Louis." *Missouri Historical Society Glimpses of the Past* 6 (January–March 1939): 5–13.

Williams   Williams, Amelia W., and Eugene C. Barker. *The Writings of Sam Houston, 1813–1863*. 8 vols. Austin: University of Texas Press, 1938–43.

Wright (1)   Wright, John Dean. *Lexington: Heart of the Bluegrass*. Lexington: Lexington-Fayette County Historic Commission, 1982.

Wright (2)   ———. *Transylvania: Tutor to the West*. Lexington: University Press of Kentucky, 1980.

Yater   Yater, George H. "Nine Young Men from Kentucky." In Yater and Denton, 1–14.

Yater and Denton	Yater, George H., and Carolyn S. Denton. *Nine Young Men from Kentucky*. Supplement to *We Proceeded On*, WPO Publication no. 11. Great Falls, Mont.: Lewis and Clark Trail Heritage Foundation, 1992.
Yurtinus	Yurtinus, John Frank George. *A Ram in the Thicket: the Mormon Battalion in the Mexican War.* 2 vols. Ph.D. diss., Brigham Young University, 1975.

Internet Resources

AF	Ancestral File, Family History Library, Salt Lake City, Utah. http://www.familysearch.org
Ancestry	Ancestry's computerized genealogy database, including census records. http://www.ancestry.com
Court	Circuit Court Case Files, Office of the Circuit Clerk, City of St. Louis, Missouri. http://stlcourtrecords.wustl.edu
Descendant	The Lewis & Clark Corps of Discovery Descendant Project. http://home.pacifier.com/karenl/lewis&.htm
Discovering	Discovering Lewis and Clark. http://www.lewis-clark.org
IGI	International Genealogical Index. http://www.familysearch.org

Acknowledgments

Thanks to my wife, Deborah, for her wonderful support and for her companionship on the Lewis and Clark trail. Thanks to our children, Isaac, Courtney, Justin, and Whitney. Among the six of us, we have seen a good deal of Lewis and Clark's route, from St. Louis to Astoria, from Omaha to the confluence of the Snake and the Columbia, from Three Forks to Lemhi Pass.

Special thanks to Dan Bial, my agent, and Lara Heimert and Phil King, my editors. Their help has been invaluable. Thanks to Keith Condon, Mary Pasti, and everyone else at Yale University Press, a first-class institution.

It was a pleasure to conduct the majority of my research at the Missouri Historical Society in St. Louis (my favorite research facility), the Family History Library in Salt Lake City, and the Harold B. Lee Library and L. Tom Perry Special Collections Library at Brigham Young University, Provo, Utah. Thanks to their fine staffs. Thanks also to those who assisted me at the Allen County Public Library, Fort Wayne, Indiana; the Chicago Branch of the National Archives; the Filson Historical Society, Louisville, Kentucky; the Illinois Historical Society, Springfield; the Indiana Historical Society and Indiana State Library, Indianapolis; the Jefferson National Expansion Monument Library, St. Louis; Lewis and Clark College Library Archives, Portland, Oregon; the Lewis and Clark Trail Heritage Foundation Library, Great Falls, Montana; the Missouri State Archives, Jefferson City; the Newberry Library, Chicago; the Ohio State Historical Society, Columbus; the Oregon Historical Society, Portland; the St. Louis Genealogy Society; the State Historical Society of Missouri and Western Historical Manuscript Collection, University of Missouri, Columbia; the State Historical Society of Wisconsin, Madison; and the Utah Historical Society, Salt Lake City.

It has been great to get to know quite a number of people who help keep the spirit of Lewis and Clark alive. Special thanks to Jim Holmberg. Thanks also to Rebecca Bogden, Carol Bronson, Jay Buckley, Esther Duncan, Doug Erickson, John F. Hall, Larry and Sandra Hargrove, Jane Henley, Tom Huntington, Donna Masterson, Jim Merritt, and Joe Mussulman. It was a particular pleasure to talk with Eugene Gass Painter, the great-grandson of Patrick Gass. My association with fellow members of the Lewis and Clark Trail Heritage Foundation (P.O. Box 3434, Great Falls, Montana, 59403) has been rewarding both personally and professionally. There is a special fellowship among those who are passionate about Lewis and Clark.

I deeply appreciate the work of Stephen E. Ambrose, Irving W. Anderson, John Bakeless, Robert B. Betts, Nicholas Biddle, Ken Burns, Hiram Martin Chittenden, Eldon G. Chuinard, Charles G. Clarke, Ruth Colter-Frick, Elliott Coues, Paul Russell Cutright, William C. Davis, Bernard DeVoto, Richard Dillon, Stella M. Drumm, Dayton Duncan, Eva Emory Dye, Vardis Fisher, LeRoy R. Hafen, Burton Harris, James J. Holmberg, Harold P. Howard, Donald Jackson, John G. Jacob, Howard R. Lamar, Robert E. Lange, Dale L. Morgan, Gary E. Moulton, Joseph A. Mussulman, Richard E. Oglesby, Milo M. Quaife, James P. Ronda, M. O. Skarsten, Jerald S. Snyder, Reuben G. Thwaites, Robert M. Utley, and Olin D. Wheeler.

Thanks to the following people who contributed information to the list of members of the Lewis and Clark Expedition in Appendix A: John A. Baker, Eleanor Buzalsky, Rita Cleary, Ruth Colter-Frick, Darlene Fassler, Richard B. Groharing, Evelyn Huggins, Pat Lowery Koetting, Jeffrey La Page, Patti Malvern, Louise Matney, Barbara Nell, Donna Phillips, Joyce Scott, and Karen E. Willard.

Thanks to those who will research the members of the Lewis and Clark Expedition in the future. The search for York, for Hugh Hall, and for the others continues.

Index

Women are listed by married surname, if known (by maiden name if otherwise). Namesakes are given in order of birth. The following abbreviations are used: JBC = Jean-Baptiste Charbonneau, LCE = Lewis and Clark Expedition, ML = Meriwether Lewis, TC = Toussaint Charbonneau, TJ = Thomas Jefferson, WC = William Clark.

Bellefontaine, Fort, 21, 36, 37, 49, 58, 76, 165
Bible, 51, 81, 119, 128
Biddle, Nicholas: asked by WC to work on
    journals, 86; on Conrad's bankruptcy, 88;
    death of brother, 251n.11; interviews WC,
    86; letter to WC regarding publication of
    history of LCE, 168; Ordway's journal and,
    238n.30; works with Shannon on journals,
    86–88, 107–8
Big Bellies. *See* Gros Ventre nation
Bighorn River and Bighorn, Mont., 40, 43,
    138, 147
Big Neck (Iowa chief), 165–66
Billings, Mont., 42
Bismarck, N.Dak., 90
bison, 18, 46
Bissell, Russell, 128
Bissonnet, Antoine, 39–40, 49–52, 78
Bitterroot Mountains, 9, 49, 101
Black Buffalo (Lakota chief), 17–18, 32–33
Blackfoot nation, 2, 3, 41, 44, 45–48, 90,
    92–95, 108, 134, 152, 154
Black Hawk (Sauk chief), 169–70
Black Hills, 77
Black Moccasin (Hidatsa chief), 7
Bonneville, Benjamin, 43
Boone, Daniel, 2, 25, 80–81, 125, 184, 242n.18
Boone, Nathan, 125, 126, 242n.20
Boone, Squire, 81
Boonsboro, Mo., 184
Bouche (first name unknown), 40, 44
Bozeman Pass, 41, 44, 48
Brackenridge, Henry M., 106–7, 109–12
Bradbury, John, 46, 71, 99–100, 111–12, 125
Brady, James, 104
Brandt, Etienne, 44
Bratton, Mary Maxwell (wife of Wm.
    Bratton), 100
Bratton, William: back problems cured by
    Shields, 79–80, 98, 231n.17; community
    leader, 100–101; complimented by ML, 99;
    death, 101; enters keelboat business, 99,
    235–36n.13; near New Madrid at time of
    earthquake, 99–100, 235–36n.13; relates
    near starvation during LCE, 101; settles in
    Indiana, 100–101; taken prisoner during
    War of 1812, 121–22; vital stats, 187
Brazeau, Joseph, 136; WC's list and, 149
Breckenridge, Lettissia, 57
Bridger, Jim, 2, 3, 137–38, 179, 239n.16
Brierly, Rachel Maria (daughter of Patrick
    Gass), 182–83, 193
Brown, William, 91

Buckley, Jay, 250n.40
Buckner, Tom, 180
buffalo. *See* bison
Buffalo River, 67
Burr, Aaron, 19, 59, 84, 225n.3

Cabeza de Vaca, Alvar Núñez, 215n.1
Calhoun, John C., 133, 164, 245n.15
Cameahwait (brother of Sacagawea), 108,
    239n.8
Carr, William, 51–52
Carson, Kit, 2, 176, 179
Cartwright, Peter, 38
Charbonneau, Jean-Baptiste, 3, 15, 16, 149,
    184; baptism of, 107, 238n.4; with
    Beckwourth, 180; birth of, 14; clerks at hotel,
    180; comforts battalion member, 177; death,
    180; departs for Montana, 180; described
    by Frémont, 179–80; Duke Paul Wilhelm
    Herzog of Wurttemburg and, 178, 253n.55;
    false conclusions concerning, 253n.55;
    fathers a child, 179; hired by Kearny to
    guide Mormon Battalion, 175–77; kills
    grizzly bears, 176; Luttig then WC named
    guardian of, 117; obituary, 188; serves as
    magistrate, 180; settles in California, 180;
    skill as a cook, 180; TC and, 172, 178; as a
    trapper, 179–80; travels to Europe, 178–79;
    vital stats, 187–88; wanders through lava
    fields, 179; WC and, 15–16, 108, 117, 177–78;
    wrongly identified as Jean-Baptiste in Utah,
    252n.49; youth, 177–78
Charbonneau, Lisette, 113, 117, 241n.32
Charbonneau, Toussaint, 3, 13, 14, 77, 123,
    149; arrives at Fort Manuel in 1812, 113,
    240n.27; arrives at Tilton's Fort, 138; arrives
    in St. Louis in 1809, 107, 238n.4; arrives in
    St. Louis in 1839, 171; assists in translation
    process, 157; death, 172; departs for Lake
    Traverse, 138; Duke of Wurttemburg and,
    178; emissary to Arikara, 135–36; escapes
    Indian attack, 171; estate, 172; at Fort Kiowa,
    136; fulfills missions for Lisa, 110, 113–14,
    116–17; with Hugh Glass, 137–38; JBC and,
    172; Lacrocque's positive impression of, 134;
    leaves St. Louis in 1811, 106–7; Luttig's neg-
    ative description of, 133–34; presumed
    dead, 117; Sacagawea's illness and, 113–14;
    skill as a cook, 171; smallpox epidemic and,
    171–72; takes young wife, 172; with trading
    venture on Arkansas River, 134, 245n.18;
    travels up Missouri in 1811, 107, 108–9;
    travels up Missouri in 1823, 136–38;

true age of, 171, 188; vital stats, 188–89;
WC and, 13–16, 106–7, 141, 171, 216n.14;
whereabouts during winter of 1811–12, 112,
239n.23

Chardon, F. A., 171–72, 240n.28

Charlo (slave of Manuel Lisa), 112–13

Cheek, James, 92, 93–94

Cherokee nation, 162–64

Chickasaw Agency, 64, 67, 204

Chickasaw Bluffs, 62, 63, 70, 195, 203–4

Chickasaw nation, 54, 64, 65, 203–4

Choctaw nation, 65

Chouteau, Auguste, 31, 106, 124; godfather to
JBC, 107; as justice at Drouillard's trial,
49–50; receives note from Lepage, 77–78

Chouteau, Auguste-Pierre: battle with Arikara,
34–35, 58, 128; escorts Sheheke in 1807, 30;
travels up Missouri, 32

Chouteau, Jean-Pierre, 31, 60, 78, 101; escorts
Sheheke in 1809, 58–59, 63–64, 89–90,
107, 115

Chouteau family, 23, 78, 107

Christy, William, 23–25

Civil War, 2, 3,

Clark, Edmund (brother of WC), 144

Clark, Edmund (son of WC), 169, 189

Clark, George Rogers (brother of WC), 25, 83,
142, 169, 184–85, 232n.4

Clark, Harriet Kennerly Radford (wife of
WC), 158, 169, 189

Clark, John (father of WC), 139, 189

Clark, Jonathan (brother of WC), 70, 77, 79,
81, 82, 85, 141, 168, 169, 184–85, 241n.2

Clark, Julia Hancock (wife of WC), 25–26, 60,
82, 85, 158, 167, 168–69, 189

Clark, Mary Margaret (daughter of WC),
168–69, 189

Clark, Meriwether Lewis (son of WC), 77, 85,
168, 170, 189, 232n.10

Clark, William, 3, 4, 12, 23, 24, 25, 26, 33, 36,
41, 43, 48, 58, 60, 71, 72, 75, 76, 82, 114, 115,
178, 184; appointed governor of Missouri
Territory, 123; and Arikara attack on Ashley,
133; asks Biddle to assist with journals, 86;
assists Gibson's widow, 77; assists Shields's
wife, 79; Bates and, 238–39n.5; Biddle and,
86–88; Black Hawk War and, 169–70;
Colter and, 9–13, 125; concerns about ML,
59–60, 70; death, 170–71; death of loved
ones, 169; establishes Fort Osage, 224n.4;
funeral procession of, 170–71; fur trade and,
31, 112; as Indian agent and superintendent
of Indian affairs, 29, 52, 56, 119–21, 123–25,

133, 142; Indian museum of, 167; influence
following LCE, 161; Irving and, 144, 169;
JBC and, 15–16, 117, 177–78; Julia Hancock
and, 25–26, 167, 168–69; and LCE journals, 72, 86–87, 167–68; letter about LCE
delivered by Gass, 184–85; letter to Dearborn, 29–30; list of LCE members, 36, 77,
115, 128, 149–50, 151, 152, 154, 157, 181, 212,
243–45n.14, 247nn.1–2; maps of, 26, 125,
153, 221nn.10 and 14; as militia general, 29,
119–21, 123–25; named guardian of TC's
children, 117; obituary, 189–90; orders construction of gunboats, 123–24; Pryor and,
29–30, 33–36, 120–21, 163; reads report of
ML's death, 70; receives report of death of
Rose and Glass, 147; receives report of
Jones-Immell massacre, 134; receives report
of ML's death from Pernia, 64–65; relations
with Indians, 7–8, 17–18, 32–33, 34, 119–21,
123–25, 170; requests help from Pryor and
Willard during War of 1812, 120–21; on
return journey of the LCE, 5–6, 13–21;
runs for governor of state of Missouri,
124–25; saves Sacagawea from flash flood,
15; sends buffalo robes from Fort Mandan,
81; Shannon and, 37, 82, 85, 86, 164, 166;
and slavery, 139–44; TC and, 13–16, 106–7,
141, 171; TJ and, 71, 170; travels to Washington in 1809, 59–60; visits TJ, 71–72; vital
stats, 189–90; and War of 1812, 168; warns
of Indian threat in 1810–11, 119–20, 241n.2;
Willard and, 120–21, 172; York and, 2,
38–40, 141–44, 148. See also Lewis and Clark

Clark, Fort, 171–72

Clark Canyon Reservoir, 107

Clark's Fork River, 43–44

Clarksville, Ind., 140–41

Clatsop, Fort, 79

Clay, Henry, 2, 163; befriends Shannon, 85,
165, 232n.7; fights a duel, 84–85; professor
and trustee at Translyvania, 84

Clearwater River, 9

Clyman, James, 127, 128, 131–33, 134–35,
243n.13

Cody, Wyo., 43

Colbert, George, 65–66

Cole party, 122

Collins, John, 4, 12, 149, 178; with Ashley, 127,
128; attacked by the Arikara, 130–31; death,
131, 133, 243–45n.14; discipline problems,
128–29; early history, 128–29; possibly goes
west with McClellan, 150–52; vital stats,
190, 243–45n.14

estate, 155, 192; marriage, 155; possibly with Chouteau, 30; vital stats, 192

Fincastle, Va., 86, 158

Fisher, Vardis, 63, 207–9, 224n.1

Fitzgerald, John, 137–38

Fitzhugh, Dennis, 143, 219n.16, 247n.21

Fitzpatrick, Thomas, 127

flatboats, 61, 65, 81

Flathead Lake, 150, 152

Flathead nation. *See* Salish nation

Floyd, Charles, 80, 155, 174; death of, 1, 3, 39, 75, 115, 149; LCE journal of, 157, 160; vital stats, 192

Fox nation, 121, 123–24, 169–70

Franklin County, Mo., 81, 157

Frazer, Robert, 140, 149; charged with assault and murder, 156; death, 157; estate, 157, 193; LCE journal of, 156, 157, 160; rushed by party of Sioux, 155–56; settles in Franklin County, Mo., 157; vital stats, 192–93, 249n.27; watch-repair business, 157

Frederick County, Md., 128

Freeharty (first name unknown), 93

Freeman, Thomas, 72

Frémont, John C., 2, 16, 174, 179–80

Fries, Anastasia Katharina, 179, 187

fur trade, 23, 30–31, 112, 179–80. *See also* beaver trapping

Galena, Ill., 120

Gallatin River, 41, 44, 48, 92

Gasconade River, 32, 157

Gass, Maria Hamilton (wife of Patrick Gass), 183, 193

Gass, Patrick, 3, 140, 149; Daniel Boone and, 184; death, 77; delivers letter announcing return of LCE, 184–85; description of, 181–82; early history, 182; final days, 184–85; LCE journal of, 3, 57, 157, 160, 168, 182; left with several young children, 183; loss of eye, 181, 253–54n.62; meets Maria Hamilton, 183; ML's gunshot wound and, 8; petitions Congress, 183–84; service in War of 1812, 181; vital stats, 193

Ghent, W. J., 212

Gibson, George, 3, 58, 78, 114, 128, 150; estate, 77, 193; gunshot wound, 35–37, 76; illness of, 76; joins Pryor's party, 29, 76; last will and testament, 76; petition to Congress, 75–76; plays fiddle, 76–77; travels up Missouri with Pryor, 32; treated with mercury for syphilis, 76; value during LCE, 29, 76; vital stats, 193

Gibson, Maria Reagan (wife of George Gibson), 76–77, 193

Gibson, Reed, 132–33, 243n.13, 243–44n.14

Glass, Hugh, 127, 130, 136–38, 147, 178, 243n.13, 243–44n.14, 245n.27

Goodrich, Silas, 4, 140, 150, 156, 159; death, 160; mercury treatment for syphilis, 160; value as fisherman during LCE, 160; vital stats, 194

Grand River, 20, 33, 136

Gravelines, Joseph, 20, 33, 202

Great Falls of the Missouri, 15, 93, 101, 152

Great Salt Lake, 239n.16, 242–43n.2, 252n.49

Grey Eyes (Arikara chief), 34

Grinder, Priscilla: describes events leading to ML's death, 67–69, 73–74; greets ML and servants, 54; mentioned by Neelly, 69; mentioned by TJ, 71; on ML's state of mind before his death, 55; suspicions about, 72, 73, 74, 224n.1; text of letters and recollections concerning, 203–7

Grinder family, 54, 55, 71, 72–74, 203–8, 224n.1, 225n.2

Grinder's Stand, 54, 67, 90, 95

Gros Ventre nation, 42, 90, 91, 114, 117, 171, 240n.28. *See also* Crow nation; Hidatsa nation

Guice, John D., 68, 207, 209, 230n.48

Guillet, Urbain, 107

Hall, Hugh, 4, 149, 150, 159, 175; census records, 250n.37; death, 160; difficulty with land warrant, 160; possibly kept LCE journal, 160–61; settles in Pennsylvania, 160; vital stats, 194, 250n.37

Hall, James, 137, 245n.27

Hall, John F., 160–61

Halsey, Jacob, 171

Hamilton, Alexander, 19, 182

Hancock, Forrest, 12–13, 19, 38, 40, 44

Hancock, George, 26, 86

Hancock, Julia. *See* Clark, Julia Hancock (wife of WC)

Harmon, Daniel W., 216n.2

Harrison, William Henry, 23, 27, 118–19, 120, 122

Hebard, Grace Raymond, 210–13, 238n.4

Hempstead, Edward, 51, 156

Henry, Andrew, 2, 41, 128, 136–37

Herzog, Duke Paul Wilhelm of Wurttemburg, 178, 253n.55

Hickman, Paschal, 121

Hidatsa nation, 6–7, 13, 14, 16, 18, 29, 42, 90, 106, 108, 111, 240n.28

History of the Expedition Under the Command of Captains Lewis and Clark, The, 168, 238n.30

Hoback, John, 39, 111

Holmberg, James J., 207, 218–19n.14, 240n.28, 247n.21, 250n.40

Holmes, Reuben, 41, 44–45, 134

House, James, 63

Houston, Sam, 162–64, 167

Houston, Miss., 64

Howard, Genevieve Roy (wife of Thomas P. Howard), 154, 194

Howard, Harold P., 239nn.8 and 23

Howard, Joseph and Louis (sons of Thomas P. Howard), 154, 194

Howard, Thomas P., 150; death, 154; discipline problems, 154; early history, 154; vital stats, 194

Hudson's Bay Company, 30–31, 106, 179

Hull (first name unknown), 93

Hunt, George, 121

Hunt, Wilson Price, 2, 109–11, 239n.16

Hunter, Jesse, 177

Idaho, 13, 41, 43, 55, 79–80, 111, 153, 180, 198

Immell, Michael, 94, 114, 116, 134, 234n.10

Indiana, 23, 27, 100, 101, 140–41, 160, 192, 231n.19

Indians and Indian nations, 1, 8, 19, 24–27, 29, 31, 38, 39, 56, 64, 71, 72, 87, 113. *See also names of specific nations*

Inskip Station, 180

interpreters, 14, 157

Iowa nation, 165–66

Irving, Washington: description of Edward Rose, 45, 220n.7; information on York, 144; visit to WC, 144, 169

Jackson, Andrew, 121, 162, 163, 165, 166

Jackson, David E., 127, 128, 130–31

Jackson, Donald, 185, 207, 212–13

Jackson Lake and Jackson, Wyo., 43

Jacob, John G., 181, 183

James, Thomas, 39, 44, 46–48, 89, 90–93, 95, 126

Jefferson, Thomas, 19, 24, 29, 85, 86, 114; hears report of ML's death, 70; as host of White House parties, 27; Indians and, 7, 17, 20, 26–27, 58, 170; and LCE, 5, 13, 23, 28; and LCE journals, 56–57, 70, 72, 168; letter from Neelly, 66, 69, 70, 74; letters from Russell, 62–63; ML and, 26, 56, 57,

58, 71, 75, 225n.7; on ML's state of mind and death, 60, 62–63, 66–67, 69–72, 72–74; WC and, 71–72, 170

Jefferson River, 41, 46, 94, 95

Johnson, David and Isidore (stepchildren of John Ordway), 102, 104–5, 236n.17

Johnson, John, 105, 236n.17

Jones, Landon, 250n.40, 251n.22

Jones, Robert, 94, 134, 234n.10

journals. *See* Lewis and Clark Expedition journals

Judith River, 26

Jusseaume, René, 7, 13, 25–27, 28, 34–36, 114, 133–34

Kansas City, Mo., 32, 178

Kaskaskia, Ill., 77, 195, 218n.7

Kearny, Stephen W., 175, 176

keelboats, 28, 32–37, 39, 40, 44–45, 60–62, 81, 89, 98–100

Kennerly, William Clark, 139, 246n.1

Kentucky, 3, 5, 8, 9, 35–36, 37, 58, 65, 70, 76; contemporary description of, 82; "nine young men from," 29, 76, 78, 98

Kentucky flatboats, 61, 65, 81

Kiowa, Fort, 136, 137

Knife River, 90, 107

Kootenai nation, 150, 247n.3

Labiche, François, 25, 80, 149, 249n.28; assists in translation process, 157; death, 158; settles in St. Louis, 157–58; value during LCE, 157; vital stats, 195; works as boatman, 157–58

Labiche, Genevieve Flore (wife of François Labiche), 158, 195

La Charette, Mo., 20–21, 125

Lacrocque, François-Antoine, 134

Lake Erie, 121–22

Lake Eustis. *See* Yellowstone Lake

Lake Traverse, 138

Lakota nation, 7, 16–18, 29, 32–33, 109

Langevin, Antoine, 138

La Raye, Charles, 215n.2

Leavenworth, Henry, 133–36, 171, 245n.15

Leclair (first name unknown), 117

LeCompt (Lecomte), François, 114

Leonard, Zenas, 145–48, 247n.20

Lepage, Jean-Baptiste, 45, 48, 150; death, 78; early history, 77; estate, 78, 195; explores Little Missouri River, 77; LCE pay, 78; with Lisa, 39, 78; married prior to LCE, 77; note to Chouteau, 77–78; vital stats, 195

Leroux, Antoine, 176

Lewis, Lucy Meriwether. *See* Marks, Lucy Meriwether Lewis

Lewis, Meriwether, 3, 4, 5–6, 20, 21, 28, 42, 43, 75, 85, 90, 149, 154–55, 184; arrives at Grinder's Stand, 54–55, 67; Bates and, 57, 58, 60, 226n.9; burial, 69, 204, 205; death, 2, 36, 68–69, 95, 107, 195–96, 203–9, 225n.2, 247n.2; debts, 56, 59, 60, 63, 64, 70, 72, 78; departs for Washington in 1809, 59–60; describes Bratton's illness and recovery, 80, 98; and escort of Sheheke, 57–59; Eustis and, 55–56, 59; events leading to death, 67–69, 115; as governor of Louisiana, 29, 36, 52, 56–60; gunshot wound during LCE, 8, 13, 17–18, 19; illnesses, 60–61, 62–63, 64–65, 99, 207, 227n.18; and LCE journals, 56–57, 59, 63, 65, 70, 72, 167–68; Lucy Meriwether Lewis Marks (mother) and, 61; mental illness in the family of, 71, 228–29n.40, 235n.12; on the Natchez Trace, 65–67; obituary, 195–96; recuperates at Fort Pickering, 62–64; report to TJ, 23; rescues Windsor, 158–59; Russell and, 62–63; state of mind prior to death, 55, 59, 60–65, 66, 67–69; suicide attempts of, 62–63; supposed drug and alcohol problems, 60–61, 62, 72; thirty-first birthday during LCE, 55; TJ and, 26, 56, 57, 58, 71, 75, 225n.7; travels to Washington in 1806, 25–27; vital stats, 195–96; wounds himself, 68, 69–70. *See also* Lewis and Clark

—accounts of death: Mrs. Grinder, as reported to Wilson, 204–6; Mrs. Grinder, as reported to unnamed schoolteacher, 206–7; Nashville newspaper, 69–70; Neely to TJ, 203–4

—post-expedition evaluation: of Bratton, 99; of Drouillard, 31, 80; of Field brothers, 30, 80, 155; of Floyd, 80; of Labiche, 80, 157; of Shields, 79–80; of TC, 14

Lewis, Reuben, 57, 73, 90, 94–95, 112–13, 229n.40, 233n.1, 235n.12

Lewis, Will, 122

Lewis and Clark, 13, 14, 15, 19, 20, 23, 28, 33, 45–46, 51, 55, 83, 87–88, 90, 106–8; attitude toward insubordination, 9; friendship of, 8–9, 19, 59–60, 64–65; honored with reception, 23–25; recruit unmarried men, 79; rewarded by TJ, 28–29; rumors regarding, 20, 217n.20; and vote on where to spend winter of 1805–6, 140

Lewis and Clark Expedition, 1–2, 5, 24, 31, 41, 49, 108, 112, 183; preparations for, 8–9; summary of, 9; supplies for, 13; translation by interpreters for, 14, 157. *See also* Lewis and Clark

Lewis and Clark Expedition journals, 13, 14, 23, 160; Floyd's, 157, 160; Frazer's, 156, 157, 160; Gass's, 3, 57, 160, 168, 182; Hall's, 160–61; ML and, 56–57, 59, 63, 65, 70, 72, 167–68; Ordway's, 101, 105, 160, 238n.30; publication of, 57, 86–88, 168, 238n.30; WC and, 72, 86–87, 167–68; Whitehouse's, 156–57, 160; Willard's, 175

—entries written: on Bratton, 79–80, 98; on celebrating Christmas, 105; on Collins, 12; on Colter, 12; on Council Bluffs, 174; on Drouillard ("Drewyer"), 12; on fiddle playing, 76–77, 151; on the Field brothers, 12; on Goodrich, 160; on Howard, 154; on hunting, 12; on Indians, 6, 7, 17, 18, 43, 76–77, 79, 155–56; on John McClellan, 150–51; on making their own clothing, 155; on ML's birthday, 55; on ML's illness, 61; on ML's wound, 8, 19; on mosquitoes, 16; on returning to St. Louis, 6, 16, 18, 19, 20–21, 22, 23; on Sacagawea, 14, 15–16; on Shannon, 28; on Shields, 79–80; on TC, 15–16; on TJ, 19, 20; on vote of where to spend winter of 1805–6, 140; on weather, 16, 18; on whiskey, 19; on wildlife, 18, 159

Lewis and Marks families, 71, 72, 73, 228–29n.40, 235n.12

Lexington, Ky., 82–83, 84, 88

Lincoln, Abraham, 84

liquor. *See* alcohol and alcoholism

Lisa, Manuel, 46, 78, 92, 96, 123–24, 156, 159; and Bissonnet's death, 39–40, 49, 50; and Drouillard's murder trial, 49–53; early history, 30; encounter with Arikara, 33–34; establishes Fort Manuel, 113; establishes Fort Raymond, 40–43; and fur trade, 30; and members of corps, 220n.3; men of, killed by Indians, 114, 116; murder charge dropped, 53; Rose and, 44–45; sends emissaries to Crow nation, 40; strengths and weaknesses noted by Brackenridge, 109; trapping expedition of 1807, 39; travels up Missouri in 1811, 106, 108–11; travels up Missouri in 1812, 112–13, 239n.23

Little Bighorn River, 42, 117

Little Missouri River, 77

Loisel's Fort, 151

Lolo Hot Springs, 43

Louisiana Purchase and Louisiana Territory, 19, 24, 29, 31, 59, 70, 73, 75, 83

newspapers, 23, 24, 69, 70, 73, 88, 133, 153, 154, 164, 166, 167. See also *Missouri Gazette*

Nez Percé nation, 49

"nine young men from Kentucky," 29, 76, 78, 98

North Dakota, 6, 12, 30, 33, 78, 90, 107

North West Company, 30–31, 93, 106

O'Fallon, Benjamin, 133–34, 178, 245n.15

O'Fallon, John, 125, 143

Ohio River, 25, 61, 65–67, 81, 84, 99, 184

Omaha, Nebr., 110

Omaha nation, 6, 17, 110

One Eye (Hidatsa chief), 90

Ordway, Elizabeth Johnson (wife of John Ordway), 102, 104–5, 236n.17

Ordway, Gracey (wife of John Ordway), 102, 236n.17

Ordway, John, 3, 12, 16, 25, 45, 77, 140, 149; accompanies ML to Washington, 101; commands separate group on Missouri River, 101; death, 104; describes arrival in St. Louis, 22; early history, 101; family troubles, 103–4; LCE journal of, 101, 105, 157, 160, 238n.30; letter to parents concerning LCE, 101; in New Madrid at time of earthquake, 98, 102–5; settles in Missouri, 102; threatened by Colter, 9; vital stats, 196

Ordway, John Jr. and Hannah (children of John Ordway), 104–5, 196, 236n.17

Ordway family, 102–5, 196, 236nn.17 and 18, 237nn.21 and 23

Osage, Fort, 52, 156, 239n.23

Osage nation, 2, 27, 163–64

Osage River, 32, 39, 50

Owen, Abraham, 119

Owyhee River, 180

Pacific Fur Company, 31

Pacific Ocean, 2, 5, 9, 14, 23, 55, 101, 107, 140, 163

Papin, Alex, 114

Parker, Eliza, 84

pawpaws, 20

Peale, Charles Willson, 86

Penrose, Clement, 60

Pernia, John, 54–55, 60–61, 64–65, 68–74, 206, 207, 208

Peruvian bark, 37, 61, 79. *See also* medicine and medical treatment

petition to Congress (signed by Joseph and Reubin Field, Patrick Gass, George Gibson, Silas Goodrich, Hugh Hall, John B.

Thompson, and Alexander Willard), 75–76, 151, 218n.14, 218–19n.40, 230n.2

Philadelphia, Pa., 56, 59, 67, 86, 87, 207, 225n.2, 232n.7, 238n.30

Pickering, Fort, 62–64, 67, 72

Pieper (first name unknown), 123

Pierre, S.Dak., 136, 151

Pike, Zebulon, 19–20

Pilcher, Joshua, 133, 134, 135–36, 152, 171, 178

pirogues, 5, 9, 14–15

Platte River, 39, 90

Plumer, William, 27

Ponca nation, 17, 110

Potawatomi nation, 119

Potomac River, 67

Potts, John, 75, 133, 150, 153; death, 46; early history, 45; estate, 46, 197, 222n.23; with Lisa, 39, 78; saves Lisa from Rose, 44–45; traps with Colter, 45–46; vital stats, 197

Prairie du Chien, Wis., 121, 124, 201

Price (first name unknown), 122

Proctor, Henry, 122

Provost, Etienne, 2

Pryor, Nathaniel, 3, 28, 38–39, 58, 114, 128, 140, 141, 149; accused of urging Osages to war, 164; appointed subagent to Osage nation, 163, 164; attacked by Arikara, 34–35; attacked by Winnebagos, 120–21, 241n.6; attends to wounded, 35–37; death, 164, 198; escorts Sheheke, 29, 76; married before LCE, 77; recommended by Sam Houston, 163–64; reports on battle to WC, 36; robbed by Cherokee, 164; serves under Andrew Jackson, 121, 163; takes horses across eastern Montana, 76; travels up Missouri, 32–33; vital stats, 197–98

Quaife, Milo M., 238n.30

Randolph, Martha Jefferson, 71

Raymond, Fort, 2, 40–43, 44, 48, 78, 90, 91, 95, 153, 156

Reagan, Jacob, 76

Reid, Russell, 212–13

Revolutionary War, 24, 25, 32, 83

Reznor, Jacob, 39, 111

Robidoux Fur Brigade, 179

Robinson, Edward, 39, 111, 220n.5

Robison, Kinsay and Elizabeth, 103–4, 237n.21

Ronda, James, 213, 240n.28

Rose, Edward: attacked by Arikara, 127,
128, 130–31, 135; conspires with TC to sell
Indian women, 134; death, 147; descriptions
of, 40, 220n.7; emissary to Crow nation,
40–41; fights with Lisa, 44–45, 78; with
Lisa in 1812, 111, 239n.23; lives among
Crow, 111; possibly seen by Leonard with
Crow nation, 146–48; warns Reuben Lewis
of Indian threat, 117
Rucker (first name unknown), 94
Rush, Benjamin, 86
Rush's pills, 79
Russell, Gilbert C., 62–63, 72

Sacagawea, 3, 4, 15, 16, 149; arrives in
St. Louis in 1809, 107, 115, 238n.4; assists in
translation process, 157; death, 2, 115, 121,
133; described by Brackenridge, 107;
deserved "greater reward," 216n.14; finds
food for corps, 15; gives birth to Baptiste, 14;
leaves St. Louis in 1811, 106–7; reunited
with friend and brother, 107–8; saves LCE
journals when boat capsizes, 14–15; saved
from flash flood by WC, 15; struck by
Charbonneau, 15, 114; taken captive by
Hidatsa raiding party, 13–14; thought by
some to have died in Wyoming, 210–13;
travels up Missouri in 1811, 107, 108–9; vital
stats, 198; votes on where to spend winter of
1805–6, 140; whereabouts during winter of
1811–12, 112, 239n.23
St. Charles, Mo., 40, 50–51, 165
St. Louis, Mo., 5, 12, 21, 38, 49, 52, 59–60, 71,
77, 78, 89, 90, 95, 106; contemporary
descriptions of, 24, 60
St. Louis Missouri Fur Company, 31, 58, 112,
218n.7, 233n.1
Saint-Mémin, Charles B. J. F. *See* Fevrét de
Saint-Mémin, C.-B.-J.
Salish nation (also called Flatheads), 44, 93,
157
Salmon River, 67
Sanford, John F. A., 147
Santa Fe, N.Mex., 134, 175, 176
Sarpy, Gregoire, 151
Saskatchewan River, 93
Sauk nation, 71, 121, 123–24, 169–70
Scott, John, 50, 52, 53
Seaman (ML's dog), 60, 227n.15
sexual relations (between members of the
corps and Indian women), 111–12. *See also*
mercury treatment for syphilis
Shannon, David (brother of George
Shannon), 165

Shannon, George, Sr. (father of George
Shannon of LCE), 32
Shannon, George, 3, 38–39, 58, 76, 78, 114,
128, 141, 149, 168, 183; appointed U.S.
district attorney, 165, 251n.11; assists Biddle
with LCE journals, 86–88, 107–8; attends
Transylvania University, 82–86; biographi-
cal summary of, 37; candidate for Congress,
166; Clay and, 85, 165, 232n.7; death, 167;
death of wife, 166–67; debts, 165, 167,
251n.12; defends Chief Big Neck, 165–66;
elected to Kentucky House, 165; joins
Pryor's party, 28; jury member at
Drouillard's trial, 49, 52–53, 82; leg
amputated, 37, 49; makes controversial
ruling in Desha case, 165; as possible
member of saltpeter cave expedition,
223n.1; possibly hears of ML's death, 85;
with Pryor's group during LCE, 76; purported alcohol problems, 167, 251n.12;
shoots wolf, 28; student essays of, 83–84;
studies law, 87–88; travels up Missouri with
Pryor, 32; visits Jonathan Clark, 82; vital
stats, 198, 217n.1; WC and, 37, 82, 85, 86,
164, 166; wounded in battle with Arikara,
35–37, 219nn.16–17
Shannon, James (brother of George Shannon),
165
Shannon, Ruth Price (wife of George
Shannon), 164, 166–67, 198
Shannon, Thomas (brother of George
Shannon), 165
Shannon, William Russell (son of George
Shannon), 37, 198, 217n.1
Shannon, Wilson (brother of George
Shannon), 165, 183
Shaw, John, 103, 237n.22
Shawnee nation, 6, 31, 95, 119, 123, 172
Sheheke-shote (Mandan chief), 13, 18, 21,
101; arrives at Fort Manuel, 113, 240n.27;
death, 114–15, 240n.28; decides to visit
TJ, 6–8; declining reputation, 89–90,
111; described by Brackenridge and
Bradbury, 111–12; failed attempt to return
to home, 28, 29, 76; returns to St. Louis
area, 36; successful attempt to return to
home, 57–59, 63–64; threatened by
Arikara, 33–34; travels to Washington,
25–27
Shelbyville, Ky., 70, 233n.16
Shields, John, 150, 172; cures Bratton's back
problems, 79–80, 98; death, 81; early history, 78–79; estate, 81, 199; married before
LCE, 77; sends buffalo robe to wife, 81, 141;

skill as gunsmith, 79; value during LCE, 78–80; vital stats, 199

Shields, Martha Jannette. *See* Tipton, Martha Jannette Shields

Shields, Nancy White (wife of John Shields), 78–79, 81

Shields family, 81

Shoshone nation, 6, 13–14, 39, 88, 91, 107–8

Shoshone River, 43

Sioux City, Iowa, 32, 39

Sioux nation, 17, 29, 129, 134–35

slavery, 5, 24, 66, 139–45, 148

smallpox epidemic, 170, 171–72

Smith, Annie Jane (daughter of Patrick Gass), 183, 184, 193

Smith, James, 183

Smith, Jedediah, 1, 127, 128, 130–31, 242–43n.2

Smith, Peter, 156

Snake River, 9, 43, 76–77, 153

Stanford, Leland, 3

Stanton, N.Dak., 107

Stephens, Aaron, 127, 128, 130, 243–44n.14

Stevens, J. H., 179

Stoddard, Amos, 63

Sublette, William L., 127, 128, 130–31

Tecumseh (Shawnee chief), 119–20, 123

Tennessee River, 65, 66, 67, 195, 203

Tenskwatawa (Shawnee chief), 119–20

Teton Mountains, 43

Teton River, 43

Teton Sioux nation. *See* Lakota nation

Texas, 162, 167

Thomas, William H., 47, 89, 90

Thompson, David, 31, 150

Thompson, John B., 133, 140, 150, 151, 248n.10; early history, 152; estate, 153, 199; possibly killed by Indians, 152, 153; vital stats, 199; widow of, 153

Three Forks, 13, 41, 44–46, 90, 92, 93, 106, 108, 152, 153

Thwaites, Reuben Gold, 156–57, 207

Tilton's Fort, 138

Tippecanoe, Battle of, 118–20

Tipton, John, 81

Tipton, Martha Jannette Shields (daughter of John Shields), 78–79, 81, 199

tobacco, 17, 42, 43, 55, 66, 71, 154

Todd, Mary, 84

Todd, Robert, 84

Togwatee Pass, 43

translation process, 14, 157

Transylvania University, 82–86, 87

Traverse, Lake, 138

U.S. Congress, petition signed by LCE members to, 75–76, 151, 218n.14, 218–19n.40, 230n.2

Valle, Francis, 94

Van Buren, Martin, 79

venereal disease, 112, 113. *See also* mercury treatment for syphilis

Vincennes, Ind., 120, 152

violin. *See* fiddles and fiddlers

Vivaldi, Canon de, 156–57

Wabash Valley, 118

Walker, Adam, 118

Walker, John H., 105

Walker, Joseph, 147

wapatos, 140

War Department, 29, 64, 74, 119, 166

War of 1812, 2, 3, 88, 105, 118–26, 152–53, 154, 162, 163, 181

Warfington, Richard, 150, 202, 247n.1

Washington, George, 24, 164–65

Washington, D.C., 20, 25–27, 36, 59, 65, 101, 123, 164, 168

Waynetown, Ind., 100–101

weapons, 13, 34–35, 42, 44, 65, 79

Weaver, Pauline, 176

Weir, James, 99

Weiser, Peter, 16, 45, 48, 133, 248n.11; emissary to Crow nation, 40–41; files for bankruptcy, 153; in Idaho, 41, 153, 221n.10; with Lisa, 39, 78, 153; possibly killed by Indians, 152–53; serves in War of 1812, 153; vital stats, 199–200

Weiser, Idaho, 153

Welch, J. E., 178

Werner, William, 150, 249nn.30–31; cook during LCE, 158; death, 158; receives loans from ML, 158; settles in Virginia, 158; vital stats, 200

Werner, William, Jr. (son of William Werner of LCE), 158

whiskey. *See* alcohol and alcoholism

White, Hugh Lawson, 79

White, James Haley, 177–78

Whitehouse, Joseph, 140, 149, 150, 248n.21; arrested for bad debts, 156; death, 156–57; desertion of, 156, 200; discipline problems, 155; LCE journal of, 156–57, 160; reenlistment of, 156, 200; tailor during LCE, 155; vital stats, 200, 249n.25

Whitehouse (White) family, 156, 200
Whitley, Thomas, 45
Whittington, Hiram, 163–64
Wilkinson, James, 19, 56, 73, 128, 150, 208, 217n.20, 225n.3, 230n.48
Willard, Alexander, 3, 16, 149, 170, 180, 184; as blacksmith, 79, 121, 172; comments on LCE, 174–75; death, 174, 200; death of son, 172–73; escapes Indian attack, 121; goes west in 1852, 173–74; LCE journal of, 175; moves to Wisconsin, 172; obituary, 201; sent to warn Pryor of Indian threat, 120, 121; settles in Missouri, 172; vital stats, 200–201; WC and, 120–21, 172
Willard, Eleanor McDonald (wife of Alexander Willard), 172, 173, 174, 201
Willard, George Clark (son of Alexander Willard), 172–73, 201
Willard, Lewis (son of Alexander Willard), 174–75
Wilson, Alexander, 208; asked by ML to make bird drawings, 67; interviews Mrs. Grinder, 67–69, 74, 204–6
Winchester, James, 122
Windsor, Richard, 28, 45, 76, 140, 149; census records, 250n.34; death, 159; with Lisa, 39, 78, 159; rescued by ML, 158–59; vital stats, 201

wine. *See* alcohol and alcoholism
Winnebago nation, 120–21
Wistar, Caspar, 86
Wolf River, 62
Woodruff, Wilford, 175
Wyeth, Nathaniel, 101–2, 179
Wyoming, 2, 43, 77, 115, 145, 210–13

Yankton, S.Dak., 109
Yankton Sioux nation. *See* Sioux nation
Yellow Corn (wife of Sheheke), 25, 58
Yellowstone Lake, 43
Yellowstone Park, 43–44
Yellowstone River, 2, 38, 40–41, 43, 44, 48, 90, 91, 127, 129, 134, 136, 138, 147
York, 4, 25, 150; concerned about relationship with WC, 143; dances, 141; death, 2–3, 144, 148, 247n.21; desires freedom, 143; endures "trouncing" by WC, 141; hired out to harsh master, 143; possibly seen by Leonard with Crow nation, 145–48; responsibilities during LCE, 5, 140; sends buffalo robe to wife, 141; takes up freight business in Nashville, 144; vital stats, 202; votes on where to spend winter of 1805–6, 140; wife and, 141–45, 148; youth, 139–40, 246n.1
York's family, 139–40, 141–42, 202
Young, Brigham, 175